Paweł **Althamer**

Frank **Benson**

Huma **Bhabha**

Maurizio **Cattelan**

Urs **Fischer**

Katharina **Fritsch**

Ryan **Gander**

Isa **Genzken**

Rachel **Harrison**

Georg **Herold**

Thomas **Hirschhorn**

Martin **Honert**

Pierre **Huyghe**

Jeff **Koons**

Paul **McCarthy**

John **Miller**

Cady **Noland**

Ugo **Rondinone**

Thomas **Schütte**

Yinka **Shonibare MBE**

Paloma **Varga Weisz**

Mark **Wallinger**

Rebecca **Warren**

Andro **Wekua**

Cathy **Wilkes**

Edited by Ralph Rugoff

the Human Factor

The Figure in Contemporary Sculpture

Foreword

Spanning the past 25 years, *The Human Factor* brings together major works by 25 leading international artists who have fashioned new ways of using the figure in sculpture. In addressing the medium's oldest subject, these artists engage in dialogues with classical and archaic as well as modernist art. They also respond to a wide array of contemporary popular representations of the human form. Rather than focusing on the body as a subject, they use the figure as a catalyst for exploring the ways in which our culture constructs identities, social positions and values. Alluding to matters ranging from political violence and voyeurism to the impact of mass media, their work holds up an uncanny mirror to our accepted codes and conventions for representing the 'human'. It provokes us to reassess and re-imagine how we respond to and make sense of this most familiar form and the myriad artistic traditions associated with it. Thought-provoking and engaging, their work demonstrates that figurative sculpture — far from being an anachronistic genre — includes some of the most dynamic art being made today.

It has been a pleasure and privilege to work with the artists in this exhibition, and our thanks go first and foremost to them. They have enriched us all by making works of art that can expand the ways in which we think about and look at the world around us, and our place within it.

The Human Factor could not have been realised without the generosity of the many lenders to the exhibition, including individual collectors, museums, galleries, foundations and the participating artists themselves. We extend to them our gratitude and appreciation for making these artworks available to the public. We are also deeply grateful to the Stanley Thomas Johnson Foundation, the Swiss Arts Council Pro Helvetia, Edlis-Neeson Foundation, Gladstone Gallery, Dakis Joannou, Matthew Marks Gallery, Maureen Paley, London, Max Hetzler Gallery, Ringier Collection Zürich, Sadie Coles HQ and Stephen Friedman Gallery.

Many individuals have provided crucial help and assistance to the Hayward Gallery team organising this exhibition, and their names are listed on page 206. Hayward Assistant Curator Eimear Martin deserves special mention for her thoughtful research, and her indispensable work in bringing this show together. Curatorial Assistant Debra Lennard provided excellent support, and Luisa Summers played an important early role in getting this project organised. For their original and thoughtful contributions to this catalogue, I wish to thank Penelope Curtis, Martin Herbert, Lisa Lee and James Lingwood. Helen Luckett also deserves a special note of thanks for her excellent texts in this book, as well as her superb interpretive materials in the gallery. Hayward Art Publisher Ben Fergusson did a superb job managing all aspects of this publication and Sonya Dyakova has earned our gratitude with her intelligent and elegant design.

I also wish to thank Hayward Operations Manager Thomas Malcherczyk, former Hayward Operations Manager Ruth Pelopida and Senior Technician Gareth Hughes for their work in planning and executing the installation; Hayward Registrar Imogen Winter for skilfully overseeing transport matters; and Hayward General Manager Sarah O'Reilly for expertly supervising and assisting with so many different facets of the exhibition. Finally, I am very grateful as ever for the support of Southbank Centre Chief Executive Alan Bishop and Artistic Director Jude Kelly, as well as Southbank Centre's Board of Governors and Arts Council England.

Ralph Rugoff, Director, Hayward Gallery

The Human Factor

Ralph Rugoff

In 1988, as part of a body of work called 'Banality', Jeff Koons exhibited *Bear and Policeman*, a polychromed wood sculpture that featured a life-sized bobby gazing up in adoration at a giant bug-eyed toy bear. Compared to the bear's vaguely menacing monumentality, the constable, an ostensible authority symbol, looks distinctly like the toy in this couple. This impression is reinforced by the bear's grip on the policeman's phallic-shaped whistle. Koons, in fact, has described this work as conveying a sense of sexual humiliation. We can also read it in another way, however: as an allegory for the artist's larger project.[1] The sculpture seemingly invites us to follow the bobby's example: to put aside our critical scruples and to enjoy its overwhelming spectacle — its bold colour and scale, virtuoso craftsmanship and, above all, its kitsch cocktail of sentimentality and sexual innuendo.

Aside from its entertaining creepiness, the unsettling impact of this work largely derives from its apparent demand to be taken seriously. By transforming an image from a tourist postcard into a meticulously produced object with the mass and volume of 'serious' sculpture, and by presenting it in the context of an art gallery, Koons insinuates that we should treat *Bear and Policeman* with the respect accorded to significant works of art. Yet at the same time, how can we not laugh at its absurdly kitschy appearance? And how can we not view its display in a gallery as a sly joke intended to deflate the aura of pompous rectitude that surrounds the reception of 'important' cultural artefacts? By mixing up competing conventions and the expectations they put into play, *Bear and Policeman* leaves us with a disconcerting uncertainty about how to position ourselves in relation to its contradictory signals.

B

In the mid-to-late 1980s, a number of other artists also began making figurative sculpture that played unsettling games with historical tropes and cultural codes and categories. Katharina Fritsch, Thomas Schütte, Martin Honert, John Miller and Cady Noland, among others, all produced sculptures that, however different from one another, shared an interest in denaturing conventional ways of representing the human form. For these artists, the figure was not — as it was for some of their contemporaries — a means of probing issues around corporeal or existential experience; nor was it a vehicle for portraiture. Instead they approached the figure as a culturally encoded representation defined by particular historical and social conventions. In other words, the human forms in their sculpture did not evoke actual bodies, so much as figures of rhetoric. As the artist Mike Kelley observed in his catalogue essay for *The Uncanny*, the pioneering 1993 exhibition that he curated around figurative sculpture and imagery, this kind of work took as its subject 'the convention and the cliché'.[2] In this regard, pop art, with its re-packaging of populist tropes, had provided a crucial precedent, but the work of these artists also took on board the 'theatricality' of minimalist sculpture, conceptual art's questioning of taxonomies and context, and the ironic formalism elaborated by artists such as Bruce Nauman and Gilbert & George.

Over the last 25 years, this rhetorical approach to using the figure has been further developed by several generations of sculptors (including those mentioned above). Indeed it is tempting to say that we are now in the midst of yet another figurative 'revival.' Certainly there is no shortage of artists currently mining this area in very different ways. Reflecting this diversity, *The Human Factor* encompasses a wide array of recent practices, from hyper-real sculptures to quasi-abstract assemblages, from works fabricated with new technologies to those made with traditional techniques. In all of them, the human figure — that most recognisable of all forms — is unsettled in ways that mix up signs of familiarity and otherness, presence and absence. Ultimately it serves not as an endpoint but as a point of departure for staging and unpicking the ways that our culture constructs identities, social positions, values and histories.

The Human Factor thus focuses on sculpture that has a distinctly 'worldly' character. In this respect it might seem to have a distant connection to the socially engaged figurative sculpture of the 1960s, as exemplified by American artists such as Edward Kienholz, Eric Segal and Duane Hanson.

C

But whereas that work was typically driven, and tightly circumscribed, by its narrative concerns, the sculpture in *The Human Factor* involves its audience in a more open-ended conversation, inviting us to root around in, and draw connections between, its far-ranging references. At the same time, this work invites us to pay attention to the particular dynamics of its staging and what we might consider its social behaviour: how it keeps us company, how it addresses and confronts us, what kind of looking it solicits and whether it greets us as a kind of surrogate, or as a fellow actor sharing the same stage. In keeping with this interest in public experience, *The Human Factor* only includes sculpture that relates to a human scale and represents or approximates a full figure. Their human size imbues these objects with a 'presence' that seems to mirror our own; it gives them the capacity to theatrically confront us, even to spook us.

Untimely Histories

For most of its history, sculpture devotedly depicted the body. In the Renaissance, the human form was seen as the medium's point of origin; as Vasari declared, 'It is undeniable that from man, as from a perfect model, statues and pieces of sculpture … were first derived.'[3] That ancient association still

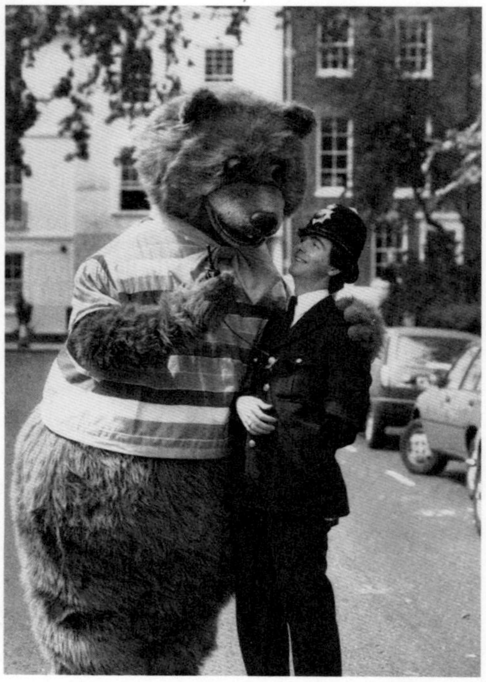

B

Image from the photoshoot that produced Mike Hollist's picture postcard, 'The Bear Fact', 1985, which Koons then used for *Bear and Policeman*, 1988

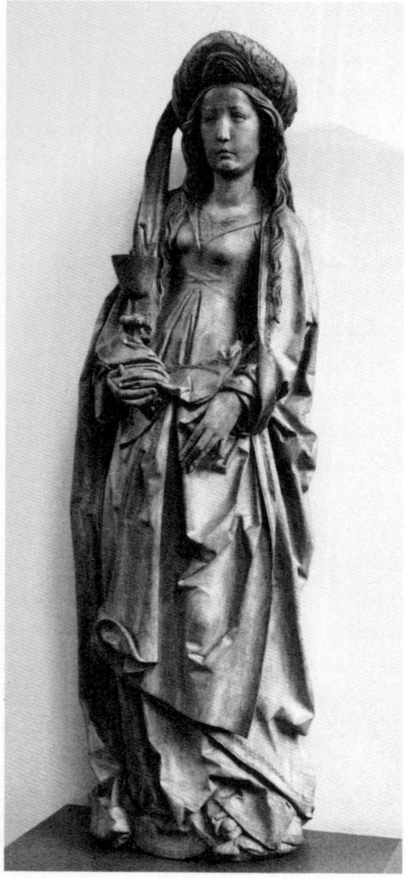

A

Tilman Riemenschneider, *Saint Barbara*, c. 1510

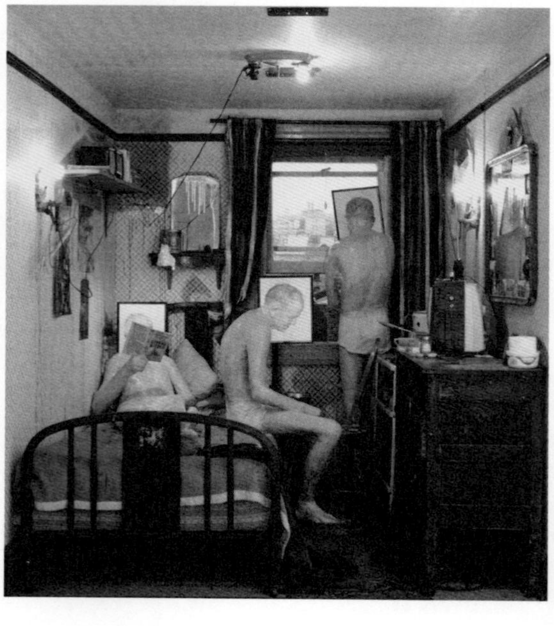

C

Edward & Nancy Reddin Kienholz, *Sollie 17*, 1979–80

clings to its contemporary iterations and so, inevitably, a hint of a retrograde aura haunts recent figurative sculpture — a predicament exacerbated by the figure's relative marginalisation within the 'expanded field' of sculptural practices from the past half-century. In the early 1960s Anthony Caro's pioneering painted metal constructions were hailed for 'liberating' sculpture from its hidebound association with the figure, while forging a more abstract and medium-specific language. With the subsequent emergence of a diverse sculptural terrain, extending from minimalism to land art, from institutional critique to various forms of 'social practice', the figure generally has been conspicuous by its absence.[4]

Yet rather than conceding the figure's irrelevance, the artists in *The Human Factor* exploit its seemingly anachronistic status to make work that evinces an acute and subversive historical self-consciousness. Their work typically conflates conventions from different eras, remixing period styles and tropes in order to suggest unexpected links between them as well as to undermine our facile habits of categorisation. In some instances it also reinterprets and updates moments from sculpture's past to comment on shifting cultural and social relationships of our own time. Conjoining fragments of collective memory with aspects of present-day experience, it opens up the narrow bandwidth of historical reference that characterises most contemporary art. In its place, much of this work presents an ambiguous or uncanny temporality.

Huma Bhabha's sculpture exemplifies this approach in an almost archaeological fashion. Made with a mix of traditional materials and consumer and industrial detritus, her figures inventively remix forms ranging from ancient Egyptian statuary to African tribal masks and Renaissance funerary sculpture, while also reflecting influences from twentieth-century modernists as well as imagery from contemporary science fiction and horror movies. Defying any attempt at pinpointing their allegiance to a single lineage, they confront us (often with abrasive humour) with unassimilable positions of difference and exoticism. A perplexing historical elusiveness, although in a quieter modality, also characterises the work of Paloma Varga Weisz. Often employing anachronistic wood-carving or wax-casting techniques, her figurative sculptures depict the features of contemporary life models while incorporating aesthetic elements from German folk traditions and the late-Gothic religious art made by sculptors such as Tilman Riemenschneider.

A

In articulating an ambivalent tension between stylised historical conventions and a naturalistic depiction of present-day bodies — between the archetypal and the personal — Varga Weisz's figures reflect a contemporary predicament: namely, our uncertainty about the degree to which our 'individuality' is forged by cultural conventions as much as our particular psychological make-up.

A number of artists in *The Human Factor* take on classical statuary's status as a 'timeless' art, a notion linked to the idealised and archetypal character of its figurative depictions. It is worth noting here that the notion of a timeless art, with its implication of an eternal aesthetic order, is a reassuring one for the ruling classes of any society. Playing against this tradition, Mark Wallinger's white marbleised resin *Ecce Homo* (1999), a life-sized figure depicting Christ posed with hands tied behind his back, eschews the conventional representation of a bearded, long-haired archetype. Cast from an identifiably contemporary model with a shaved head and wearing a crown fashioned from barbed wire, *Ecce Homo* replaces an evocation of the eternal with a timely allusion to present-day concerns about political prisoners and struggles for social justice.

Modern art derived a key component of its aesthetic — and moral — code from the popular misconception regarding the unadorned material surface — the transcendent whiteness — of ancient Greek and Roman statues, which, as scholars now assure us, were in fact painted to simulate flesh tones. From a modernist viewpoint, the alleged plainness of ancient statuary comprised a type of aesthetic honesty; sculpture remained 'true' to the enduring character of its materials by refusing to adulterate them with the deceptions of paint and colour. To hard-line modernists, a painted statue was an idol of fraudulence inasmuch as it involved masking the object's physical reality. Mischievously revisiting this history, Frank Benson's *Human Statue* (2005) presents a cast fibreglass sculpture of a naked man that has been painted with *trompe l'œil* realism to resemble a 'living statue' street performer. Simultaneously gesturing to the timelessness of classical art and the 'live' time of performance, to high and 'low' traditions, eternal truths and kitsch masquerade, *Human Statue* is a humorously uncanny conflation. *Human Statue (Jessie)* (2011) further elaborates Benson's off-kilter mixing of Greco-Roman and contemporary conventions by also incorporating particular stylistic cues derived from 1980s pop culture.[5] Cast in bronze, its classically posed female figure sports a slicked-back Grace Jones-style coiffure along with giant sunglasses and a minimalist dress painted in matte black. Meanwhile, the anonymous formalism of the figure's rigid pose and bronze colouration is countered by its hyper-realistic anatomical detailing (achieved through a high-tech, computer-assisted production process), resulting in an uncanny figure that simultaneously embodies the present-ness of an actual body and the atemporality of an archetype.

Exploring the way that art's 'timeless truths' reflect social values constructed by particular classes, cultures and periods, both Yinka Shonibare MBE and Ryan Gander revisit the same anomaly of modern sculpture: Edgar Degas' *Little Dancer Aged Fourteen* (1880–81, cast c. 1922), a two-thirds life-size wax figure dressed in a cloth tutu which the artist purportedly kept in his studio until his death.[6]

D

For classical and modernist tastes attuned to the archetypal, *Little Dancer Aged Fourteen* is too vivid in its evocation of a particular body, too close to being a fetishistic surrogate rather than a 'timeless' work of art. Scaled up to life-size and rendered with a light brown skin tone, Shonibare's headless *Girl Ballerina* (2007) is dressed in a top made of batik fabric, a material with a complex relationship with the history of colonial trade in Africa; holding a large pistol in one of the hands clasped behind her back, the figure conjures insurrection and resistance rather than a demure acquiescence. In a very different manner, Gander also updates Degas' sculpture into a figure that evinces an independent agency. His *Come up on different streets, they both were streets of shame Or Absinth blurs my thoughts, I think we should be moving on* (2009) recasts Degas' dancer in a very different pose: having apparently abandoned a nearby plinth, the bronze figure is shown standing on her tiptoes atop a blue cube in order to peer through a gallery window into an adjoining space. No longer passively displaying herself for the spectator's pleasure, Gander's ballerina is transformed from an object of desire into a figure enacting its own desires to explore the surrounding world.

Theatricality

In the early 1960s, a conspicuous theatricality characterised a new wave of figurative sculpture by artists such as Ed Kienholz, George Segal and Duane Hanson. While pursuing very different aesthetic agendas, these artists often presented sculpted figures in stage-like tableaux replete with props and furniture. Typically driven by narrative and social commentary, their works were often presented in an almost pictorial manner inasmuch as they were staged to be viewed from particular perspectives (Kienholz, in fact, once described himself as a painter working in three dimensions).[7] While theatrical in a conventional sense of the word, their self-contained sculptural scenes rarely broke the 'fourth wall' to address the surrounding space of the gallery and the spectator.

In contrast, much recent figurative sculpture explores theatricality as a way to draw attention to the specific manner in which our visual encounters in a gallery are staged. For many artists making this kind of work, minimalism has been a key reference point, particularly for the way it shifted the viewer's focus from contemplating an object's internal formal dynamics to exploring the shifting relationships that develop between sculptural forms and their architectural setting as one moves through the space of a gallery. Rejecting the modernist assumption that art's formal content was exclusively authored by the artist, minimalism emphasised its process of reception: the work's 'content', rather than being seen as something inherent in the art object, emerged through its audience's subjective response. In his oft-quoted critique of minimalism, the critic Michael Fried famously denounced this tendency as 'theatrical' because the work seemed to engage the viewer as a participant in an encounter, rather than as a transcendent witness.[8]

The theatrical 'presence' of figurative sculpture, of course, derives in large part from the way that it mirrors our own physical form and solicits our irresistible anthropomorphic impulse to project aspects of our mental life onto any object in which we discern a semblance of human features. Taking advantage of this tendency, contemporary sculptors stage the figure in ways that make us self-conscious of this emotional displacement while also drawing our attention to ways in which, as spectators, we perform a scripted role and way of looking in the gallery. Through its overt theatricality this type of work can also contaminate the gallery's ostensible neutrality as a display space, prompting us to reflect on conditions and conventions of showing art that we might otherwise take for granted.

In a series of sculptures begun in the late 1980s, John Miller has used store-bought mannequins as proxies for exploring the viewer's subjective positioning in the gallery transaction. In Miller's *Now We're Big Potatoes* (1992), we encounter a male mannequin anachronistically attired in a one-piece bathing suit and standing with a foot mired in one of several shit-coloured mounds on the floor around it. Mannequins, however cheaply produced, represent an idealised norm; but as the apparent protagonist (or victim) of an abject slapstick routine, Miller's figure is humorously de-idealised. Confronted by this displaced and absurd figure, our habit of projection is disrupted: rather than imagining how its clothing might look on us, do we instead feel a vicarious embarrassment on account of its humiliating public predicament? Have we also somehow 'put our foot in it'? Or does Miller's denatured retail surrogate lead us to wonder whether the gallery itself is a bit like a dysfunctional department store — a place where commodities are elegantly displayed?

Maurizio Cattelan's *Him* (2001) likewise solicits our participation in an ambiguous theatrical encounter. Cattelan carefully stages this figurative sculpture so that our perception of it unfolds in two distinct stages: initially viewed from its back and at a distance, it appears to represent a young boy kneeling in prayer. From this viewpoint, the 'empty' space surrounding the sculpture functions to dramatically heighten its apparent vulnerability and isolation. But once we have circled around the figure and discovered its disconcerting hybrid identity — a realistic, adult-sized head depicting Adolf Hitler sits atop its shoulders — we experience this same 'empty' space as being charged (and filled) by the emanation of a sublime, unbounded evil. In both moments of our encounter, the work's scale is delimited not by the figure's actual size but by the emotional aura generated by its staging. In abruptly shifting our perceptions in this way, Cattelan's sculpture alerts us to the constructed character of our 'subjective' encounters in the gallery.

Thomas Schütte also plays disquieting games with scale to imbue his pair of *Krieger* sculptures (2012) with a dramatic and spatially disorienting presence.

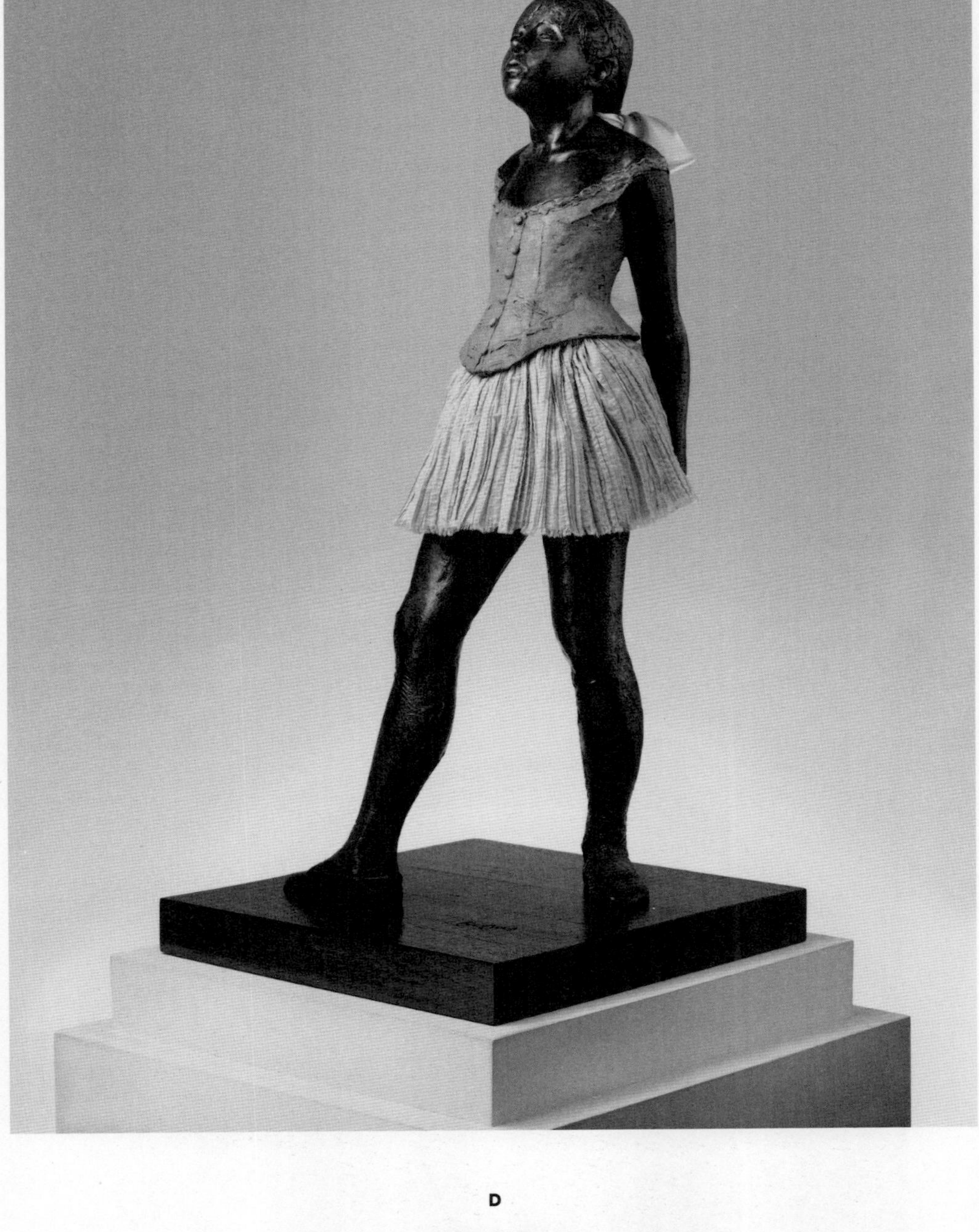

D

Edgar Degas,
***Little Dancer Aged Fourteen*,**
1880–81, cast c. 1922

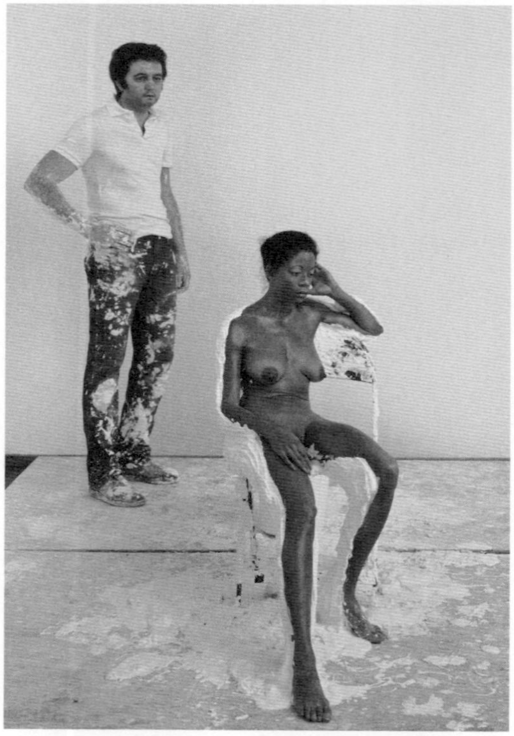

E

John De Andrea,
***Untitled (Studio Scene)*, 1977**

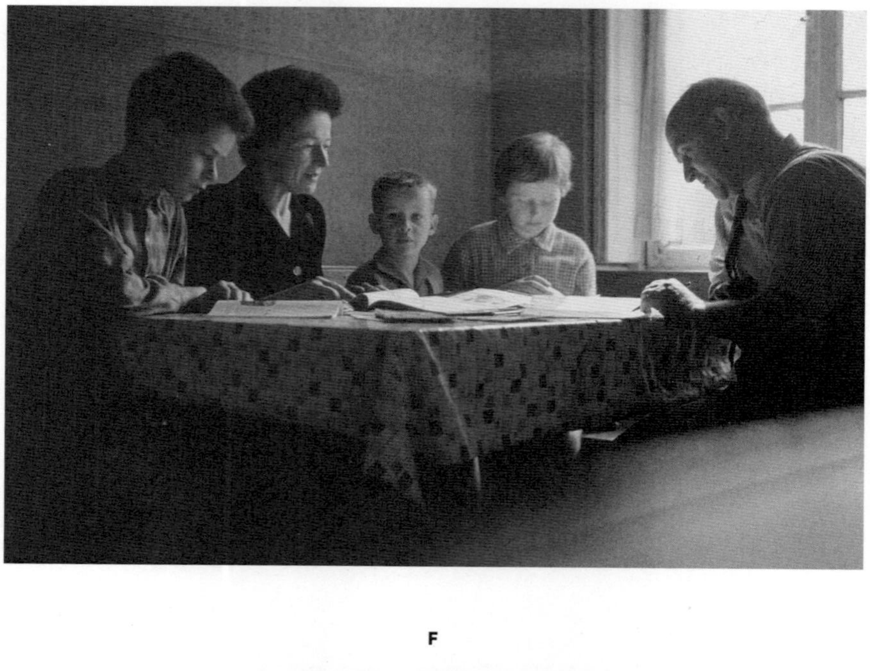

F

Photographic basis for Martin Honert's
***Foto* (Photo), 1993**

In stark contrast to the heroic language of neoclassical war monuments, these stained wooden sculptures depict two giant 'warriors' whose aggressive posturing is belied by their pathetic, misshapen anatomies. Thirty per cent larger than life-size, they appear simultaneously commanding, absurd, belligerent and vulnerable. Both figures wear helmets shaped like screw-top bottle caps, and this detail clues us in to the fact that these sculptures have been scaled up from table-top models. This is evident as well when we pay attention to their seemingly improvised and hand-modelled formal articulation. Thus even while they tower over us in the intimidating fashion of public monuments, they simultaneously invoke the intimacy of toy-sized figures. This contradictory demeanour unsettles the certainty of our own position and perspective — not only in relation to the spaces that they occupy, but also to the histories that they summon.

Whereas modernist sculpture traditionally activated the space around it through its internal formal relationships, works such as these re-orient our experience of the gallery as an arena for constructing a certain way of looking at and relating to objects. Several artists in *The Human Factor* engage with this territory by addressing the explicit manner in which art objects are typically presented and arranged. Rather than submitting to our unimpeded inspection, these sculptures seemingly embody an ambivalence about their display in the gallery; playing with codes of public and private behaviour, they make us self-conscious about how we perform our role as spectators.

As with many of his installations, Andro Wekua's *Sneakers I* (2008) places its wax and painted cast figure on a dramatic platform: a table that in turn rests on a cast aluminium pallet. But while this exaggerated display rhetoric focuses our attention on the figure as if it were an actor on a stage, its defensive posture — sitting hunched over with face buried in its arms — conveys an introverted withholding that seems aimed at shutting the viewer out. Conjuring this same tension between revealing and concealing, Gander — in the initial work from his ballerina series — places the figure out of view behind the pedestal that she has apparently vacated; posed sitting on the floor and smoking a cigarette, the model seems to be enjoying a private break from the imperative of eternally displaying herself. Whether we regard the sculpture from above or get down on the floor for a better look, the work's mise-en-scène theatricalises our scrutiny as an intrusive act.

Sculptures like these invite us not simply to look *at* an object but also to question what kind of looking it solicits. Taking on this concern in a more jarring fashion, Paul McCarthy's *That Girl (T.G. Awake)* (2012–13) confronts the etiquette of public viewing through its explicit display of three unnervingly lifelike versions of the same naked female figure, all posed in seated positions with knees apart and resting atop glass-plated white tables. The figures' astonishing verisimilitude imbues them with a truly uncanny presence; as one critic observed, 'They achieve such a high degree of realism that approaching them feels like an invasion of personal space.'[9] Consequently when we scrutinise these figures, our normal gallery behaviour seems to be disconcertingly transformed into a public act of voyeurism. Due to their heightened realism, in other words, our relationship to these objects is inappropriately but unavoidably shifted into an ethical, rather than an aesthetic, register. Our act of looking in the gallery becomes a self-conscious and problematic performance in which we become keenly aware of how our sense of morality is entangled with, or even produced by, our responses to particular visual conventions.

Sculpture As Image

In one of the salient tendencies of figurative sculpture over the past 25 years, artists have responded to the pervasive (and invasive) presence of mass media in contemporary life by making work that draws on photographic sources while reflecting the ways in which our photographically inflected habits of seeing have flattened our spatial perception and experience. In contrast to the sculptural photo-realism pioneered in the 1960s by artists such as Duane Hanson and John De Andrea, which sought to return the medium's primary focus to representation, this more recent work is concerned with fashioning figures that evince a provocatively indeterminate presence, hovering between object and image. Mixing temporal registers, it entangles sculpture's present-time physicality with photography's indexical yet ghostly trace of a past moment.

E

In a culture over-saturated with photographic media, our perception and engagement with concrete spatial and physical relationships — the traditional arena of sculpture — takes on a diminished and detached character. As we spend more and more time gazing at electronic screens, from smartphones to computers and televisions, we develop a chronically split consciousness: our attention is increasingly divided between the physical and virtual spaces that we simultaneously inhabit. Exploring this kind of psychology, Katharina Fritsch's 'space picture' sculptures present life-sized cast figures in front of large screen prints of exterior scenes that function like photo backdrops. In *Riese und 4. Postkarte (Franken)* (Giant and 4th Postcard [Franconia]) (2008), we encounter a tall male figure, holding a club and dressed cave-man style, who stands before a green-tinted mural-sized image of a mountain gorge as if guarding his territory. Cast from a real person, Fritsch's sculpture engages our attention through the immediacy of its lifelike details, but its matte-grey painted surface, which reflects neither light nor its surroundings, lends it a distinctly ghostly demeanour. Oscillating between signs of actual and ideal, real and unreal, it stages what the artist has called an experience of 'inaccessibility' — it places before us an object that, for all its size and substance, remains difficult to grasp or categorise, and that leads us to also question our apprehension of the surrounding space in which it exists.

Martin Honert explores similar concerns with his painted sculptures that comprise painstakingly crafted, three-dimensional reconstructions of the artist's childhood photographs. *Foto* (Photo) (1993), a sculpture depicting a small boy seated alone at a dining table, is painted with an evocative yet muted realism that reproduces the lighting and shadows of its source image. This imbues it with a contradictory character: for all its vivid presence in the gallery, it clearly references another time and space. By cross-wiring the conventions of not only sculpture and photography but also painting, Honert endows this figure with an eerie elusiveness that hints at the haunting quality of memories. *Englischlehrer* (English Teacher) (2010), fabricated and painted in a manner that cannily approximates the grain of an old black-and-white photograph, imbues its banal subject with the uncannily frozen quality of an image. Yet in translating his personal photographs into material objects, Honert distances his work from photography's claim to 'truthfully' represent reality; his sculptures appear stranded in a no man's land between portraiture, fiction and memory.

F

Other sculptures that draw on photographic materials also extrapolate on the social impact of the mass media — how it colours and shapes our understanding of both collective and personal histories. Cady Noland's *Bluewald* (1989) features an enlarged news photo of Lee Harvey Oswald, shown doubled over after being shot by Jack Ruby, silkscreened onto an aluminium panel that is propped up with a crude wooden support and perforated with several large circular 'bullet' holes around Oswald's midsection and face. The format recalls the life-sized, cut-out photos — sometimes called 'standees' — that are a fairground staple; usually depicting historical figures or movie stars, they offer the public a fictional photo opportunity to pose alongside the famous. In restaging the image of Oswald's assassination through this 'low' sculptural form, Noland underscores the way in which America's mass media carnival reduces social reportage to a sideshow spectacle. The reflective surface of the aluminium panel, meanwhile, hints at our complicit participation, as does the way in which the sculpture stands before us like a pop-up shooting target.

Alluding to the perceptual impact of filmic, rather than photographic, experience, McCarthy's *That Girl (T.G. Awake)* disconcertingly reconfigures sculpture's temporal coordinates. The three figures in this work depict the same model in poses that are only subtly varied; seemingly capturing the subject in contiguous moments of time, they conjure a three-dimensional sequence of film stills. But whereas a finished film assembles its discrete parts into a seamless whole, McCarthy's installation foregrounds the fractured material reality of cinema; it spaces its three figures in such a way that we cannot properly take them all in at the same time. Each figure, while representing a whole body, is also presented as only a fragment of a temporal sequence. In effect, figurative sculpture of this kind constitutes a subversive realism; instead of reassuringly confirming our sense of a concrete 'reality' out there, it engages us in reflecting on the media-derived conventions that inform our perception and understanding of the 'real.'

Materiality As Convention

A number of artists in *The Human Factor* deliberately foreground the material aspects of their sculpture, as well as traces of its production process, as a means of disrupting our tendency to read the figure primarily as a representation, a screen for our anthropomorphic projections. In contrast to much modernist sculpture, in which movement and spatial dynamics are fundamental themes, this kind of work often highlights the static, object-like character of the sculpted figure. This emphasis is evident in Ugo Rondinone's series of 'nudes' (2010–11), which depict seated naked figures, cast in wax from the bodies of young dancers and posed on the floor as if resting after a strenuous rehearsal. The realistic detail of their cast forms, along with the flesh-like tactility of wax, endows them with a visceral immediacy, but their individual specificity is undermined by the way the artist has coloured the various parts of each body with different monochrome earth tints. The exposed metal armature of their jointed construction, meanwhile, makes us keenly aware of their status as a compilation of fragments. For all their particularity, these sculptures evince an object-like anonymity that undercuts our anthropomorphic response. Rather than engaging us as performers in a theatrical event, they confront us with the void and inertia of its aftermath.

Other artists seek to disrupt our usual ways of looking at and thinking about the figure by making work that pits its representational aspirations against the base spectacle of an energetic materiality. Though very different in appearance, figurative sculptures by Rebecca Warren and Georg Herold share this desublimating tendency. Venturing into the far reaches of figurative semblance, the work of both artists deploys a seemingly improvised and clumsy mode of facture to give their work an insistent physicality that undermines our habit of projecting a sense of human life onto sculptural objects.

SHE (2003), Warren's grouping of six carnivalesque grotesques, speaks to a long legacy of work by male artists who have fetishised the female form, from Pablo Picasso and Willem de Kooning to Helmut Newton and R. Crumb.[10] Modelled in unfired clay, Warren's outlandishly sexualised ur-females appear to have only half-emerged from the primordial ooze. With gleeful and biting absurdity, they parody modernist games of formal distortion, revealing and revelling in their sublimated cruelty. At the same time, Warren's bulky yet fragile sculptures confront us with a contradictory physicality: animated by a suggestion of capricious movement, they nevertheless seem mired in an excessive, inchoate materiality that undercuts their figurative evocation. Herold's over-sized figures achieve a not dissimilar effect by foregrounding the banality of their DIY facture and materials. For all their imposing scale and energetic construction, the deliberate 'dumbness' of their slapdash and schematic presence brings them close to a degree zero in terms of their anthropomorphic values. Emptied of any suggestion of inner life, Herold's and Warren's figures focus our attention on their crude physicality as a way of mocking the 'humanist' pretentions and anthropomorphic romance accommodated by both fully-embodied and abstract sculpture alike.

Reconfigured Ready-Mades

Several artists, including Thomas Hirschhorn, Isa Genzken and Rachel Harrison, make use of ready-made figurative representations — in the form of store-bought mannequins and masks — in sculptures that possess a collage-like character. Recalling the dismemberment and ornamentation of the figure in early-twentieth-century sculptures by Dada and surrealist artists, much of this work compromises or dissolves the ostensible 'identity' of its ready-made figurative components by dramatically modifying or combining them with other sculptural elements. In Hirschhorn's *4 Women* (2008), four female mannequin bodies are partially covered with hand-written messages and accretions of formless blue matter (the artist refers to the latter as a manifestation of a 'hardening' forming over the figure like a kind of character armour) to evoke the body as a material surface on which society inscribes its various constraining texts and codes. As with the artist's *Resistance-Subjecter* (2011), Hirschhorn encases his distressed mannequin bodies in a vitrine-like structure that highlights the public character of their display while also invoking the dematerialising effects of spectacle culture (as evident in our unconscious habit, for example, of looking at the world as if from behind a glass lens or mediating screen). Indeed, the group of mannequins in *Resistance-Subjecter* appears to be dematerialising before our eyes, their bodies punctured by large, gaping 'wounds' that seemingly register the socially corrosive force of our detached consumer's gaze.

In her recent series of untitled mannequin sculptures, Isa Genzken treats the figure as an armature for freakish assemblages of masks, clothing and fabric. Dominated and defined by their exuberant material decoration, these figures exude a minimal, stillborn 'human' presence. We may be drawn in by their festive eccentricity, but we are kept at a distance by their blatant lack of any emotive or empathetic signals. These sculptures invert the classic tradition of 'breathing life' into dead materials; instead they present anthropomorphic figures as objects immersed in a pile of dead things. Genzken's open-ended formalism infuses her fashion-forward figures with the melancholy of still lifes, while recalling Walter Benjamin's remark that fashion 'was never anything but the parody of the gaily decked-out corpse'.[11]

Rachel Harrison's sculpture also tellingly mixes figurative and formal concerns, often drolly addressing the legacy of monumental statuary through an anti-heroic and funky physicality. Typically, the ready-made figurative components in her sculptures — store-bought masks and mannequins — are framed within collage-like scenarios that conjoin and contrast items of clothing, consumer bric-a-brac, photographs and vertical (and vaguely anthropomorphic) abstract forms. In *Jack Lemmon* (2011), two primary components compete for our attention: an abstract, colourfully painted cement blob and a child-sized mannequin with a Janus-style head, displaying masks that respectively depict the adult faces of a young woman and a grinning Dick Cheney.[12] Through its implied equivalence of these opposing elements, and fuelled by the antic, slapstick energy produced by its contradictory swarm of signs and materials, *Jack Lemmon* pulls the rug out from under our staid anthropocentrism. Simultaneously summoning and subverting figurative conventions, it lures us into a delirious encounter with sculptural 'otherness'.

Material Process

In classical sculpture, the figure was pointedly made from enduring materials — whether stone or metal — that offered a contrast to the impermanence of our own bodies. Reluctant to embrace our condition as mortal material beings, we have historically honoured the sculpted figure as an ideal surrogate impervious to the passing of time. Yet the connection of sculpture to death is an ancient one. Indeed, it has been said that the first statue was a corpse inasmuch as that was the first inert *object* from which an aura of life emanated.[13] Like every ideal form, then, classical sculpture inevitably calls to mind its degenerate twin.

Artists such as Paweł Althamer and Urs Fischer dramatically recast sculpture's pretence to permanence by fashioning figures from distinctly ephemeral materials. Featuring two nude standing figures (representing the artist and his first wife) who respectively hold a video camera and a mobile phone, Althamer's *Monika and Pawel* (2002) suggests an Adam and Eve reconceived for the digital era. While they boast realistically painted plaster faces, wigs and porcelain eyes, their bodies were fabricated with straw stuffing and covered with a 'skin' made from animal intestines. Resembling failed mummies (the works suffered significant damage from moths in 2008), Althamer's figures evoke an unsuccessful attempt to fix the appearances of living persons. Their now partially decomposed forms lend this sculpture the character of a work-in-progress, something yet to be finished. (It is worth noting that Althamer has said that he wanted the mobile phone and video camera to function for as long as possible, in order to anchor the piece more fully in an unfolding present moment.)[14] *Monika and Pawel* thus alludes to classical figuration only to reject its enduring physical form for a visceral and time-bound materiality.

Urs Fischer's *Untitled* (2001) likewise undermines the notions of permanence, stability and solidity associated with traditional figurative sculpture. Cast in wax from a form roughly carved in Styrofoam and tinted with crudely lifelike colouring, it depicts a standing nude woman with a candlewick emerging from the top of her head. As a condition of its display, the wick is lit and burns throughout the course of an exhibition, during which time the sculpture's man-made form gradually melts into an inchoate mound, as if returning to a state of raw matter. In *vanitas* still-life paintings, the candle is a common symbol of transience, but in configuring a sculpted body as a candle Fischer seems less interested in questions of human mortality than in staging a process of transformation. Animated by the movement of flickering flame and the changing aspect of its melting, dripping, ever-shifting form, Fischer's sculpture essentially takes on the character of a 'live' event. Besides calling to mind the built-in obsolescence of consumer products, its timed self-destruction speaks to our insatiable using up (or 'burning up') of things and images. Accustomed to the perpetual novelty of the marketplace, we now find little comfort in classical sculpture's evocation of an unchanging temporality; indeed, for today's sensation-seeking consumer, eternity has all the attraction of a graveyard.

Pierre Huyghe transforms a sculpted figure not into an event but into a component of a living system. *Liegender Frauenakt (Untilled 2011–2012)* (2012) is a concrete cast of a neo-classical reclining nude. Obscuring the statue's head with an active beehive, Huyghe disfigures the statue, creating a living mask, a new organ, a hybrid between a mineral form made by a human being and a living organism, a fixed object and an evolving structure. The work was originally presented in a composting area of Kassel's baroque park during DOCUMENTA (13) as one of the elements within Huyghe's biotope project *Untilled*, which reflects the exhibition's focus on 'imagining a universe that's less anthropocentric, a world of thought and active life that's not based especially on humans'. By adding a living organism to the existing sculpture, Huyghe recasts it as a part of a system linked to the surrounding environment through the bees' foraging and communicative behaviour.

G

In their unstable materiality, sculptures such as those discussed above engage us in the drama of a human form taking on a character for which we have no ready-made categories. Through their on-going processes of change, such works conjure the material flux of the world that lies concealed beneath the surface of our traditional forms; indeed, such forms are precisely tasked with masking this chaos. In drawing attention to this, these sculptures underscore their own status as works of artifice; foregrounding their constructed 'nature', they call into question the seeming 'naturalness', as well as the constraints, of our familiar figurative representations and clichés. They also lead us to look sceptically at the 'human' truths and values to which these conventions give form.

By various means, all of the artists considered here similarly make use of the human figure to unsettle, rather than confirm, its associations with the familiar and the known. As we have seen, the figure is not the *raison d'être* of their work so much as a rhetorical point of departure. It is engaged not to affirm our existing notions of subjectivity and identity, but as a means of looking askance at them. Far from invoking some universalised aspect of humanity, the sculpted figure is treated here as a network of multiple and contradictory meanings. Reflecting our physical presence in the gallery, it functions as a catalyst that provokes us to reflect on how we ourselves are 'figured' by aspects of our shared social reality.

One last point: there is nothing nostalgic about this kind of sculpture. In taking on the figure's various histories and conventions, it opens up bygone sculptural genres to renewed scrutiny and re-invention by repositioning them in relation to contemporary concerns and dilemmas. Ultimately, its thought-provoking realignment of historical tropes confronts us with the time-bound contingency of all our 'human' representations, current as well as past. In this respect, it offers a tonic contrast to our cult of contemporaneity, which grants us the perspective of 'molecules without history who drag themselves from one instant to another'.[16] The sculptures in *The Human Factor*, on the other hand, involve us in working through our cultural memory of the figure in order to reach an understanding of how this most familiar form — once regarded as an artistic anachronism — can still be reconfigured in ways that enhance our questioning and our understanding of our present time.

1 Jeff Koons, interview in 'Fantasy', *Art 21*, Season 5, PBS, first broadcast: 14 October 2009, 22:00 (EST). Available at: www.art21.org/images/jeff-koons/bear-and-policeman-1988 (last visited: 26 March 2014)

2 Mike Kelley, *The Uncanny*. (Fred Hoffman: Los Angeles, 1993), exh. cat. (*Sonsbeek 93*, Arnhem, The Netherlands, 5 June–26 September 1993), p. 24. Three of the artists in *The Uncanny* — Jeff Koons, Paul McCarthy and John Miller — are also included in *The Human Factor*

3 Giorgio Vasari, *Le Vite de' più eccellenti pittori, scultori, e architettori da Cimabue insino a' tempi nostril* (Lives of the Most Excellent Painters, Sculptors, and Architects), (Torrentino: Florence, 1550) quoted in W.J.T. Mitchell, *What do Pictures Want: The Lives and Loves of Images*, (University of Chicago Press: Chicago, 2006), p. 245

4 This is not to say there were not significant artists making innovative figurative sculpture during this period. Besides those already mentioned, artists such as Paul Thek, Alina Szapocznikow, John Davies and Tadeusz Kantor all made important figurative sculptures. But their work was the exception

5 Benson cites 1980s influences ranging from Robert Mapplethorpe to Patrick Nagel's pop-noir illustrations, Ridley Scott's *Blade Runner* (1982) and the 1980s album covers designed by Jean-Paul Goude for Grace Jones (Conversation with the artist, October 2012)

6 The bronze cast of Degas' *Little Dancer Aged Fourteen*, the form of this work that is most commonly exhibited, was not made until 1921, four years after the artist's death

7 Cited in Robert L. Pincus, *On A Scale That Competes with the World: The Art of Edward and Nancy Reddin Kienholz* (University of California Press: Berkeley/Los Angeles, 1990), p. 71

8 Fried maintained that the 'grace and presentness' of truly great art was predicated on its maintaining the 'supreme fiction' that its audience did not exist. See Michael Fried, 'Art and Objecthood', *Artforum*, Issue 5, June 1967, pp. 12–23

9 Joseph R. Wolin, 'Anna Plesset: "A Still Life"', *Time Out: New York*, 28 June 2013

10 Warren's vigorous modelling of raw clay also more generally evokes the myth of modernist sculptors — both figurative and abstract — grappling with the 'truth' of their materials

11 Cited in Susan Buck-Morss, *The Dialectics of Seeing: Walter Benjamin and the Arcades Project* (MIT Press: Cambridge, MA 1991), p. 101

12 Dick Cheney is the former Vice President of the United States and one of the key architects of the second U.S. invasion of Iraq in 2003. In Harrison's sculpture he is shown holding a lemon in an outstretched fishing net — a possible reference to the foreign policy 'lemons' he helped create as Vice-President?

13 Kelley, *The Uncanny*, p. 19

14 Paweł Althamer in conversation with Sven Spieker, *ArtMargins*, 12 November 2003, available at: www.artmargins.com/index.php/5-interviews/304-interview-with-pawel-althamer (last visited: 1 April 2014)

15 Pierre Huyghe in conversation with Carolyn Christov-Bakargiev, artistic director of DOCUMENTA (13), available at: www.hatjecantz.de/carolyn-christov-bakargiev-5197-1.html (last visited: 1 April 2014)

16 Jean-Paul Sartre, quoted in Alex Potts, *The Sculptural Imagination: Figurative, Modernist, Minimalist* (Yale University Press: New Haven, CT, 2000), p. 212

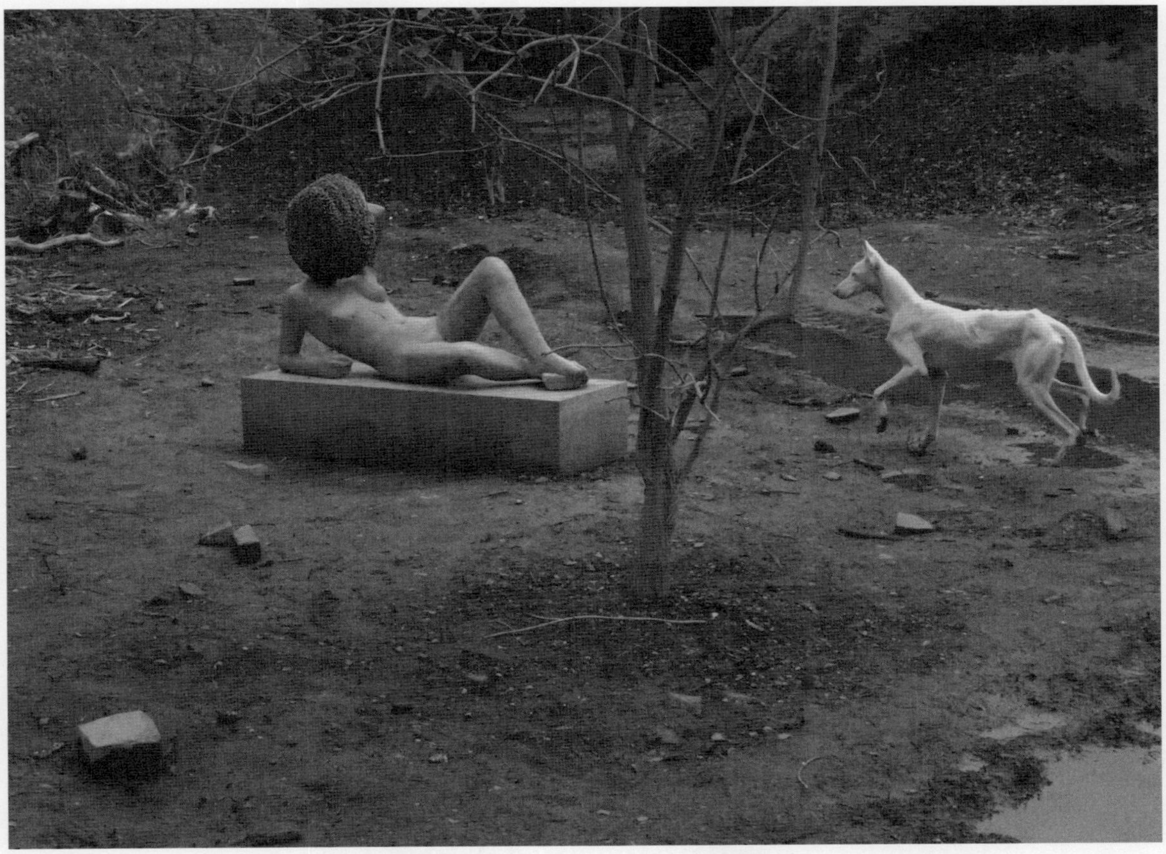

G

Pierre Huyghe,
***Untilled*, 2011–12**

Penelope Curtis

Standing Sculpture at the Turn of the Century

Exchange Values and Metamorphoses

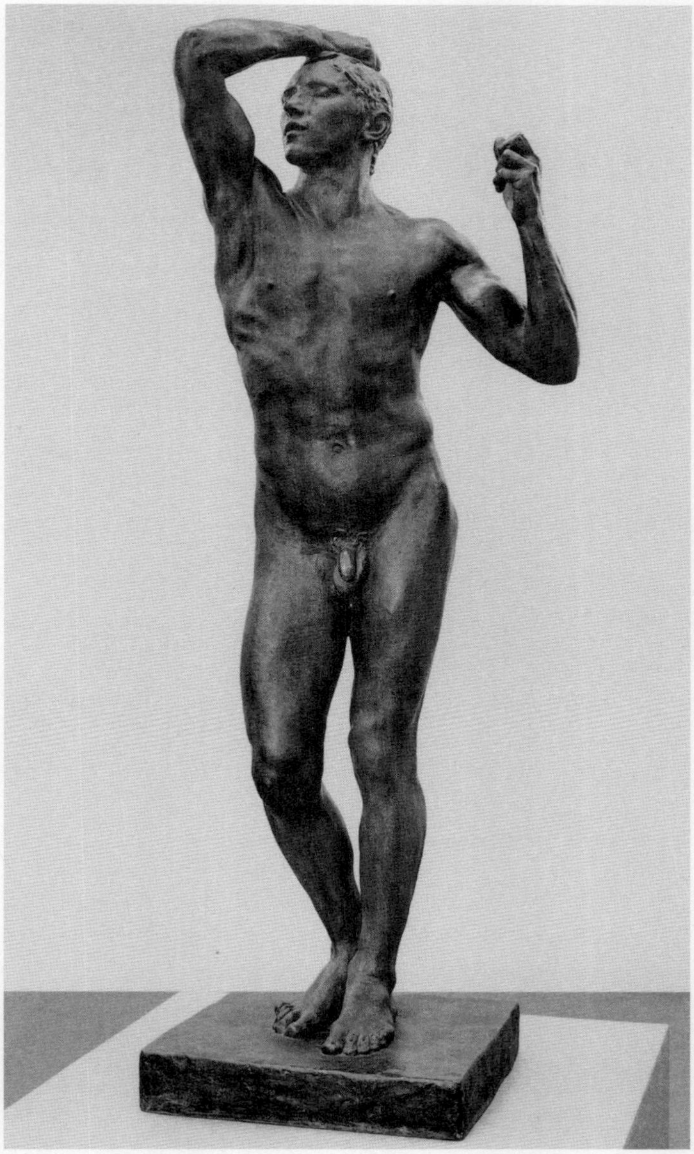

A

Auguste Rodin,
***The Age of Bronze*, c. 1876**

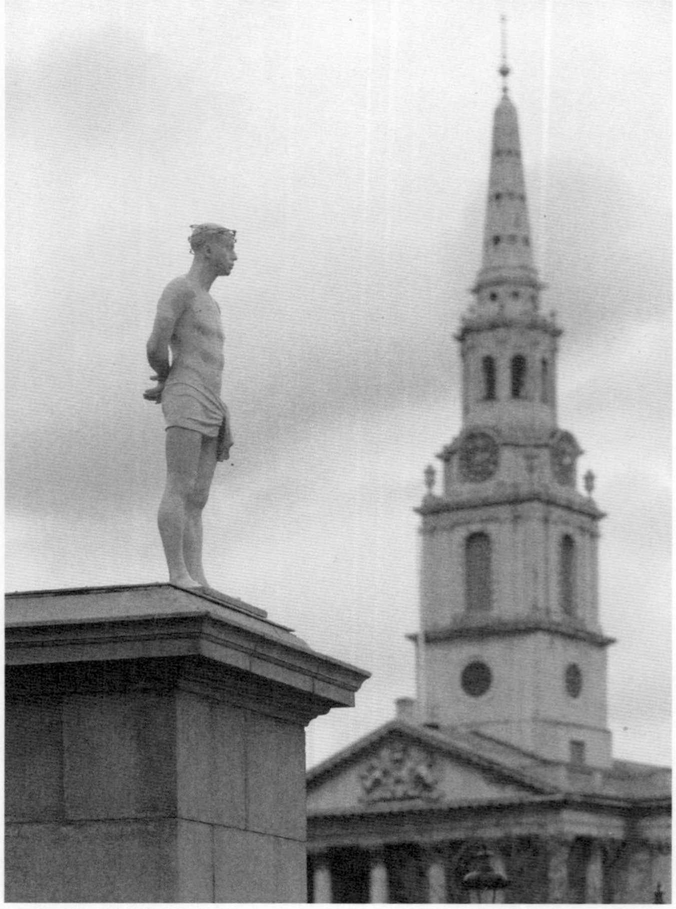

B

Mark Wallinger, *Ecce Homo*, 1999

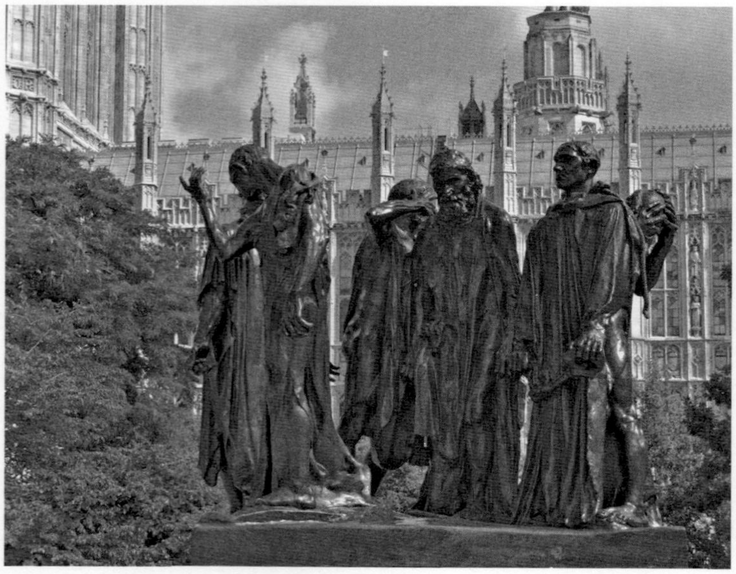

C

Auguste Rodin, *The Burghers of Calais*, 1889

There is a striking image which Charles Ray composed for the cover of a 1998 exhibition catalogue.[1] The artist appears alongside Anthony Caro's *Early One Morning* (1962), one of his favourite works. So far, so good. What catches the eye, however, is the quality of the image, or at least the image of the artist, both in terms of its positioning and his appearance. This is the more meaningful if one has any knowledge of Ray's work, which plays with mannequins and scale as a key trajectory.[2]

At the time of Caro's Tate retrospective in 2005,[3] Ray went into some detail about this picture within a more general interview with Michael Fried, because it had a rather complicated genesis. When he had been preparing for his earlier show at the ICA,[4] Ray had asked Caro if he might place and photograph a nude female model on the arm of the sculpture, and though Caro clearly understood the point, he asked that no image be disseminated which might suggest that the sculpture, which is in fact quite fragile, be used for this purpose. On the other hand, he gave Ray permission to take a photograph with a standing model. Apparently Ray ran out of time and this was never realised, but it is an interesting starting point and one that serves our purposes well.

This photographic image might be seen to represent the space between figurative and abstract sculpture, but in fact it slowly but surely demonstrates how little space there is between them, and how both elements of the image take us toward questions about scale, support, colour and expression. It is not merely a local affair, and not just because we know that Ray was educated through the work of Caro (by the Saint Martin's trained Roland Brener, who had moved to Iowa), and inspired by Edward Hopper's painting of a woman on a bed, that we know that this image makes an important point. It is as much about equivalence as about difference, and this is why it is useful for thinking about the works in this exhibition.

One might quibble and say that this image shows an artist and an artwork, rather than two artworks, but I think the fact that much of Ray's work at this time involved representations and casts of his own body, as well as making his own clothes, allows us to think of him here as an artwork. So what we see are two sculptures sharing adjacent space, both resting on the same ground. And though we may have been schooled to cite that Caro abandoned the plinth, the truth is that abstract sculpture was never on the plinth, and what has been more remarkable, over the last thirty years, is to see how figurative sculpture has decided to try being down on the ground as well as trying to get up on the plinth.

Abstract sculpture depends upon human scale for its effect and impact. Ray upsets the nicety of that balance by introducing outsize scales into his human figures. By placing his own figure next to Caro's most famous sculpture, he at once pays homage and undermines its power. Some of Ray's earliest work was more conventionally abstract, exploring as it did the languages of geometry and gravity in a perhaps consciously derivative language. Nonetheless even his most minimalist forms often included a human as well as a commemorative element.[5] He made works that remind us of Robert Morris and of Caro himself. He found his voice, however, when he realised that he could be more abstract by being figurative. This unexpected equation sees the tradition of figurative sculpture in the twentieth century swing round on itself like a figure of eight. In the early years of the century figurative sculpture was highly abstracted; it lost much of this formal restraint after the war, only to refind it in a different guise at the end. In the twenty-first century, this abstraction through the figurative is evident in the detached hyperrealism of Frank Benson's *Human Statue* (2005) and *Human Statue (Jessie)* (2011), as well as the *Untitled* (2012) assemblages of Isa Genzken.

Nineteenth-century sculptors wished to be statue-makers (*statuaires*) rather than mere sculptors. They understood that their art's highest ambitions were vested in the figure and, more than simply figural, they wished to be offered the medium of the standing figure (*statue en pied*). It was around this form that they grouped their own aspirations, because these reflected those of the public more widely. The standing figure dominated the new public sculpture of Europe and the United States; it monopolised the physical and conceptual framework of sculpture. There are of course notable exceptions, including the equestrian statue, the seated (enthroned) figure and the composite, but the *statue en pied*, on its feet, was simply accepted as the standard. It was raised up because it was in public space; the plinth displayed and protected it at the same time (and public statues often needed protection).[6] Another sculptor whose impact is often linked to the absence of plinth is Auguste Rodin. The paradigm is most often ascribed to *The Burghers of Calais* (1889), a work in which the remarkable composite quality is therefore unjustly overlooked. Surely what is singular about this monument is not its height (which varied, but was never without plinth) but the fact that it is a group portrait with an internal dynamic which in many ways excluded the onlooker, who is the more impressed as a result. It is not a low sculpture which allows for audience participation; on the contrary it is an introspective sculpture which keeps its audience out. It is in this respect, rather than in its height, that it comes to mind when we look at Ugo Rondinone's 'nudes' (2010–11). Even Paweł Althamer's pair, *Monika and Pawel* (2002), share its downward cast.

B, C

What was striking about Mark Wallinger's *Ecce Homo*, commissioned to stand on Trafalgar Square's 'Fourth Plinth' in 1999, was that it was a sculpture made within the new conventions of late-twentieth-century plinthless sculpture. It looked so defenceless, so underpowered, so human, because it was placed in public, outdoors, on an outsize plinth. Much of the sculpture which we see in this exhibition is made, like most gallery sculpture, to share our ground. In this respect figurative sculpture is enabled to be abstract, to work on equal premises, and to eschew the qualities required by the monument.

Wallinger's *Ecce Homo* has quite a lot in common with Rodin's *The Age of Bronze* (c. 1876). Both assert their lifelikeness and the sense that the life-size is a little bit less than sculpture-size. Both are closer to the naked than to the nude, and their symbolism lies in the very fact that they carry very little symbolical trapping. Rodin's figure betrays its former accessories in the arrangement of its arms; Wallinger's is more simply positioned.[7] While Wallinger's figure was cast from life, Rodin's was not, but thought to be. This, a heavy accusation at the time, and one which Rodin fought hard to repudiate, is of course also why it has such enduring strength. It seems very little removed from us but so exposed in its humanity that it protests its Christlikeness as much as its lifelikeness.

A

Many of these standing statues do use a plinth, or some more quotidian support, whether for reasons of stability or to play upon notions of sculpture as either a durable or an ephemeral form, or both. Althamer, Katharina Fritsch, Georg Herold, Martin Honert (and John Miller, to a degree) are surprisingly unusual in standing their sculpture on its own two feet in the gallery. In contrast, as many figures here are pretending to be sculptures, as are pretending to be figures. There are in fact rather few simulacra, and more composites, in which the figure itself is eroded, truncated, blinded, disembowelled, burnt and generally travestied, dressed up or dressed down, somehow returned to a more primal state in which the figure does battle with its *prima materia*.

The tension between the form and the image, as with Fritsch, or the form and the material, as with Rachel Harrison, is striking, and almost like an equation in which the result is contested. This has something to do with the relationship between raw material and made material. In another age it might have been expressed in the form of the fight between the savage and the civilised, as seen in works such as Emmanuel Frémiet's *Gorilla Abducting a Woman* (1887). There is something almost as sexualised at play in the pairings seen here as in those more overtly eroticised couplings of the late nineteenth century. The figures of Althamer express in the rawness of their material a struggle that has resulted in their return to nature; those of Thomas Hirschhorn too seem to hang in the balance between becoming and unbecoming, as their innards threaten to spill as much as to fill.

D

These sculptures echo those of the nineteenth century in another way: they are effectively chryselephantine, or made in a mixture of materials, each of which lends its specific characteristics to the creation of 'reality'. Deriving its name from Greek sculpture in precious stone and ivory, chryselephantine sculpture came to apply to a wider range of materials, but suggesting still the relationship between exposed flesh and its adornments, between vulnerability and invulnerability, between woman and man. Life-size sculptures such as Maurice Ferrary's *Salammbo* (1899) exemplify the interaction between materials, and thus across the body. This admixture of 'soft' materials hardening, and 'hard' materials softening, is as, if not more, apparent in the works on show.

The way in which matter becomes image is expressed in another way in an (in)famous work like the *The Tinted Venus* (c. 1851–56) of John Gibson, in which the tinting of the lips and nipples reminded the viewer that this was about more than mere marble. That same interplay, if updated, is at work in many of the exhibits, which slip between object and image, raw material and the human figure. Rebecca Warren's figure group *SHE* (2003) speaks clearly of this, and makes a nice comparison with Gibson, while Frank Benson's *Human Statue (Jessie)* (2011), draped but masked, seems almost to respond to the gaze of the Venus.

E

Caro gives us more reality than Ray, whose work is frankly deceptive. Nonetheless, Caro's colour unifies disparate elements, and thus creates a single image.[8] Fritsch deploys a comparable strategy in her painted figures, which thus shed their realism to become more sculptural and less pictorial, more like objects and less like images. Yet colour also negates their materiality, which is expressed instead in the massing of the photographs which act as their backdrops. Such interplay as seen between Caro and Ray is similarly at work in Harrison, Hirschhorn and Cathy Wilkes.

Indeed we might well compare these pairings — and especially Fritsch's *Riese und 4. Postkarte (Franken)* (Giant and 4th Postcard [Franconia]) (2008) — to Frémiet's woman and ape. There is a recourse to a binary proposition, and one detects a default position which allows for the twinning of rough and smooth, made and unmade, uncoloured and coloured. This nearly haptic exchange between figure and ground, between body and material, unites an apparently eclectic range of artwork, and discourages us from making any simple conclusions about figurative sculpture in the early twenty-first century, other than to accept that it is being as abstract as it is figurative.

1 Paul Schimmel (ed.), *Charles Ray*. (The Museum of Contemporary Art/Scalo: Los Angeles/Zürich, 1998)
2 When Ray made his catalogue for the Los Angeles MOCA retrospective, he found his chance to use the idea that had been there for a while. The credit for the cover image reads: 'Caro, courtesy Tate Gallery London; Ray, photo by Joshua White'. This work is not a work, or is only a cover, and as such is more than usually confusing. Ray appears to stand behind Caro's work, giving it a scale which may or may not be right. We might think this is a sculpture of Ray by Ray, but it is merely a photo of Ray, by someone else, placed behind a photo of the sculpture. 'CHARLES RAY' are the words placed above the photos of *Early One Morning* and above the photo of the artist
3 *Anthony Caro*, Tate Britain, London, 26 January–17 April 2005
4 *Charles Ray*, ICA (Institute of Contemporary Arts), London, 24 June–14 August 1994
5 His interest in the Forest Lawn Memorial Garden (Springdale, California) must be relevant here
6 For examples of this practice, see the essay by Greg Sullivan in Tabitha Barber (ed.), *Art under Attack: Histories of British Iconoclasm*. (Tate Publishing: London, 2013)
7 First exhibited as *The Vanquished*, Rodin's figure had carried a lance and worn a simple wreath on its head
8 The way in which colour brings sculpture to life is further developed by Ray in his *Unpainted Sculpture* of 1997, which to my mind is like the direct inverse of Gibson, draining out the colour of an image (a Pontiac car) so as to make it into sculpture

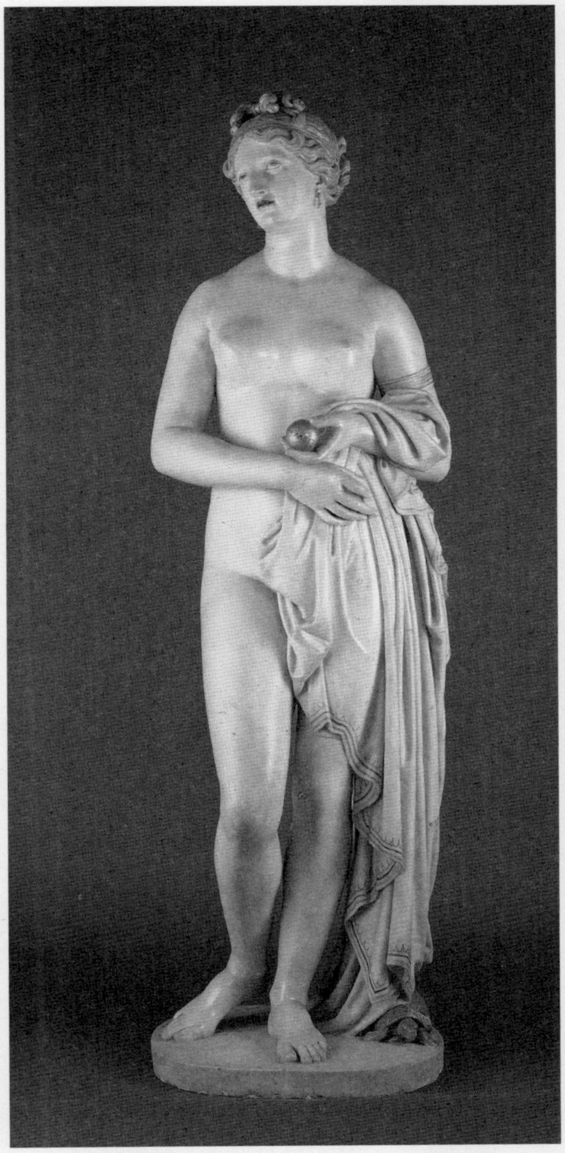

E

John Gibson, *The Tinted Venus*, c. 1851–56

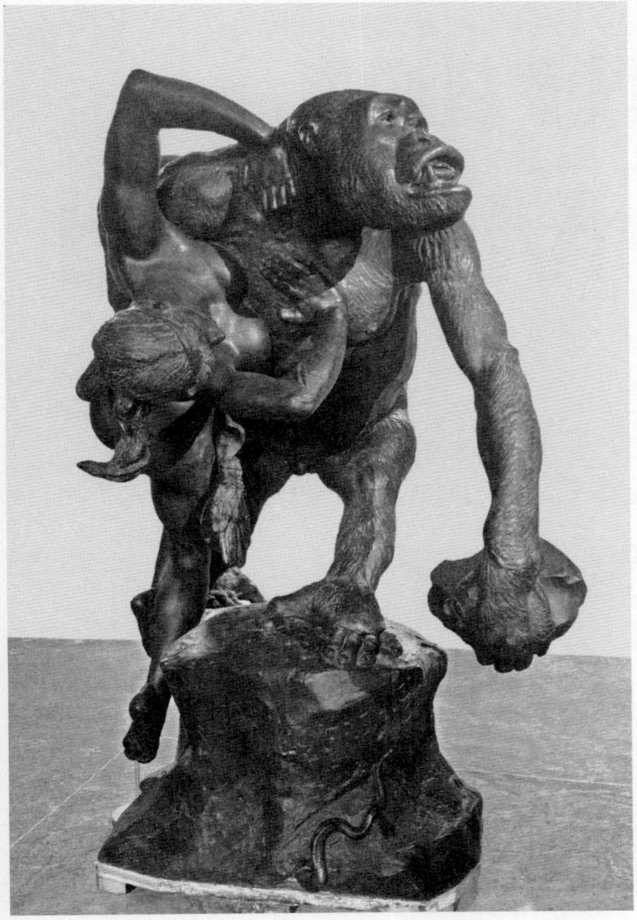

D

Emmanuel Frémiet, *Gorilla Abducting a Woman*, 1887

Martin Herbert

Post-Abstract and Data-Mapped

The Conditions of Contemporary Figure Sculpture

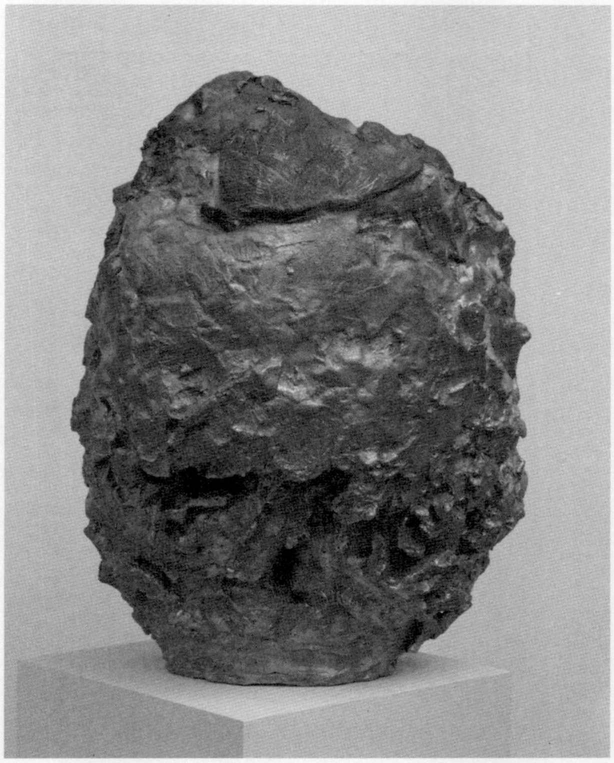

A

Rebecca Warren, *Head*,
2001

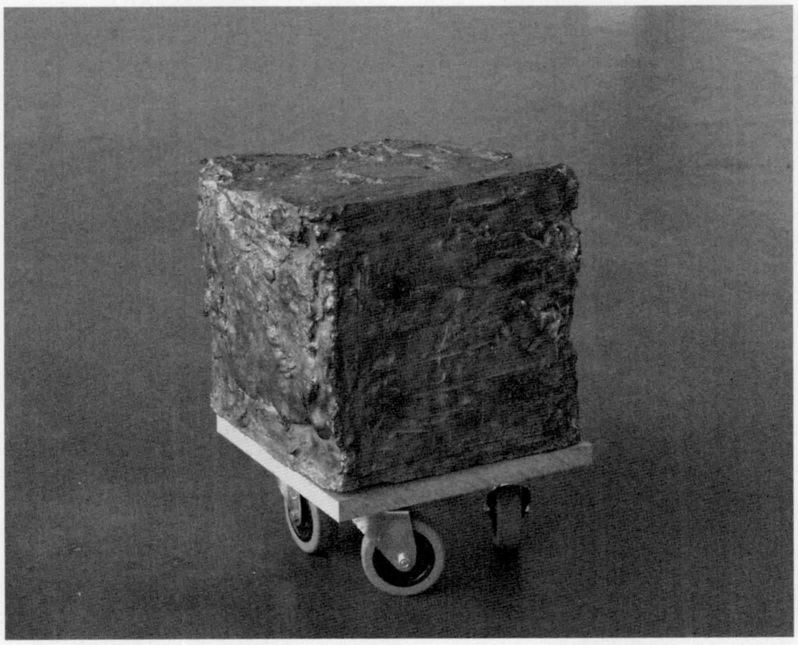

B

Rebecca Warren, *Cube*,
2003

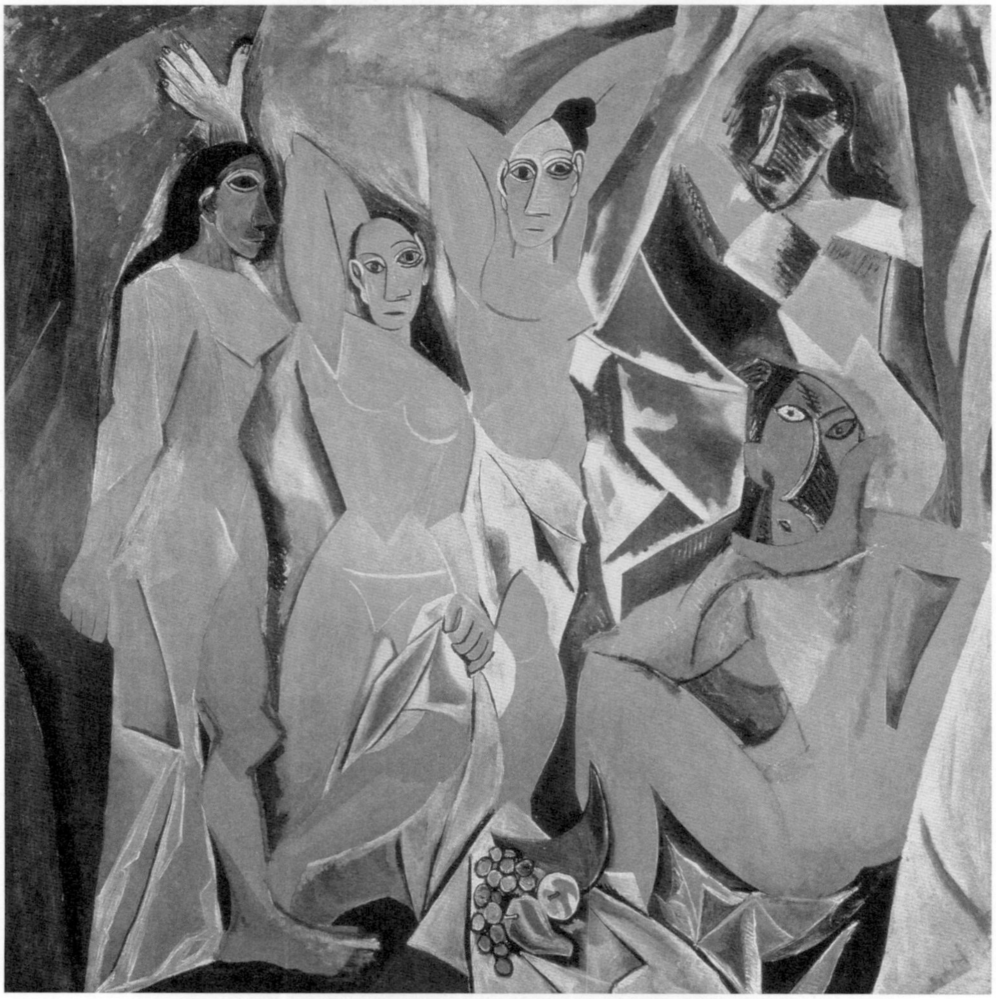

C

Pablo Picasso, *Les Demoiselles d'Avignon*, 1907

In a 1964 conversation with Alberto Giacometti, David Sylvester reminded the artist of something strange he'd once said: that, while working on a standing figure, the more clay he took away, 'the bigger it gets'. After Giacometti acknowledged saying so, but added that he didn't know why it was, the critic hazarded a rationale: 'that when the thing is narrower, and therefore denser, it has more pent-up energy. And if this energy, this contained violence, goes on increasing, you have the impression that the sculpture dominates more space.'[1] In such a reading, there's an interpenetration of the sculpture and the very air around it. Relatedly, in his 2001 essay, 'Thinking of Sculpture as Shaped by Space', Charles Ray recalls reading an interview in which Giacometti noted that 'four beautiful women who had just entered the lobby could not be seen separately from the space the shiny marble floor generated between him and them. I think,' Ray went on, 'Giacometti's sculptures somehow carry that space with them.'[2]

Such sculptural space is expansive and complexly tiered: it might, for example, be said to encompass time. But for the moment let's limit ourselves to physical dimensions. It's perhaps not wholly irrelevant to Sylvester's style of questioning, and Ray's later choice of what to highlight about Giacometti's work, that the 1960s was a period in which the relationship between a sculpture and the space around it was being revised and performed via minimalism. If the Italian sculptor's etiolated figures might be characterised as carved and compressed by the anxiety-creating world through which they move — this would be the approximate existentialist reading — then minimal artists more coolly asserted that sculpture, and reception, is indivisible from physical context. For all that the artistic results were typically geometric, this expansion was never wholly an act of abstraction, for minimal art was forever reminding viewers of the presence of their own bodies in the room. 'The better new work', wrote Robert Morris in 'Notes on Sculpture, Part 1', 'takes relationships out of the work and makes them a function of space, light and the viewer's field of vision.'[3] When Sylvester interviewed Morris the following year, he told the artist that what Morris's work most reminded him of, in terms of physiological effect, were the carved figures from one wing of the Parthenon.

In Giacometti's work, the figure merges with abstraction, with an idea of what the world is and what being in it does to one. In minimalism, abstraction merges with the figure. Over the last quarter-century, while abstract sculpture has inevitably continued to be made, artists have returned to the sculpted human form. (Artists are intransigent, wilfully curious types: close a door and they'll try to pry it open.) They have done so, when intelligently, with no illusions about the possibility of a pre-modernist *tabula rasa,* yet also without being able to forget the past. If abstract sculptors could not shake off the figure, figurative sculptors cannot disregard the lessons of abstraction. The latter constitutes unerasable knowledge, and behoves them to operate somewhere in the overlap between two spheres.

Consider, for example, the first half-decade of Rebecca Warren's career. In the late 1990s, Warren first drew attention for working in unfired clay (at a point where her Young British Artist contemporaries were having their work commercially produced) and specifically for conjoining the iconographies of counterculture cartoonist R. Crumb and photographer Helmut Newton in *Helmut Crumb* (1998), a pair of gate-like nested sculptures that reduced bodies to legs and vaginas. This work was in some sense already a dehumanising abstraction and, given Warren's gender, also a work of apparent feminist critique, but all its parts were readable. By 2001, though, Warren was making works like the tartan-patterned, mutely featureless lump *Head.* And by 2003 she'd produced *Cube,* a rough-edged cuboid, sprayed gold, and a series of ungainly, womanly sculptures in which the human figure is dissolving and detaching in increasingly complicated ways, losing defining contours in a manner that reflected Warren's own thought process concerning the iconography she was using.

A, B

Teacher (M.B.) (2003) is one of a trio of works, along with *Teacher (R.)* and *Teacher (W.),* that come with a fictional narrative attached: according to Warren, they've ostensibly been made by an art tutor, a sexually frustrated and rancorous one, at a regional English college. As in Crumb's notorious 1992 cartoon 'A Bitchin' Bod',[4] where the character Flaky Foont happily has sex with a headless woman, here the seat of thought is effectively obliterated, semi-abstracted, reduced to a grotesque, Gorgon-like snake-pit of hair. The figure also has only one monstrous breast and is clubfooted. It sits on a pair of trolleys, the square, skateboard-like sort that artists use to move works around their studios. Mobility is apropos. *Teacher (M.B.)* appears laceratingly critical of art's permissions of sexism, the cold male gaze sanctioned by exceptional skills such as Crumb's and Newton's (and Pablo Picasso's, for such a work also echoes his abstracting aggressions upon the female figure). But it also, Warren has said, reflects a conflicted, involuntary admiration of their ability. The sculpted woman is made of unfixed, unfired clay and is also on wheels. This all makes sense, since what she represents for the artist — a swirl of mixed emotions regarding masters, teachers, predecessors — won't stay still.

C

A figurative sculpture today, *Teacher* admits, must productively acknowledge the multifarious weight of the past. Warren has never shied away from this; she has, rather, used the fact to generate zones of ethical ambiguity. Also in 2003 she produced *Pony,* a pneumatic take on Edgar Degas' small sculpture *Little Dancer Aged Fourteen* (1880–81, cast c. 1922), a work the French artist kept, fetish-like, in his studio. His thought process regarding that work, and its model, is a black hole, a historical ingress that permits a proposal such as Ryan Gander's *I don't blame you, or, When we made love you used to cry and I love you like the stars above and I'll love you 'til I die* (2008). A bronze of a girl in a leotard sits propped against a white plinth, smoking, gazing at a small blue cube. The girl, in Gander's cosmology, is

Degas' teenage model; and this is a moment we never saw — the *danseuse* off-duty, between poses, and, according to the title (which, we might think, is Degas' speech), snarled up in something more than a professional transaction. Times are tangled here, or time is curved. The dancer, taking a fag-break between big historical moments, seems to be contemplating the aesthetic world that will come out of Degas' early modernism — a floating offcut from De Stijl — but also the unknown. The blue cube is a mute thing, like a miniature obelisk dropped from the sky, and it reoccurs enigmatically in Gander's work. (Another one features in *The Artwork Nobody Knows*, 2011, where a tiny, immobilised model of Gander has fallen before it, as if overcome, from his wheelchair.)

D

I don't blame you is turned playfully relativist by its title, which fast-forwards us into the 1980s (it is, in part, a lyric from Dire Straits' 'Romeo and Juliet' [1980], a song based on Shakespeare's 1597 play) while bending chronology to infer, perhaps, the timelessness of human desire and doomed love. Here, and in the companion work *Come up on different streets, they both were streets of shame Or Absinth blurs my thoughts, I think we should be moving on* (2009), again sporting a title partly taken from a 'Romeo and Juliet' lyric), where the girl stands on a larger blue cube to peer through the gallery window, there's an elastic sense of possibility in shuttling between time periods. If the monolithic weight of the aesthetic past derives in part from its being arranged, like standing stones, in a modernist timeline — development appearing to follow development with retrospectively crushing inevitability — then one way of treating it with liberating lightness might be to use it as an opportunity for recombinant fiction. And such fiction is necessarily subjective, so Gander's oeuvre as a whole has suggested since his early, dizzying lecture performances, by making lively, six-degrees-of-separation connections between disparate subjects. These, for all Gander's apparent mental agility, never let you forget that they're just one person's relativist take on the forbidding sprawl of knowledge. This isn't even his truth, just a hand-cut path through the forest.

We might not, today, be able to think of *Romeo and Juliet* without a pop song springing to mind. (We might even prefer the pop song.) Picture a succession of doors slamming shut, over time: no return to purely figurative sculpture, no return to abstraction — which, as we've seen, was ghosted by the figure in any case — and, after pop art, perhaps no possibility of art as a discrete space where the barbarians can't get in. How to speak profoundly in a sullied language?

In Jeff Koons' *Bear and Policeman* (1988), from his 'Banality' series, a smiling bear looms over an English policeman, or 'bobby', who gazes raptly into its eyes. The work, in polychromed wood, has a sweet 1950s feel that is a foil to its roiling psychosexual intent. The bear, in a semi-sexual and definitely dominating move, has grabbed the bobby's whistle, his symbol of authority and the thing that he uses to maintain order, morality. Koons has suggested in several interviews that the creature represents art, which ought to be a powerful, challenging thing that vaults over petty aesthetic niceties; at the same time, though, Koons maintains (in classic Koonsian democratic-uplift style) that art ought not to act in its own interests but in those of the public. In the gaudy universe of his 1988 body of work, 'Banality' — wherein Koons claimed he wanted to create art for the common person to recognise themselves rather than being cowed by oracular high art, an artwork (or artist) — art ought not to steal the whistle, act selfishly.

The irony-proofed blandishments of such work, and the unlikely intellectual challenge posed by Koons' apparent straight-talking and populist ambition, made clear at the time that it was possible to revisit wholly figure-based sculpture without being *retardataire* or simplistic. (Indeed, it is Koons' transparency that turns out to be difficult.) Temporal, spatial, contextual displacement of the existing can be as eloquent as the invention of new forms. In Koons' recent 'Gazing Ball' works, for example, the artist has rewound to antiquity, or something like it. There is a demotic cultural-mainstream vein running through these white plaster sculptures, each engaging with a blue ball; gazing balls, positioned like middle-class trophies in gardens, were a fixture from Koons' childhood. If the laser-cut figures of Aphrodite, Pan, etc. themselves recapitulate classical statuary, they are also tinted with popular culture: plaster casts were, Koons has also noted, very popular in the nineteenth century. And, undoing preconceptions again, for him there are verities in their iconography (sexuality, temptation) that still speak to modern reality, just as the figure of a nineteenth-century dancer might do, if we actually attend to their nuanced body language and altered context rather than merely classifying them.

E

So let the sculptural figure be, at least to some degree, the still point of a turning world. Antique stone newly set, or at least newly cut. Koons, these days, spends much of his time consulting with scientists over rarefied, submolecular developments in 3D printing, and he's far from the only sculptor awake to the widescreen horizons of the digital. Frank Benson's *Human Statue (Jessie)* (2011), though made of bronze, flaunts enough verisimilitude that, when it was installed on New York's High Line, some passers-by mistook it for a bronze-painted, stock-still 'human statue' performer. In actuality, *Human Statue (Jessie)* is an artefact of twenty-first-century bleeding-edge tech. It derives from a 3D rendering of a photograph of Benson's friend, dancer and musician Jessie Gold, which was then 3D-printed using a compound technique called rapid prototyping, before the prints were cast in a New York foundry.

How technology is driving sculptural practice can be measured in the fact that Benson's sculpture is a sequel of sorts to *Human Statue* (2005), a silver-painted male figure who explicitly resembles one of those aforementioned frozen street performers, except that he's dissonantly nude. This work was made in a relatively conventional, analogue way, casting a figure in fibreglass. The six

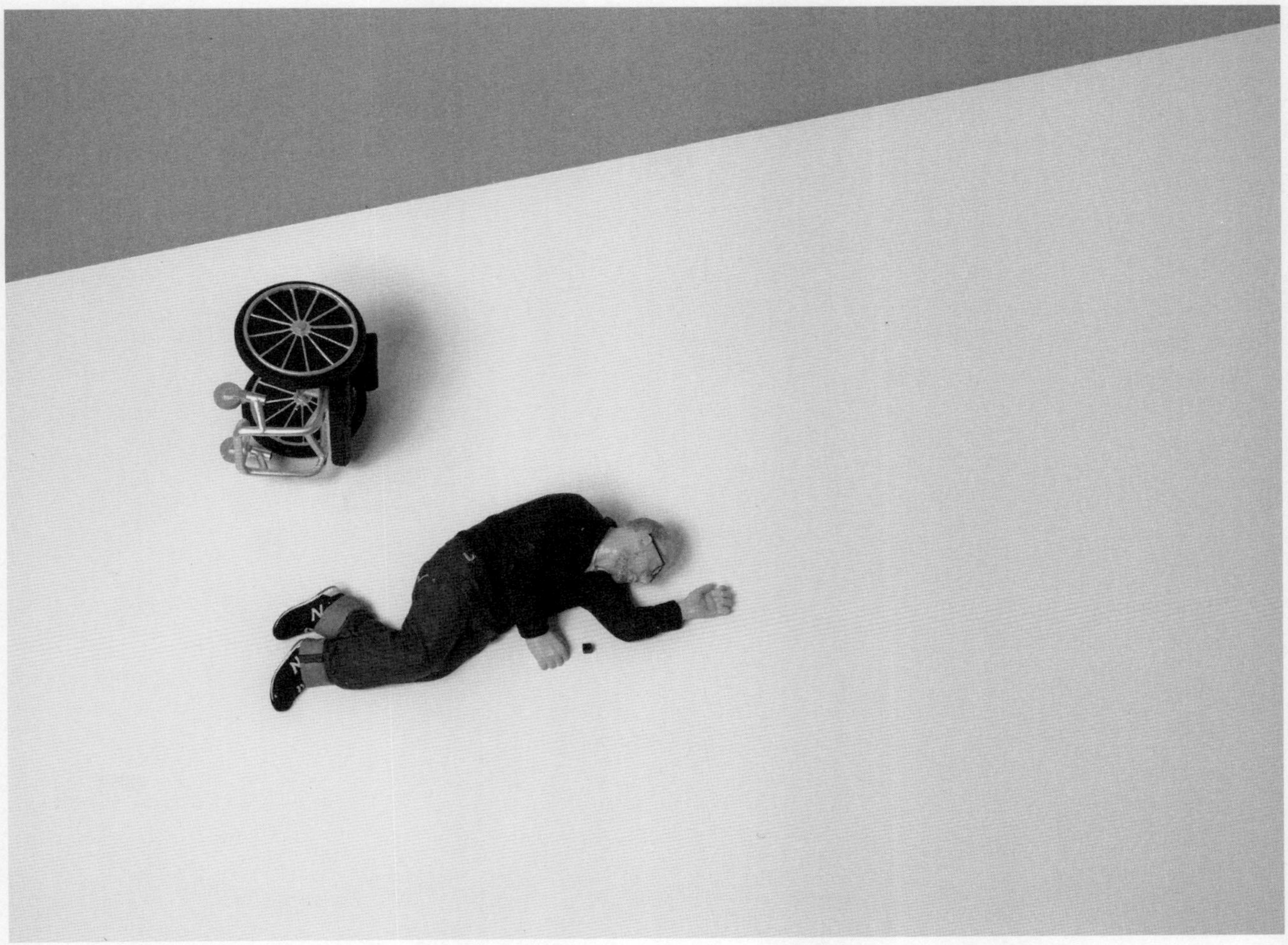

D

Ryan Gander,
***The Artwork Nobody Knows*,**
2011

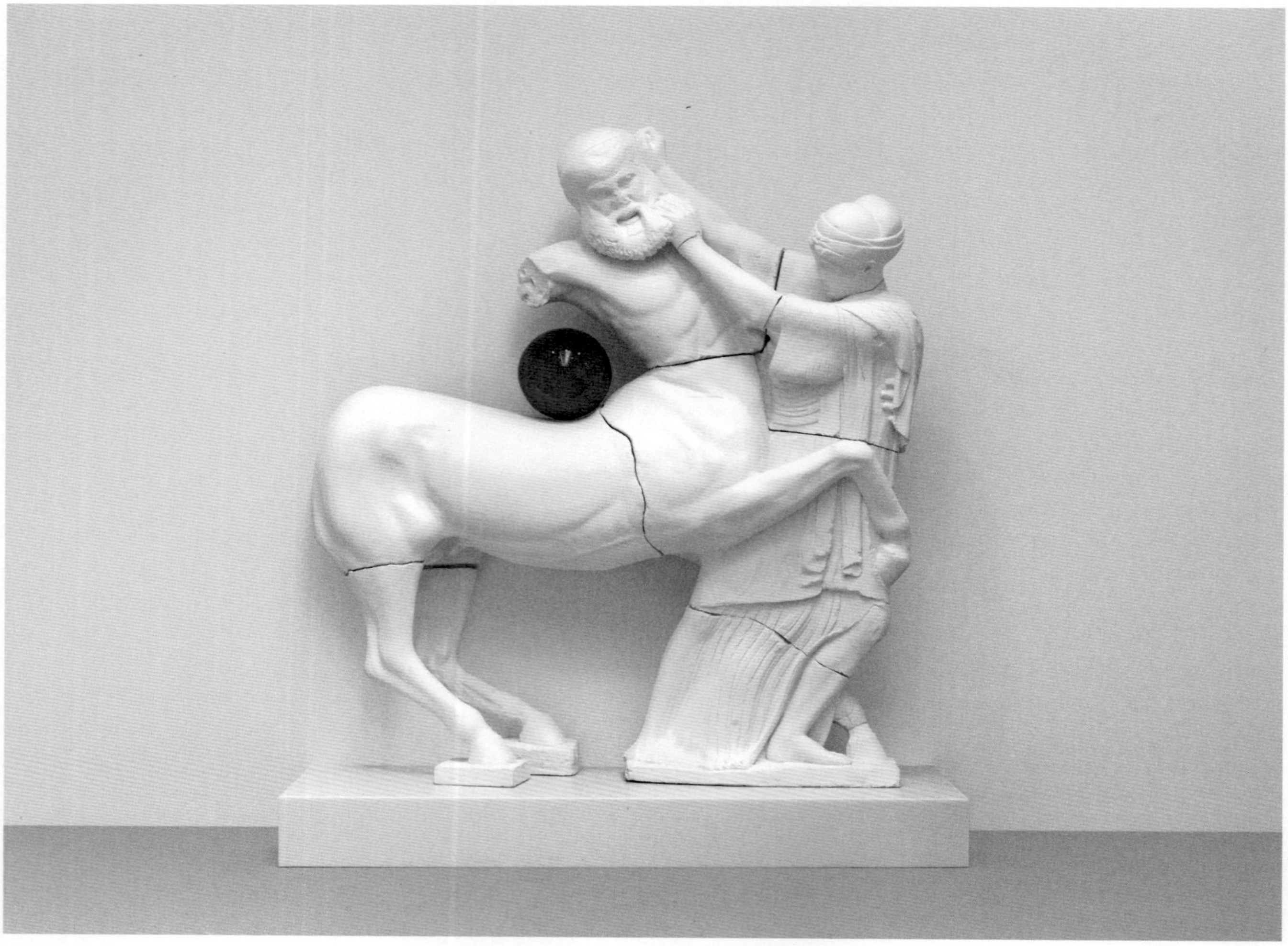

E

Jeff Koons, *Gazing Ball (Centaur and Lapith Maiden)*, 2013

years between the sculptures adumbrate a quantum leap in terms of representational control, since *Human Statue (Jessie)*'s techniques, which didn't exist in 2005, are sensitive enough to render veins in the feet. Reemphasising this technological dominion over the bodily, Benson plays with degrees of fidelity: some areas of the figure are unreally smooth, like an airbrushed magazine cover, others roughed up. But what the artist likes most about the work, he told the blog of *The New York Times,* is the fact that it is 'hard to place chronologically'.[5]

'Jessie's' body is *contrapposto*, a sculptural attitude that dates back to at least 480 BC. At the same time, she's wearing what looks like a sleek, synthetic, very modern black dress. While there's a shield at her feet, and a classical harmony between its shape and the bend of her arms, she sports an androgynous hairstyle and sunglasses that tie her to the 1980s. It's antiquity. It's that first age of retro, the Renaissance. And it's the 80s that looked forward to *Blade Runner*'s 2019. It's the early 1990s of 'posthuman' sculpture. It's 2011, a moment not only of looking backward — when the specific 80s fashions that Jessie wears were being revived on catwalks and are now already, doubly, retro again — but also of looking into an increasingly technologised future, predicated on mapping, observing, panoptic controlling: a decade after the sequencing of the human genome was completed, as CCTV cameras observe our every move, as Google Earth scours the globe. *Human Statue (Jessie)* thus registers, with spectral precision, not only a cultural obsession with glamour and surfaces, and something of end-of-empire decadence, but, more fundamentally, how we live now: strung between present, future and a myriad of pasts. (Even 3D printing has its roots in nineteenth-century methods of creating contour maps and the experimental technique of 'photosculpture'.[6])

One reason we don't have a fixed sense of the present, of course, is that we're now perpetually in the grip of imposed nostalgia cycles, past eras wheeled back onto catwalks and stages for commercial gain and recombined for creative frisson, particularly by the generation brought up with the Internet's opening up and flattening of the historical/cultural archive. Meanwhile, and ironically given the current mania for revivalism, certain things that it would be *useful* to bring back seem all but impossible to meaningfully resurrect. The present writer, for example, regularly finds himself in the studios of artists, hearing of their internal attitudes and watching them prowl embarrassedly around the word 'existentialism'. Sometimes they use it, usually they don't, because existentialism is a black-polo-necked, Gauloise-huffing, Camus-paperback-flaunting cliché. Still, it offers a useful, sincere vocabulary for dealing with human loneliness, the cruelty of the world, the brevity and possible pointlessness of life, where otherwise there's only religion. And some artists, if not many, do dare to engage with it.

Ugo Rondinone's 'nudes', a series of seven from 2010–11, look at once like they're posing for an artist, trying to get some needed rest and inwardly becalmed. The figures, in their facture, look back to classical techniques: they have nothing to do with 3D printing, being cast from the body in wax mixed with earth pigments. They're emphatically unstable — the body parts are sectioned, composite, seamed and run to varied tones of earth, flesh and grey — and, in terms of affect, occupy borderlines between being here and being taken apart, alive and inert, melancholic and relieved. Nudity, here, means allegorical exposure: defences and covers stripped back, reduced to primal being. (The press release for the work's first showing in New York didn't shy from using the word 'existential'.)

These are also perhaps works, though, to be seen in the context of Rondinone's formally diverse career as a whole. What they recall most insistently is his series, from 2001–02, of fibreglass clowns, also propped against gallery walls or laid flat. The clowns, at least, were wearing something, whether leotards or sackcloth or towelling; and the paint plastered over their faces resembled, naturally, greasepaint. Rondinone's nudes have lost even that protection. Off the pedestal and off their feet, they have little to do with the proud tradition of statuary; if, formally, they update anything from antiquity, it might be the ancient Roman *Dying Galatian* (220–30 BC), a portrait of a defeat. They are the human figure reduced to bare life.

As such they remind us that those ostensibly historical concerns animating Giacometti's art are not irrelevant, because the fundamental terms of being in the world have not changed. We have not become immortal, overcome war, collectively reanimated God, etc. What has changed is the texture of the space that surrounds the figure sculpture today. À la minimalism, the work is the sum of itself and its context. And what hangs invisible in the air around the sculpted figure, giving it 'pent-up energy', is the phantom continuum of the figurative sculptures, and also the abstractions, that preceded it. These at once make it difficult to make something new and, as we've seen, also offer opportunities for the inventive to engage the human body on the double-faced (forward-looking, backward-looking) terms of the present. The oldest figure sculpture is between 35,000 and 40,000 years old.[7] Between that point and the present there was a period of perhaps just 40 years when it was not particularly acceptable, and then only in the rarefied world of avant-garde art, to make such work. We want to see ourselves reflected, in the place we are now. If where we are now has never before had so much *then* in it, and nor, perhaps, so much scary and thrilling futurity, we'll see it in the images we build of our bodies and each other's before — à la Rondinone's nudes — our patchwork selves fall apart at the seams.

1 'Interview', in David Sylvester, *Looking at Giacometti*. (London: Pimlico, 1994) pp. 215–16
2 'Thinking of Sculpture as Shaped by Space', Charles Ray, *New York Times*, 7 October 2001
3 'Notes on Sculpture, Part 1', Robert Morris, *Artforum*, February 1966, pp. 42–44
4 R. Crumb, 'A Bitchin' Bod', *HUP*, 4 (1992)
5 'Visiting Artists: Frank Benson', *nytimes.com*, 9 September 2011
6 See NSF JTEC/WTEC: 'Rapid Prototyping in Europe and Japan', p. 22, www.wtec.org/pdf/rp_vi.pdf (last visited: 4 March 2014)
7 The oldest verifiable sculpture of a human figure is the *Venus of Hohle Fels* discovered in Schelklingen, Germany, in 2008 and currently being researched at the University of Tübingen

James Lingwood

After the Fall

The Re-emergence of the Figure in Sculpture

Over the past two decades, the field of contemporary sculpture has become so populated with figures of every conceivable kind, doing almost every conceivable thing, that it's hard to believe there was a time not long before when the figure was out of sight and out of mind.

The reconstruction of the 1969 exhibition *When Attitudes Become Form* at the Fondazione Prada in Venice last year was telling in this regard. Amongst the wide range of radical approaches to sculpture presented by European and North American artists, the figure was almost nowhere to be seen. The only exception was Alighiero Boetti's floor-based sculpture, *Io che prendo il sole a Torino il 19 gennaio 1969* (Me sunbathing in Turin 19 January 1969) (1969). The hand-moulded clumps of concrete arranged on the floor in the rough shape of the artist's body served to accentuate the comprehensive absence of the figure elsewhere in the show. 'Living in Your Head', to paraphrase the subtitle of the exhibition, meant not showing a body or a figure in any shape or form.

In *The Production of Space*, published in 1974, the French sociologist Henri Lefebvre articulated spatial experience as a combination of everyday spatial practices, the spatial imaginary and representations of space.[1] Exchange the word 'body' for 'space', apply it to sculpture in the 1970s and you get bodily practices, the bodily imaginary and representations of bodies. Bodily practices, in the form of performances and actions, became increasingly prominent through the decade. The bodily imaginary — the implication of the body of the viewer in the experience of minimalist and post-minimalist sculpture — was an article of faith. By contrast, the representation of a body, a figurative form in three dimensions, was almost heretical.

Figurative sculpture was tainted by multiple associations: in particular, the toxic attraction of totalitarian ideologies to monumental neoclassical statuary, but also the post-war humanist project to revisit the figure as a site of affliction, damage and pain. The traditions and materials of classical sculpture — standing man or reclining woman, carved marble or cast bronze — had predominated for long enough. Add to this troubling set of associations the manufactured figures of an emerging consumer culture — kitsch souvenirs of ancient sculptures for rapidly growing tourist markets — and the ever-proliferating displays of models and mannequins in department stores and shopping malls, and it's easy to understand why the figure in sculpture was so problematic. There were occasional sightings — within Edward Kienholz's installations or Paul Thek's sprawling multi-media environments, Duane Hanson's highly realistic sculptures of everyday men and women, or Antony Gormley's lead casts from his own body — but making a sculpture of a figure, or with figures, was regarded as regressive and outmoded throughout the 1970s and 1980s. The connection to classical sculpture had to be severed. Like Adam and Eve, shamed and expelled from the Garden of Eden, the figure had been exiled from the field of contemporary sculpture.

How then to explain the ubiquity of the figure in sculpture today? How did an emerging generation of sculptors prise open a position in which the figure was not automatically tainted with guilt by association? What kinds of strategy enabled uses of the figure in sculpture which were not immediately criticised as a 'return' (as had happened with neo-expressionist painting in the late 70s and 80s) but rather as an opening up of a space for sculpture in which the figure could once more be deployed and displayed?

The trajectory of the figure in the work of Thomas Schütte over the past three decades is symptomatic of this gradual opening up. In the early 1980s, not long after completing his studies at the Kunstakademie Düsseldorf, Schütte conceived much of his work in the form of sketches, scenarios and models. He used little *Star Wars* toys on stage-sets and groups of figurative wooden silhouettes to bring a sense of scale and a degree of absurdity to various architectural models. A series of small sculptures such as *Mann im Matsch mit Hund* (Man in Mud with Dog) (1982), and *Zwei Männer im Matsch (1:20)* (Two Men in Mud [1:20]) (1985) were laconic propositions for public sculptures. The little figures were symbols of stasis — political, cultural,

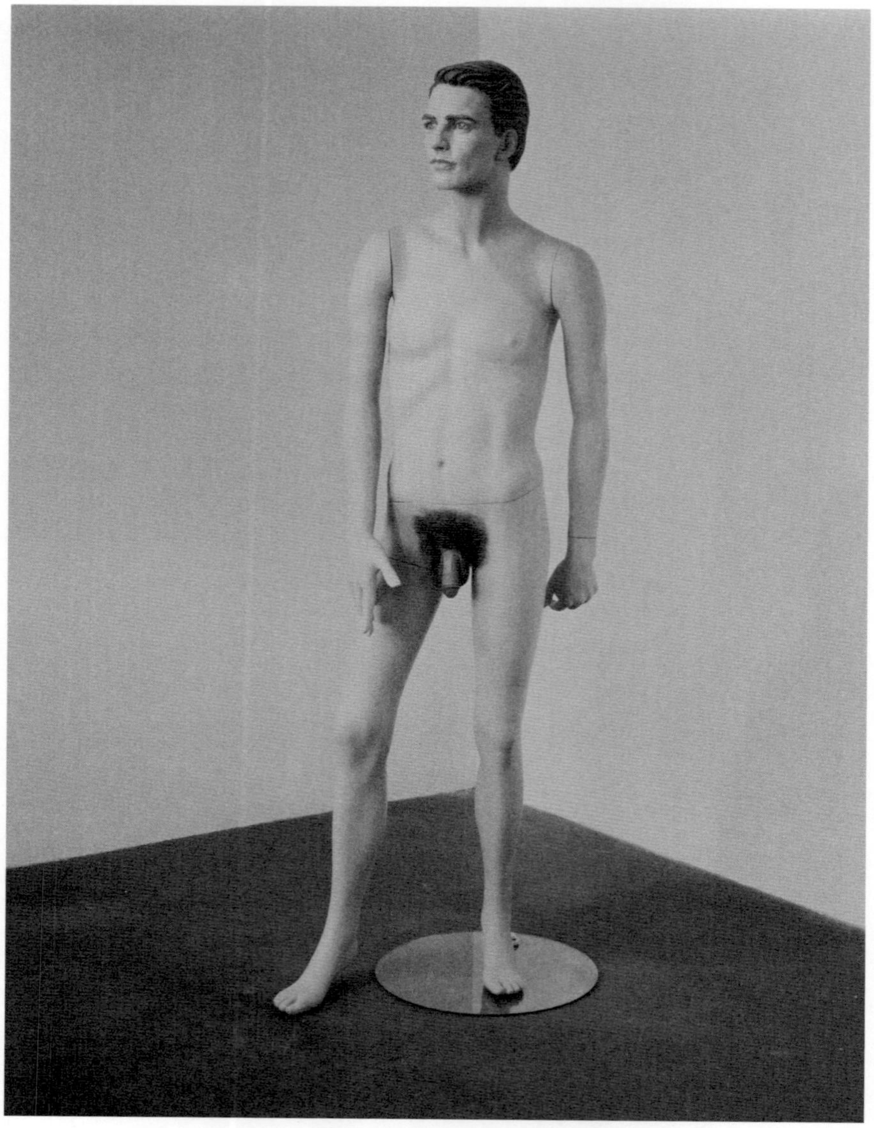

A

Charles Ray,
***Male Mannequin*, 1990**

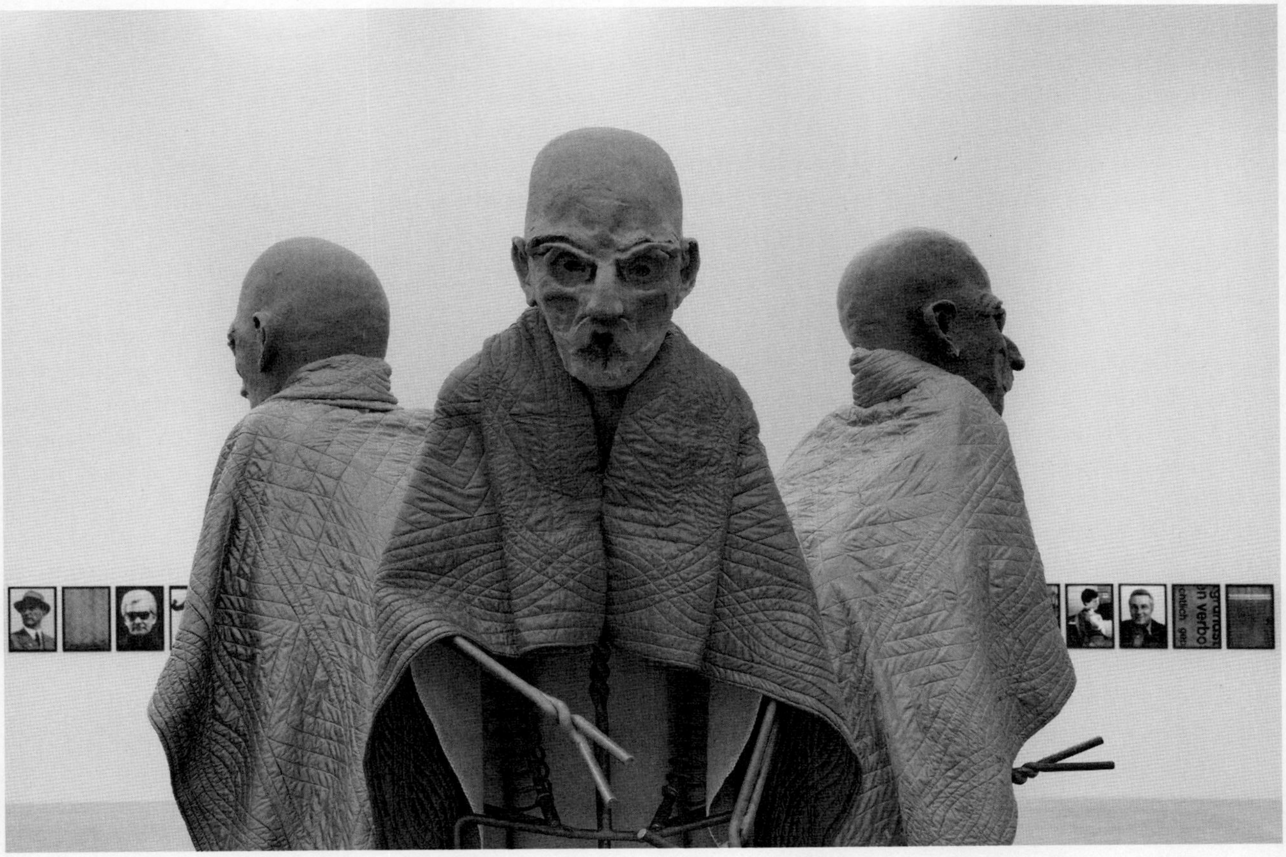

B

Thomas Schütte,
***Three Capacity Men* (detail),**
2005

sculptural? — stuck in the mud, going nowhere. At first used in a seemingly offhand way, the figure gradually moved from the edge of Schütte's sculptural practice to centre stage. He made more specific mises-en-scène: a small-scale tableau of an artist with a visitor in a studio, with two puppet-like figures dwarfed by a display of old socks on a display rack (*Mohr's Life*, 1988); and a few years later *United Enemies* (1993), an extended family of puppet-like heads, modelled out of coloured Fimo, dressed and bound together and displayed under glass bell-jars. The figures began to take on expressive characteristics that could be read as personality traits or personifications of power.

It seems that each successive use of the figure opened up for Schütte the possibility of another. A lineage in his family of figurative work can be traced directly back from the larger-than-life-size sculptures of the past 15 years to smaller predecessors. The free-standing *Three Capacity Men* (2005) relates to the puppet-like figures in *United Enemies*. In a similar vein, *Krieger*, the monumental wooden figures from 2012, are part of the same family line as the much smaller models in Schütte's proposals for war memorials of the early 1990s, such as *Kleiner Respekt* (1994). The large *Große Geister* (1996), cast in aluminium, steel and bronze, were scaled up from smaller 'originals' which Schütte made by hand in his studio and initially deployed in a collaboration with Richard Deacon, *Them and Us* (1995). However monumental some of Schütte's figurative sculptures have become, they retain their connection to the early idea of a repertoire of 'playthings' to be orchestrated in different scenarios. As they grew in size, the sculptures were loosened from more evident narrative constructions to function as free-standing, open-ended groups of figurative forms.

B

Elsewhere in Europe, and at almost exactly the same time, Juan Muñoz was on a parallel track. With the exception of a few very early sculptures from 1984, Muñoz's work started off by implying the presence of the figure through absence. There were banisters and empty balconies attached to gallery walls, and a model of a minaret on a carpet. As Muñoz began to expand his work to the scale of a room, he began to need some kind of figurative presence to animate the space. In his first room-sized work, *The Wasteland* (1987), a ventriloquist's dummy was positioned on a shelf at the far end of a room. The viewer walked over a patterned floor filling the whole of the room to approach the little figure. A year later in *The Prompter* (1988), the figure of a dwarf was partially obscured, seen by the viewer from behind, looking over an empty stage towards a drum. Next came *Dwarf with Three Columns* (1988), the diminutive figure this time fully in view. Like Schütte, Muñoz was gradually opening up a space, giving himself permission to play with a different kind of figurative presence, situated somewhere between a scenic prop and a lifelike representation.

D

Initially on guard against the dangers of appearing to turn back, by 1990 Muñoz was emboldened to declare: 'We have become aware of the millions of stories that we did not allow ourselves to tell over the last ten years, because of our suspicion of the conditions of expression [...] The doors are swinging open for everything to occur, but I don't know how much of the landscape we are actually going to travel.' [2] Muñoz began to make groups of figures — or more accurately, semi-figures — that revealed just how far he was prepared to travel. First, small bronze sculptures of ballerinas, with the upper part of the body merged into spherical bottoms as if they could be rocked from side to side, and then the larger *Conversation Pieces* from 1991–92, groups of several bronze sculptures with expressive faces and gestures, the upper half of the sculpture fully human, the lower half still spherical. As they grew in scale, the figurative ensembles became stages on which the sculptures stood and viewers moved. In their different ways, through a combination of conceptual agility and contrariness, Schütte and Muñoz had by the early 1990s both foregrounded the figure in their sculpture in an increasingly unguarded way.

Around the same time, the figure in sculpture was also materialising in other guises. A number of works in the 1987 *Skulptur Projekte Münster* signalled this development in an emphatic way. There, amongst a familiar range of abstract structures and critical propositions were sculptures of figures standing in the streets of the city, inhabiting civic space and revisiting that most outmoded of all figurative modes, the statue. Katharina Fritsch's *Madonnenfigur* (Madonna Figure) (1987) arrived like an apparition in the predominantly Catholic city. Based on a souvenir mass-produced for purchase at sites of religious pilgrimage, such as Lourdes, the bright yellow Madonna, a little smaller than life-size and placed in the middle of a busy pedestrian street, could scarcely have been more prominent. The sculpture involved a shift in size and a dramatic change of colour. It suggested a dislocation from one context to another; from one belief system to another. It was hard to place. Was it a well-meaning gesture or an irreverent act? Statues are supposed to stand for something, a value or a belief, to offer certainties rather than questions. But the status of Fritsch's statue remained elusive; it was a blank surface onto which different beliefs and anxieties could be projected.

C, E

In other public spaces in the centre of the city, Stephan Balkenhol's *Mann mit grünem Hemd und weißer Hose* (Man with Green Shirt and White Trousers, 1987), a painted wooden sculpture of an anonymous man, was attached to a wall above a shop and Jeff Koons' *Kiepenkerl* (1987) statue stood outside a restaurant of the same name. The status of Koons' contemporary copy of a much-loved folkloristic sculpture in Münster was, like Fritsch's Madonna, also ambiguous. What might the act of producing a new copy in polished stainless steel of a well-known bronze sculpture in this provincial German city mean? What was it saying about values, identities, beliefs? Was Koons casting himself as a contemporary equivalent of the *Kiepenkerl*, a pedlar coming to Münster market with a basket overflowing with abundance? Koons enigmatically suggested that the remade statue was concerned with recreating 'an icon that could once again meet the needs of the public'.

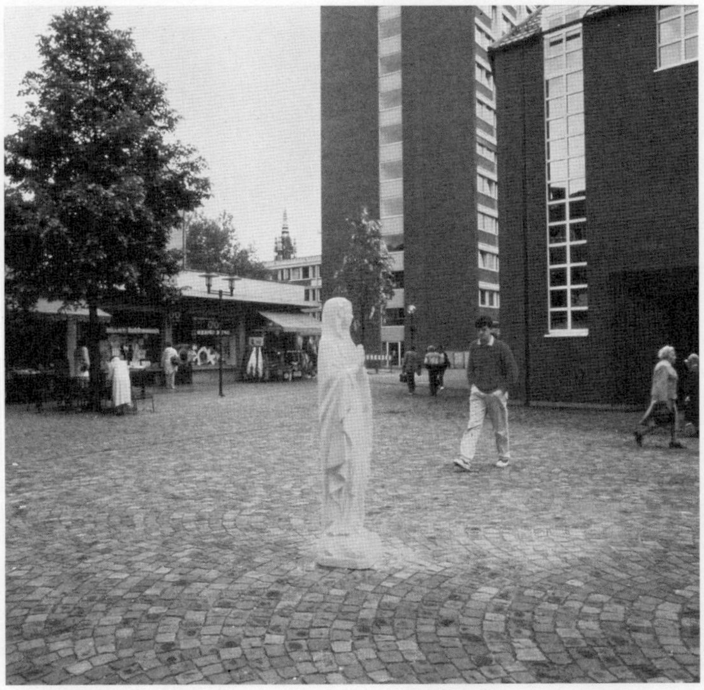

C

Katharina Fritsch,
***Madonnenfigur* (Madonna Figure), 1987**

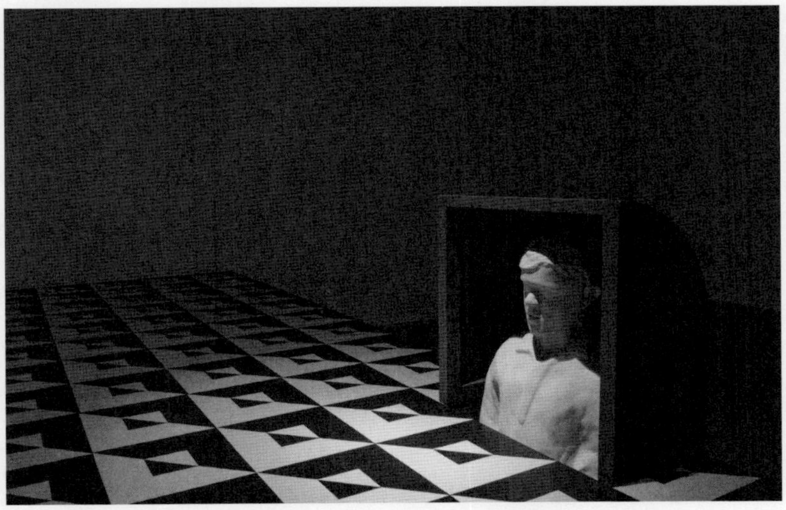

D

Juan Muñoz,
***The Prompter*, 1988**

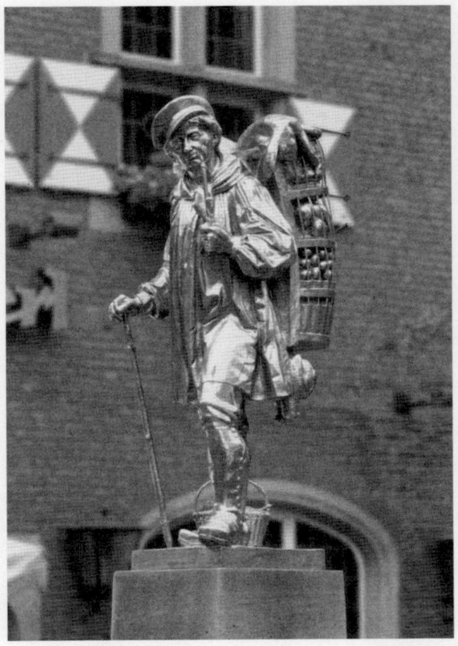

E

Jeff Koons,
***Kiepenkerl*, 1987**

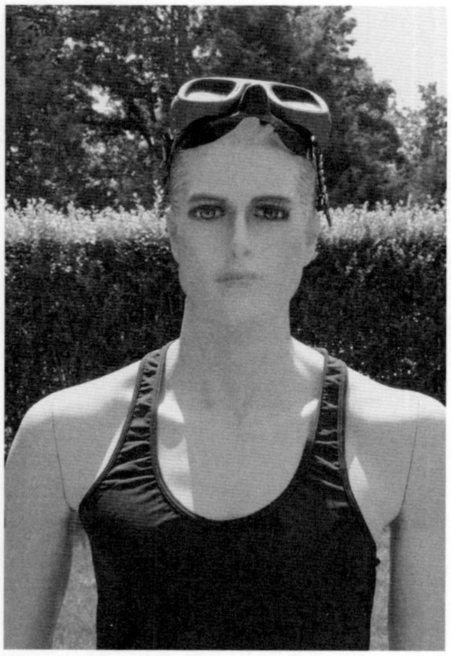

F

John Miller,
Composition in Black and Tan
(detail), 2010

Importantly, both Koons' and Fritsch's sculptures began with a found figure, a common object already in the world which they could then remake. The anonymous status of the figure afforded both artists the space to step into the contested arena of public sculpture, with statue-like sculptures which were open and uncertain. The remade figure could be multiplied again. Beyond the streets of Münster, Fritsch's yellow Madonna continues to circulate in an unlimited edition, bought by a different kind of believer.

This possibility of sculpture drawing from the vernacular world of consumer objects led to another kind of figure animating the spaces of art in the early 1990s. Both lifelike and lifeless, the mannequin had offered a rich repertoire of possibilities for the surrealists. Its latent potential as a site of the uncanny had been of particular interest to several photographers who roamed the shop windows and flea-markets of pre-war Paris to capture mannequins in various states. Picking up on this potential, a number of artists in the US, including Charles Ray and John Miller, took the mannequin as a ready-made or as a figure to be remade. Like the kitsch tourist objects remodelled by Fritsch, the mannequin was an artless everyday object, a surrogate ready to be remade and displayed within the white walls of the gallery.

Charles Ray's *Male Mannequin* (1990) comprises an unnerving combination of the generic and the singular, the anonymous and the personal. Most of the sculpture resembles a regular mannequin, fresh off the production line, with that odd pink/brown colour that only mannequins have. This part is pure artifice. Then Ray cast his own genitalia, seamlessly integrated the cast into the rest of the figure and added pubic hair for further naturalistic effect. Displayed entirely naked in the space of the gallery, the human and the artificial are fused into an unsettling new entity.

A, F, G

In parallel with Ray, John Miller began to use the mannequin as a found object for his sculpture. The first of Miller's mannequin sculptures, *My Friend*, was realised in 1989. A second-hand male mannequin was purchased from a store near the Bowery in New York, and was clothed, painted and exhibited. Miller's title suggests a child's fantasy, the desire to turn an inanimate object into an intimate friendship. The mannequin is a life-size plaything, just human enough to be the site of an almost pathetic projection. The little plastic figures that Schütte had played with in his studio become, in Miller and Ray's work, full-size protagonists in a different kind of playground. The simple pleasures of transgression, of feeding off forbidden fruit, shouldn't be entirely discounted either. A group of life-size sculptures of a dressed male mannequin, hands held behind his back, were made by Martin Kippenberger from 1989 onwards. The English translation of their title reads *Martin, into the Corner, You Should Be Ashamed of Yourself*.

Across a range of different contexts, in Europe and the United States, artists had found a way forward with the figure. Making singular sculptures related to commonplace objects — toys, puppets, tourist mementos, mannequins — they repositioned representations of the human body within the vernacular world. Stripped of interiority, they shaped and placed it into different scenarios both within and beyond the setting of the gallery. Only two decades after its fall from grace, the figure had found its way back into the field of contemporary sculpture.

1 Henri Lefebvre, *La production de l'espace* (The Production of Space) (Anthropos, Paris, 1974)
2 Juan Muñoz in conversation with Iwona Blazwick, James Lingwood and Andrea Schlieker, *Possible Worlds: Sculpture from Europe* (ICA/Serpentine Galleries: London, 1990), p. 61

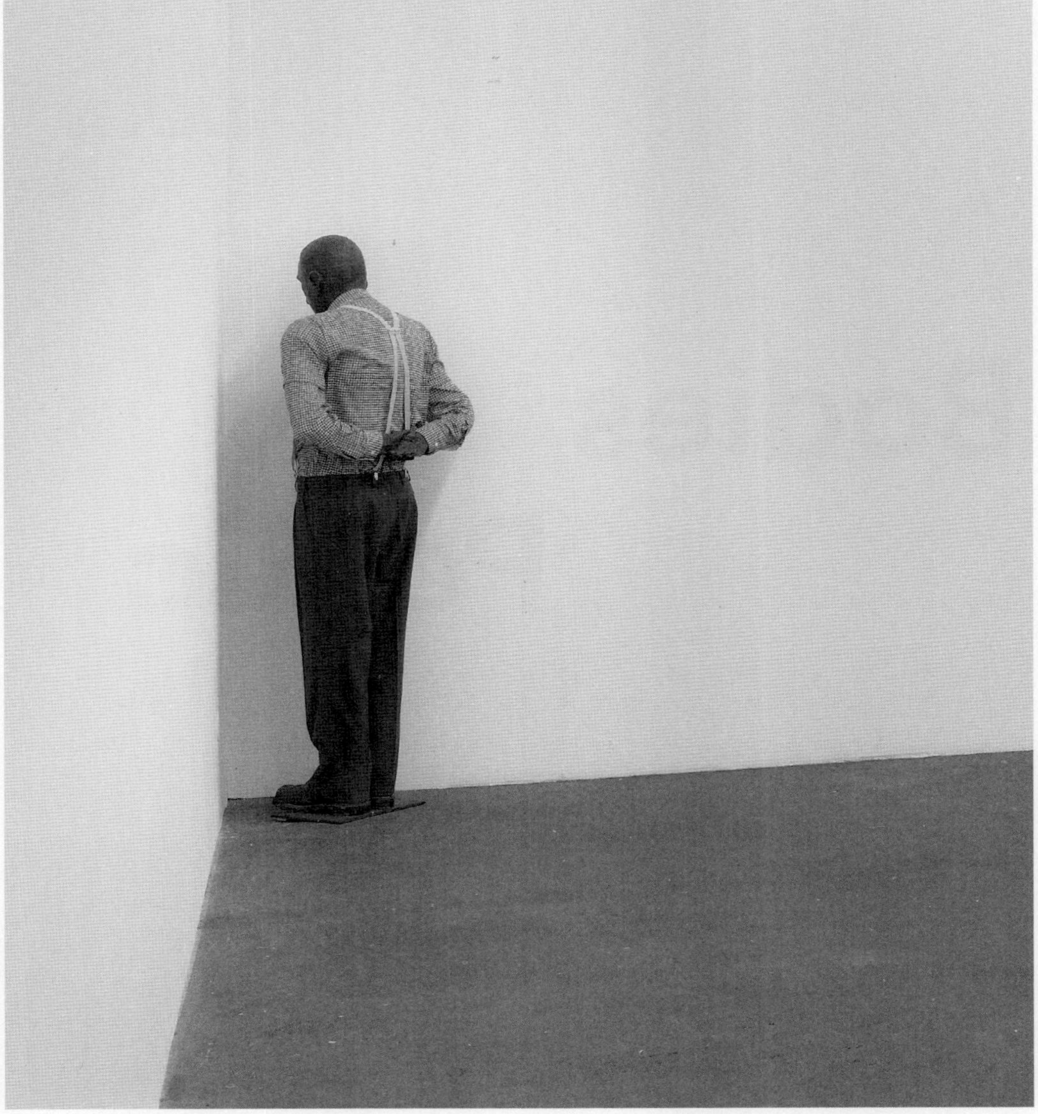

G

Martin Kippenberger, *Martin, ab in die Ecke und schäm dich* (Martin, into the Corner, You Should Be Ashamed of Yourself), 1989

Lisa Lee

Bodies Politic

Étienne-Maurice Falconet, charged by his friend Denis Diderot to pen the entry on sculpture for the *Encyclopédie*,[1] averred that the medium's highest purpose, 'considered from the moral point of view, is to perpetuate the memory of famous men and to provide models of virtue'.[2,3] In the context of a burgeoning public sphere, sculpture addressed the newly constituted Enlightenment subject by presenting paragons of citizenship and nationalism for emulation. The force of such *exempla virtutis* cannot be considered separately from the formal vocabulary in which they are expressed. Whether taking on the ideal proportions inherited from antiquity or adopting a distinct physiognomy (and sometimes evincing both strategies), whether suspended in a moment of decisive action or captured in an attitude of introspection, the body of commemorative statuary is rendered legible and persuasive through dynamic modelling of form, rhetorical clarity of gesture, interplay of light and shadow across an animated surface and transformation of stubborn matter into something (or someone) that seems vitally present. With the French Revolution, the subject of sculpture shifted from illustrious men to the body of the people. Throughout this period, the Enlightenment public sphere was thus intimately bound up with commemorative figurative sculpture, which, as Erika Naginski writes, lays claim to 'the collective as [its] dominion'.[4]

To contemplate John Miller's *Composition in Black and Tan* (2010) is to confront the radically altered expectations we have for figurative sculpture in the present. In lieu of a pedestal, which literally and metaphorically elevates what rests upon it, a mass-produced display dummy stands in a small plastic paddling pool. Its generic features and smooth carapace partake of none of sculpture's expressive potential. The title's evocation of abstraction is especially ironic, given the emphatic figuration the work involves. (In Miller's work, neither figuration nor abstraction are unscathed. The latter's historical presumptions of autonomy, self-reflexivity and non-objectivity are punctured by its relation to consumer culture.) Or consider *Composition in Black and Tan*'s

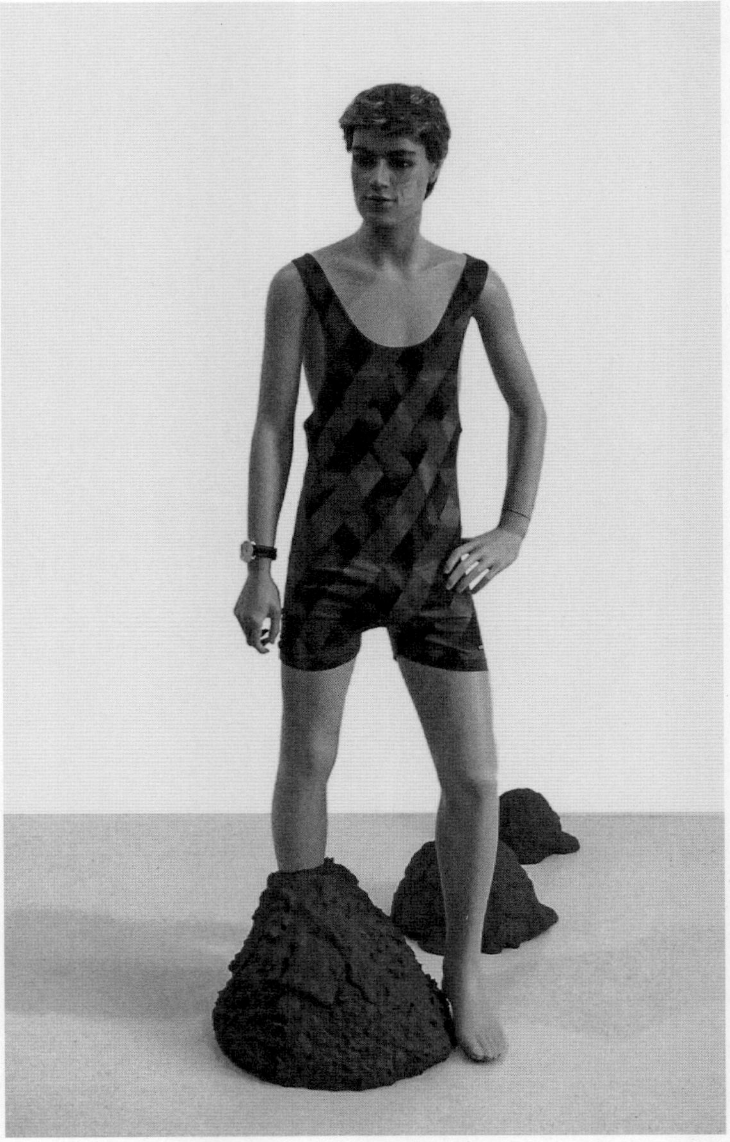

A

John Miller,
Now We're Big Potatoes,
1992

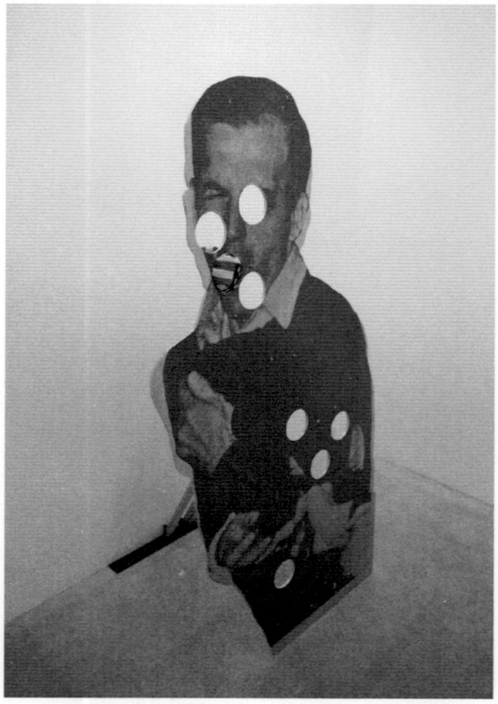

B

**Cady Noland, *Bluewald*,
1989**

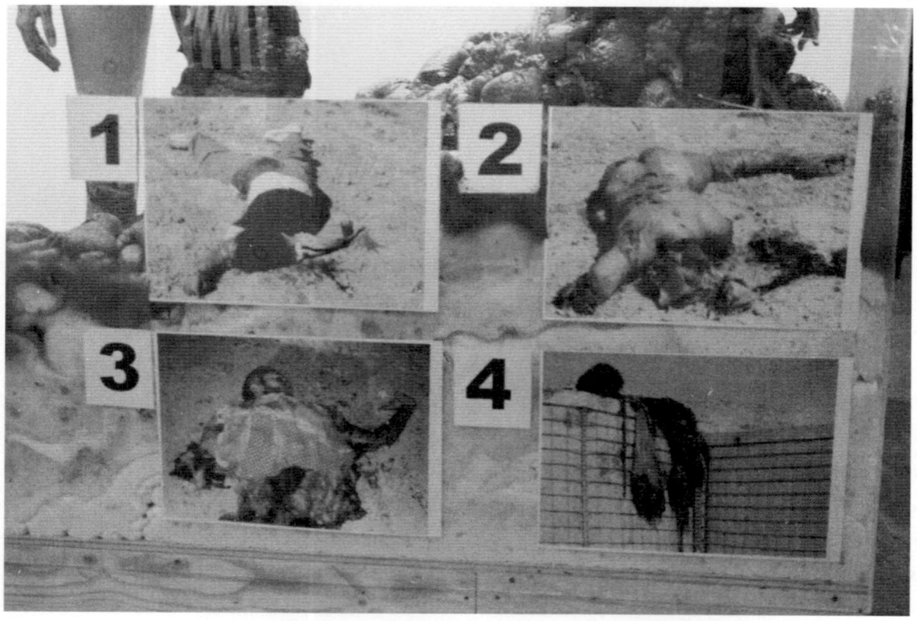

C

**Thomas Hirschhorn, *4 Women*
(detail), 2008**

more ephebic antecedent in *Now We're Big Potatoes* (1992). Dressed in a harlequin's diamond-patterned singlet, the fellow seems unperturbed by the fact that his right foot is lodged in a shit-brown mound, base matter that refuses to be sublimated by art.

A

I write of altered expectations for sculpture, but it would be equally to-the-point to write of altered sculptural possibilities. For if sculpture played a role in providing the Enlightenment public sphere with images of itself, participating thereby in its constitution, what happens with the dissolution of that sphere? Jürgen Habermas argued that the separation of public authority from private autonomy in the seventeenth and eighteenth centuries gave rise to a context in which private individuals could gather to engage in disinterested rational-critical debate.[5] By the nineteenth century, however, this public sphere had all but disintegrated with the rise of commodity capitalism. Penetrated by corporate interests, the public sphere becomes a pseudo-private vehicle for advertising and propaganda.[6] Under these circumstances, negotiation takes the place of rational debate; public opinion is no longer hashed out among private individuals, but is a product of PR efforts; subjectivity itself is the domain of co-optation.

The extreme difficulty, if not the impossibility or absurdity, of imagining a contemporary commemorative statuary devoted to 'illustrious men,' to 'the citizen' or to 'the collective' marks the degree to which the structural transformation (i.e. disintegration) of the public sphere has called into doubt the function and form of secular and civic sculpture as it developed in the Enlightenment period. Monumental and figurative sculpture suffers this crisis of relevance most acutely. Cady Noland, ever the astute observer of American culture, addresses these expectations head-on in *Bluewald* (1989). The work offers us not an illustrious man, but an infamous one: Lee Harvey Oswald at the moment he was shot by Jack Ruby. *Bluewald* embodies minimal three-dimensionality even as it occupies literal space. Noland's use of flatness responds explicitly to the photographic medium, and more broadly to the issue of mediation, drawing the motif of Oswald's crumpling body directly from Bob Johnson's iconic photograph of the incident. Noland posits that it is photography, not sculpture, that offers the indelible public images of our time. No modelling of solids and voids, but literal holes suggest the impact of gunshots, as well as the lapses of knowledge and the violence implied by photography.

B

Additional misgivings about representing the body persist as a consequence of the ubiquity of sculptural representations of idealised types under the totalitarian regimes of the late-1920s and 1930s, which harnessed figuration's capacity to symbolise collectivities that were brutally enforced in actuality. On the one hand, then, figural sculpture faces a loss of orientation with the erosion of the authentic public sphere that had once given it purpose. On the other hand, it endures a loss of credibility due to its more proximate history as a preferred instrument of ideology under totalitarian regimes. This historical situation provides a lens — one of several — through which to understand the significance of the resolute turn to abstraction in the sculptural production of the post-war period. For the most part, those sculptural forms deemed 'advanced' — whether according to modernist, minimalist, or post-minimalist criteria — refused the refinements of modelling and declined to represent the human form. Indeed, the way in which the accusation of anthropomorphism was lobbed back and forth, by Donald Judd and Michael Fried to name the obvious examples, suggests that even the residue of figuration within abstraction prompted discomfort.

In the resurgence of sculptural figuration over the past few decades, one can detect a subset of artists for whom the political dimension of a return to the human form is paramount. The most compelling of their works, it seems to me, confront and thematise the possibility or impossibility of sculpture in the face of an equally precarious public sphere. The foregrounding of a lost sculptural plasticity in these works — and by lost I mean a sense of historical remoteness that renders plastic qualities unavailable — emphasises the difficulty of (literally) figuring either the *exemplum virtutis* or the body of 'the people'. Put in different terms, the politics of recent figurative sculpture resides in its expression, through its formal and material means, of the troubled state of subject-object relations, of intersubjective connections, and of coherent selfhood that would have served as a basis for participation in the public sphere.

The cadre occupying Thomas Hirschhorn's harshly lit *Resistance-Subjecter* (2011) forms a collective of a particularly terrifying kind. Gaping cavities underscore the hollowness of the mannequin forms as crystalline growths, held on with clear packing tape, overtake the breach. Their purposeful strides, implied by *contrapposto* stances, seem unimpeded by the excrescences, and are perhaps even activated by them. From bulbous masses of paper and packing tape to bristling nails (a reference to so-called 'fetishes'), Hirschhorn has developed an entire lexicon of such material accretions. Self-nourishing, metastatic and perhaps communicable, these 'concretions' manifest a psychic hardening that results in a hardening of human relations.[7] The interior-to-exterior dynamic is reversed in *4 Women* (2008), where a foamy substance, evidently synthetic but suggestive of the organic, progressively consumes the encased mannequins. The encroachment of formless matter is doubled by language: from left to right, the mannequins are increasingly inscribed with text — snippets of slogans, clichés and headlines. Four images of devastated bodies, adhered to the vitrines, suggest a correspondence to the mannequins. (Former and latter bear labels numbered one through four.)

C

The logic of correspondence remains inscrutable, yet we are induced to compare the unyielding surfaces of the mannequins with the tattered and pulpy corpses in the pictures, the former's wholeness with the latter's fragmentation, verticality with horizontality, the inanimate with the dead. The inscriptions and photographs suggest mediation and violence as unavoidable aspects of the constitution of the contemporary subject, while the mannequins foreground the role played by commodity capitalism. With their mass-production, standardised proportions, limited repertoire of poses, impassive faces and uniform surfaces, the mannequins also manifest the eschewal of sculptural plasticity. We are offered no dream of collectivity or image of the people, but rather a nightmare of non-differentiation or, as David Joselit has suggested, of a '"distributed" subjectivity'.[8]

An obvious historical precedent for salient social critique through the contraction of sculptural means can be located in John Heartfield and George Grosz's assemblage *Der wildgewordene Spießer Heartfield. (Elektro-mech. Tatlin-Plastik)* (The Petit-Bourgeois Philistine Heartfield Gone Wild. [Electro-Mechanical Tatlin Sculpture]) (1920). A child-sized tailor's dummy-turned-soldier, decorated with makeshift epaulets and medals, stands at attention. To his right thigh is attached a lamppost — simultaneously evoking a prosthetic limb and the display mount for fragmented classical statuary.[9] The crisis of subjectivity in the aftermath of the First World War, with its corollary in the fragmentation of the body, is thus coupled with a direct citation and debasement of the heroic and idealised human form as represented in antique sculpture. '*Der wildgewordene Spießer Heartfield* stands for the disenchantment of the work of art', writes art historian Brigid Doherty.[10] Not only is aesthetic beauty called into question, but also art's redemptive promise.

D

The contemporary figurative works under discussion here have greater affinity with the bitter travesties of Dada than with the uncanny disturbances offered by Surrealism, which are perhaps more commonly associated with the presence of dolls and mannequins in art. This is true of Isa Genzken's outlandishly costumed figures, each more extravagant than the last. Where might one go in such a makeshift cape, reflective leggings and spangled headgear, complete with transparent antennae three feet tall? For all the masquerading, nothing is being masked. When encountering Genzken's motley gatherings of mannequins I'm always prompted to think of Fredric Jameson's discussion of the 'waning of affect' in the postmodern period. The intoxicating play of decorative surface effects takes the place of expression, which is predicated upon 'some separation within the subject, and along with that a whole metaphysics of the inside and outside'.[11] Genzken's emphasis, in these works, on colour and reflectivity, on the *thinness* of the textile and the glitz of reticulated foil, is all outside and no inside, all stuff and no soul. Overtly anthropomorphic, these sculptures are utterly evacuated of subjectivity.

By modelling many of the human figures in his works, Thomas Schütte engages with the sculptural tradition rather than circumventing it. Yet traditional means appear distinctly diminished here. Or, I should say, diminished and also writ large: the entirety of *Krieger* (2012) was moulded in the hand and then greatly enlarged, such that summary marks are rendered crudely expressive — hence the lumpy quality of the *Krieger*, with their bottle-top helmets. Schütte takes up the history of monumental sculpture, and specifically the subcategories of 'great men' and war memorials. But he eschews realism or idealism, offering instead dysmorphic soldiers, more haunting than comic, and stooped, skeletal personages. Where traditional sculpture built upon metal armatures for structural stability and sculptural dynamism, the armatures of the *Three Capacity Men* (2005) are laid bare, rendering them simultaneously menacing and frail.

Rachel Harrison's knobby, garishly daubed monoliths are named after thinkers, politicians and celebrities. If not all 'great men', they are at least notable ones. Spurning statuary's erectness, long equated with moral rectitude, *Schmatte with President* (2006) lists and teeters. The preposition of the title renders the heroic figure — Abraham Lincoln, in this case — supplementary. (One might remark upon Harrison's obvious delight in the play of prepositions, especially when it comes to the commodities she includes in/on/over/against/beneath/beside her cement-coated forms.) Indeed, the President's likeness, in the form of a flimsy latex mask, has been deposed (literally lowered) to the column's mid-region and set off-centre. A politician of more recent vintage is evoked in the two-headed, epicene man-child, *Jack Lemmon* (2011). From one side, Dick Cheney's smug visage tops a child mannequin's too-small body. The jaunty figure has no backside but a second front, this one featuring breasts and a female mannequin's head (wearing the Cheney mask as a hairdo). Sharing its platform is an abstract form, all protuberances and dappled colour. Ungainly in its massing, Harrison's abstract figuration is strangely articulate. An entire vocabulary of posture and bodily gesture comes across through her congealed forms. The mannequin and polychrome abstraction engage in a sort of duet of rhymed form (weight is similarly shifted in both bodies, their 'limbs' are similarly extended) even as they are a study in contrasts (mass-produced and handmade, anthropomorphic and abstract). The incommensurability of *Jack Lemmon* makes vivid the figure as disunity, internally split and outwardly doubled, with implications for both subjectivity and sculpture. But if this sounds metaphysically weighty, Harrison carries it off with insouciance.

Faced with a disintegrated public sphere in which sculpture's traditional significance and function are rendered moot, artists responded in the 1950s, 60s and 70s by turning to abstraction and to various forms of withdrawal as the means for advancing the medium. More recently, however, a generation of artists — the ones I discuss here are but a subset — have revisited the statue, vehicle of civic values, as precisely the means to register, interrogate and critique the altered conditions of self and other, public and private, individual and collective. In this way, loss is converted into a critical tool for the examination of the root causes of that loss. The return to the human figure, which finds precedents in Berlin Dada's assemblages, refuses sculptural plasticity, long equated with a kind of expressive wholeness, in favour of debased materials and deskilled means. Yet through disjunction, crudeness, frivolousness and savagery, this contemporary mode of figuration has achieved formal and rhetorical power.

1 Denis Diderot/Jean le Rond d'Alembert (eds.), *Encyclopédie, ou dictionnaire raisonné des sciences, des arts et des métiers* (Encyclopaedia, or a Systematic Dictionary of the Sciences, Arts and Crafts), (André le Breton: Paris, 1751–72)
2 Étienne-Maurice Falconet, 'Sculpture', in *The Encyclopedia of Diderot & d'Alembert Collaborative Translation Project*, Nelly S. Hoyt/Thomas Cassirer (trans.), (MPublishing: Ann Arbor, 2003), available at hdl.handle.net/2027/spo.did2222.0000.166 (last accessed: February 3, 2014). Originally published as 'Sculpture,' Diderot/le Rond d'Alembert, *Encyclopédie*, 14, pp. 834–37
3 The pedagogical role of sculpture gained particular urgency in the mid-eighteenth century, as Erika Naginski's scholarship has shown. My discussion of late-eighteenth century commemorative sculpture is indebted to her excellent study: Erika Naginski, *Sculpture and Enlightenment*. (Getty Research Institute: Los Angeles, 2009)
4 Ibid., p. 2
5 Jürgen Habermas, *Strukturwandel der Öffentlichkeit. Untersuchungen zu einer Kategorie der bürgerlichen Gesellschaft* (The Structural Transformation of the Public Sphere: An Inquiry into a Category of Bourgeois Society), (Luchterhand: Neuwied, 1962)
6 See Oskar Negt and Alexander Kluge's response to Habermas's influential text, revising and extending its terms to account for the significance of media conglomerates in the construction of consciousness and publicness in the late-twentieth century. Oskar Negt/Alexander Kluge, *Öffentlichkeit und Erfahrung. Zur Organisationsanalyse von bürgerlicher und proletarischer Öffentlichkeit* (Public Sphere and Experience: Toward an Analysis of the Bourgeois and Proletarian Public Sphere), (Suhrkamp: Frankfurt am Main, 1972)
7 See Thomas Hirschhorn, 'Letter to Frédéric (Regarding "Concretion")', *Critical Laboratory: The Writings of Thomas Hirschhorn*, (MIT Press: Cambridge, MA, 2013), pp. 279–82
8 David Joselit, 'The Subjecters,' *The Subjecters: Thomas Hirschhorn*. (La Casa Encendida: Madrid, 2009), p. 51
9 Brigid Doherty, 'The Work of Art and the Problem of Politics in Berlin Dada', *October*, 105 (Summer 2003), pp. 78–88
10 Ibid., p. 81
11 Fredric Jameson, *Postmodernism, or, The Cultural Logic of Late Capitalism* (Duke University Press: Durham, NC, 1991), p. 11

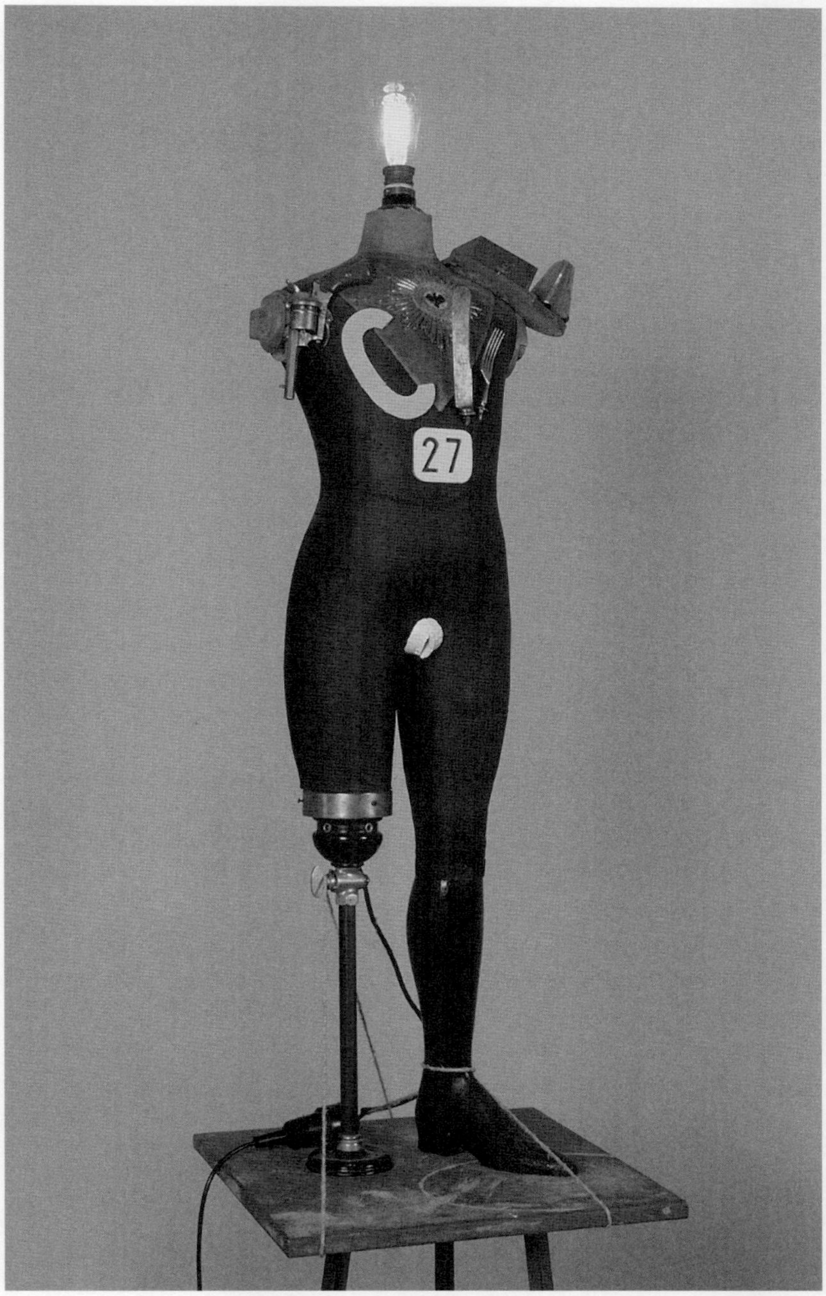

D

John Heartfield and George Grosz,
Der wildgewordene Spießer Heartfield
(Elektro-mech. Tatlin-Plastik)
(The Petit-Bourgeois Philistine Heartfield Gone Wild [Electro-Mechanical Tatlin Sculpture]),
1920

Plates

Paweł **Althamer**

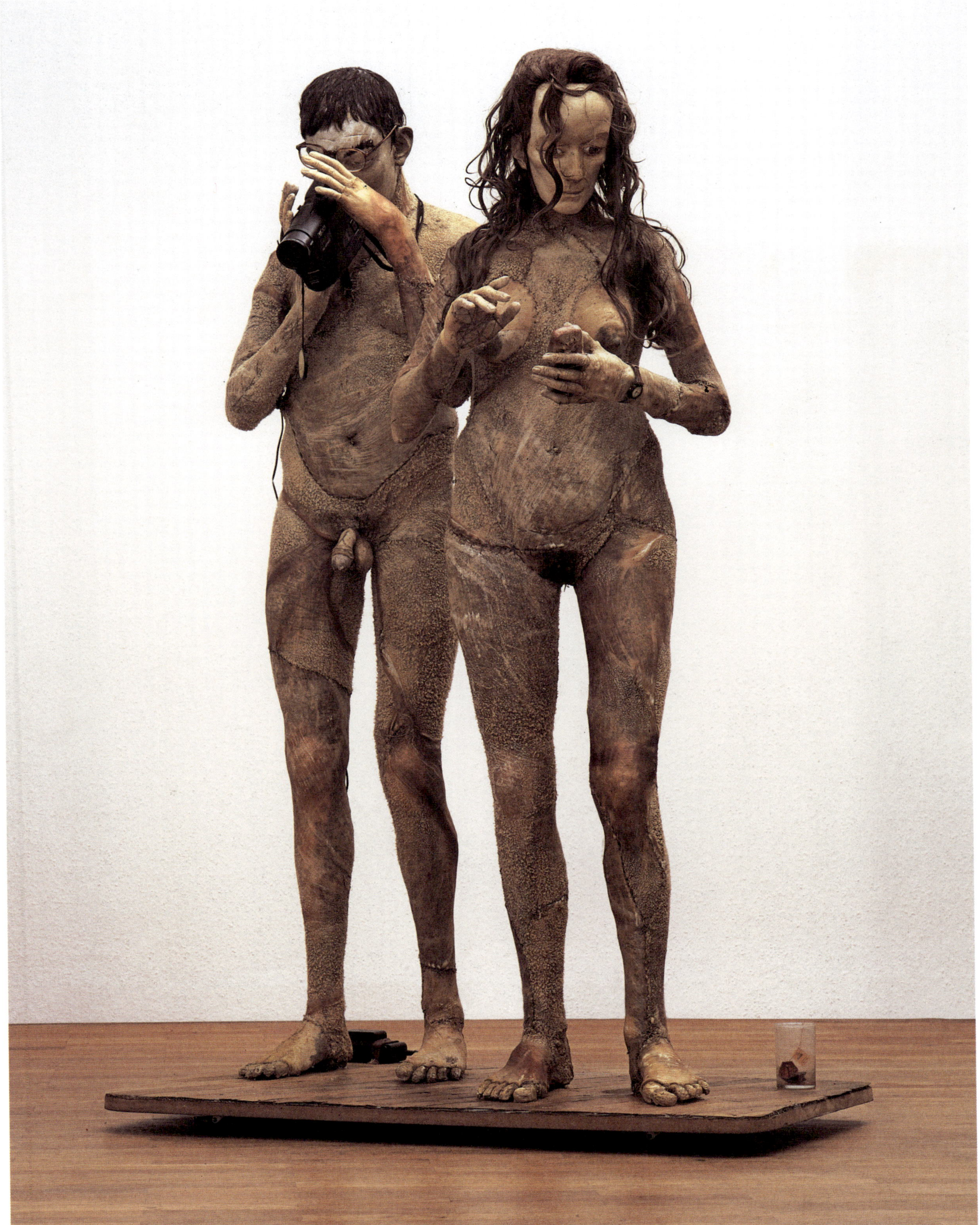

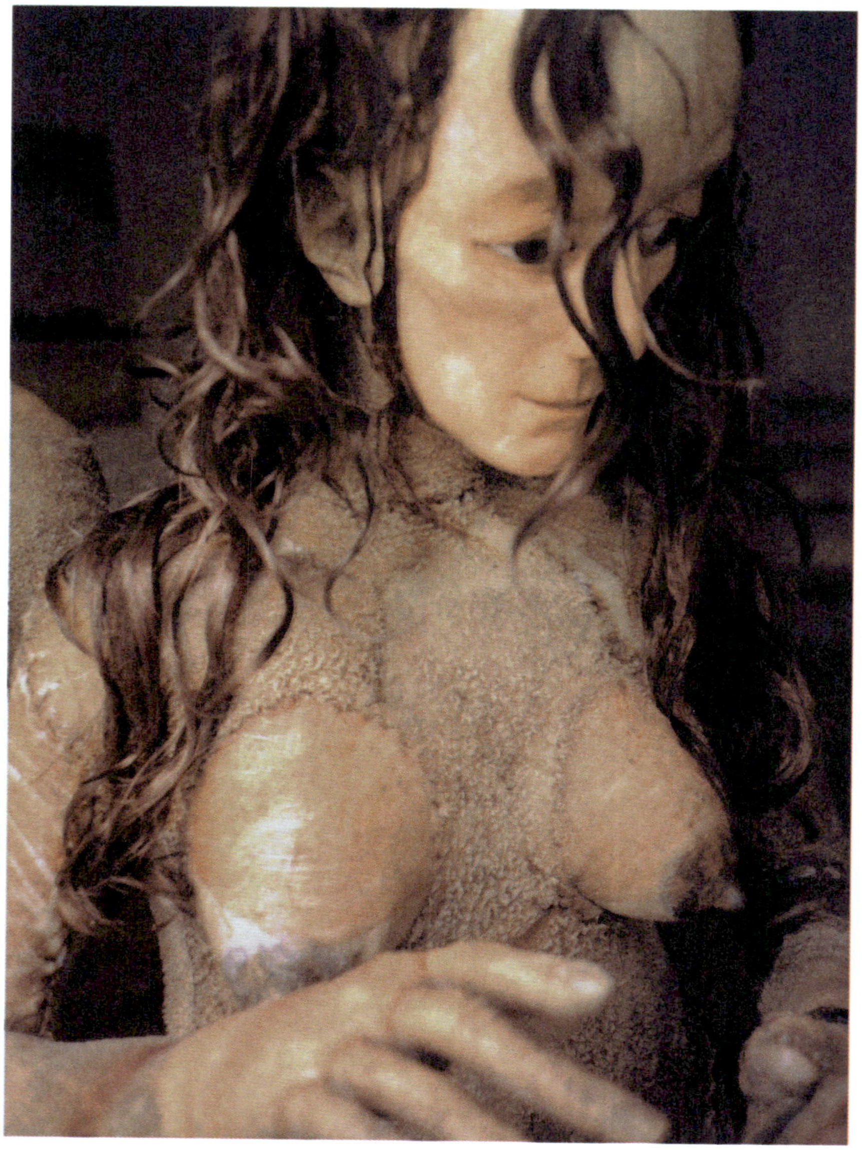

← *Monika and Pawel*, 2002

↑ *Monika and Pawel* (detail), 2002

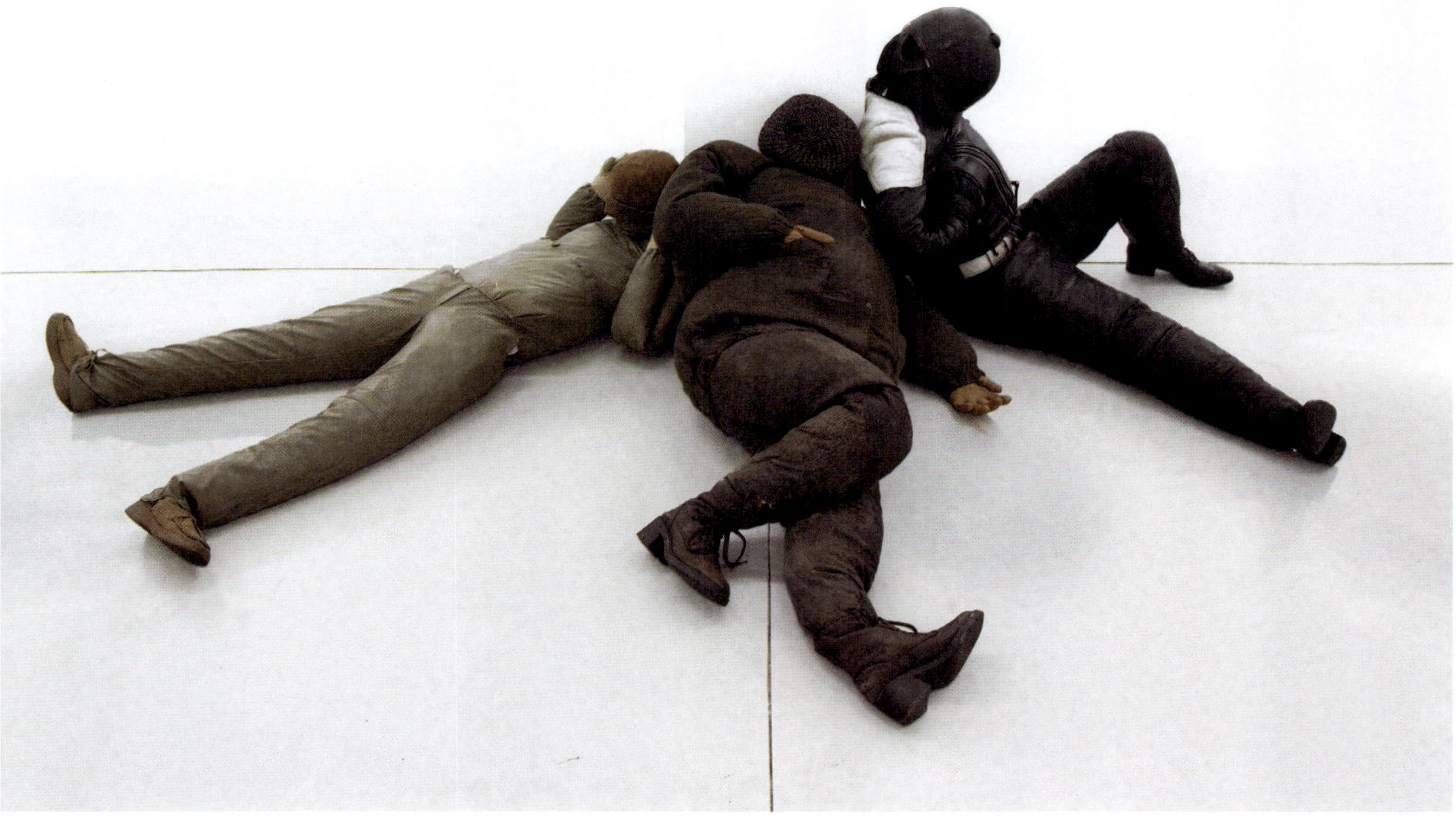

Paweł Althamer's art focuses on what it means to be human. His quasi-shamanistic, socially-motivated work revolves around the body, either as sculpture or in the form of living people, of those who are often on the margins of society, and sometimes the viewers themselves. Althamer considers all his sculptures to be different manifestations of the self: 'it's like saying, "Notice me, I'm here".' He thinks of these works as totems whose purpose is 'to connect people, to integrate them, and to create a common narrative; they are just signs for people to gather round'.

Monika and Pawel (2002) portrays Althamer and his then wife as a twenty-first-century Adam and Eve, absorbed with the fruits of a technological Tree of Life. As in many of his earlier works, the bodies are constructed mainly from animal guts and grass sewn onto a hidden metal armature. Like figures in anatomical drawings, their precisely rendered bundled-grass muscles are apparent beneath the lifelike skin, with its visible scars, sutures and lesions. Their nakedness and open wounds recall the Renaissance anatomists' motto 'Know Thyself', indicating that anatomy was a means of physical and psychological self-knowledge. *Monika and Pawel* speaks of impermanence, mutability and the temporary nature of existence. Although the video recorder, mobile phone and wristwatch may still work, they are no longer state-of-the-art, and the figures have become subject to decay. Althamer is reconciled to this: he has said that the work is about 'serious themes like dying; a dying body, a dying material world'.

Althamer's works also venture into what he calls the 'deep space of history, art history especially'. While Adam and Eve is a common motif in Western art, *Untitled* (2006) quotes a particular image, Pieter Bruegel's *The Land of Cockaigne* (1567), in which three sluggards sprawl in a glutton's paradise where pigs and geese run about already roasted, and houses are roofed with cakes and pies. The only obligations are to eat and sleep. But in Althamer's version there is no food or drink, or comfort of any kind. The hoodlums, hobos, homeless, or whoever they are, have only each other for company and support.

↑ ***Untitled*, 2006**

Frank **Benson**

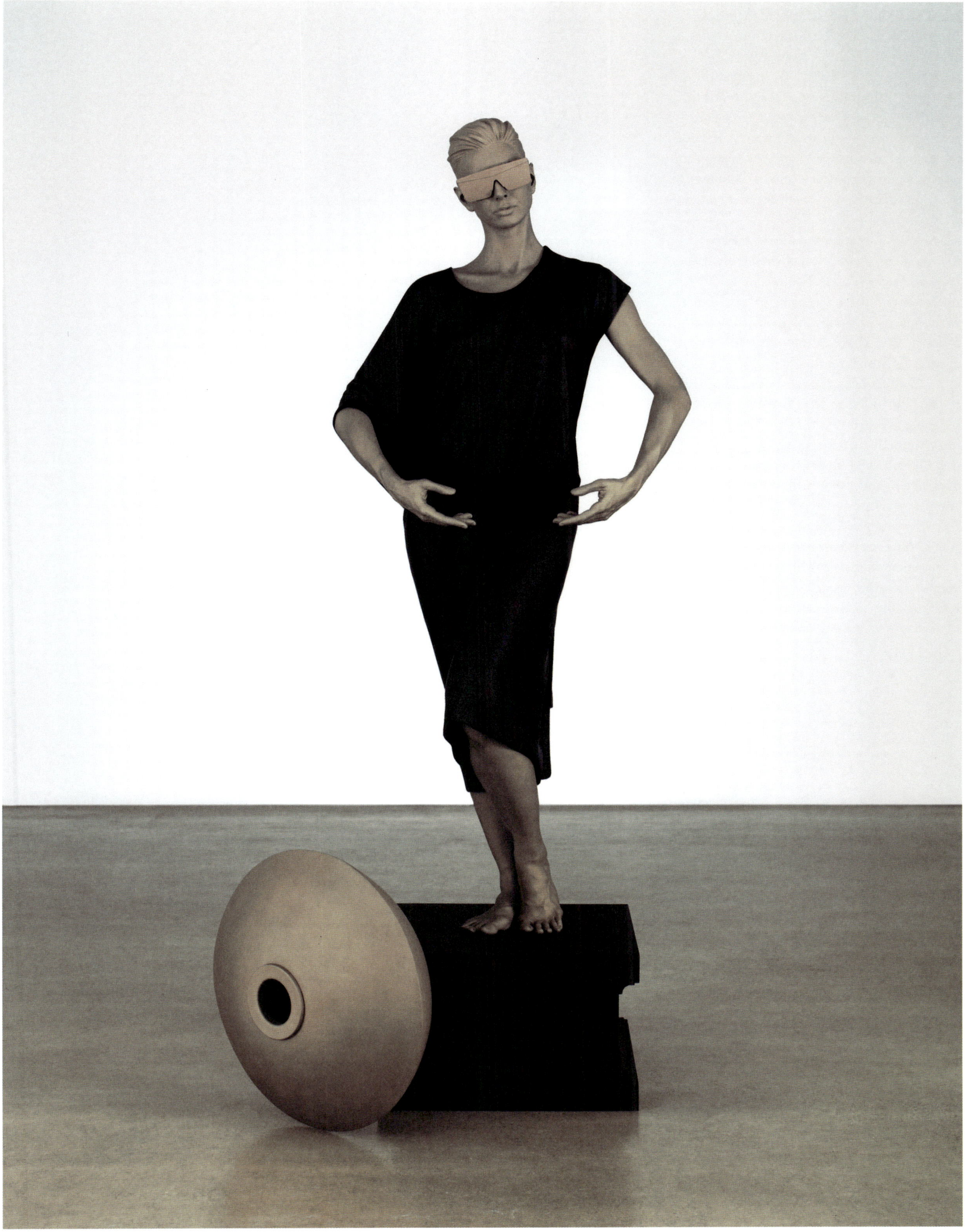

Frank Benson's classically posed, near-lifelike sculptures draw on the motif of the living statue, familiar from pedestrianised urban centres around the world. For Benson, this subject holds transgressive appeal as a 'folk form of performance art' rarely seen in a fine art context, which — due to its uncanny relation to normal human appearance — is also prone to provoking discomfort; 'a lot of people hate those performers', the artist has commented.

An interest in tapping into these effects informed the production of the highly realistic *Human Statue* (2005); Benson 'wanted it to appear as if there was an actual performer in the space'. Working with a mould maker from the special effects industry, the artist created a silicone mould capable of capturing every last detail of a model's body. To provide the illusion of living flesh, Benson painted the resulting fibreglass cast in airbrushed acrylics, using naturalistic flesh tones. In a *trompe l'œil* flourish, a layer of silver oil paint was then applied by hand using cosmetic sponges to simulate the smeared application of grease-paint, leaving pinkish tones showing through. A credible pretence of posed life, *Human Statue* sparks a dialogue between reality and its imitation through art that twists back on itself, making, in Benson's words, 'a sculpture of a person posing as a sculpture'.

Human Statue (Jessie) (2011), initially conceived as a 'mate' for the male nude, advances this conceptual game. Though the bronze sculpture clearly portrays a woman, its appearance is ambiguous: standing atop a pedestal, weight shifted onto one leg, the figure looks classical, yet its visor sunglasses recall 1980s fashion. At the same time, its hands are stiffly held out in front of its waist, as if the disc-like pot resting against the sculpture's base had just slipped from their grasp. Two years in the making, the sculpture's fabrication history is similarly complex. With the aim of creating a sculpture using digital technology, Benson scanned the body of New York-based dancer Jessie Gold with a camera that records in three dimensions. The artist manipulated the photographic data before translating it into a wire-frame model, amplifying the skin's natural puckering, smoothing the surface of the loosely flowing dress, and simplifying the contours of the model's hair in a process that moves beyond realistic representation. Two separate methods — 3D printing and computer-aided (CNC) milling — were then used to transform the virtual model into a physical mould for lost-wax casting, melding sophisticated modern technology with ancient analogue techniques. The resulting sculpture — Pygmalion hyper-real in parts, declaring its own artifice in others — proposes a formal riddle, in line with Benson's reflection on his work: 'over time I have developed an exacting form of representation to create sculptural and photographic works which are, at their core, formal abstractions.'

← ***Human Statue (Jessie)*, 2011**

→ ***Human Statue*, 2005**

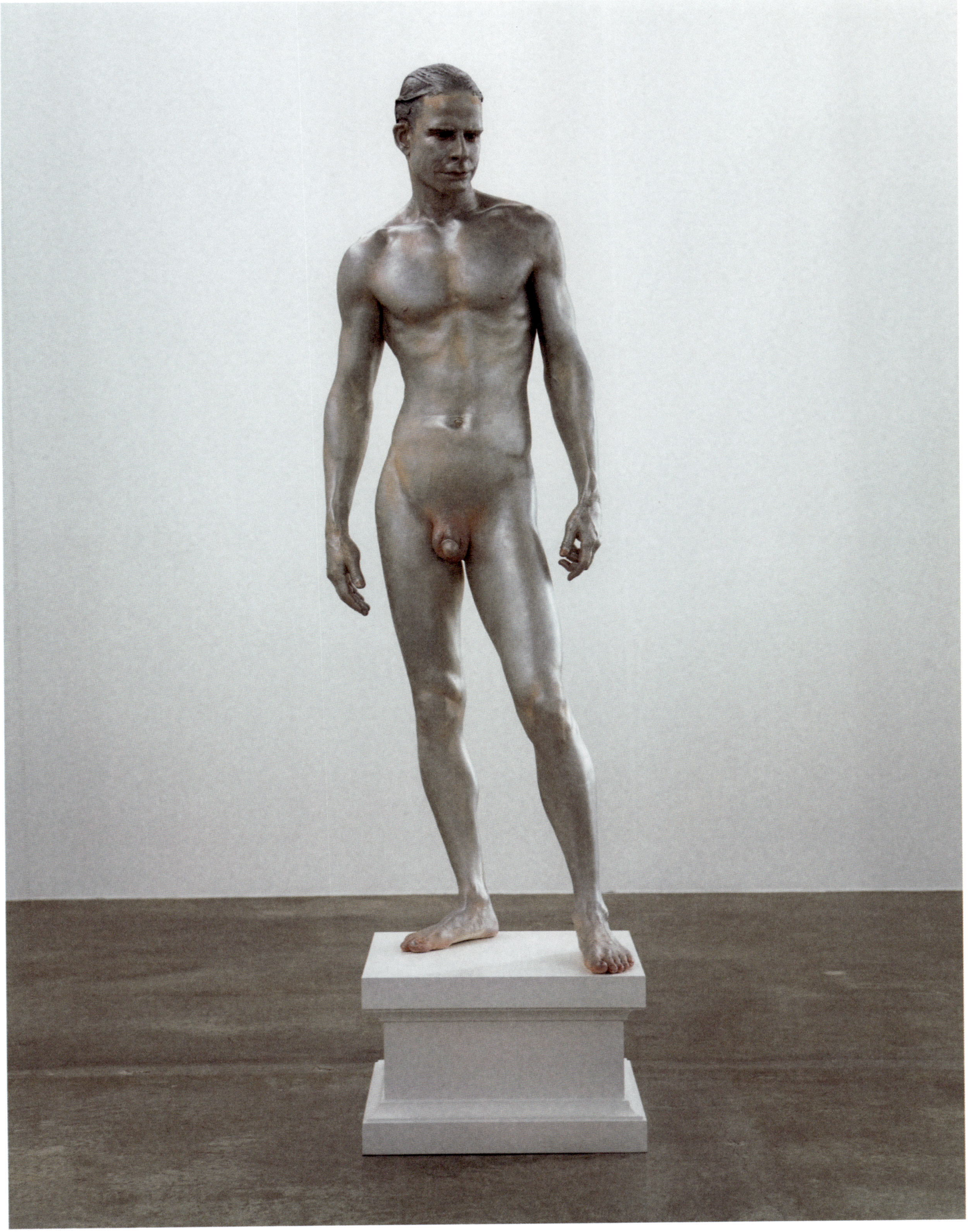

→ *Human Statue*, 2005

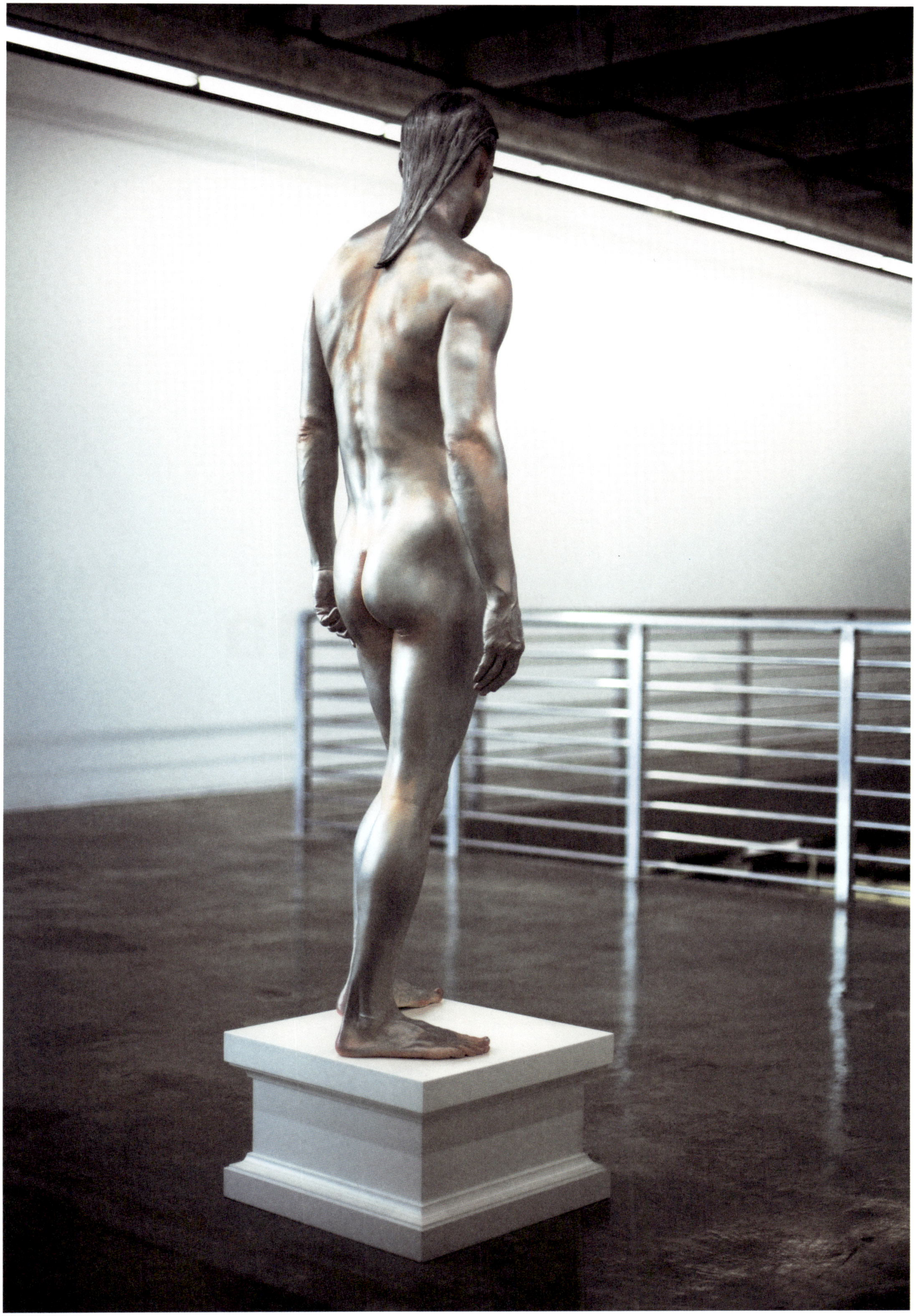

Huma Bhabha

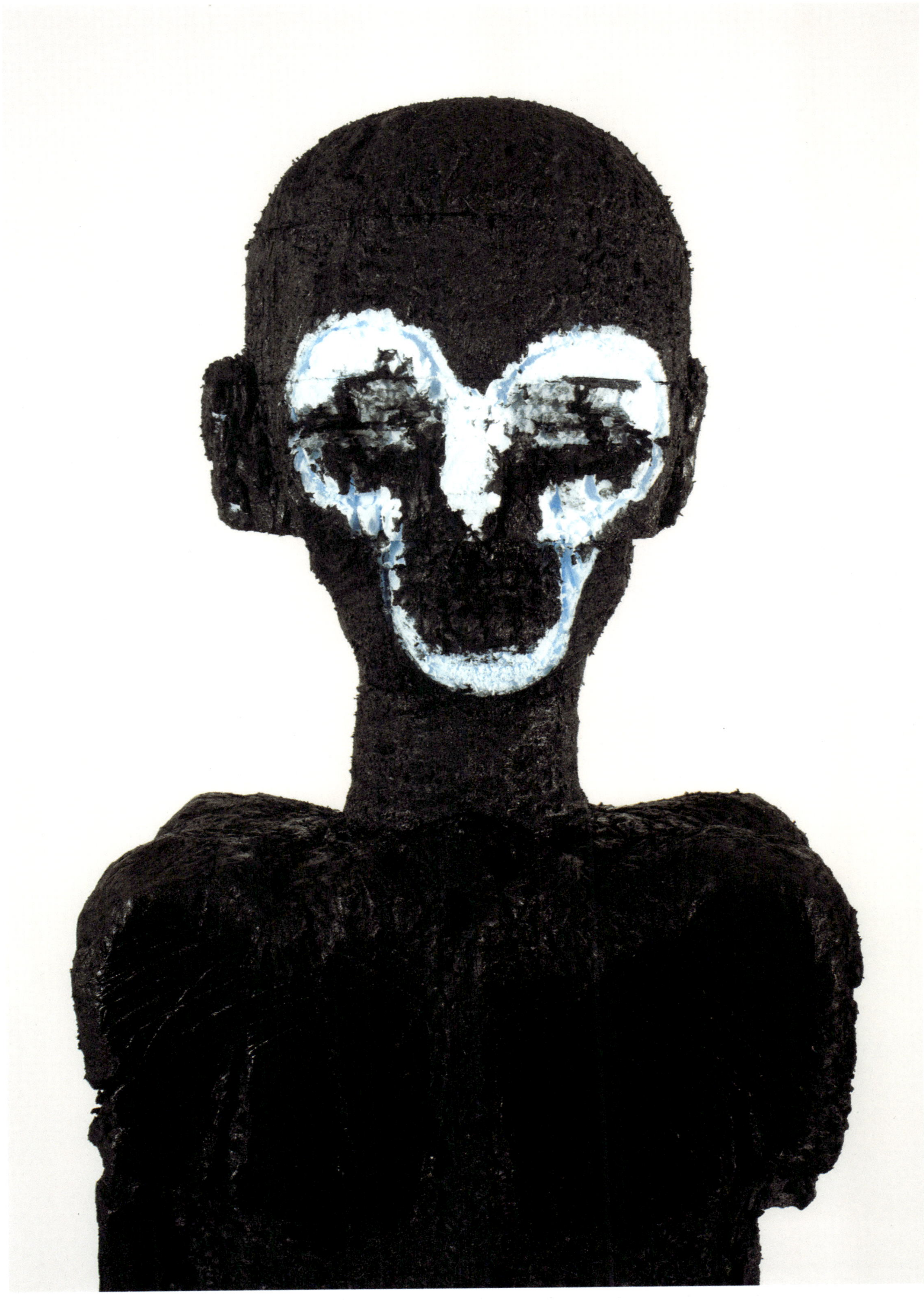

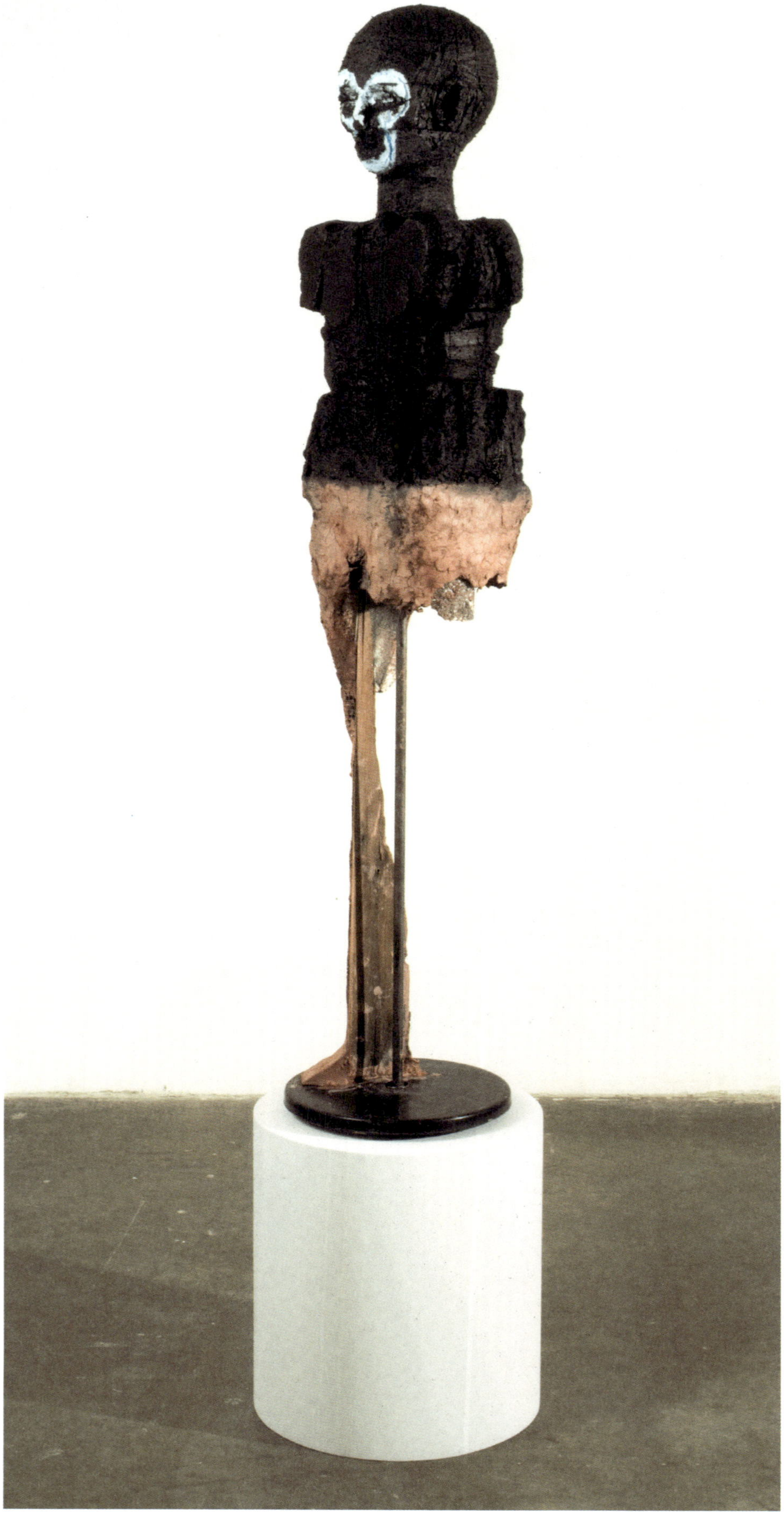

← *Bourne Darkly* (detail), 2008
↑ *Bourne Darkly*, 2008

↗ *The Immortal Story*, 2007

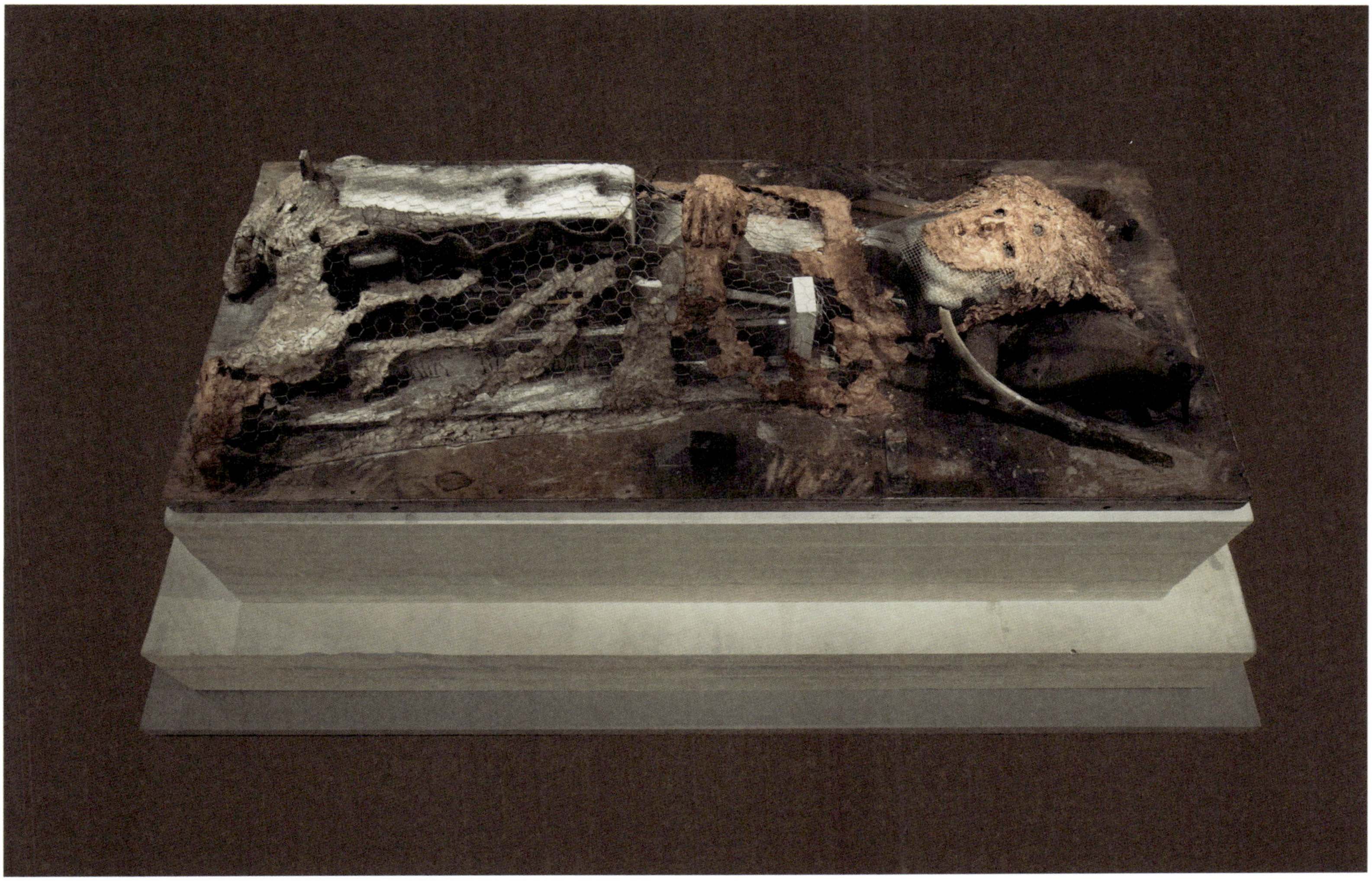

In Huma Bhabha's work, ancient history, an imagined future, present time and memory collide. Besides alluding to works by modern masters such as Constantin Brancusi, Alberto Giacometti and Pablo Picasso, her references extend from Greek and African art to horror and science fiction movies. Bhabha's sculptures are constructed mainly from waste materials, which have histories of their own. Describing her figures as 'landscapes of human debris', she explains: 'my use of materials relates to artists like Robert Rauschenberg and the history of assemblage, but I also see the use of discarded materials relating to how, in places like Pakistan, everything is used or saved no matter how seemingly useless.'

Bhabha thinks of her assemblage-based figures and mask-like heads as 'characters'. Speaking of *The Orientalist* (2007), one of her very few cast works, she says that it is 'a portrait not of a specific person, but of an ideology, and since orientalism is a destructive ideology the figure is monstrous'. As she elucidates: '*The Orientalist* is very much a cyborg, with a mask-like face that reminds me of *The Picture of Dorian Gray*. And giving it that title seemed to link Oscar Wilde's metaphor to Edward Said's critique of Western hubris.' The work's starting point was a chair that Bhabha found which suggested the base for an Egyptian seated figure. She made the sculpture in the way she makes most of her works — using Styrofoam, wood, metal, wire and clay — but knowing that in this case the original would be destroyed to make the bronze.

Emphasising that there is 'no hierarchy' in her looking, Bhabha's works draw inspiration from a wide-ranging array of sources, including Renaissance tombs (*The Immortal Story*, 2007) and Robert Ludlum's popular novels and their related films (*Bourne Darkly*, 2008). 'As I work on the pieces', she notes, 'I'm aware of them in a very abstract way — I mean that literally and figuratively — and I go back and forth between things that I know I'm referencing and things I'd like to reference. Viewers won't necessarily make the same connections, but I want them to have the pleasure of looking at something that calls other things to mind.'

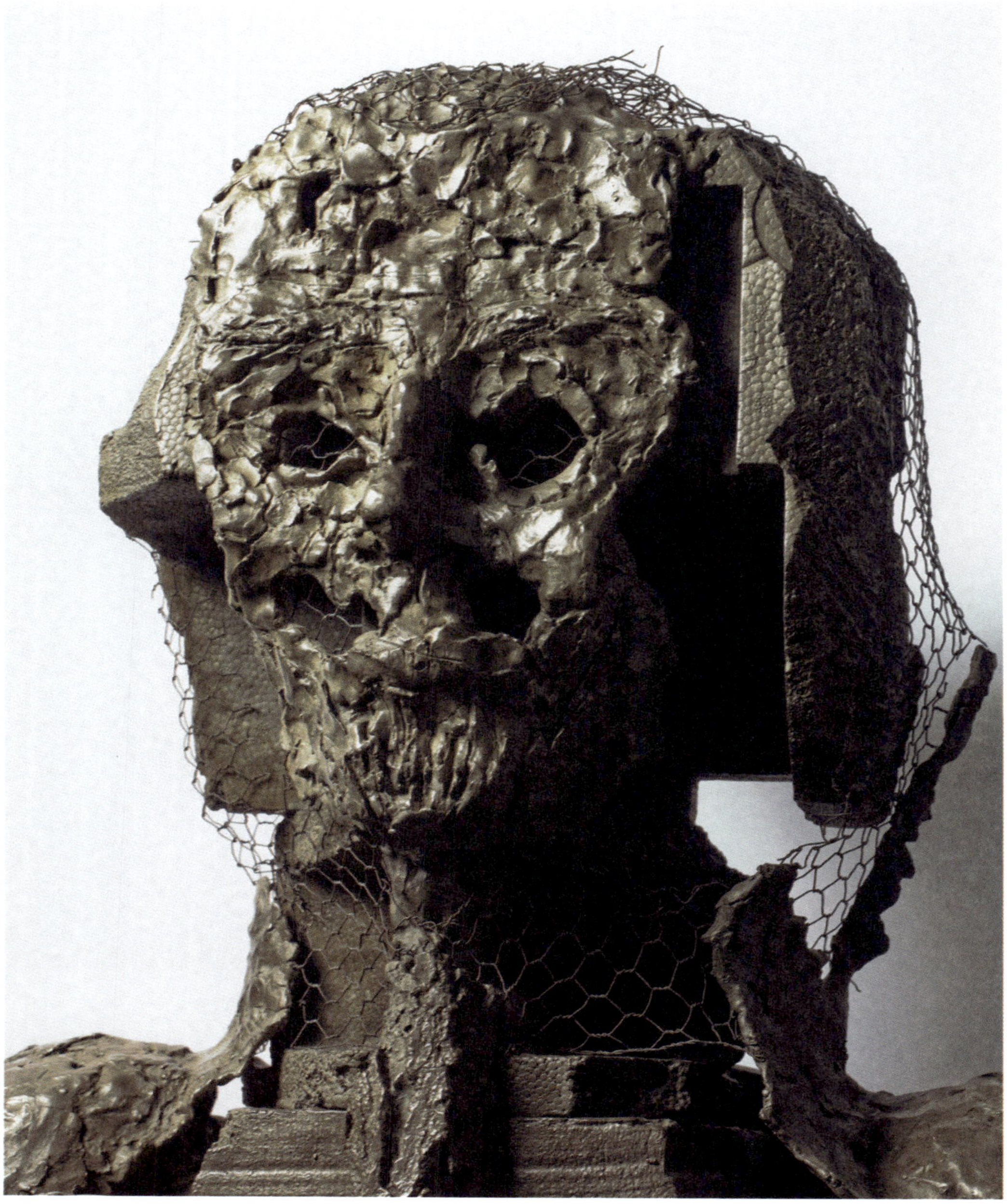

↑ ***The Orientalist*** **(detail), 2007**

→ ***The Orientalist*****, 2007**

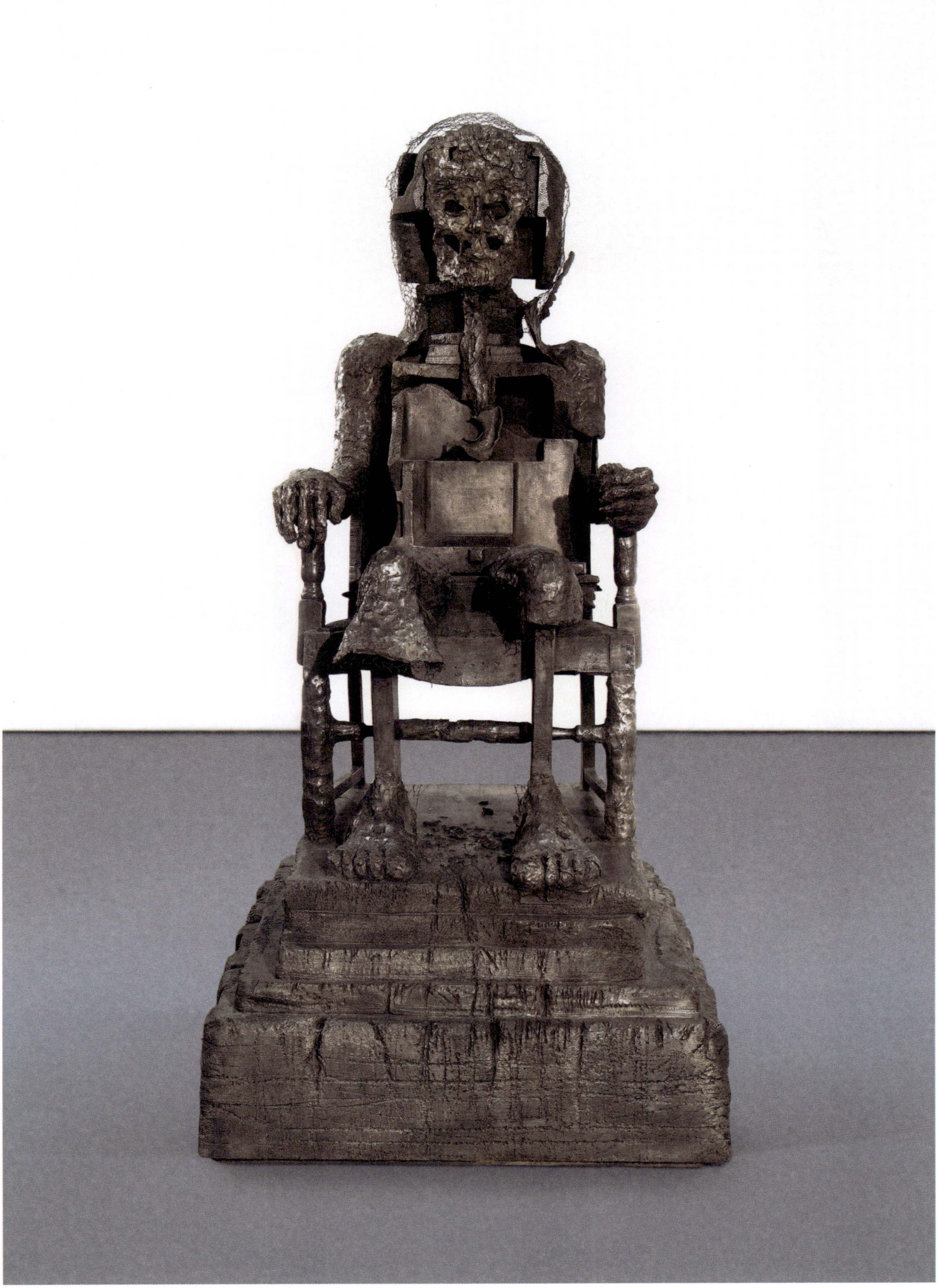

Maurizio **Cattelan**

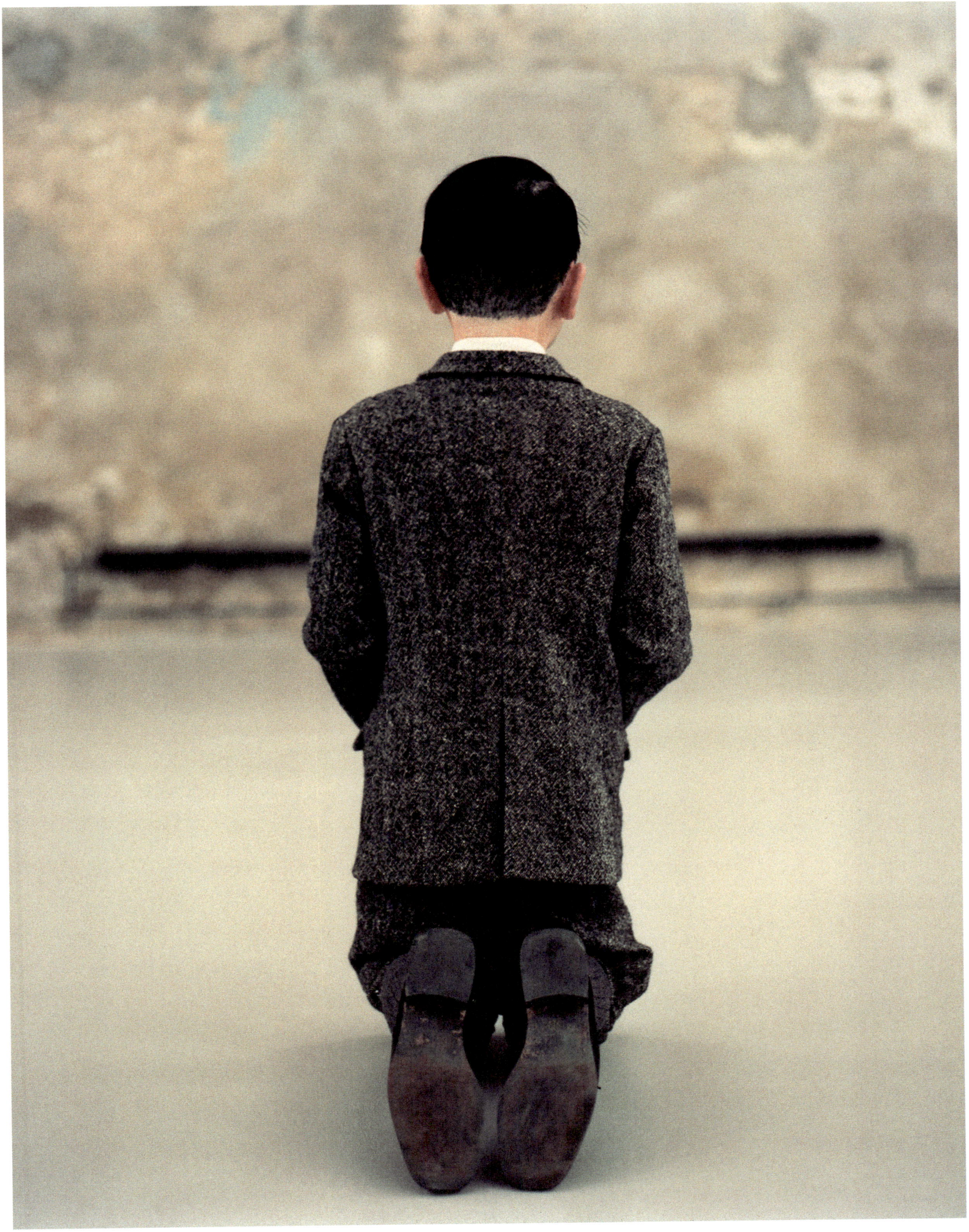

Maurizio Cattelan believes that art has to become a 'catalyst for different opinions, a mirror for our paranoias'. His work incites controversy, and its effrontery can generate extreme responses. In the case of *Him* (2001), a kneeling, child-size figure is seen from behind. It is only when the viewer walks around it and sees it face-to-face that the praying boy reveals itself as a diminutive Adolf Hitler. The double-take is a double shock; as Cattelan points out, 'you don't know if he's praying to have six more million people to kill, or for forgiveness', and it poses the question, if Hitler asked for absolution, would God forgive him?

Many of Cattelan's works are concerned with deception and how deceptive appearances can be. He describes *Him* as 'a rough image about peeling off masks and roles', and says that he is more interested in images than sculptures. While he creates concepts and their staging, the physical objects are fabricated by other people.

← ***Him*, 2001**

→ ***Him*, 2001**

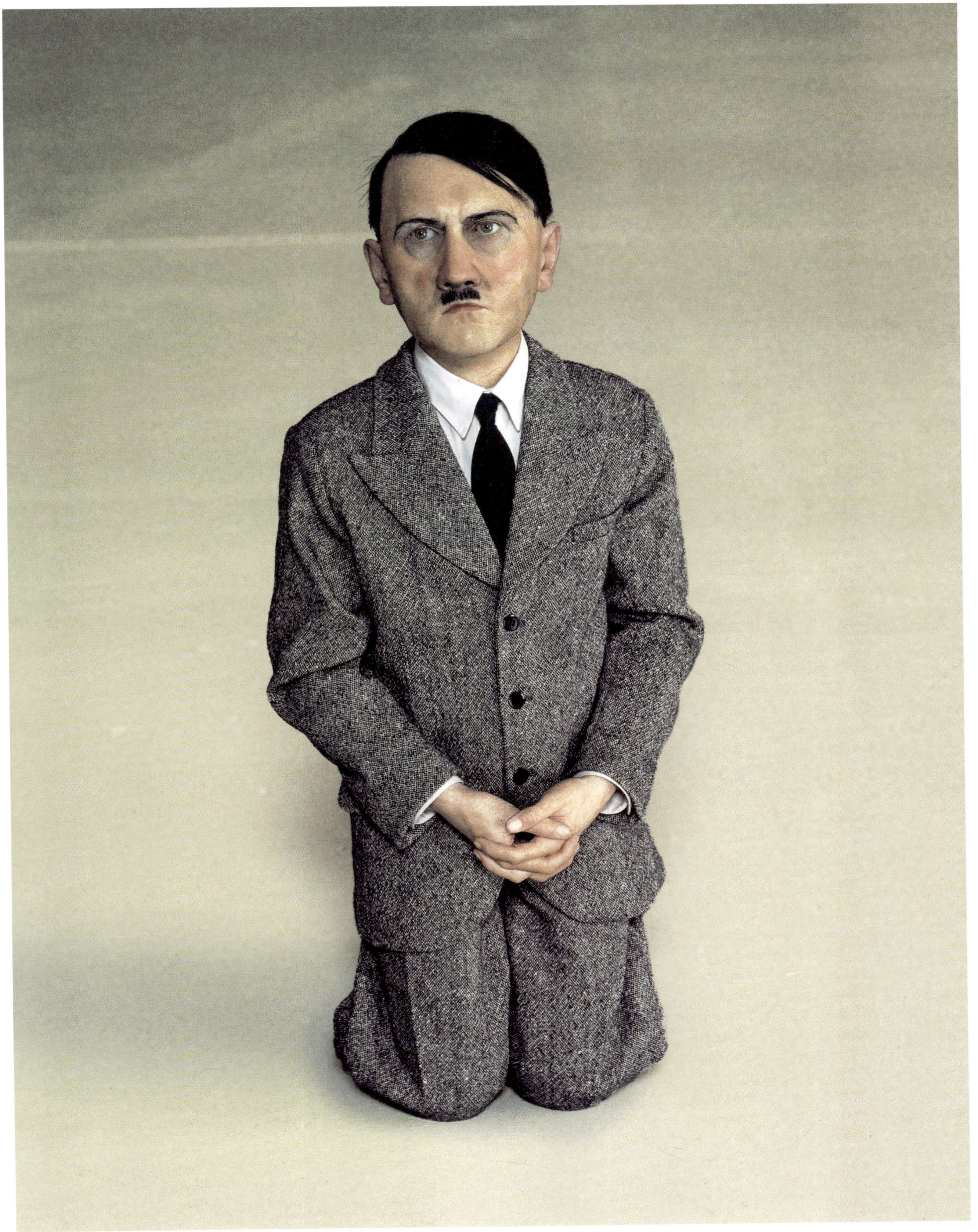

Though Cattelan considers *Him* to be an icon of fear, he sees *Now* (2004), his life-size effigy of John F. Kennedy lying in state, as a symbol of optimism, in the sense that 'the fact that there was someone like him makes you hope there must be another one somewhere'. At the same time, the work is an attempt at closure: 'certain deaths never end; they are eternal, they continue in the present. Putting Kennedy in a coffin, for me, meant making him die once and for all, interrupting this cycle of hypotheses, eternal reincarnations in the news.'

Cattelan, who once dealt with real corpses when he worked in a morgue, thinks of sculpture as dead, distant, deaf. Paradoxically, he chooses to make many of his works appear as lifelike as possible. The figures of both Hitler and Kennedy were fabricated by Cattelan's frequent collaborator, the Parisian waxwork sculptor Daniel Druet, who models the figures in plaster and then — like an embalmer in a funeral parlour — paints the skin and adds the finishing touches. Speaking of *Now*, Cattelan remarks that he didn't have any special reason for removing Kennedy's shoes and socks: 'I just think you shouldn't wear them in a coffin. It's like going to bed.'

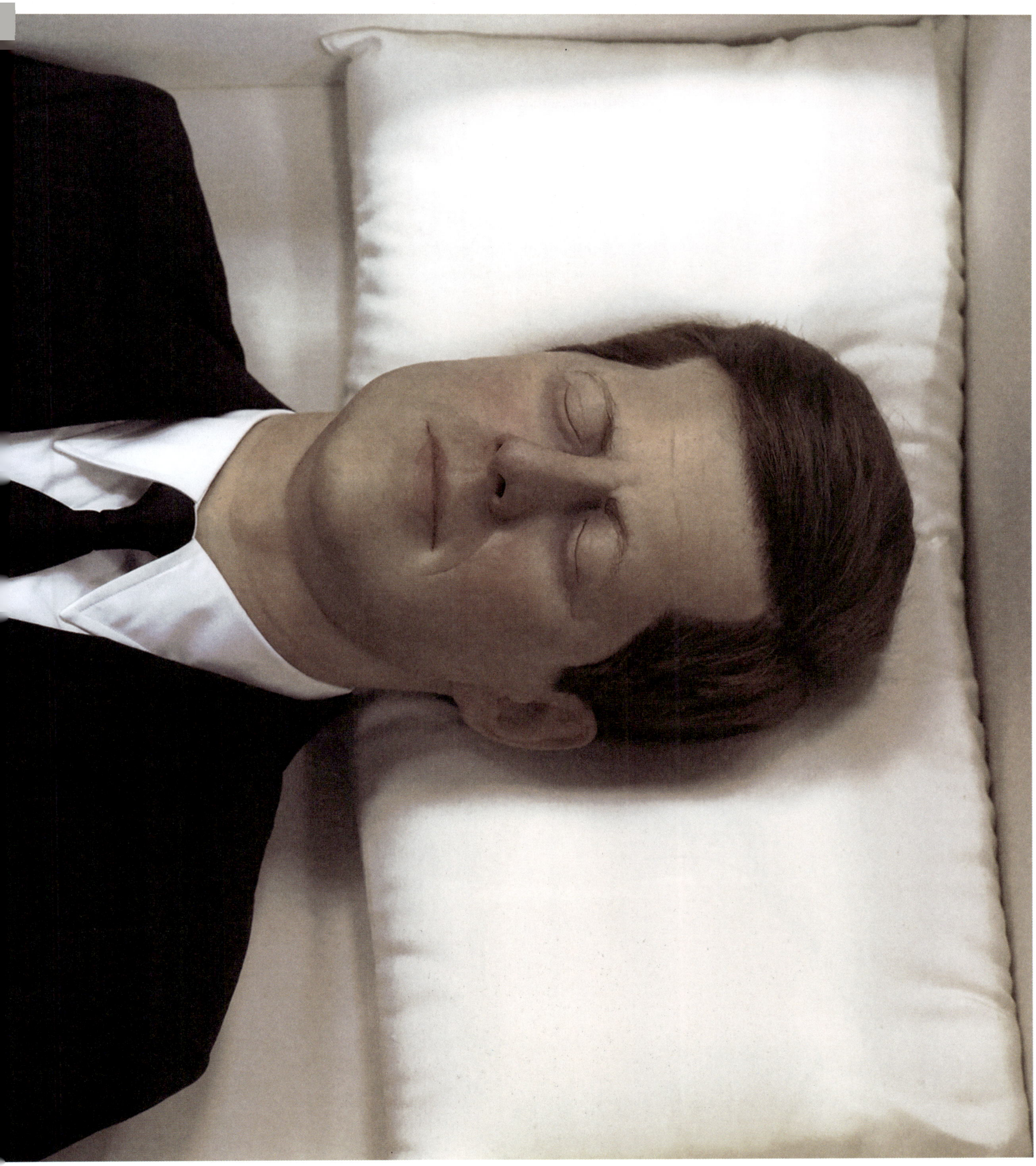

↑ ***Now*** **(detail), 2004**

→ ***Now*****, 2004**

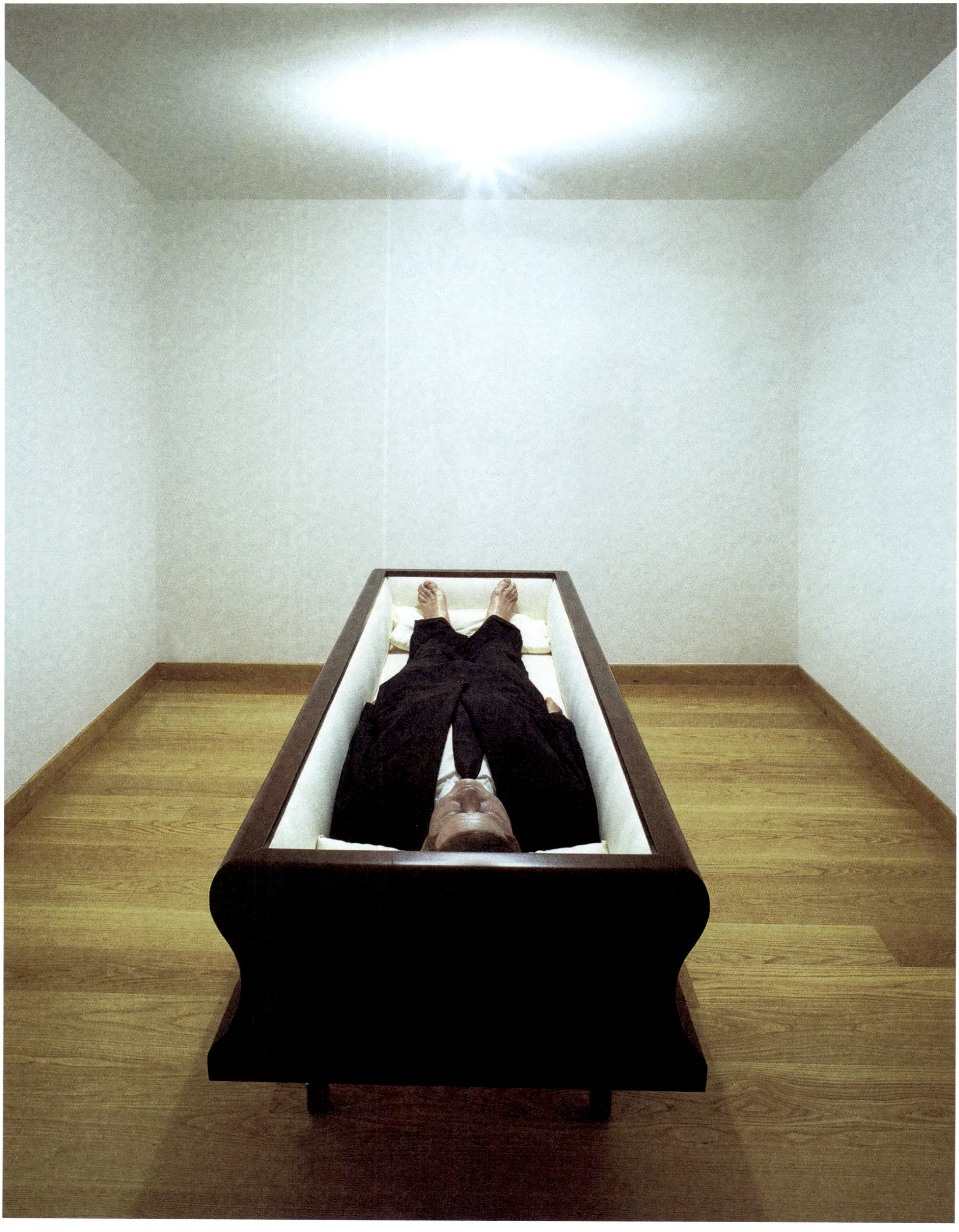

Production

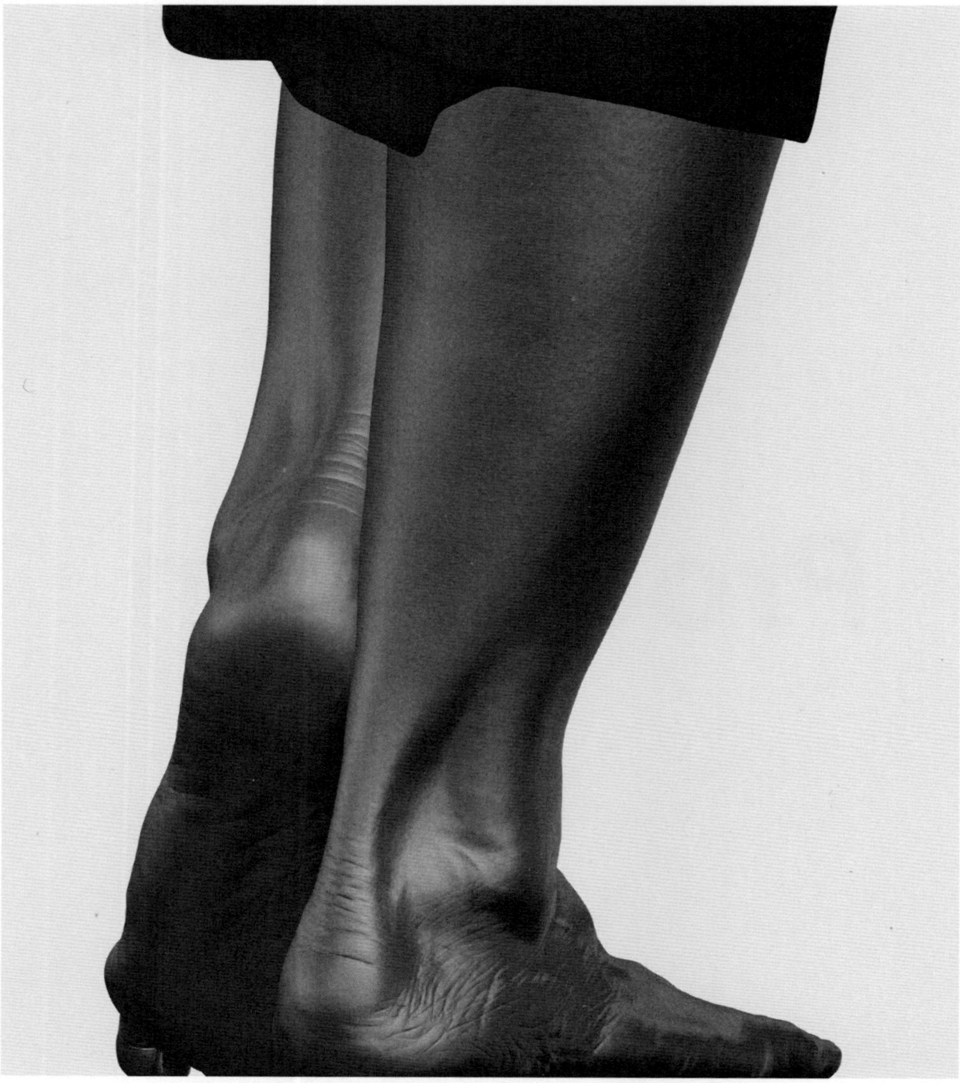

Frank Benson Digital preparatory image for
Human Statue (Jessie), 2011

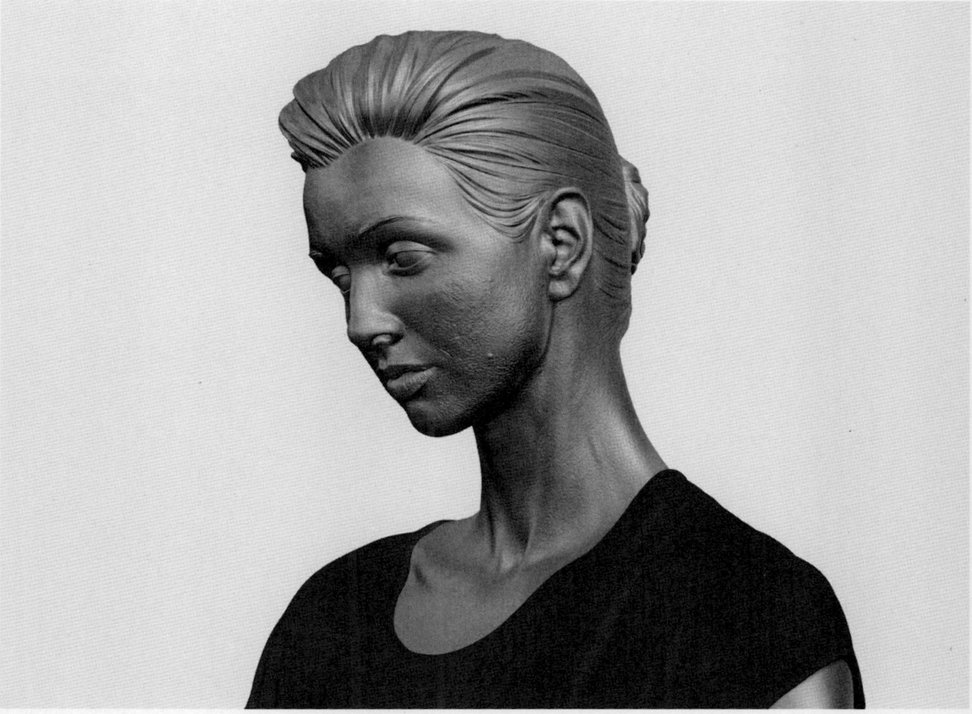

Frank Benson Digital preparatory image for
Human Statue (Jessie), 2011

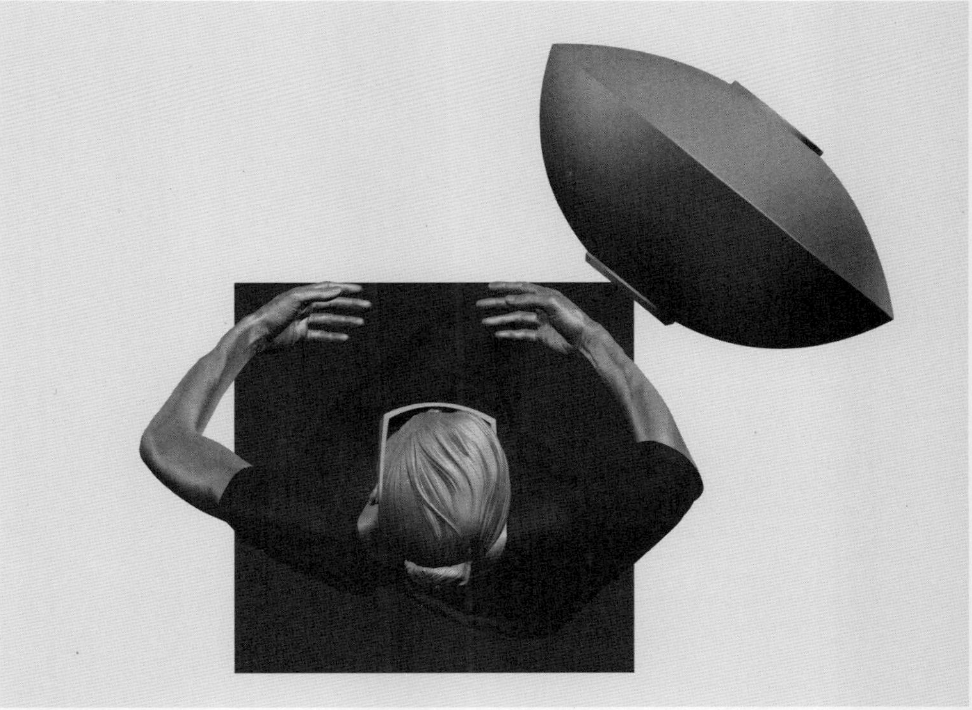

Frank Benson Digital preparatory image for
Human Statue (Jessie), 2011

Frank Benson

To create *Human Statue (Jessie)*, Benson scanned the body of his subject with a camera that records in three dimensions, and manipulated the texture of the skin and hair using 3D-modelling software (pictured). Digital light processing and a computer-controlled milling machine were then used to translate this virtual model back into a physical mould that was cast using the lost-wax technique. It was finished with a clear matte varnish, which halted the patination process and allowed the metallic colour of the bronze to show through on the head, limbs, glasses and vase. Once the bronze was sealed, a matte black outdoor paint was applied to the base and to the dress with an industrial spray finisher.

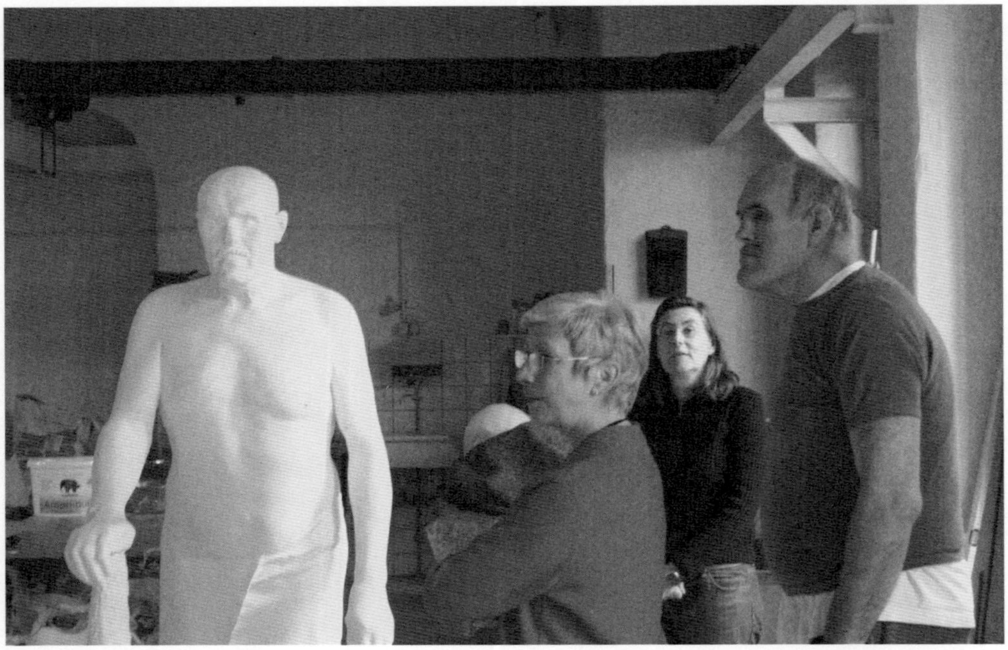

Katharina Fritsch *Riese* (Giant), 2008, photographed alongside the life model for the work

Katharina Fritsch

Fritsch's works are produced using both plaster casting and 3D-scanning methods, which faithfully replicate their live models. The sculptures are then painted in monochrome colours with a light-absorbing matte finish. *Riese* (Giant) was modelled on a taxi driver the artist met (photographed above, alongside his likeness) who was acromegalic — a condition caused by an excess production of growth hormones.

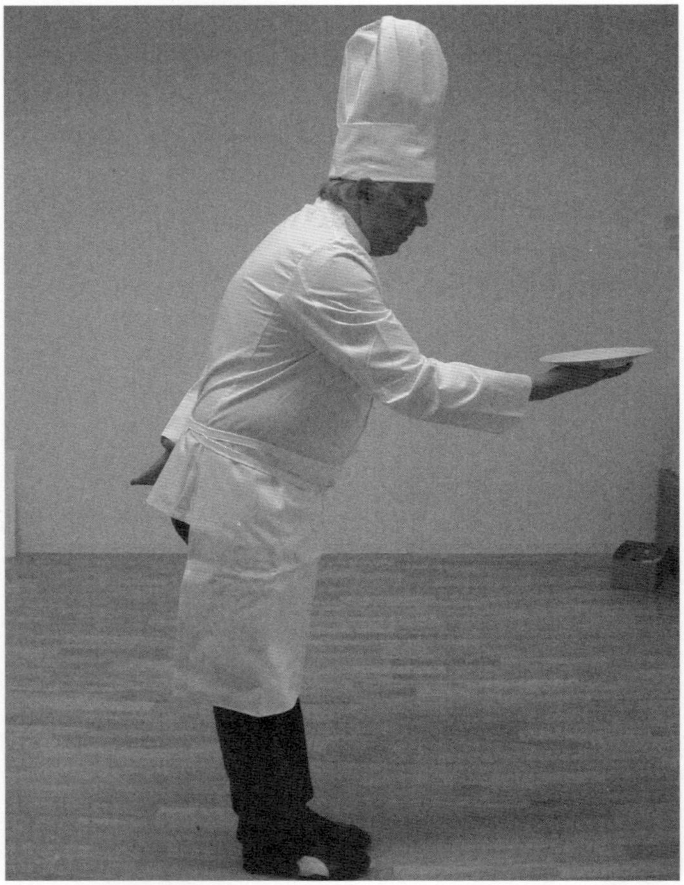

Katharina Fritsch Model for *Koch und 6. Foto (Schwarzwaldhaus)* (Cook and 6th Photo [Black Forest House]), 2006/2008

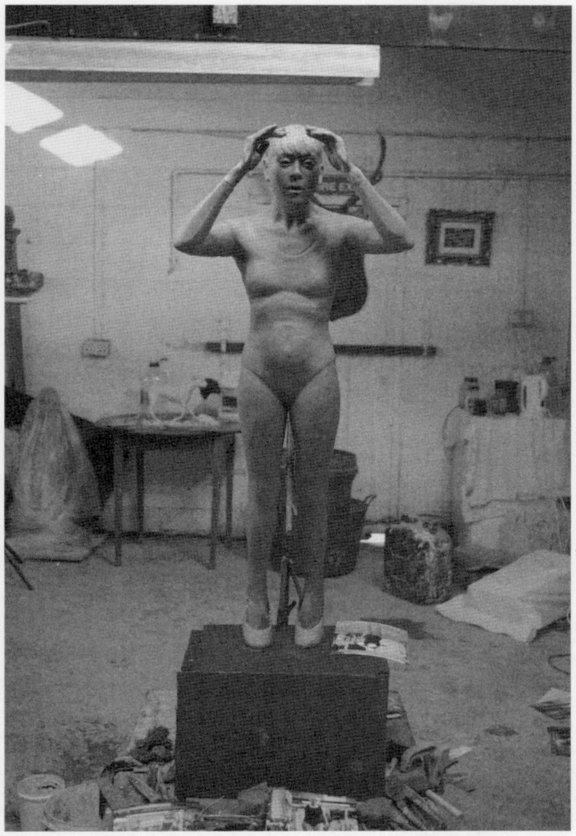

Ryan Gander *Come up on different streets, they both were streets of shame Or Absinth blurs my thoughts, I think we should be moving on*, 2009

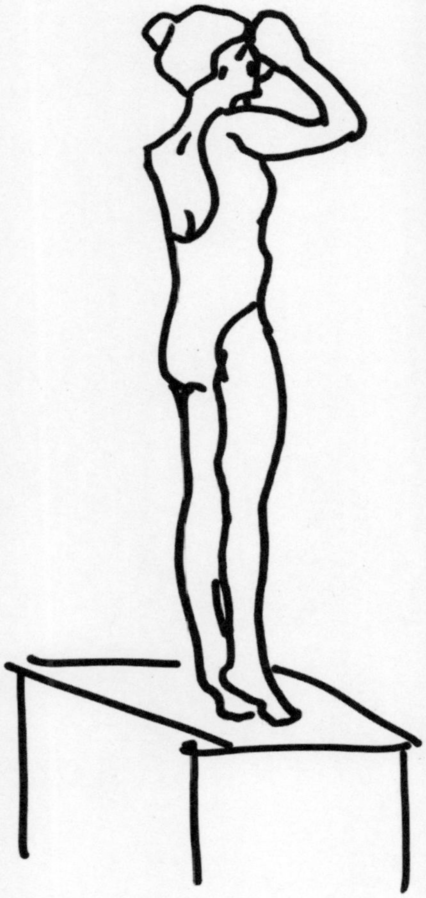

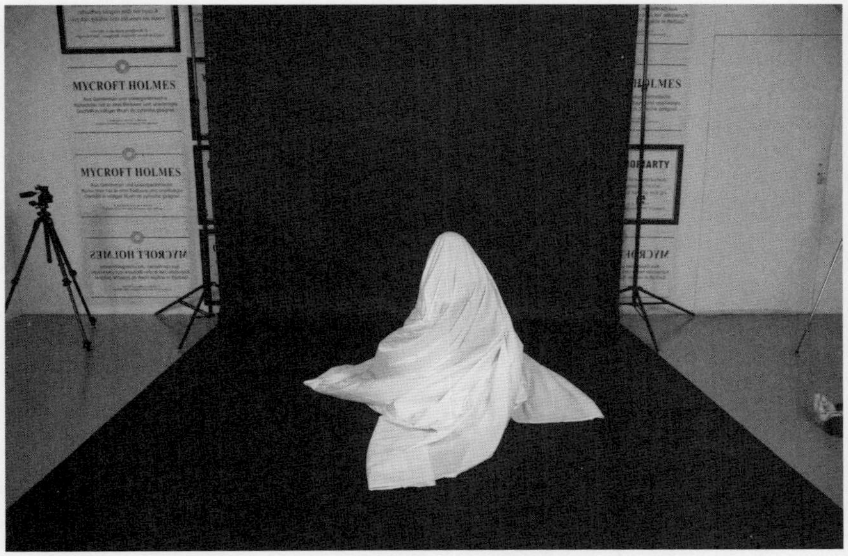

Ryan Gander Preparatory photograph for *Tell my mother not to worry (ii)*, 2012

Ryan Gander

Gander created his ballerina figures by taking photographs of a posed model (in the case of the work, illustrated above, his wife, the gallerist Rebecca May Marston), which are then used to produce two-thirds life-size figures sculpted in wax. Each figure is then sent to the foundry to be cast in bronze. The appearance of the finished sculptures are intended to resemble the little ballerina sculpted by Edgar Degas, and indeed the physical process has similarities with that of the *Little Dancer Aged Fourteen* (1880–81, cast c. 1922); Degas sculpted the original ballerina figure in wax and this was used forty years later by the inheritors of his estate to cast two separate versions in bronze.

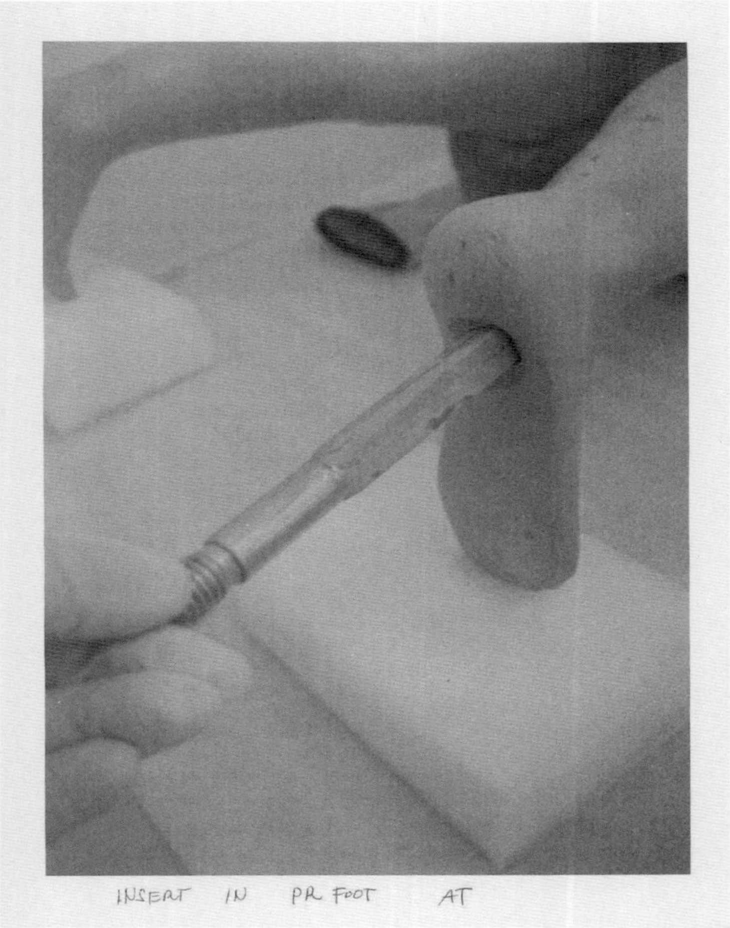

Rachel Harrison Installation instructions
for *Jack Lemmon*, 2006

Rachel Harrison

Rachel Harrison's works are a mixture of fabricated forms and found objects, from telephones and cardboard boxes, to drinking straws and snakeskin. The rough-surfaced sculptures that form the basis of many of her works are handmade using simple materials, such as chicken wire, cement, polystyrene and wood. These are then finished with paint, often in colourful, sometimes pearlescent tones, which is frequently also applied to the pedestal – an element present but indistinguishable from the sculpture itself. These forms are then adorned with photographs and found objects; in the case of *Schmatte with President* (2006), it is a mask of Abraham Lincoln and a scarf, for *Jack Lemmon* (2011), the mask is Dick Cheney's, hung on the head of a female mannequin on the body of a child, dressed in a gold tracksuit top, holding a fishing net and a lemon.

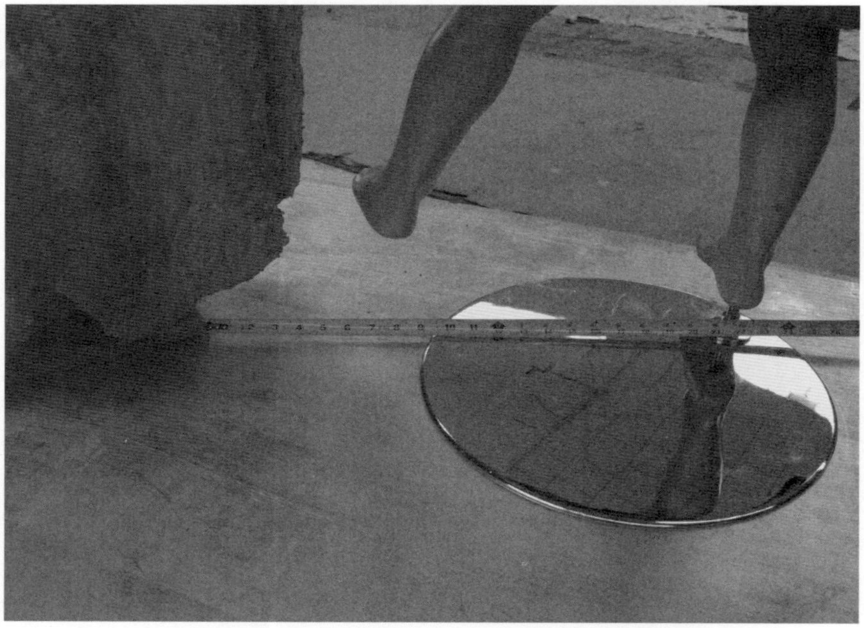

Rachel Harrison Installation instructions
for *Jack Lemmon*, 2006

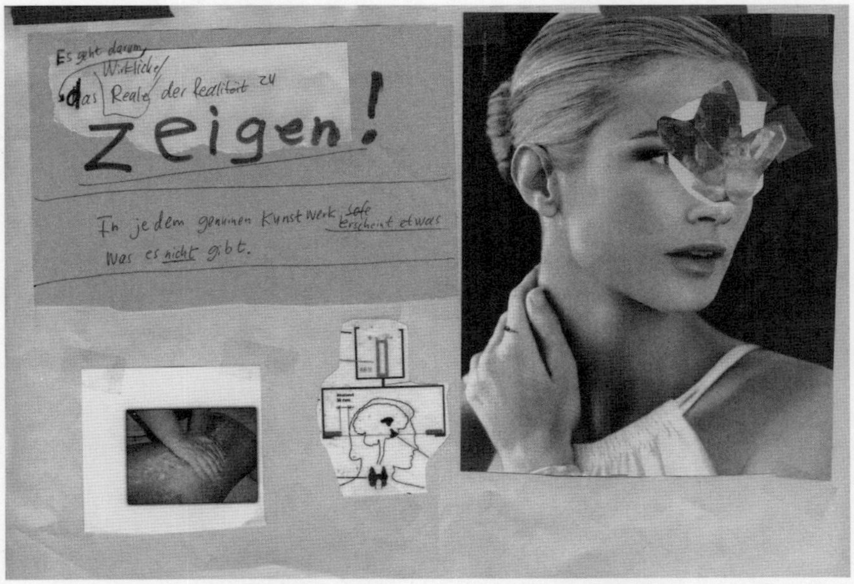

Thomas Hirschhorn Preliminary sketch
for 'Crystal of Resistance', 2011

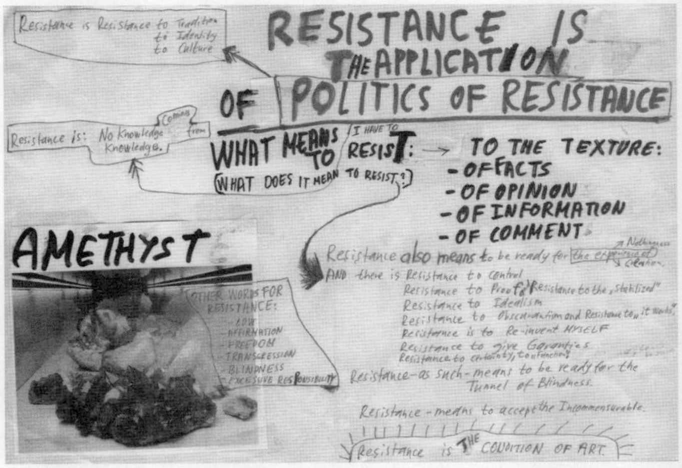

Thomas Hirschhorn Preliminary sketch
for 'Crystal of Resistance', 2011

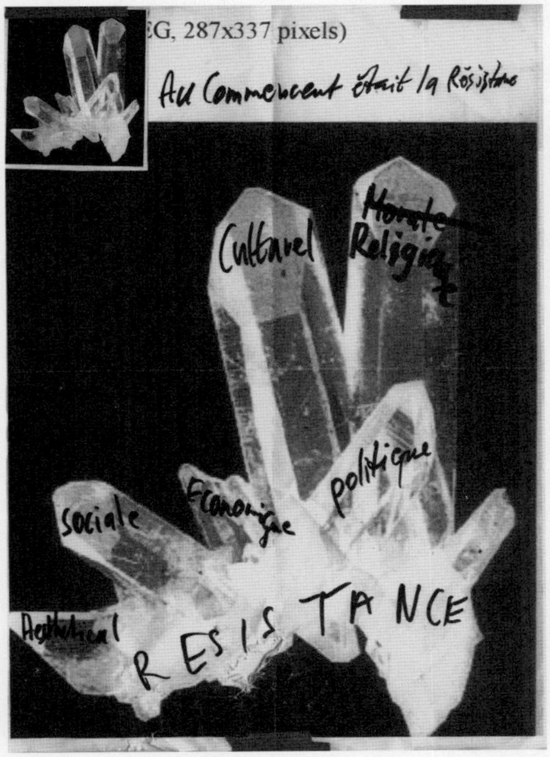

Thomas Hirschhorn Preliminary sketch
for 'Crystal of Resistance', 2011

Thomas Hirschhorn

These sketches were made at the time of Hirschhorn's 'Crystal of Resistance', his installation at the Swiss Pavilion for the 2011 Venice Biennale, which included the sculpture *Resistance-Subjecter*. Hirschhorn uses two- and three-dimensional collage as a key tool for producing what he understands as 'new worlds' made up of elements of the existing world. The artist views this practice of reconfiguration as a method of public and political engagement; in the artist's words, 'collages resist facts, collages resist information and collages resist documents. Collages create a truth of their own.'

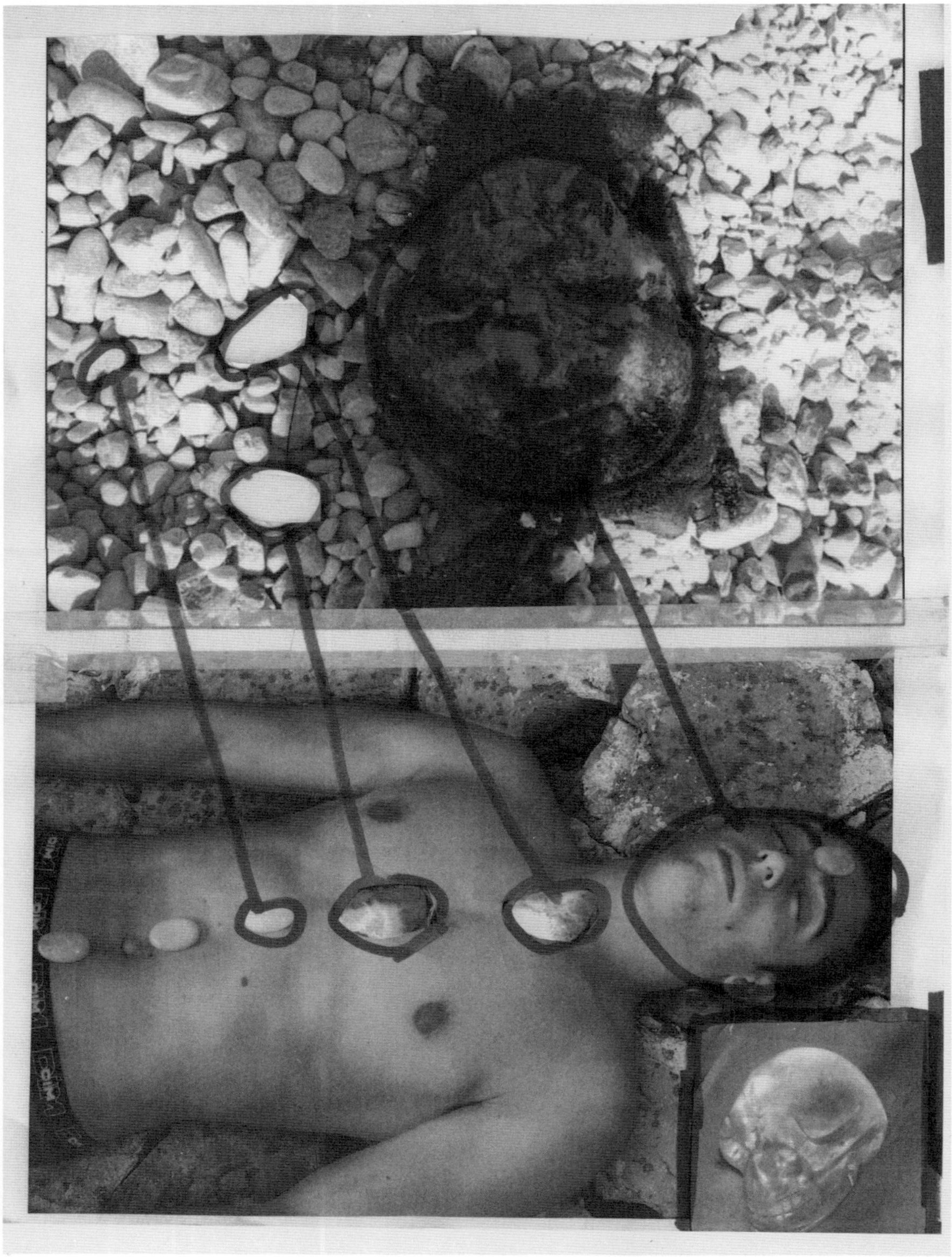

Thomas Hirschhorn Preliminary sketch
for 'Crystal of Resistance', 2011

Urs Fischer

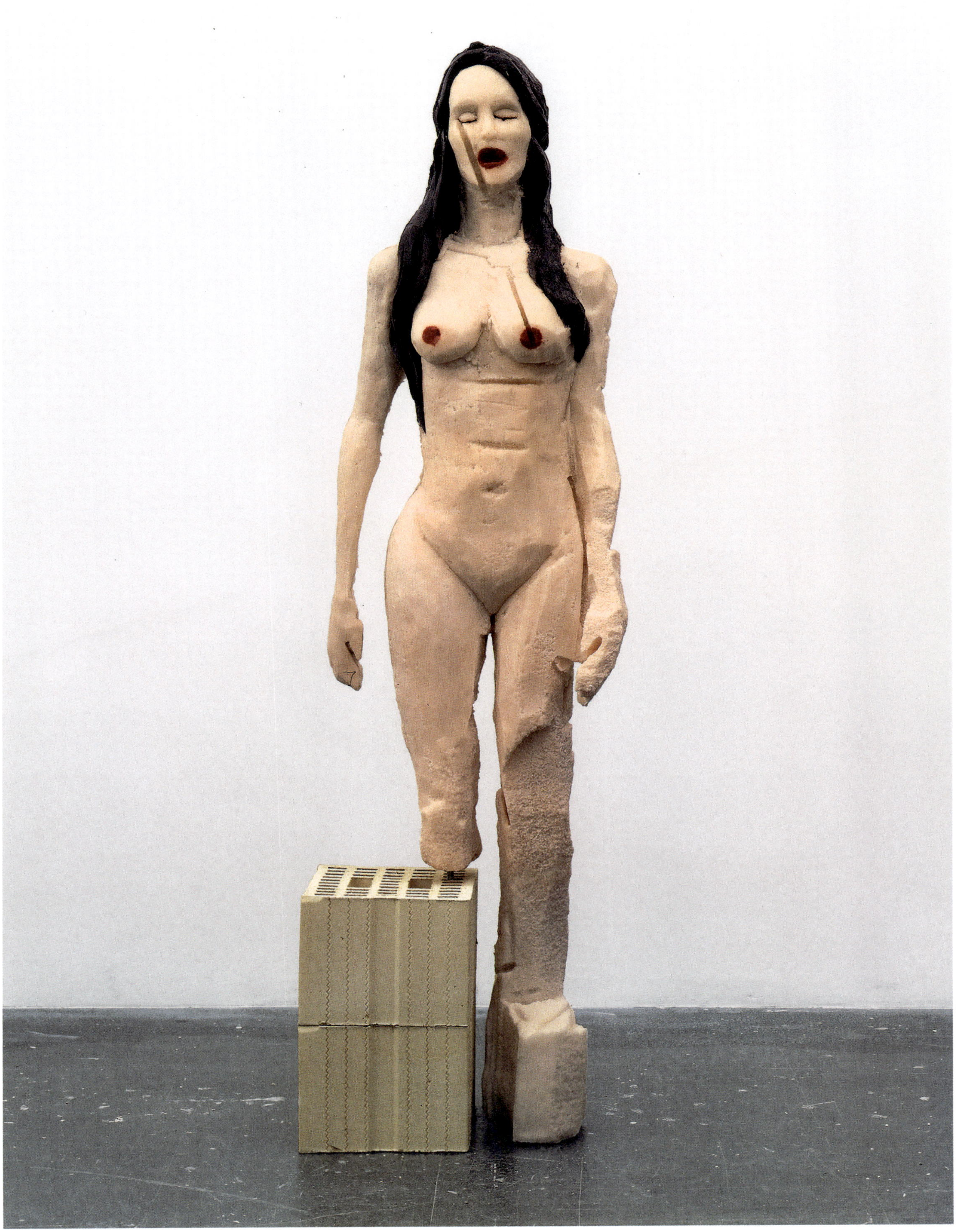

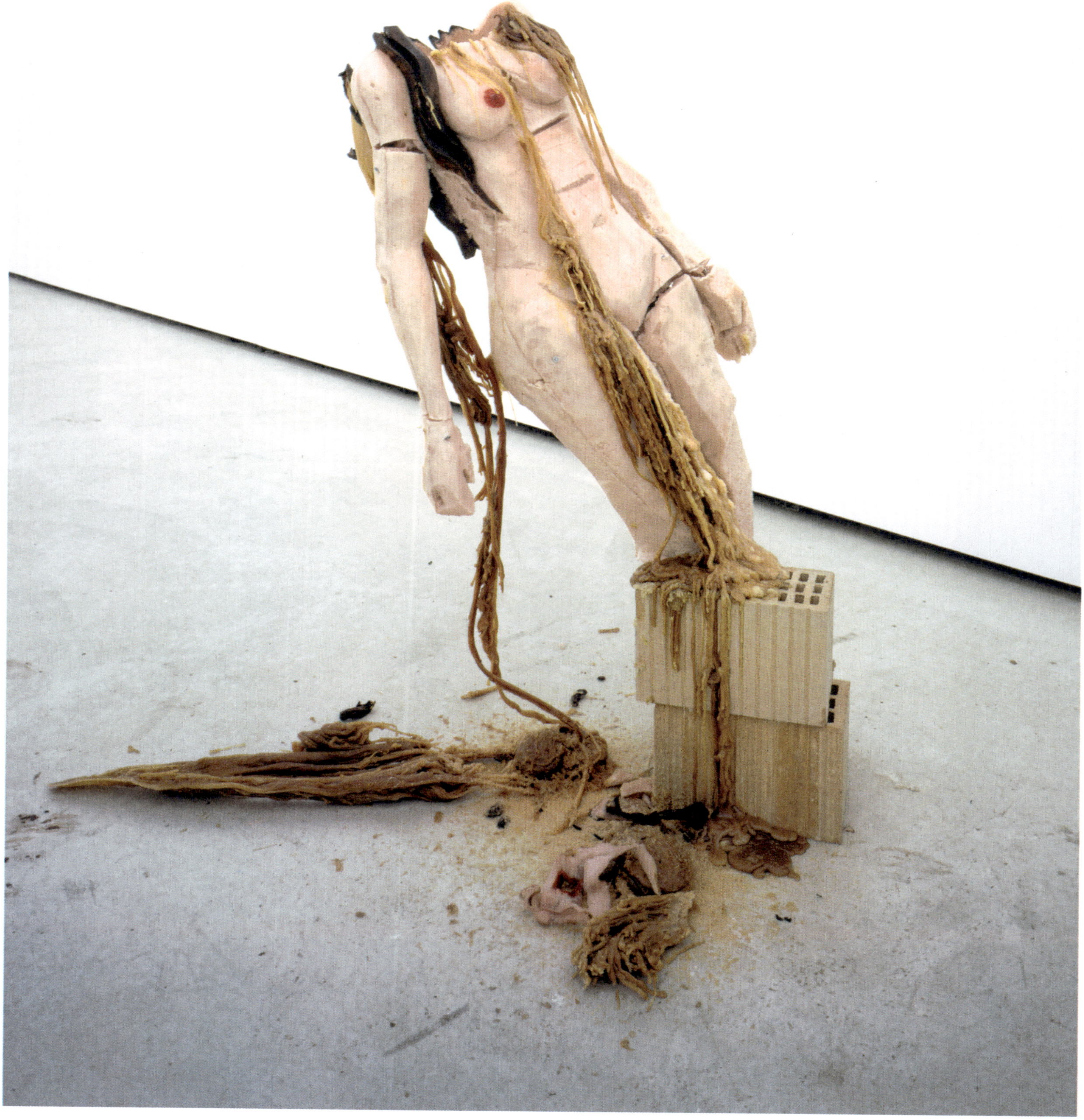

← *Untitled*, 2001

↑ *Untitled*, 2001

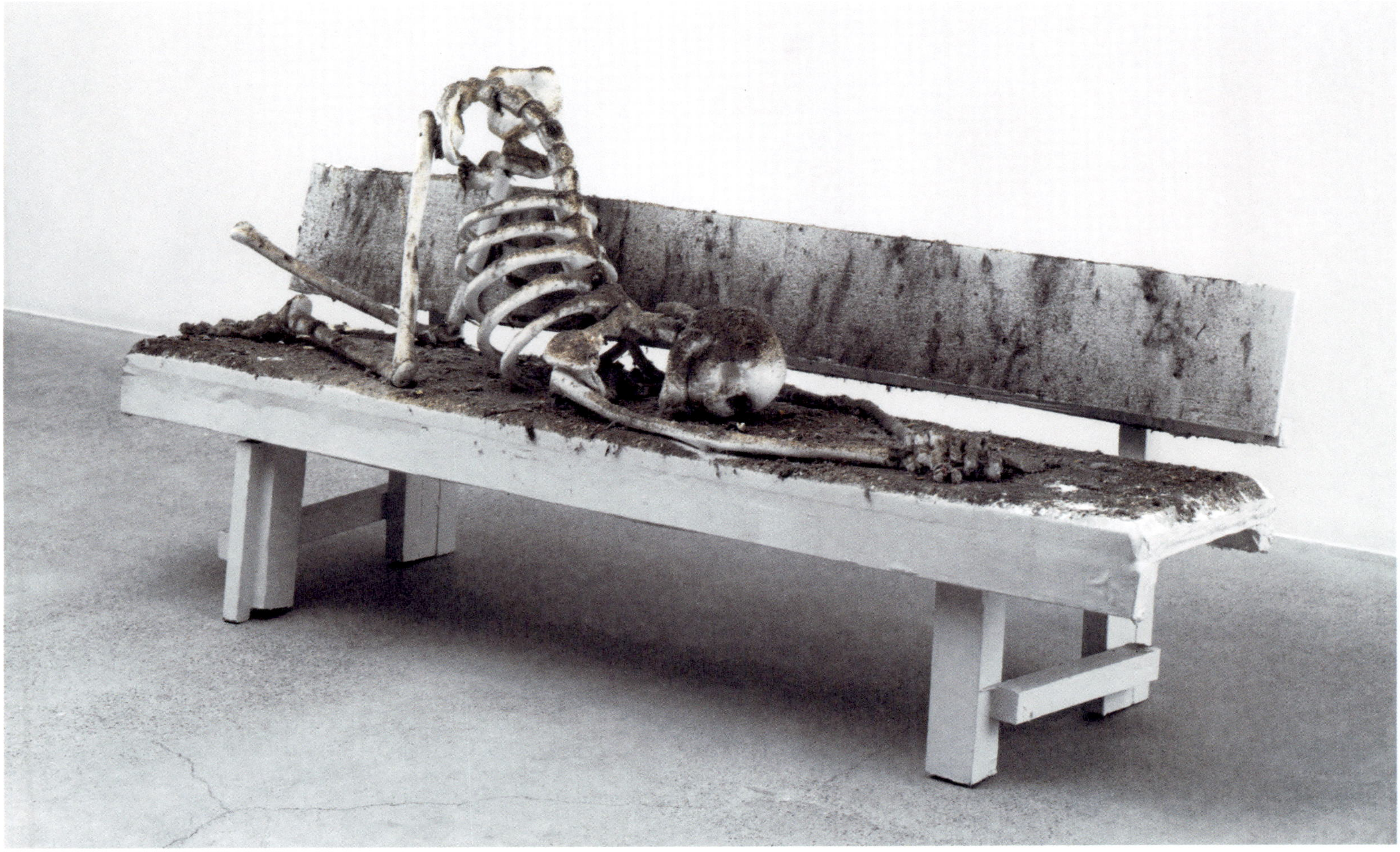

Like many of Urs Fischer's sculptures, at first glance *Skinny Sunrise* (2000) and *Untitled* (2001) appear to be explorations of mortality and decay; modern *memento mori*. In historical *vanitas* paintings, images of skeletons and lighted candles are standard props symbolising the brevity of life and the inevitability of death. Yet, for all his interest in art history, Fischer sees these objects quite differently. His skeleton sculptures are not about death: 'they are very much alive,' he says; 'they are characters, they're funny.' Similarly, his wax candle sculptures, which burn throughout the duration of an exhibition, are not about transience. Although they eventually become puddles of molten wax, Fischer points out that 'they aren't destroyed, they create new images'.

Recently, when speaking about the sculptor Medardo Rosso (1858–1928), whose unique working method involved the use of cast wax, Fischer reflected that 'a lot of sculpture gains its singular power by replacing something fleeting with something concrete and non-ephemeral. The notion of time is largely absent in this game. Sculpture as the real living dead. You can place a sculpture art historically, but when encountering a three-dimensional form in space, you're always inclined to consider it as something current, of the present. You and a sculpture share space. Sculpture can be very social, if you don't mind the company.' With his *Untitled* wax nude, which is gradually transformed as it burns down, Fischer marks the passing of time while ensuring that the sculpture, whose mutability is beyond his control, is always very much of the present. By the end of the exhibition, the sculpture has exchanged its manmade nature for its physical nature. The resulting pool of molten wax is then collected and recycled once the show is over. The work is then remade for its next reincarnation using fresh wax.

In contrast to the protean nature of the wax sculptures, which are always in a state of flux, Fischer's skeletons represent a sort of permanence. In his view, they are 'pretty likeable figures… They are simple, like prototypes; they are an easily workable form of figuration, and for me they have a pleasurable, curious liveliness.'

↑ ***Skinny Sunrise*, 2000**

Katharina **Fritsch**

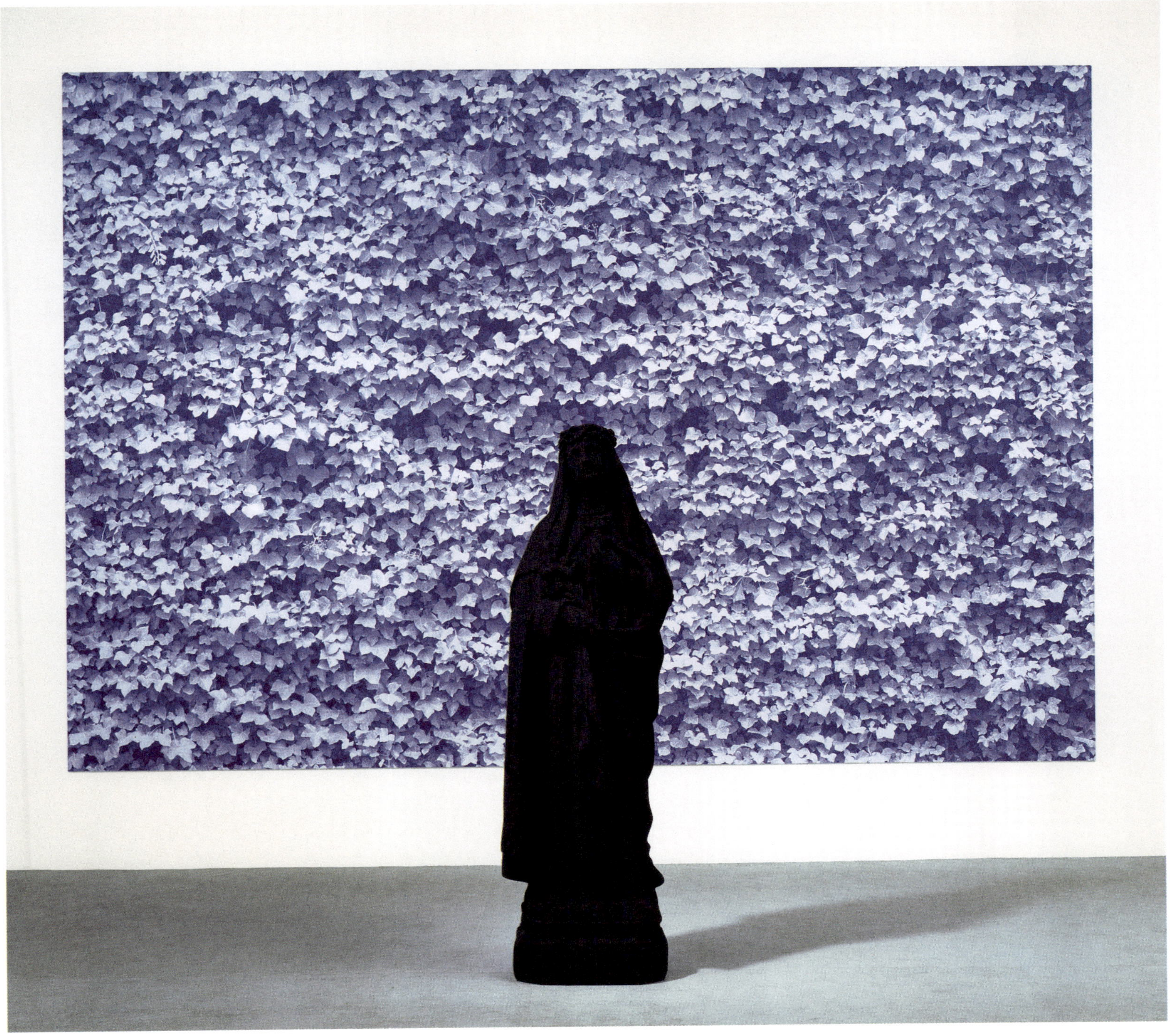

↑ *St. Katharina und 2. Foto (Efeu)*
(St. Katharina and 2nd Photo [Ivy]), 2007

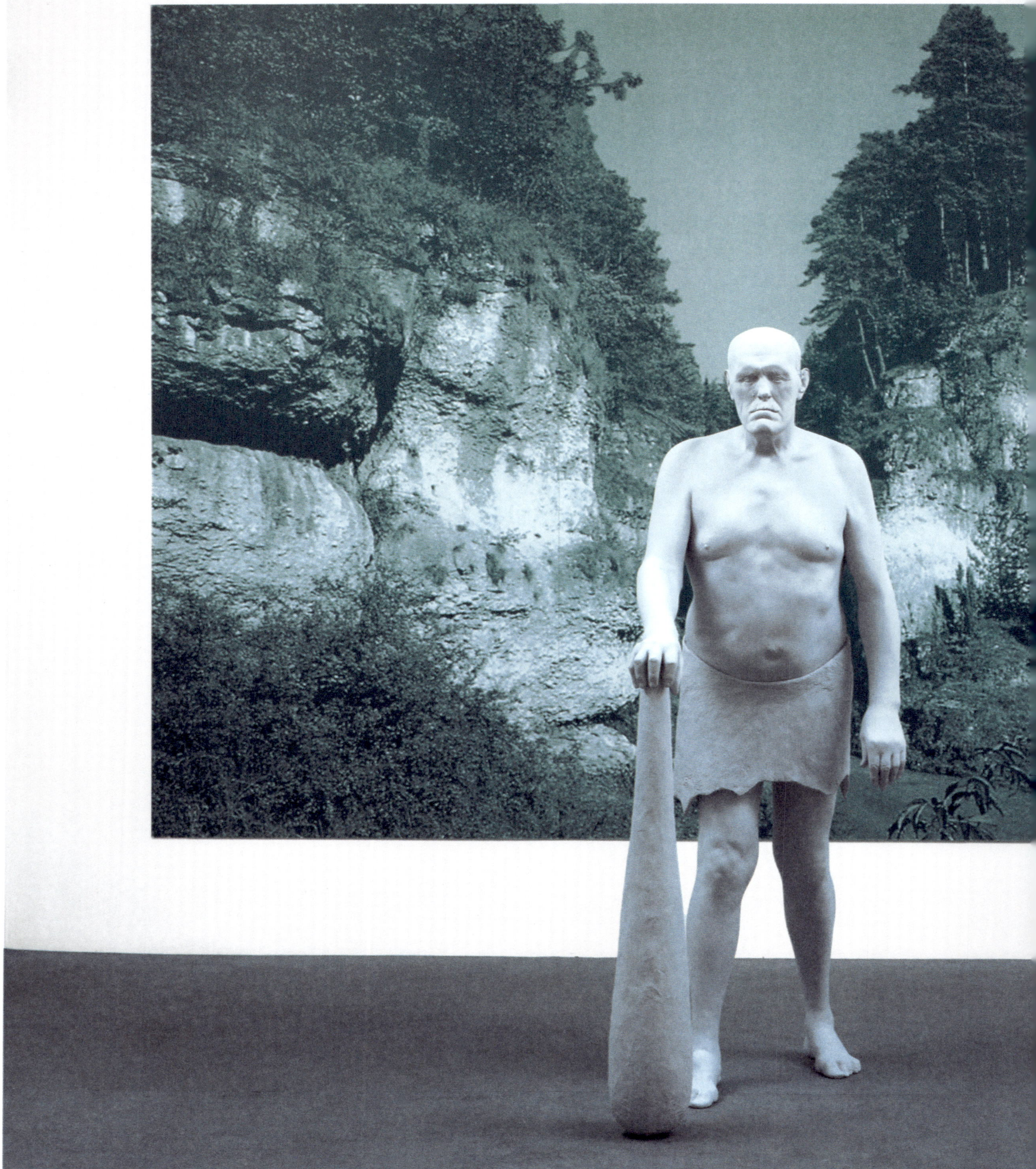

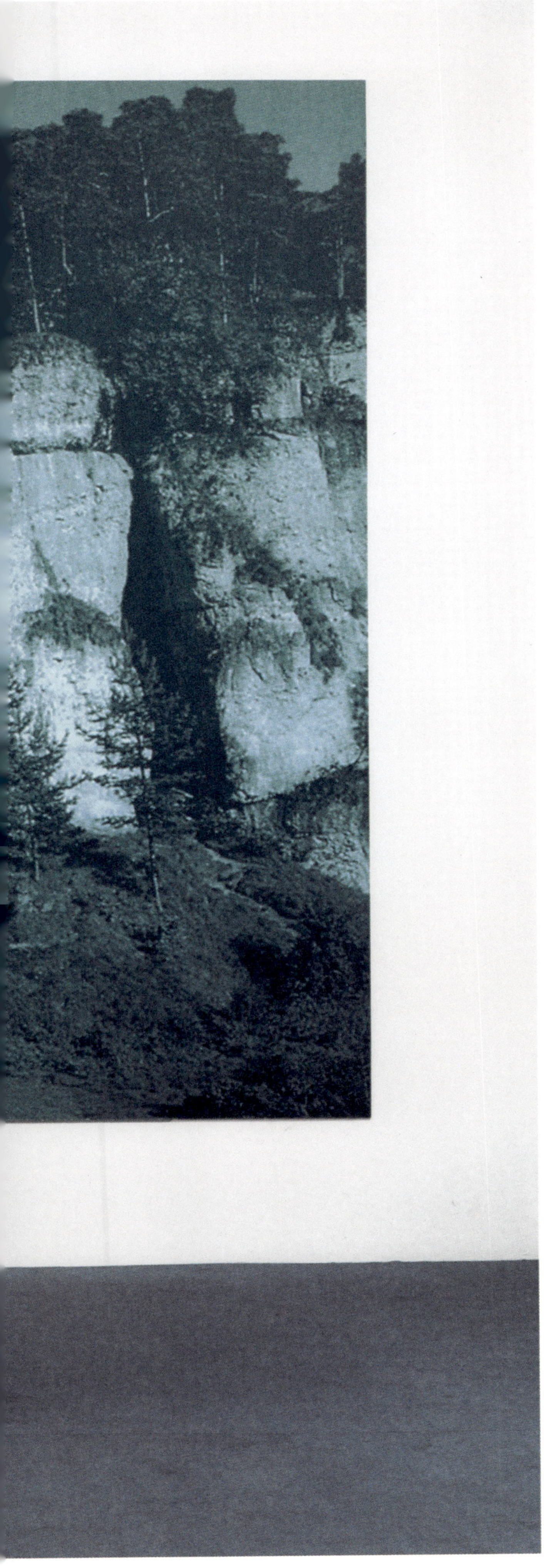

← *Riese und 4. Postkarte (Franken)*
(Giant and 4th Postcard [Franconia]), 2008

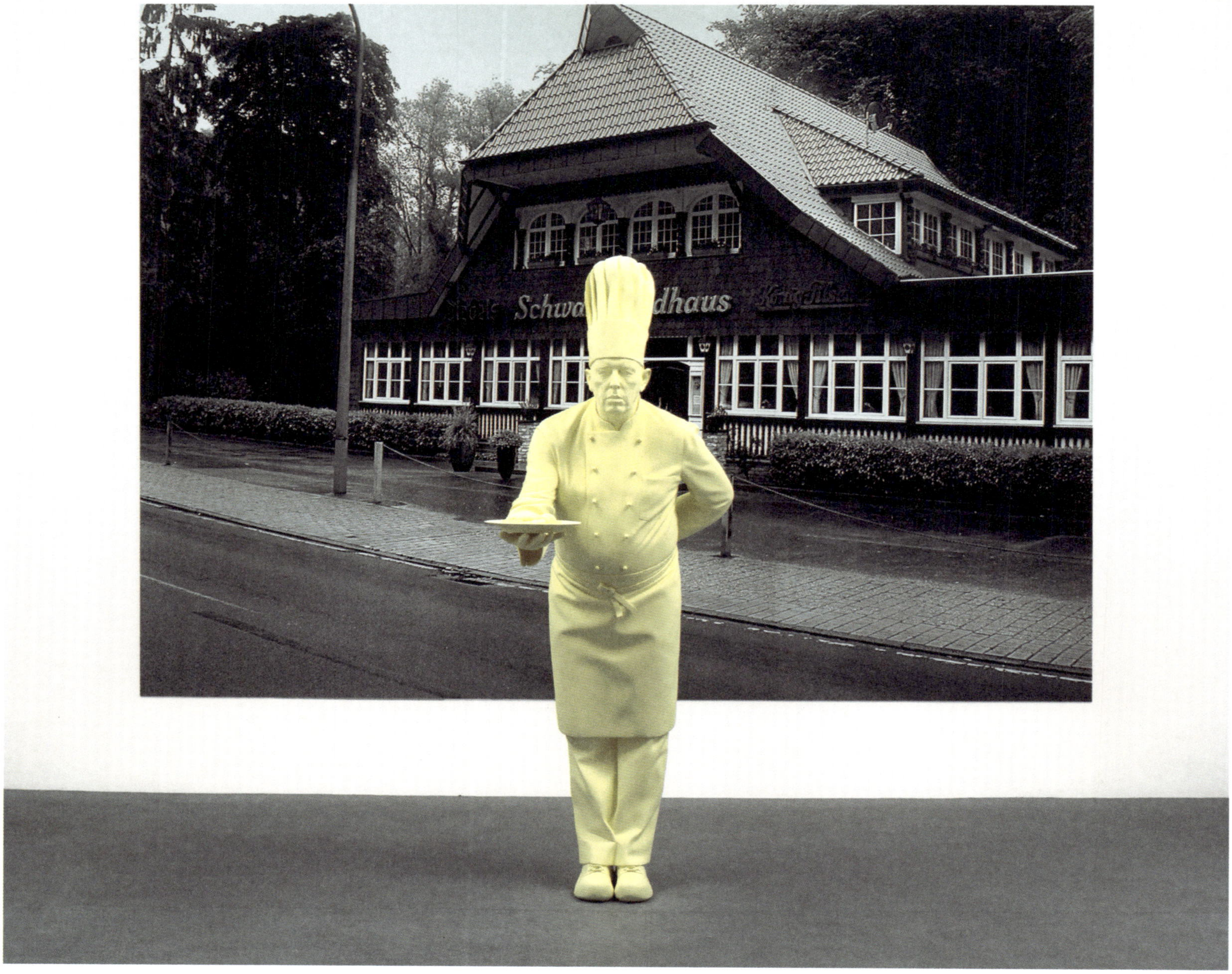

↑ ***Koch und 6. Foto (Schwarzwaldhaus)***
(Cook and 6th Photo [Black Forest House]),
2006/2008

Katharina Fritsch's sculptures are characterised by their simplicity and meticulous execution. The handmade or industrially crafted figures, animals and everyday objects she produces are often rendered in single colours and presented in unusual arrangements that mine personal and collective images, narratives and motifs. Fritsch has said that she thinks in images and is less concerned with sculpture than with 'making three-dimensional pictures'. This is achieved by a painstaking production process designed to simultaneously bring about the heightened presence of the three-dimensional figure and a concurrent flattening effect.

St. Katharina and 2nd Photo (Ivy) (2007), *Giant and 4th Postcard (Franconia)* (2008) and *Cook and 6th Photo (Black Forest House)* (2006/2008) exemplify this approach. In all of these works, backdrop images, based on postcards the artist collected as a child, provide a context for the figures: *St. Katharina and 2nd Photo (Ivy)* presents a matte black replica statue of Catherine of Siena with her emblems standing before a screenprint depicting a nearly abstract wall of lush ivy rendered with a blue tint; *Giant and 4th Postcard (Franconia)* depicts a huge grey primeval-looking man posed in front of an acidic green landscape of rocks and grottos; backed by a nostalgic and grim looking roadside restaurant, the lemon-coloured chef in *Cook and 6th Photo (Black Forest House)* greets visitors with a stereotypical host's bow, while presenting a platter of unenticing food. By juxtaposing sculpted figure and background, these works create a pictorial impression that evokes, in turn, a 'tableau', a fake cinematic green-screen and the perspectival illusion of Renaissance portraiture.

On the one hand, these figures seem familiar. They are immediately identifiable, due in part to their context and high degree of naturalism, but also to the store of popular imagery they draw on: religious iconography in the case of St Catherine; fairy tales and myths in the case of the giant; and promotional clichés of rotund chefs outside tourist restaurants for the cook. On the other hand, Fritsch's use of monochrome colouring and the light-absorbing quality of her matte finish, which denies reflection and depth, have rendered them strange. Nearly industrial in their flawlessness and absolutely motionless, these figures take on a quasi-spectral tone. Figure and background hover between presence and absence, the ordinary and the uncanny, evoking a process of derealisation.

Whether Fritsch casts her figures from live models (the 'giant' was cast from an acromegalic taxi driver and the cook from a model) or pre-existing cultural and commercial artefacts (in the case of St. Catherine), her approach suggests a reification of the human body. Modelled in plaster casts or by 3D scanners, the body becomes yet another object of reproduction, stripped of its individual traits so that it may acquire the status of an image.

Ryan Gander

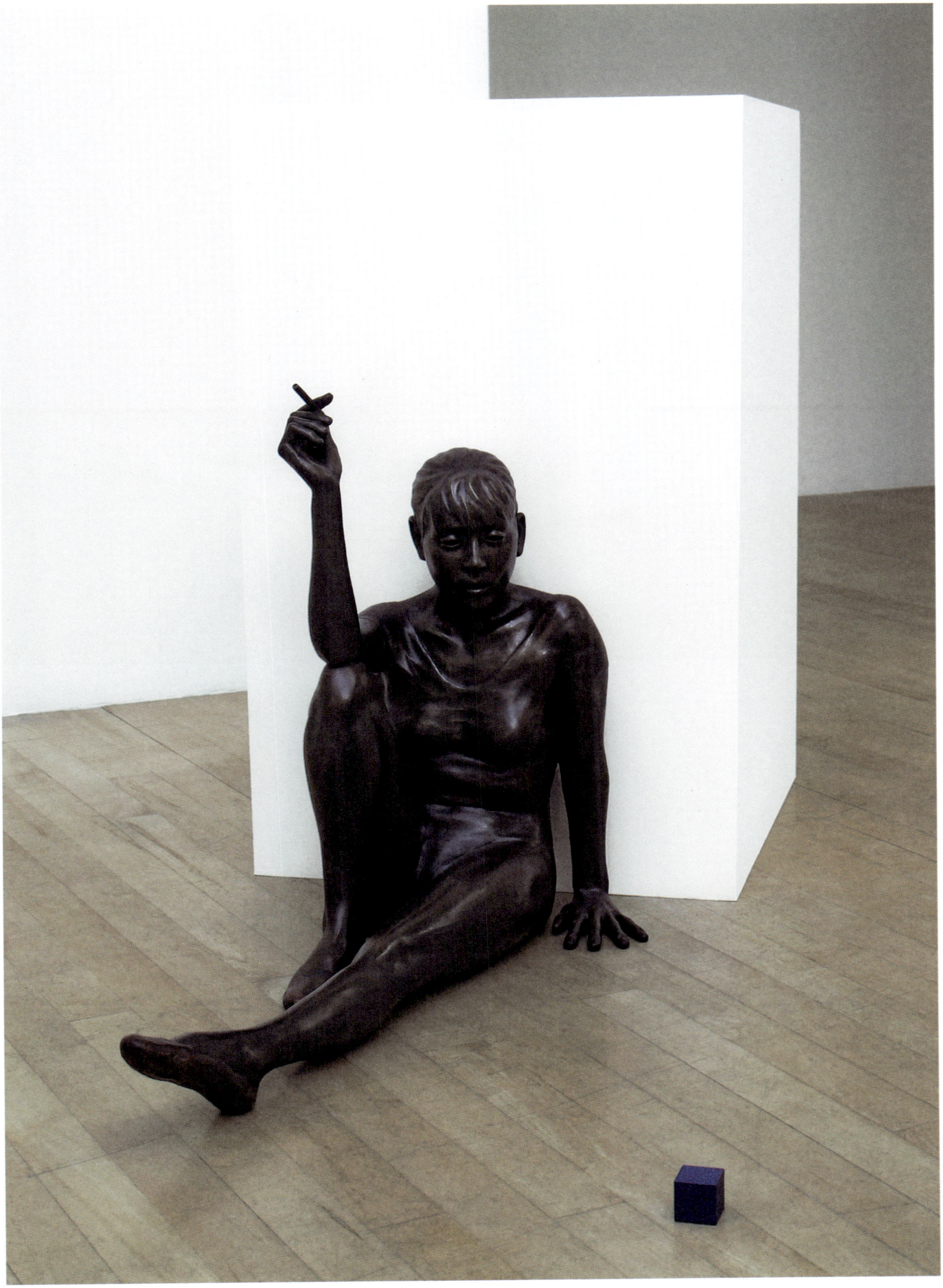

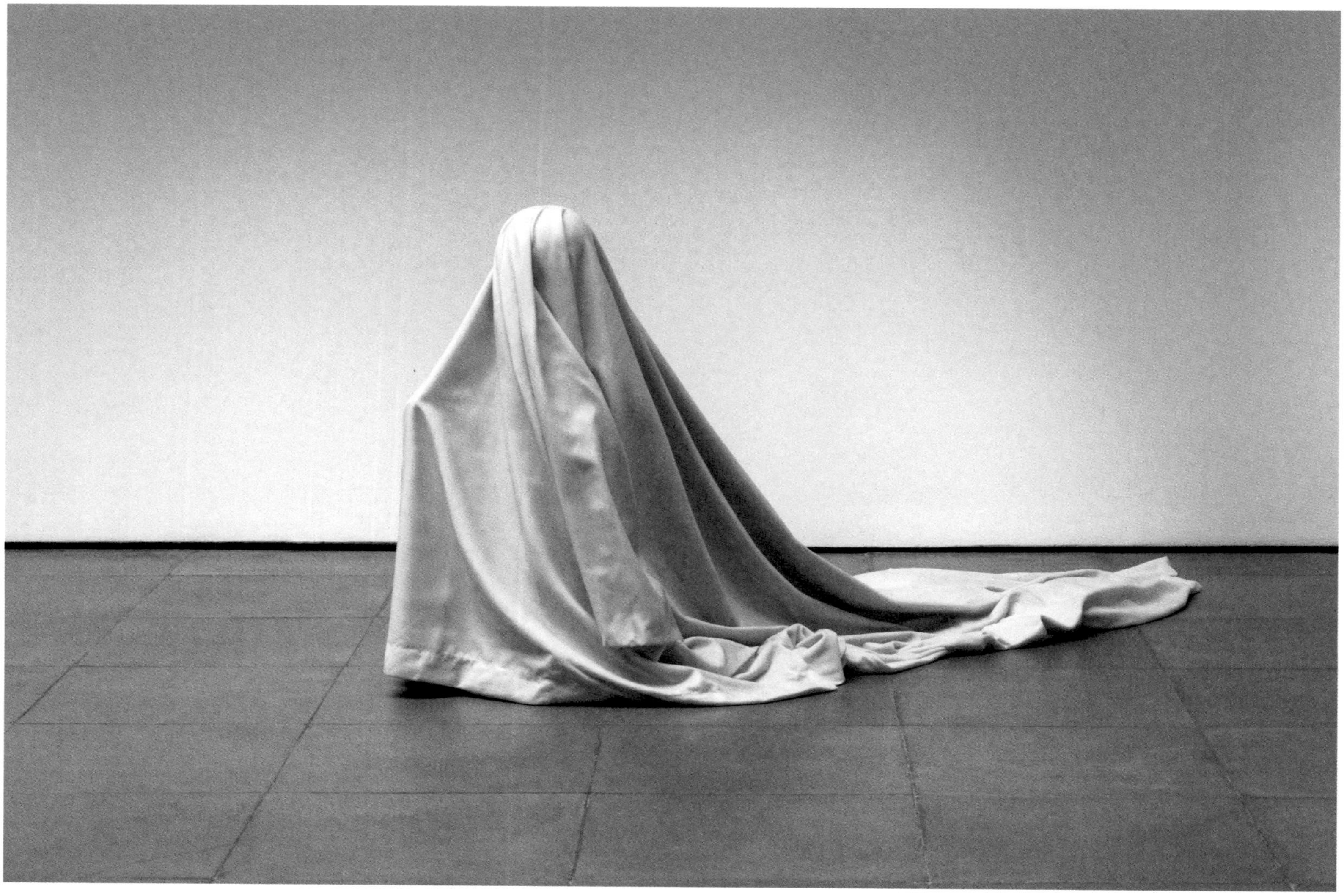

Ryan Gander is a thinker and producer of art, an imaginer and storyteller who sometimes uses events in art history as starting points for works. Since 2008, he has brought into being a succession of sculptures featuring a young ballerina. This bronze figure is based on Degas' *Little Dancer Aged Fourteen* (1880–81, cast c. 1922), which started life as a coloured wax statuette, dressed in a gauze tutu, with real hair and shoes. Apart from a single outing in Paris in 1881, the *Little Dancer* was not seen in public until the 1920s, when bronze casts of it were made and bought by museums.

← ***I don't blame you, or, When we made love you used to cry and I love you like the stars above and I'll love you 'til I die*, 2008**

↑ ***Tell my mother not to worry (ii)*, 2012**

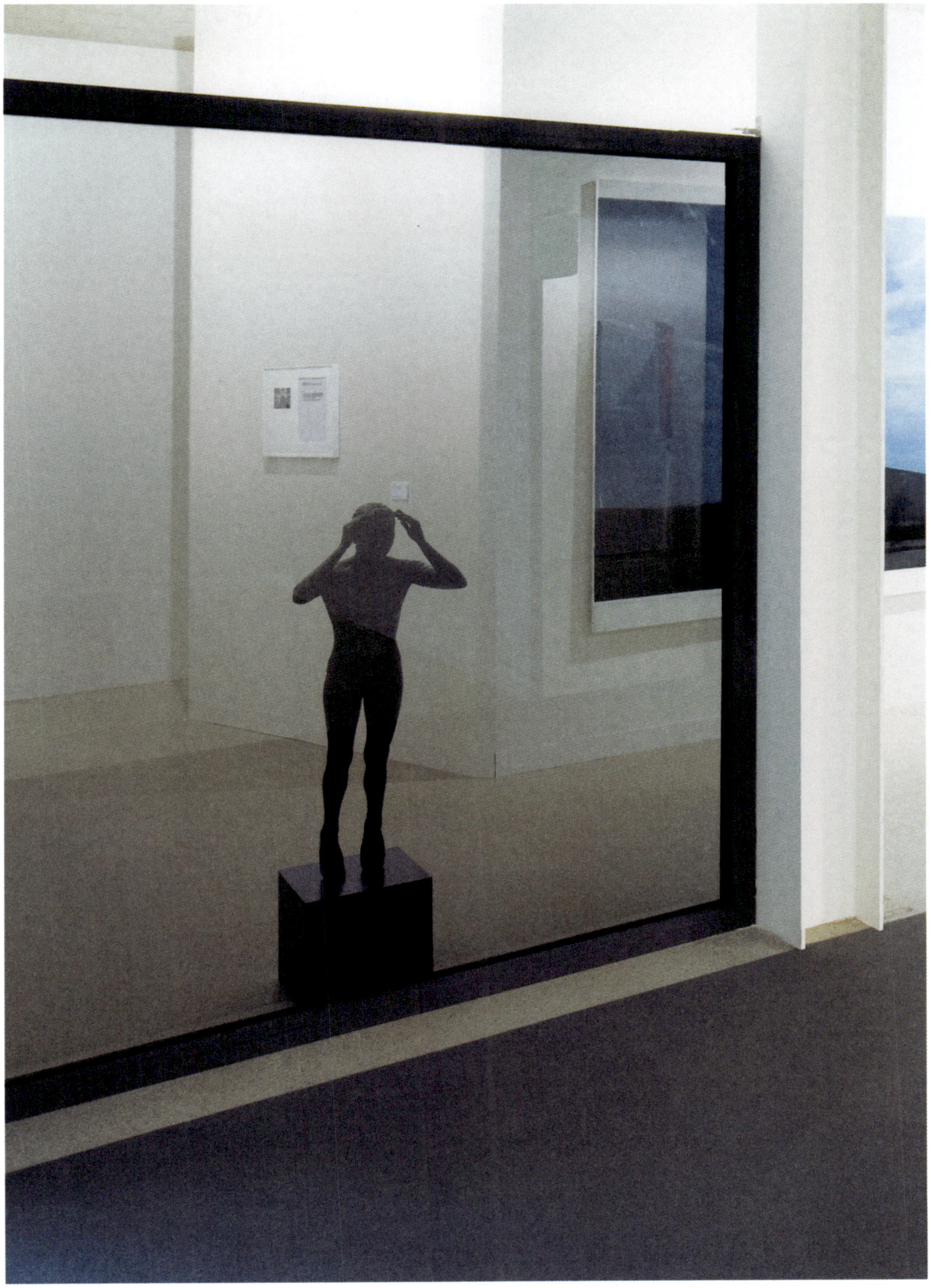

↑ ***Come up on different streets, they both were streets of shame Or Absinth blurs my thoughts, I think we should be moving on*, 2009**

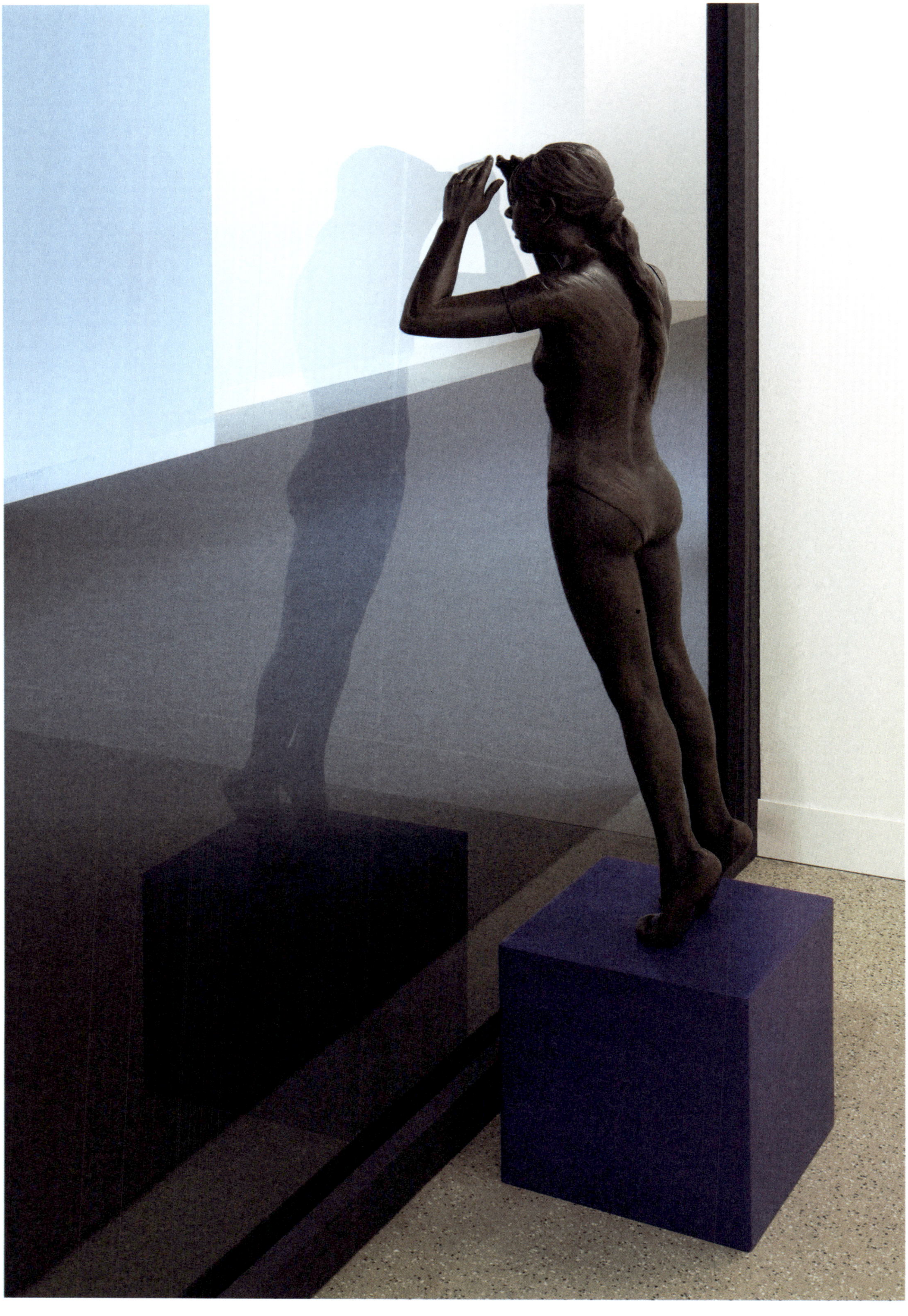

After Degas' *Little Dancer* had been standing on her pedestal for more than 80 years, Gander took pity on her. He let her get down from her plinth for a cigarette break, and provided a small blue cube — a piece of modern art — for her amusement. He also gave her a title for the work that included a line from Dire Straits' 'Romeo and Juliet': *I don't blame you, or, When we made love you used to cry and I love you like the stars above and I'll love you 'til I die* (2008). Since then, Gander has created further episodes in the dancer's afterlife. Each of the works contains the same three elements: a bronze ballerina, a white plinth and a blue cube, and the setting is always an art gallery. While the plinth and the cube change size from work to work, the scale of the figure remains constant. At two-thirds life-size, it is the same proportion that Degas used for the original. In almost every other way, however, the two dancers differ. As Gander points out, his work is not at all in Degas' style; 'it's not about reproducing his work, but about reproducing the character of the ballerina who posed for him.' Over time, as Gander's sequence progresses and his ballerina gets older, she shows less and less respect for the institution of art. In *Come up on different streets, they both were streets of shame Or Absinth blurs my thoughts, I think we should be moving on* (2009), she stands on the blue artwork in order to look through a window — at other art, or perhaps at no art at all. In later works her behaviour becomes increasingly transgressive.

The figure of Gander's ballerina is modelled on his wife (who happens to be a gallery owner). The process is this: she poses, he takes a photograph, a sculptor makes the figure in wax, which is then sent to a foundry and cast in bronze. A similar process takes place with *Tell my mother not to worry (ii)* (2012). But here the material used is marble resin, which gives this life-size sculpture of Gander's four-year-old daughter playing ghosts with a bed sheet the disquieting appearance of funerary art.

← ***Come up on different streets, they both were streets of shame Or Absinth blurs my thoughts, I think we should be moving on*, 2009**

Isa Genzken

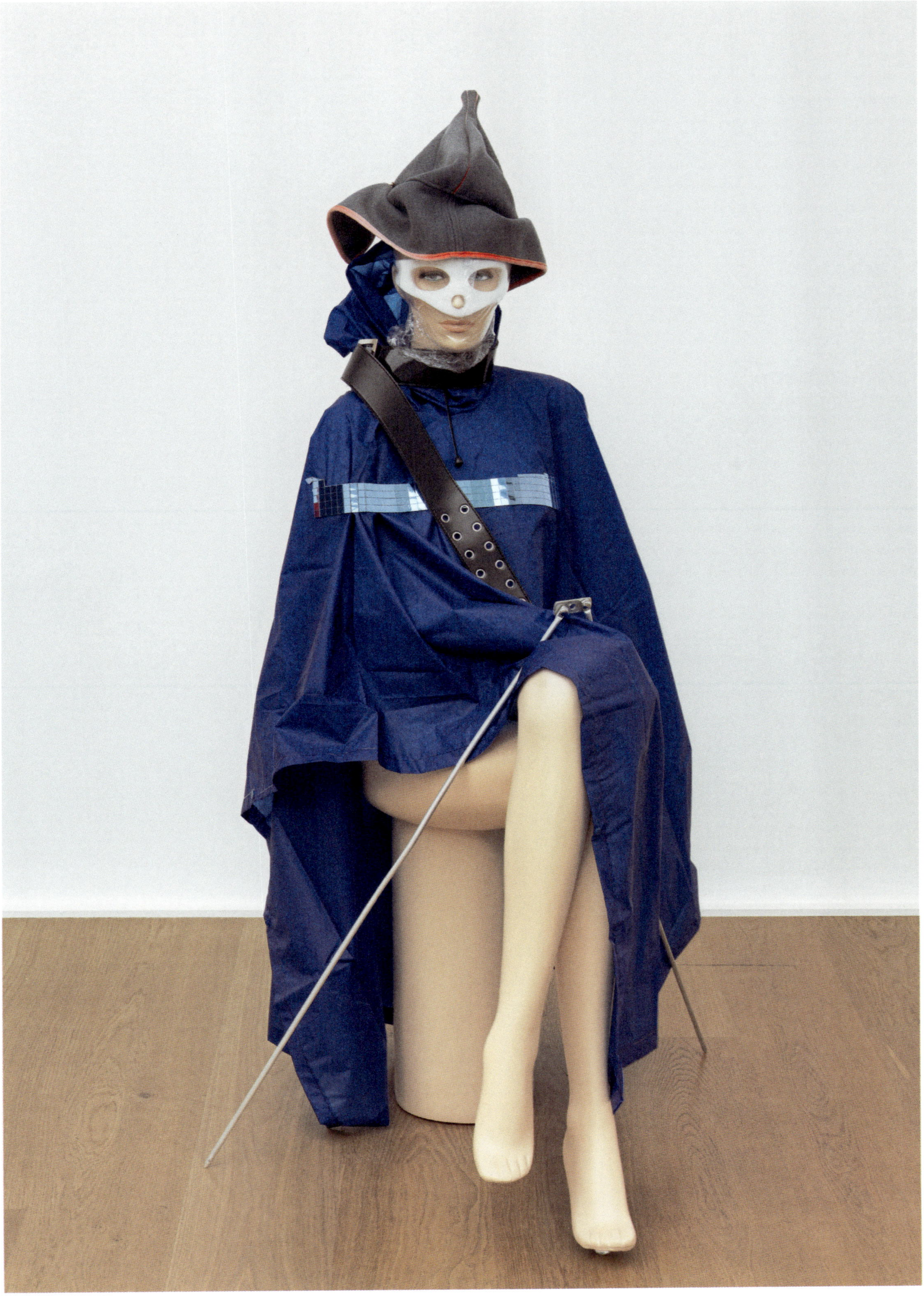

Resembling android clubbers, Isa Genzken's carnivalesque mannequins are apparelled in a sort of 'deviation chic'. As alarming as they are in their inscrutable remoteness, these outlandish beings invite close inspection. Both of these *Untitled* works (2012) wear clothes borrowed from Genzken's own wardrobe or fashioned from salvaged materials which she has carefully chosen and assembled. Every detail, from dribbles and grunge to masks, stickers and reflective surfaces, is pertinent.

Mentioning that there is 'a permanent misunderstanding' regarding the materials that she uses, Genzken says, 'I am not interested in ready-mades. The meaning is in the combination of things… I want to animate the viewers, hold a mirror up to them'. Her choice of cheap or discarded materials reflects her concern with environmental issues, and a horror and fascination with the excesses of contemporary urban life. She uses similarly low-grade materials in other works concerned with the experience of the metropolis: sculptures that express her thoughts about architecture, and about buildings as sculpture, and their effects on everyday life.

The *Untitled* works shown in *The Human Factor* are part of a series of seven mannequin sculptures that are themselves a sort of dress-rehearsal for a larger work made in 2013, called *Schauspieler* (Actors), which has a cast of twelve characters. With each of these groups, there is a strong sense of audience participation: visitors are encouraged to mingle with the figures, walk around them, and become part of the crowd. As Genzken said, with regard to an earlier work: 'I had wanted to make sculptures portraying a scene from a film, that is, rather like models: not sculptures in the traditional sense but a flow of figures and perspectives. You could think of them as scenes in a sci-fi film.'

← ***Untitled*, 2012**

→ ***Untitled*, 2012**

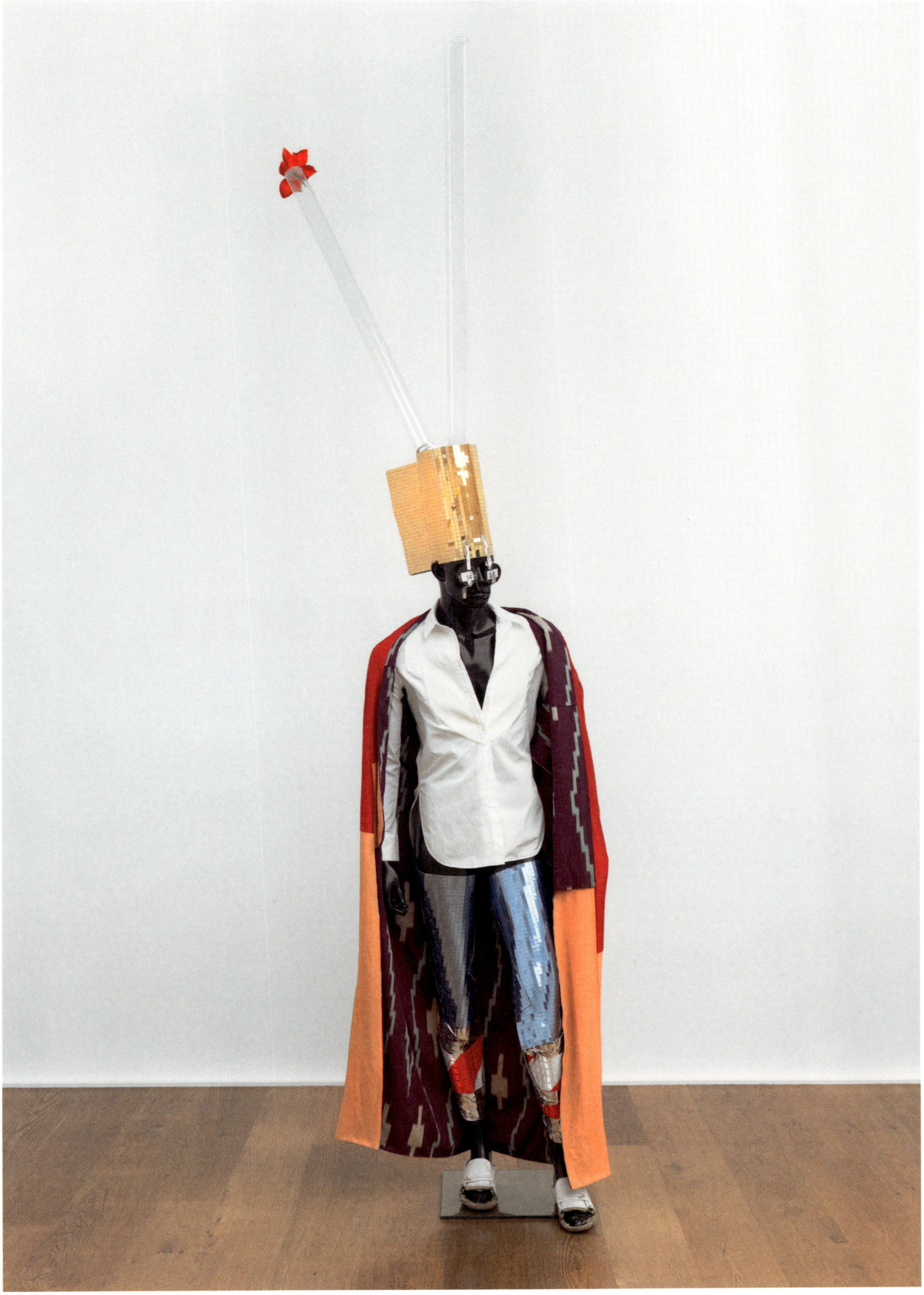

Rachel Harrison

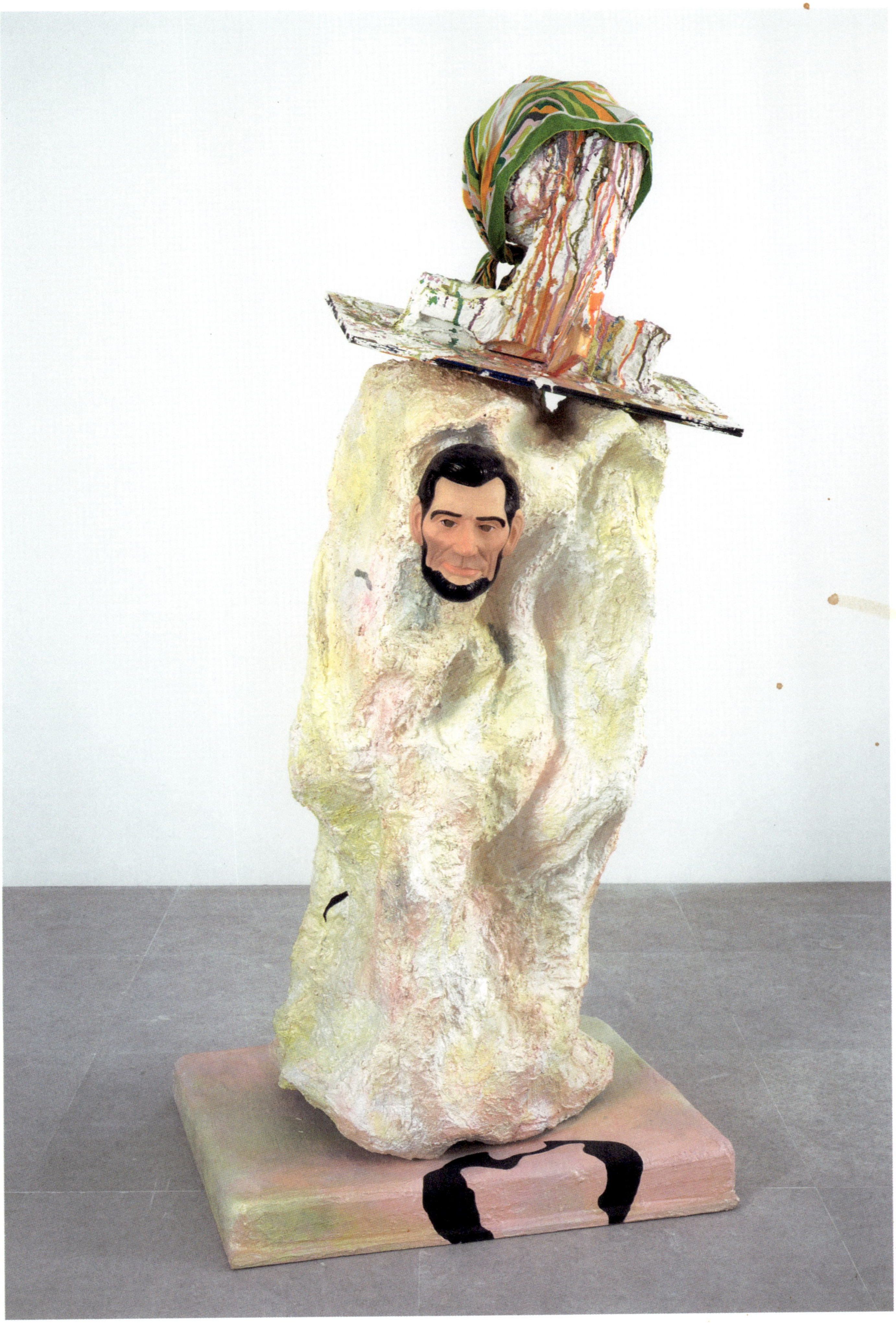

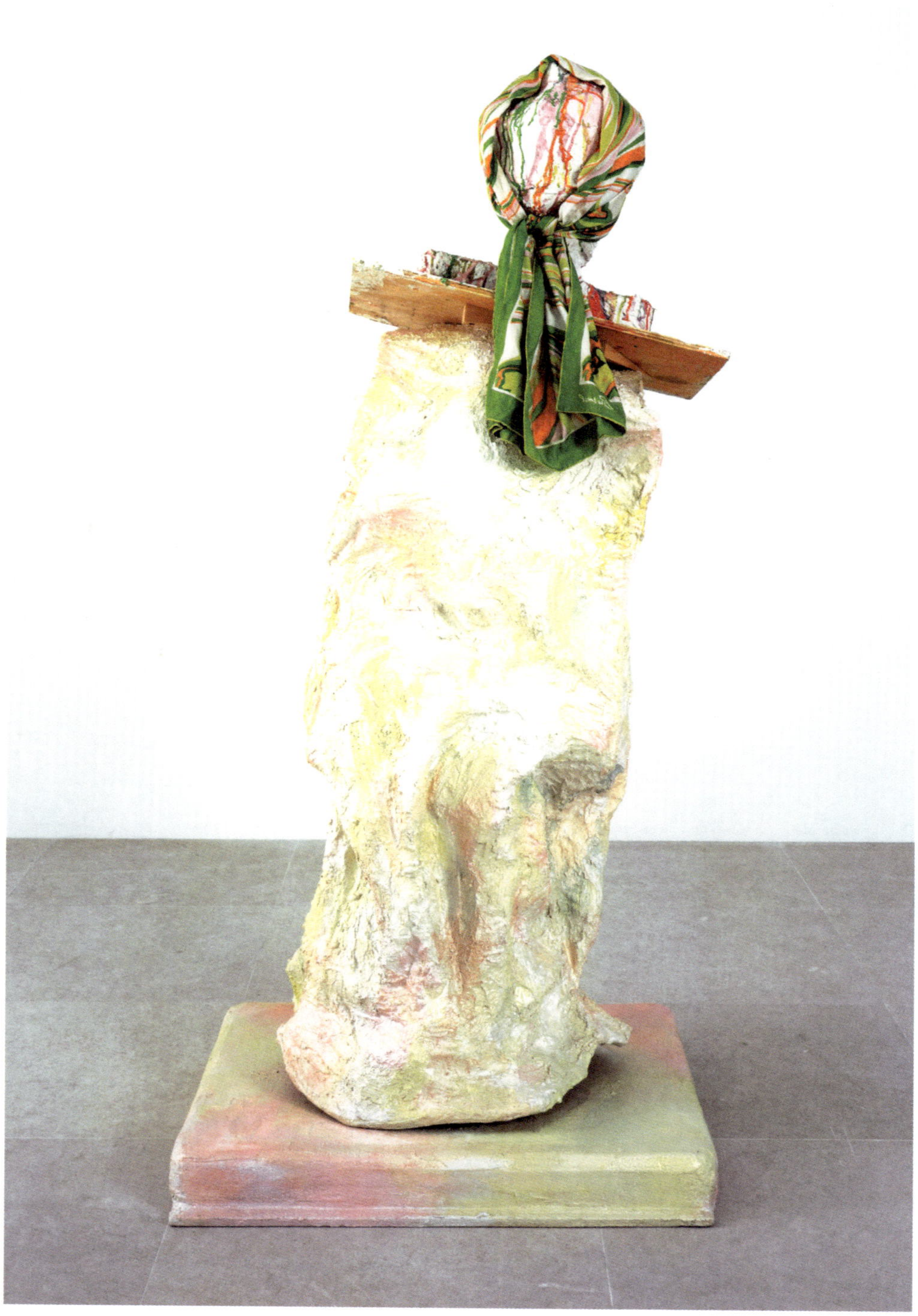

Rachel Harrison's apparently casual assemblages always contain far more in the way of matter, allusion, humour and meaning than a first or second glance suggests. They play with dualities: figuration and abstraction; painting and sculpture; the found and the made; art history and popular culture; the legible and the illegible. They also often deal with the human figure in surprising ways.

In *Schmatte with President* (2006), the body is a shapeless menhir, reminiscent perhaps of Auguste Rodin's bundled-up *Monument to Balzac* (1891). Harrison's figure is topped with a faceless head wrapped around, mammy-like, with a headscarf, which may or may not be the *schmatte* of the title. (According to the authors of *Meshuggenary: Celebrating the World of Yiddish* (Simon & Schuster, 2002), 'When referring to stuff, [*schmatte* is] rags and shoddy merchandise, no matter what the price tag. Referring to people, it can mean someone not worthy of respect or someone who is a brown-nosing sycophant.') While the pale monolith is delicately painted in pastel colours, the head — back and front — is covered in bright streams and trickles of runny acrylic. Below the plasterer's board shoulders, a mask of President Lincoln is embedded as in a comic Mount Rushmore. Is it worn as a giant badge of allegiance, or is it simply a slippage? And what about the black outline painted where the figure's feet might be — what does that signify?

If *Schmatte with President* brings to mind images of slavery, and the fact that in recent years America's foremost national martyr and abolitionist has been accused of racism, *Jack Lemmon* (2011) takes such free association much further. As with *Schmatte*, the work's main element is a painted concretion, but in this case it forms a garish bulwark, a ruined

← ***Schmatte with President*, 2006**

↑ ***Schmatte with President*, 2006**

safeguard for the small body that cavorts beside it. The figure itself is two-faced, a Janus-like kidult he/she. Depending on which way you approach it, you are met with either the calm, bespectacled face of shop-window-mannequin womanhood, or the smirking mask of Dick Cheney, 46th Vice President of the United States, perpetrator of what many consider to be one of the biggest foreign policy blunders of modern times, and code-named 'Angler' by the US Secret Service.

In Harrison's assemblages, the title is as much part of the work as any of its other elements. As she herself has said, 'a title is an object; it is another place where I can add a "thing".' In *Jack Lemmon*, the riffs on lemon as a colour and as slang for a defective thing are as significant as the reference to the great comic actor, who dressed in drag to escape the mob in *Some Like it Hot* (1959), and was known as 'Dickhead' in one of his later roles.

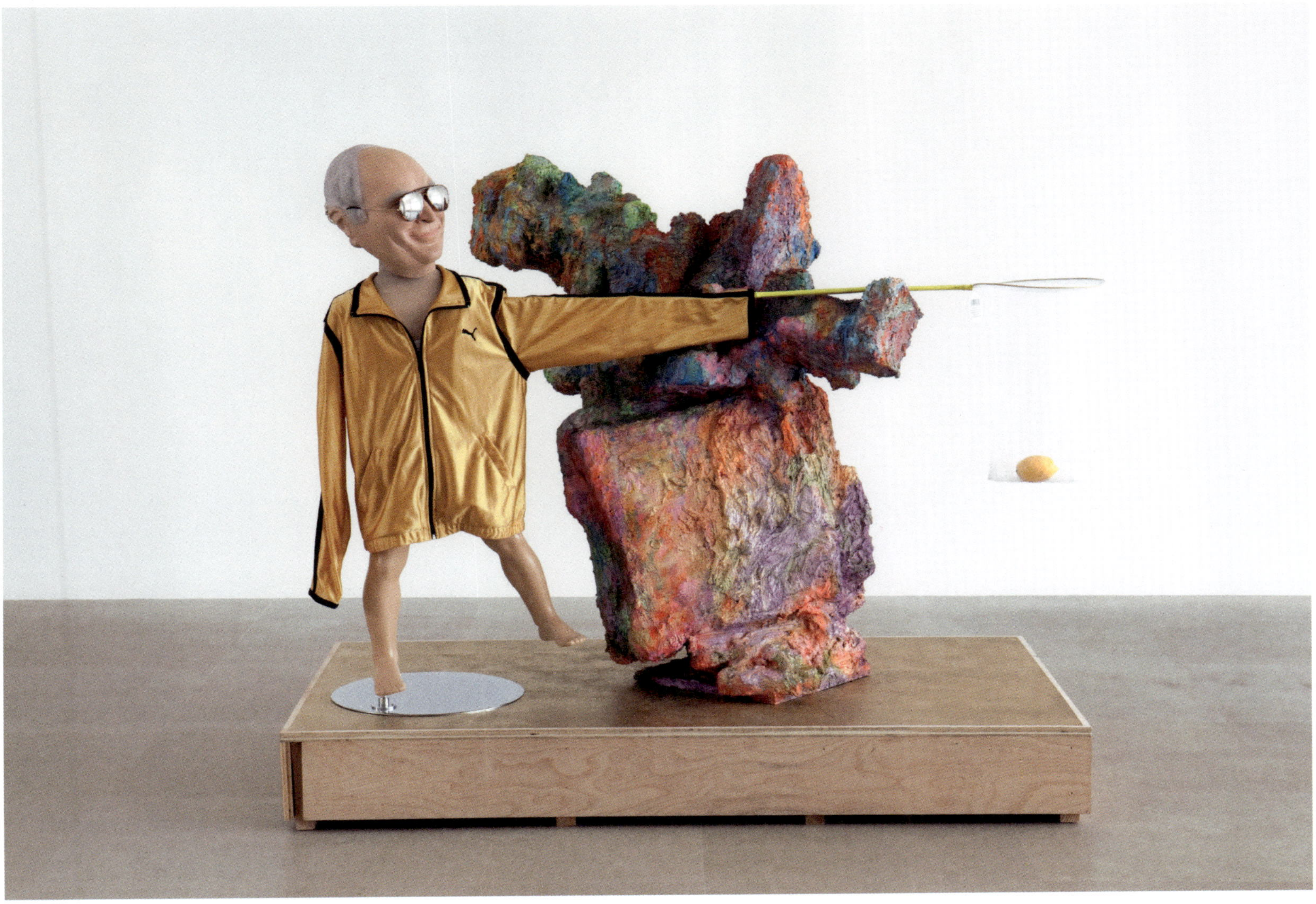

↑ ***Jack Lemmon*, 2011**

→ ***Jack Lemmon* (detail), 2011**

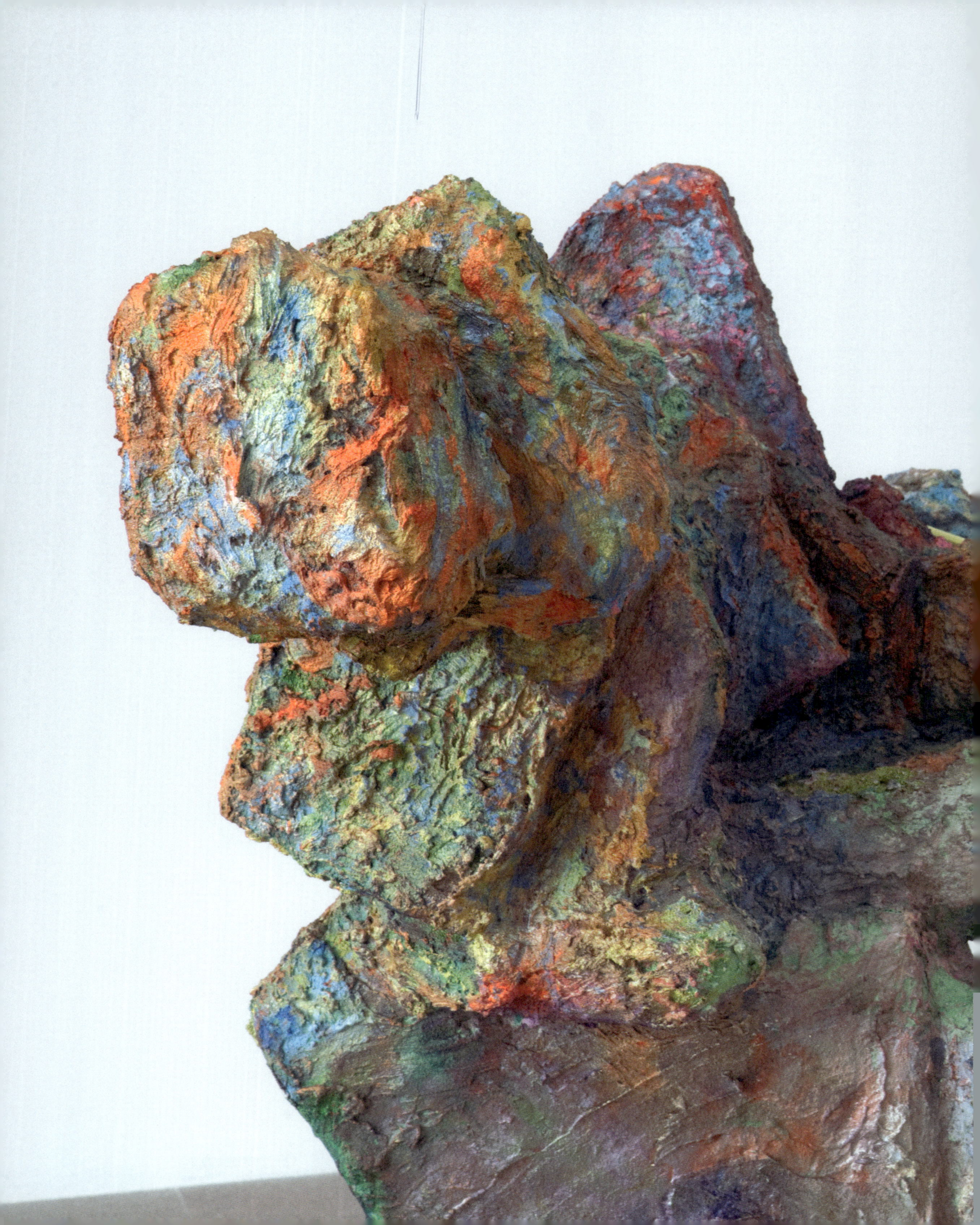

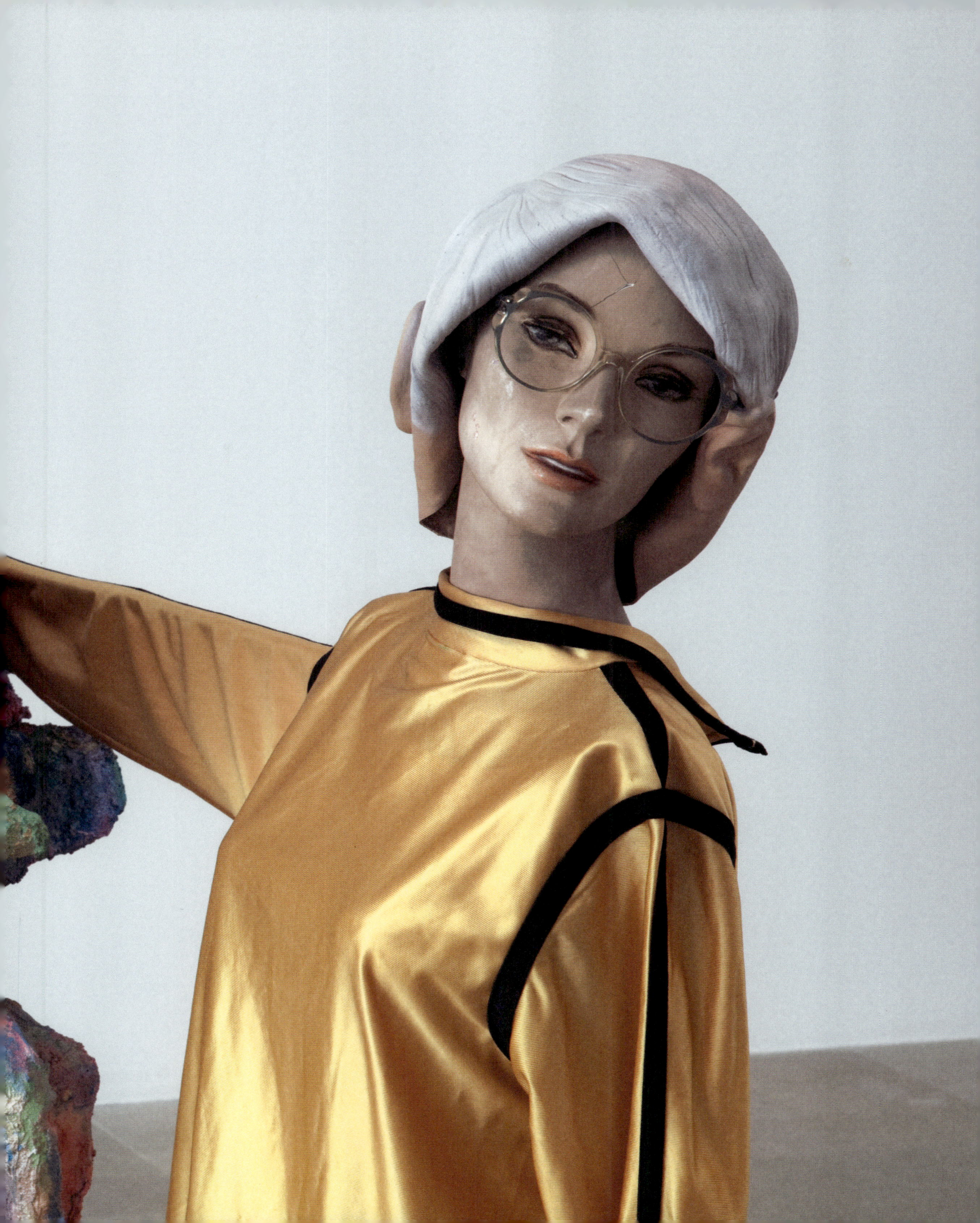

Georg **Herold**

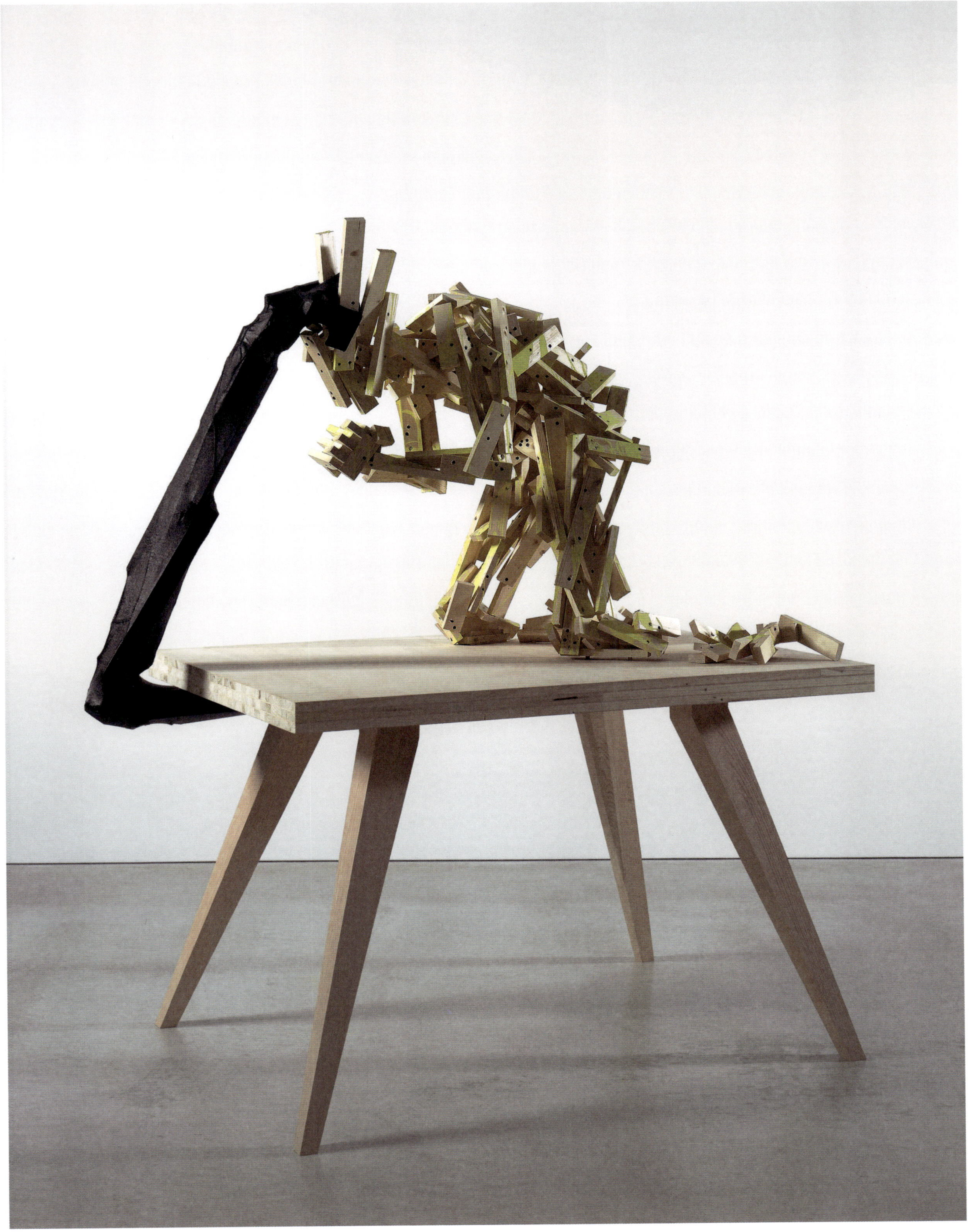

One day in 1977, when he was still a student, Georg Herold fixed a strip of timber to the studio wall and called it *Präsentation der ersten Latte* (Presentation of the First Batten). Since then, plain wooden roofing battens — which are cheap, and available in every hardware store — have continued to play a leading role in his work. At first, even though they sometimes had titles that referred to real people, Herold's batten-sculptures were abstract structures. *Goethe-Latte* (Goethe Batten, 1982) consists of two battens which become yardsticks, leaning against the wall. One, which is more than two metres long, bears the name of the great writer and thinker, while the other, which measures only 60 centimetres, carries an inscription that translates roughly as 'by comparison, some loser' (in German, the word 'latte' is slang for an erect penis).

Over the past few years, Herold has created figurative sculptures from battens, producing works that are at once attention-grabbing and frustratingly minimal. Some of these, such as *My Sweet Lord* (2009), are more or less life-size; others, like *Blühendes Leben* (2009), are vast. In the case of *My Sweet Lord*, the work is constructed from a mass of short sections clustered to form a schematic, stereometric shape, like an exploded three-dimensional drawing of a body. The kneeling figure is clamped by a gigantic canvas-covered arm whose robot-like hand grips the supplicant's head with such force that its lower legs have shattered.

In works such as the emaciated and wantonly provocative *Blühendes Leben*, Herold encases almost the entire wooden framework in wet canvas which shrinks as it dries, constraining and contorting the battens and pulling the figure's body parts this way and that. After this, the work is sprayed with glossy car body paint. Speaking about the whole process, which becomes a battle for domination between the art and the artist, Herold describes how the figures resist him and how they struggle and fight back. 'I intend to reach a state that is ambiguous and allows all sorts of interpretations', he says. The title *Blühendes Leben*, which translates as 'Life in full bloom', is a mocking swipe at kitsch images of reclining female nudes. About this impossibly posed, aggressive, DIY structure that is barely a figure, Herold asserts: 'beauty was never the goal, rather an attempt to develop and implement a technology, and suddenly you realise that nice things can be created in this way.'

← ***My Sweet Lord*, 2009**

→ ***Blühendes Leben*, 2009**

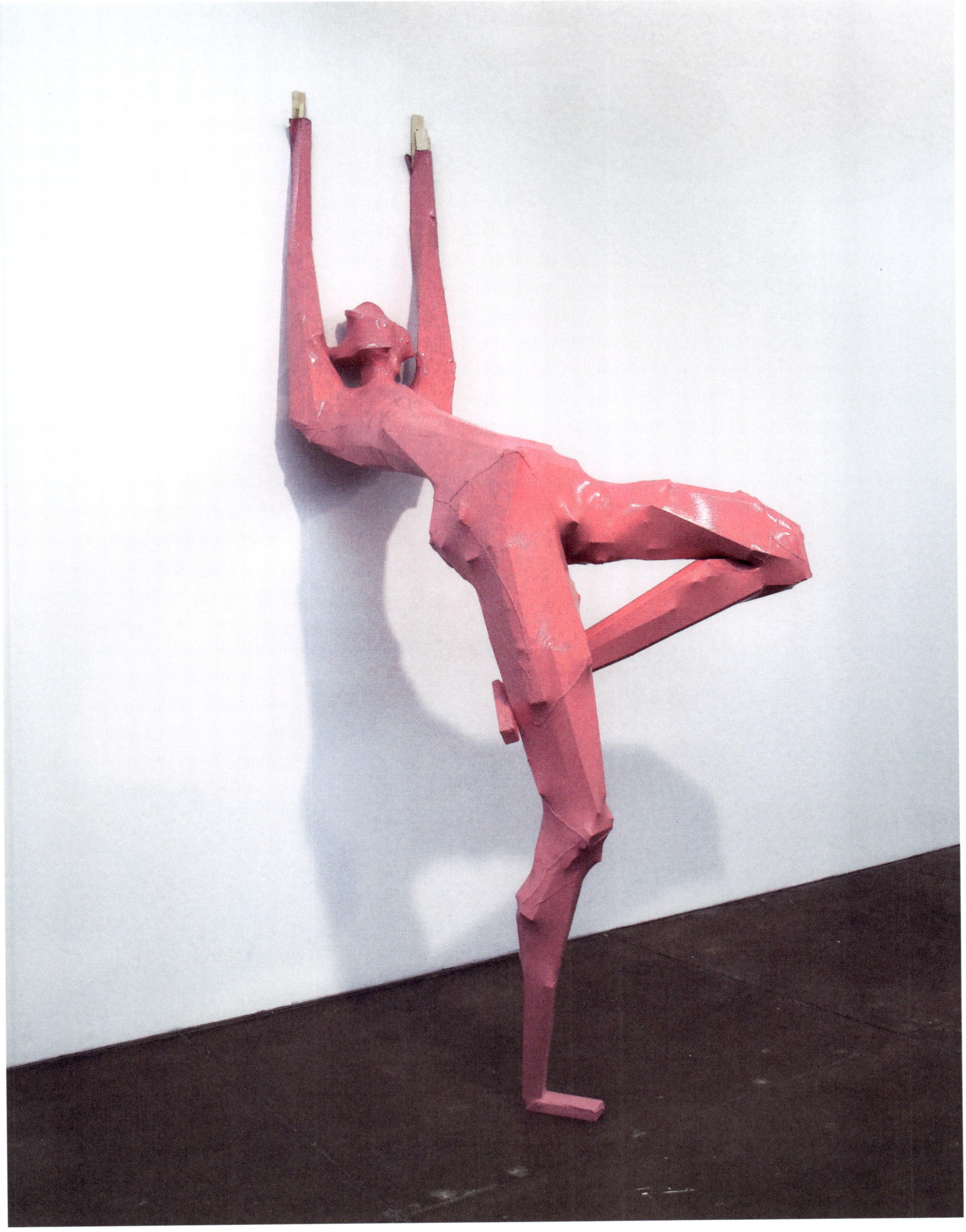

Thomas **Hirschhorn**

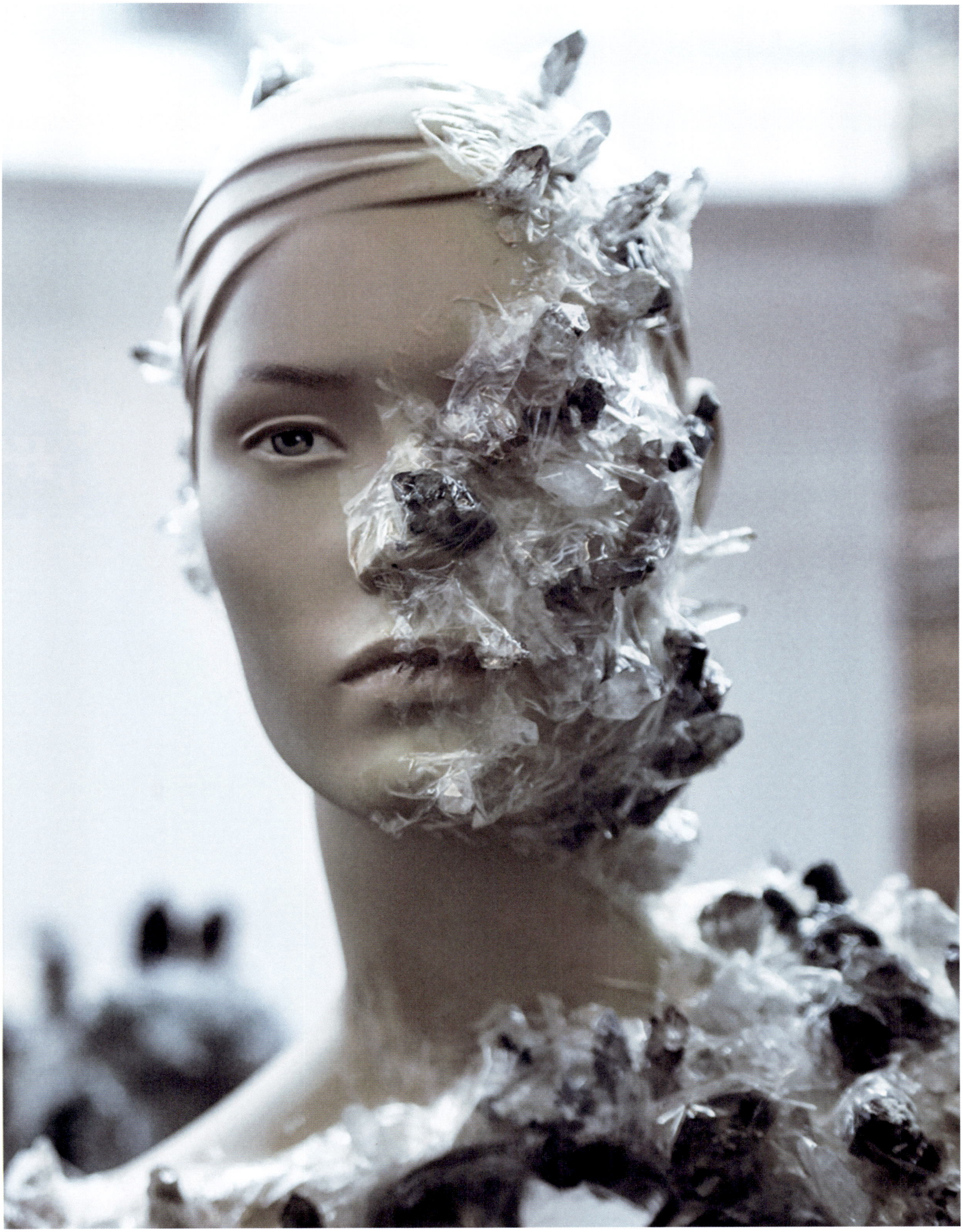

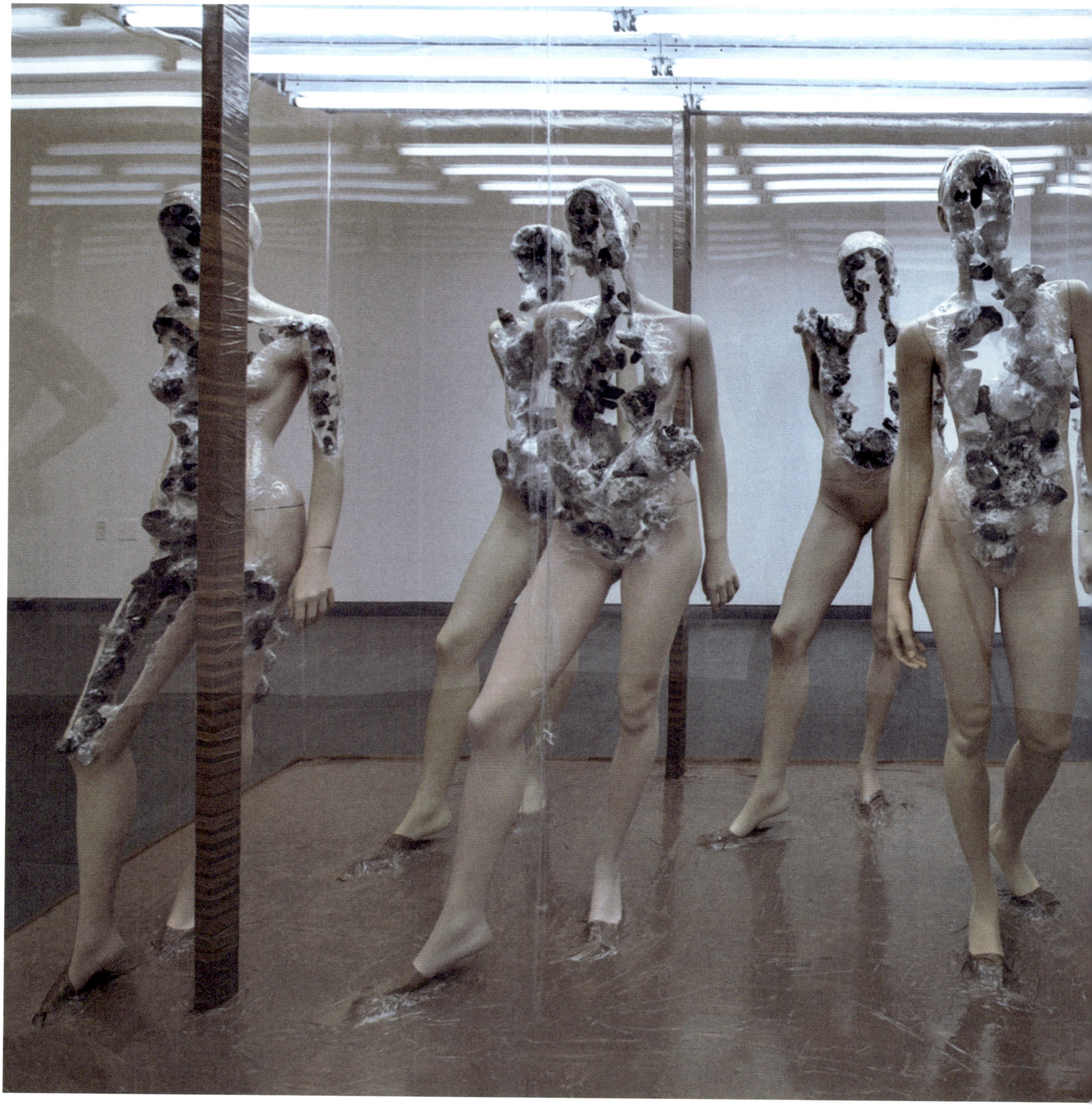

← *Resistance-Subjecter* (detail), 2011

↑ *Resistance-Subjecter*, 2011

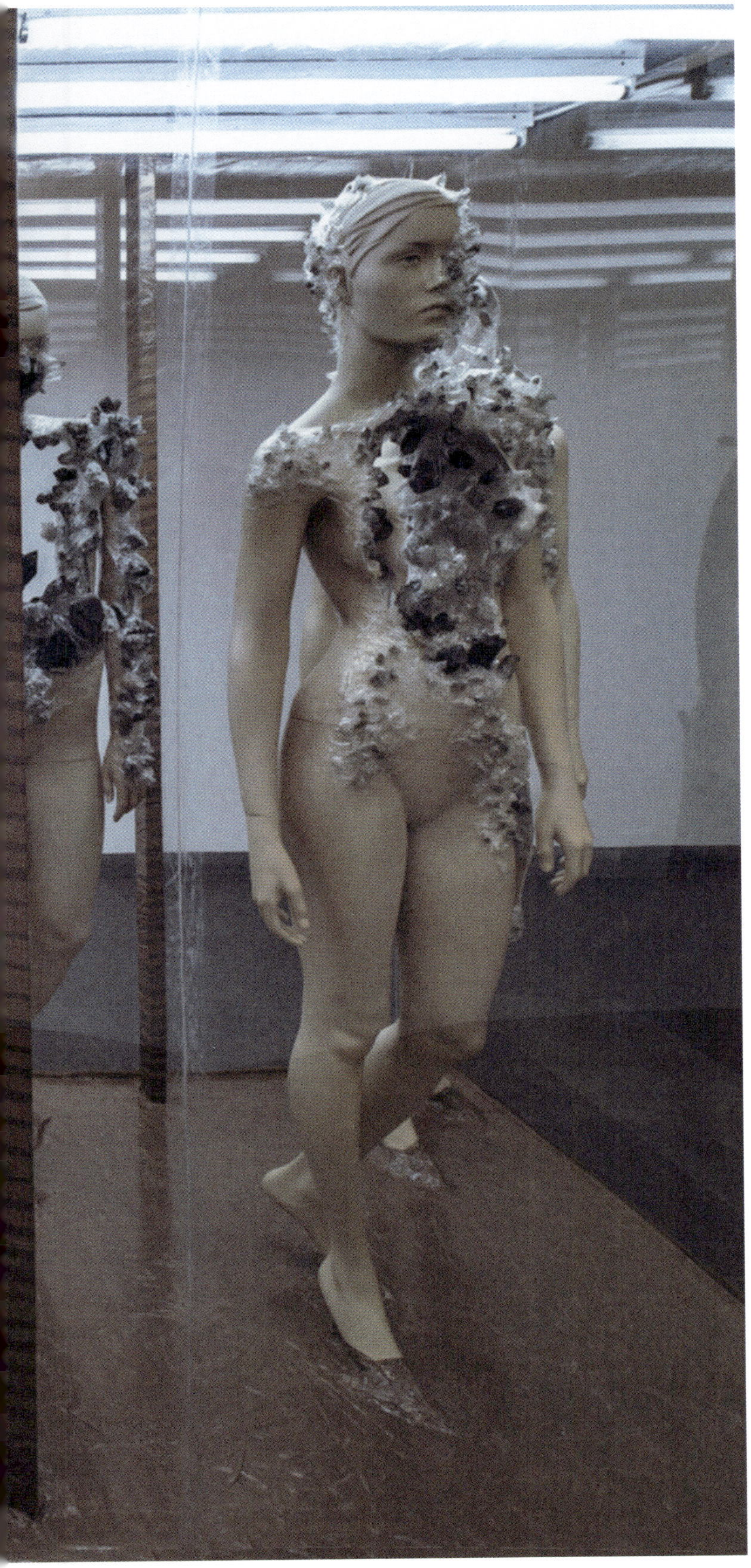

Thomas Hirschhorn describes himself as 'an artist, a worker and a soldier', explaining that he fights 'hierarchy and demagogy'. His complex sculptural environments explore contemporary social conditions, combining philosophy with the debris of modern life and piling concepts and materials together in vast, rambling accretions. They are often constructed from plywood, cardboard, aluminium foil, packing tape, photocopies and printouts — commonplace elements that 'everybody knows and uses in their everyday life, not for doing art'. He regards these works, which address subjects as various as war, protest, pop culture, fanaticism and fundamentalism, as 'collages in the third dimension', defining this as 'putting things together that are not meant to be put together'.

Hirschhorn's works are equally striking for the worldview they express, often colliding images of violence with objects of fashion or art in settings that mimic shop-window displays. *4 Women* (2008) juxtaposes images of mutilated male bodies, culled from the internet, with female mannequins standing in a harshly lit showcase. The vitrine, or 'display' as Hirschhorn terms his environments, and its associations with commercial consumer culture, also features prominently in *Resistance-Subjecter* (2011), where gaping body cavities and proliferating crystalline formations puncture the familiar seductive poses of the mannequins.

For Hirschhorn, the mannequin constitutes 'a material like any other, it is an inclusive material, unintimidating, unpretentious and democratic [...] like cardboard or pictures torn from a magazine'. The mannequin serves as a surrogate other, a stand-in for our own selves and for the subjectivity of others. In his words, it 'represents the smallest distance between me and the image of another. A mannequin is another form of me, a surface of projection.' It becomes a surface of inscription in the case of *4 Women*, where two of the mannequins are tattooed with a plethora of messages and slogans. At the same time, all four figures exude a foamy substance, the ink-blue colour suggestive of chemical, artificial matter. These eruptions progressively consume the bodies, while the increasingly dense body writing speaks of our conscription into a social and ideological text.

In *Resistance-Subjecter*, the body becomes a surface of impact. Here, the mannequins have been blasted apart, eviscerated and colonised by makeshift crystalline shapes. In both cases, the mannequin stands as a surrogate body that is easily invaded, brutalised, even destroyed. Central to Hirschhorn's explorations of the human form is the idea of concretion — a process through which a form is impacted and hardened. *4 Women* sees the body engulfed and disfigured by the action of external forces, social or physical. In *Resistance-Subjecter* — which was part of a much larger 'environment' presented at the Swiss Pavilion in the 2011 Venice Biennale — the hardening comes from within, as the body is transmuted into crystalline shapes and mineral form. Both capture our contemporary condition as one marked by fragility, where exposure to the world, the reality of war, the surfeit of media images and excessive consumption leaves us either broken by its violence or inured to it.

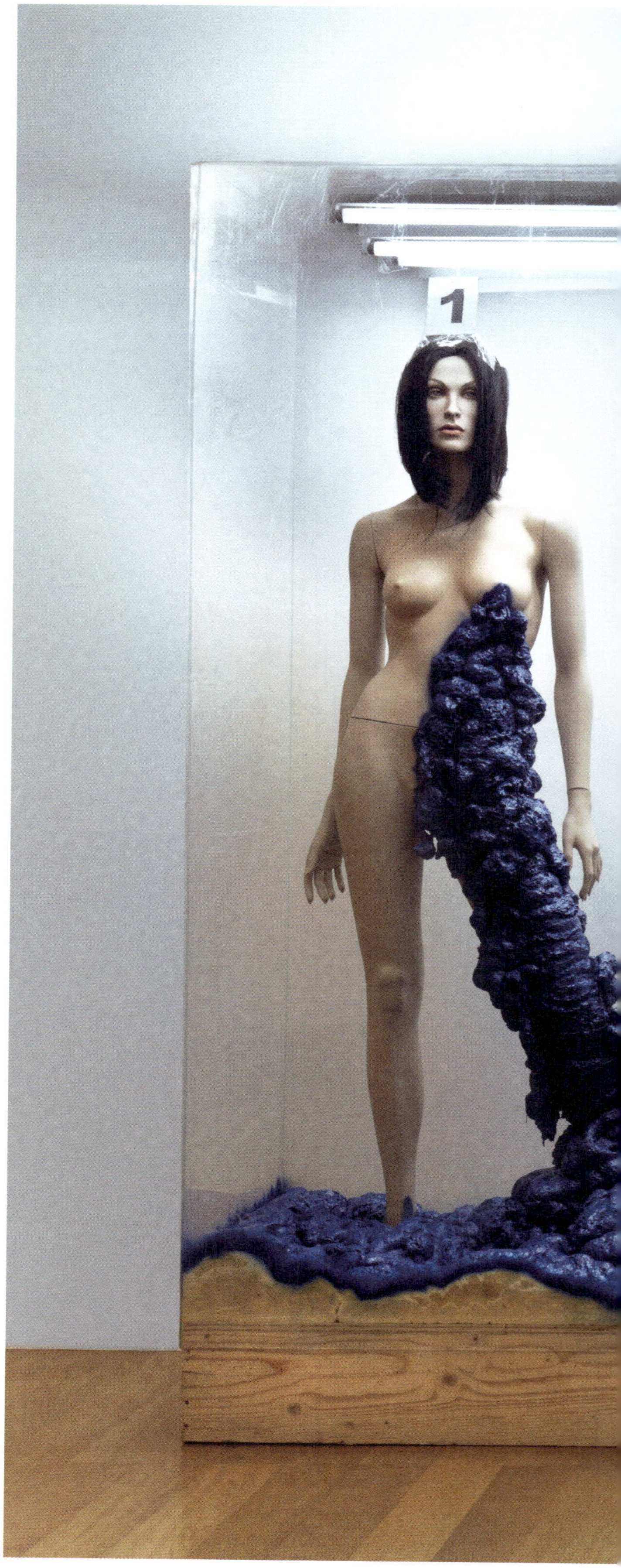

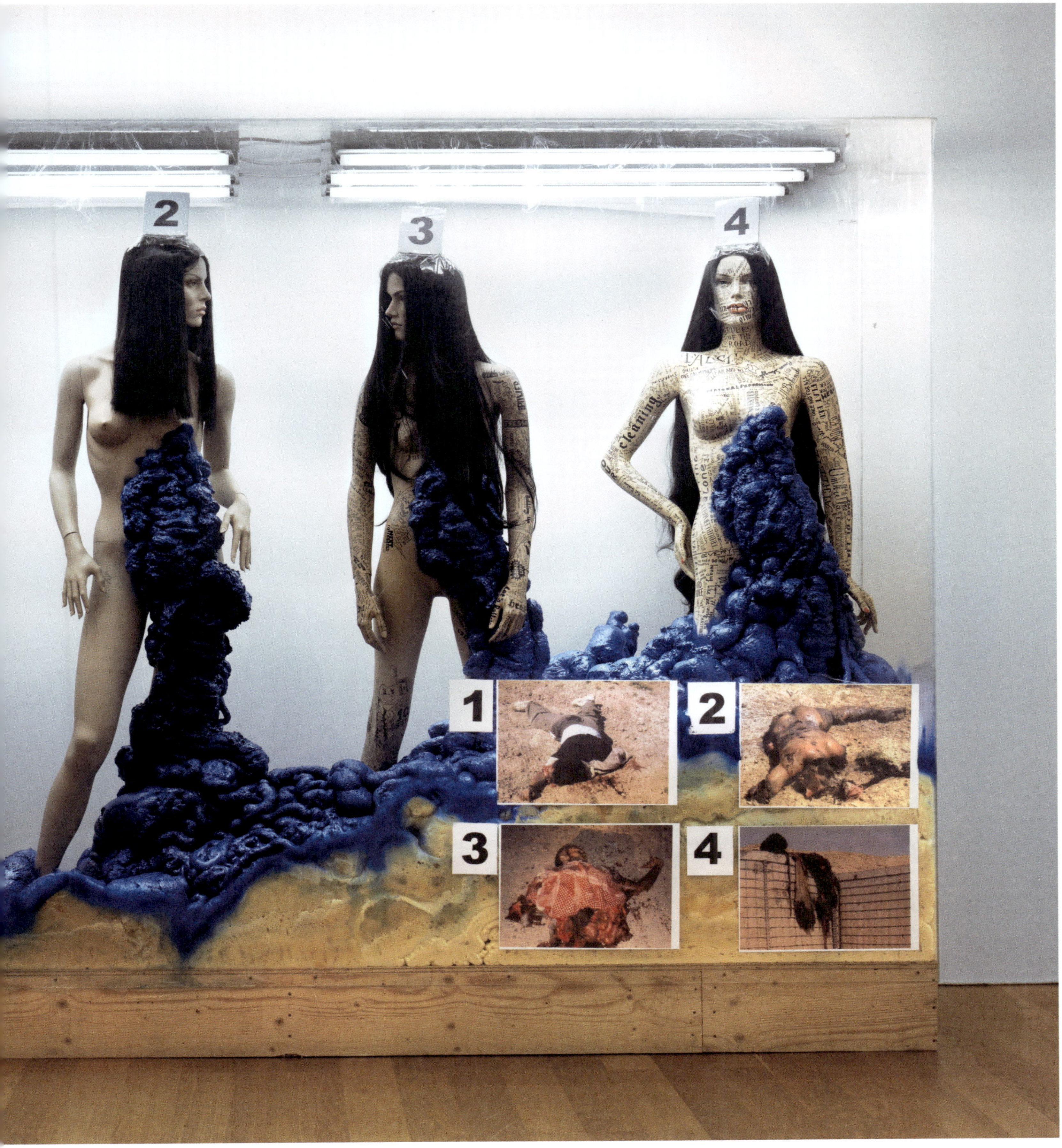

↑ ***4 Women*, 2008**

→ ***4 Women* (detail), 2008**

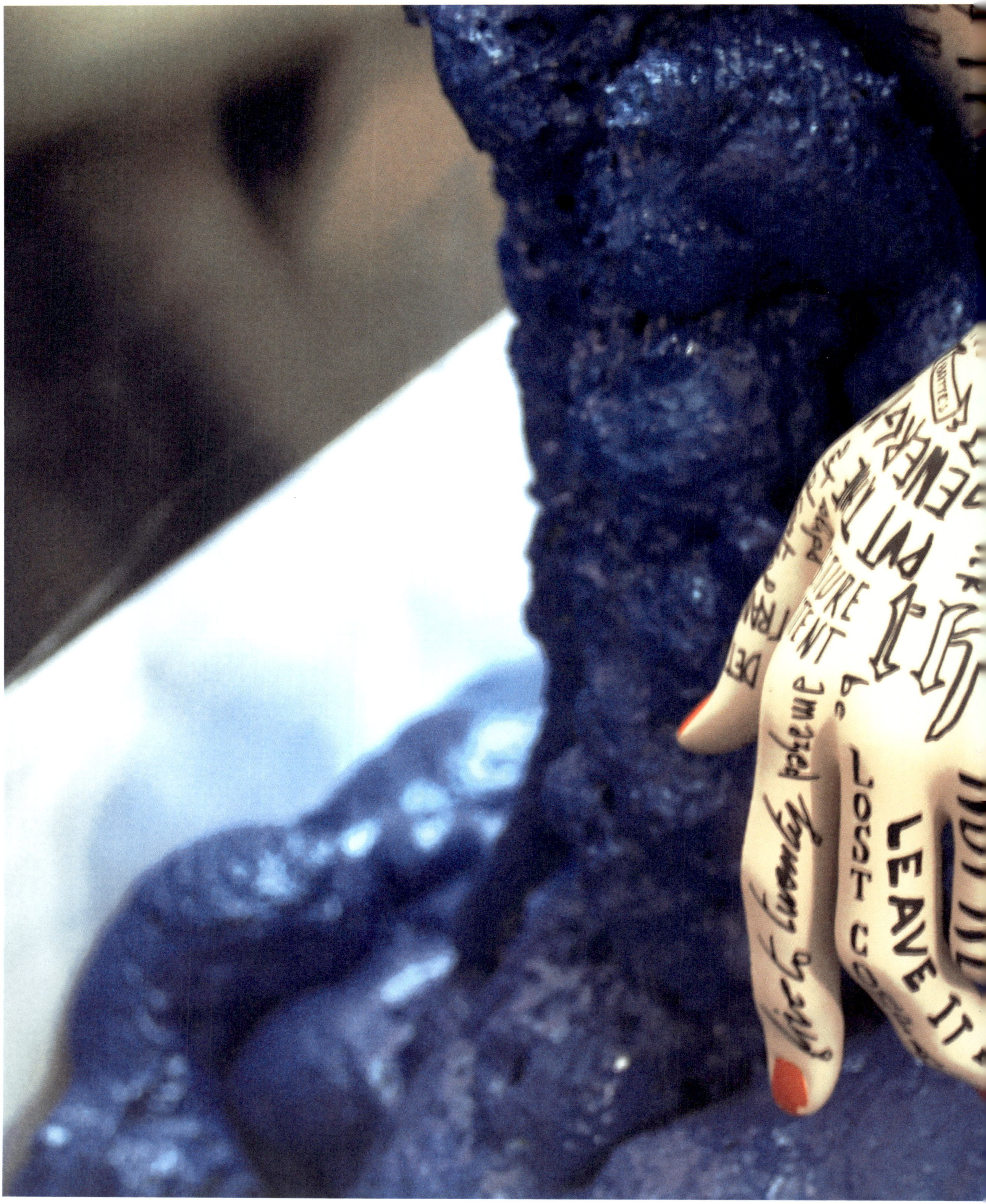
LEAVE IT

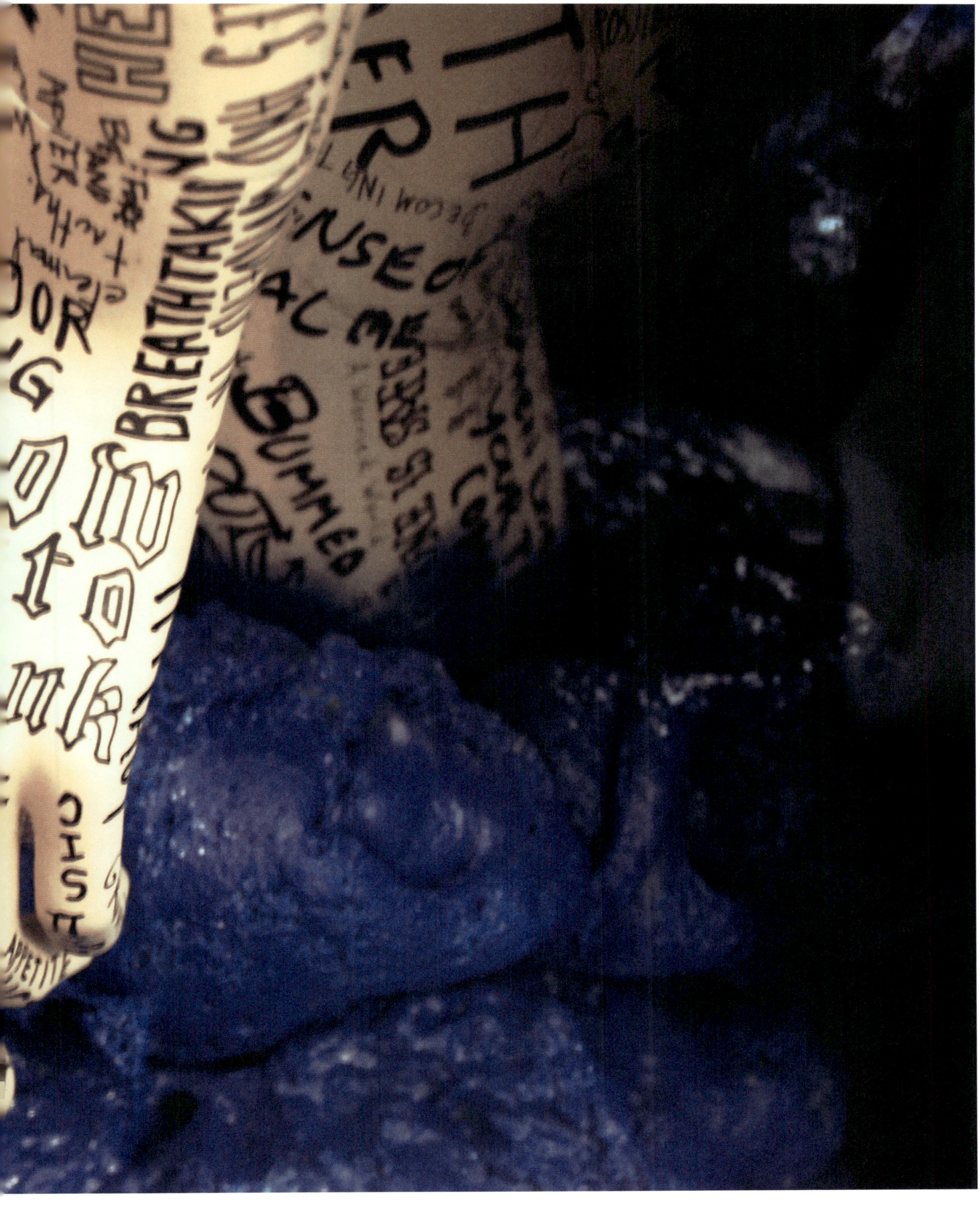

Martin **Honert**

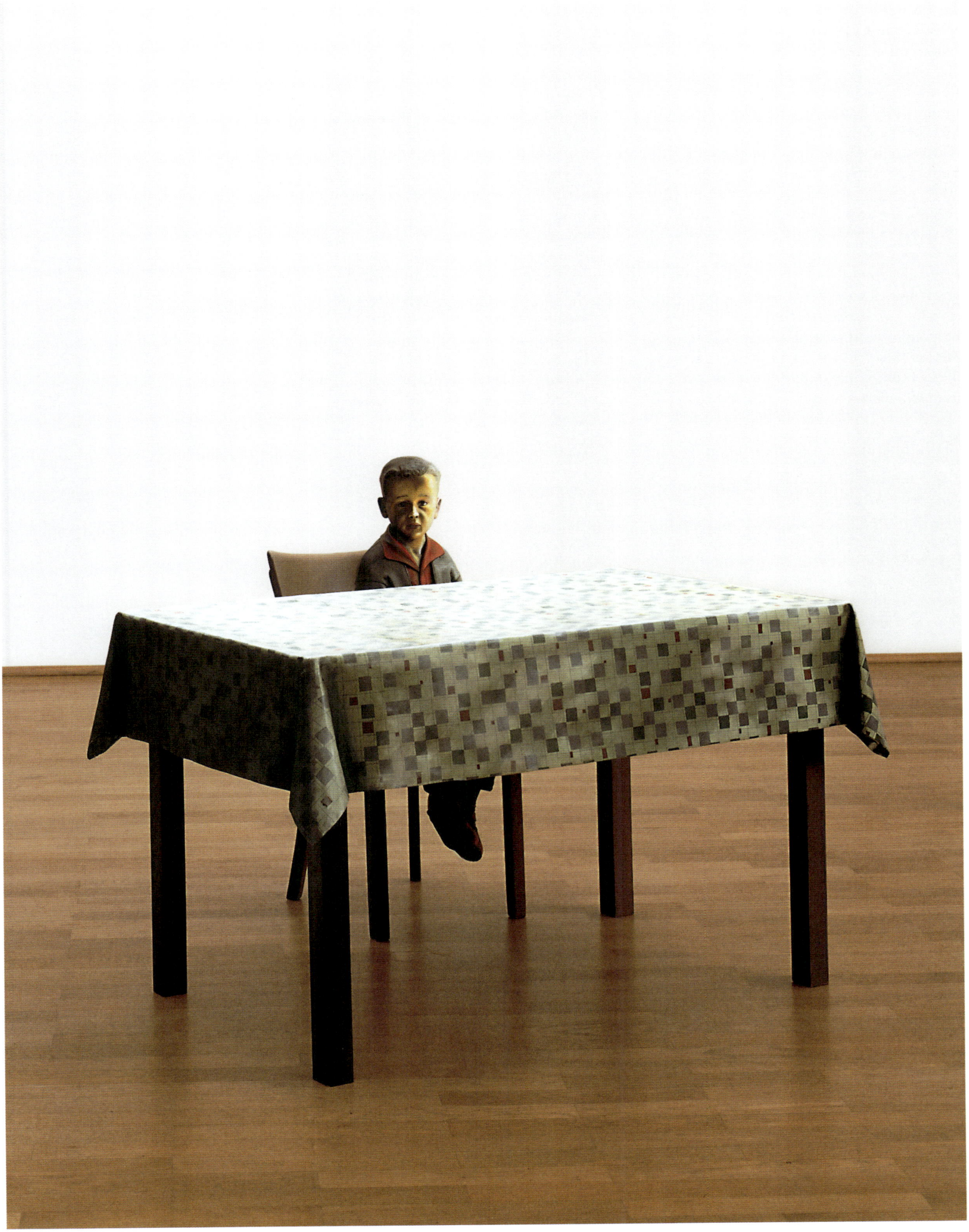

Martin Honert's handcrafted figures have their origins in the artist's past. Both *Englischlehrer* (English Teacher) (2010) and *Foto* (Photo) (1993) are based on photographs from Honert's childhood in post-war West Germany: the former depicts a teacher from his boarding school in the Ruhr, while the little boy in *Foto* is a self-portrait, extracted from a family holiday snap taken in Spain.

Though Honert takes his subject matter from a personal archive, he is not interested in psychoanalytic concerns. 'I don't want my work to get too personal', he has said, explaining his preoccupation with childhood not in terms of emotional significance, but rather 'because I think it's important to discover what's way past but still in the memory as an image'. It is the enduring mental picture, frozen in time, that Honert painstakingly sculpts. 'I always want to freeze things into an image, a "scene"', he has remarked. In excavating the memories subsumed in a photograph, Honert distils his source images to a single detail: contextual elements — the schoolroom, family members poring over Spanish guidebooks — are excised, leaving solitary, static figures. Working alone, Honert fills the photographs' gaps, reconstructing from memory the back of his teacher's comb-over and the instinctive arrangement of his own feet age five, suspended far off the floor when seated. What results is a three-dimensional fragment of externalised consciousness that can be inspected objectively from every angle.

Though narrative details are stripped away, Honert's working method ensures that each sculpture remains tied to a specific photographic moment. Both the cast polyester and fibreglass boy and tablecloth in *Foto* have been painted to reflect the strong sunlight flooding in from the window in the original over-exposed Ektachrome slide; the colour of the imitation wipe-clean cloth is drained from the tabletop's illuminated surface, while the right side of the boy's face is fixed in deep shadow. A similar tactic is used for *English Teacher*, whose body and suit (cast in layered polyurethane containing sand and glass particles to replicate the grainy vintage photograph) are painted to suggest a light source from the left, while the sculpture's diminutive one-half scale implies the distanced perspective of the back of the classroom. Refusing to accord with the conditions of their actual circumstances, Honert's figures — part photograph, part sculpture — occupy at once the temporal spaces of both past and present.

← **_Foto_ (Photo), 1993**

→ **_Englischlehrer_ (English Teacher), 2010**

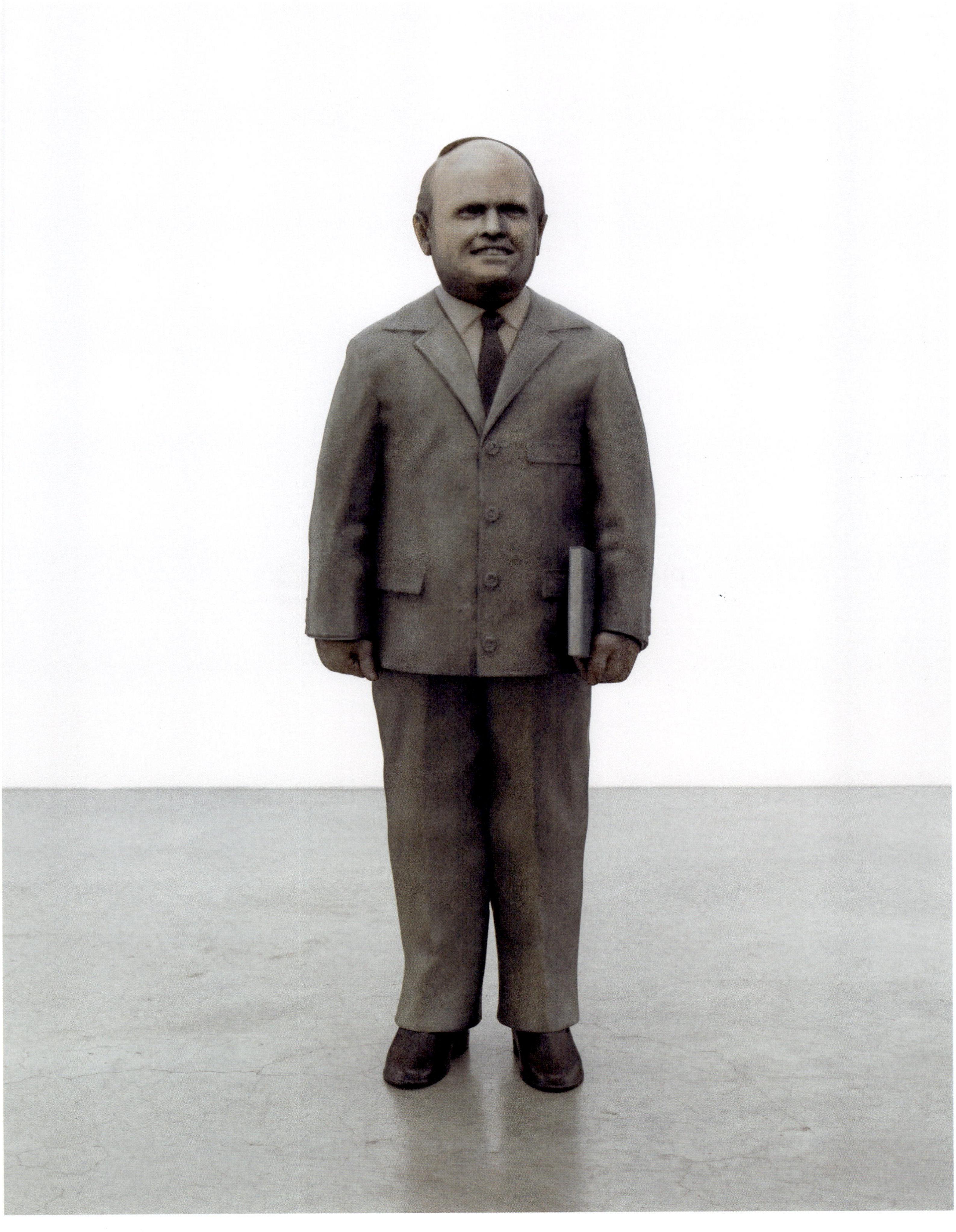

Pierre **Huyghe**

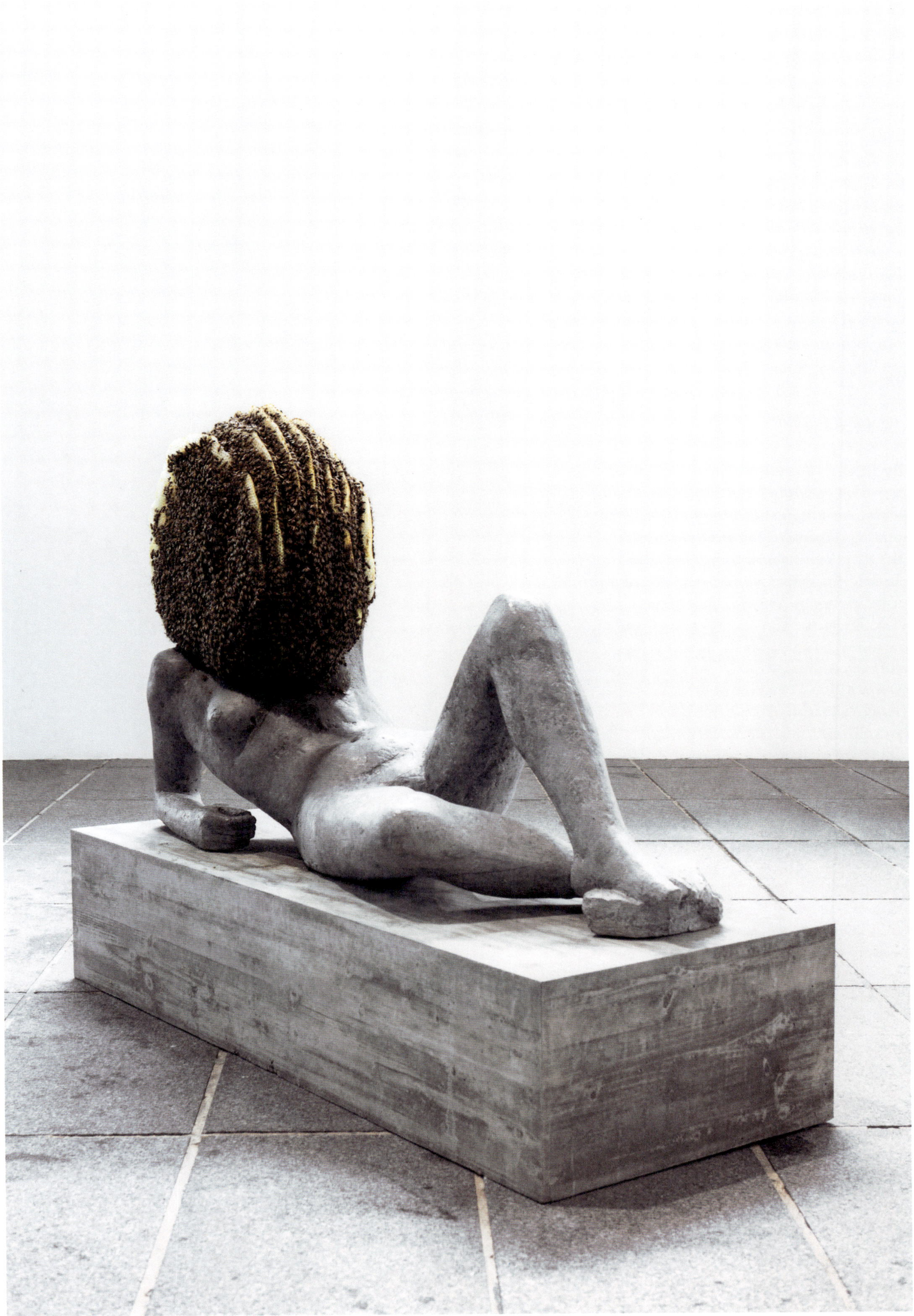

Pierre Huyghe creates time-based situations. When humans or human forms appear in his works, they are often part of complex networks, including living organisms such as animals and plants. What interests Huyghe is 'constructing situations that take place within a particular reality as an auto-generating system which exists within itself'. He also speaks of 'intensifying the presence, creating the conditions for an emergence to occur and grow'.

This is precisely what happens in *Liegender Frauenakt (Untilled 2011–2012)* (2012). The reclining female nude is an existing sculpture that has undergone a transformation. The original sculpture, a classical work by Max Weber, a twentieth-century Swiss sculptor, has been cast in concrete and a swarming beehive obscures the head.

The head of *Liegender Frauenakt (Untilled 2011–2012)* is inhabited by thousands of bees who communicate constantly with each other, creating a complete biological community. The statue was originally conceived as an element in a biotope that Huyghe created for dOCUMENTA(13) at Kassel, in Karlsaue Park. Artefacts, inanimate elements, living organisms, plants, animals, human beings and bacteria, were left to create a growing system within a composting area. The title *Untilled* alludes to the fact that the area was not cultivated, non-dependent on and indifferent to the viewer's presence. *Untilled* reflects the aspiration of dOCUMENTA (13) to move beyond our anthropocentric bias and imagine a world of thought and active life that is not based solely on humans.

Metamorphosis and auto-generating systems are central to Huyghe's practice: 'I look at how things in co-presence change, vary in intensity or metabolise and grow something beyond themselves', he remarks. As producers of honey and wax, bees are an apt metaphor for this process.

← ***Liegender Frauenakt (Untilled 2011–2012)*, 2012**

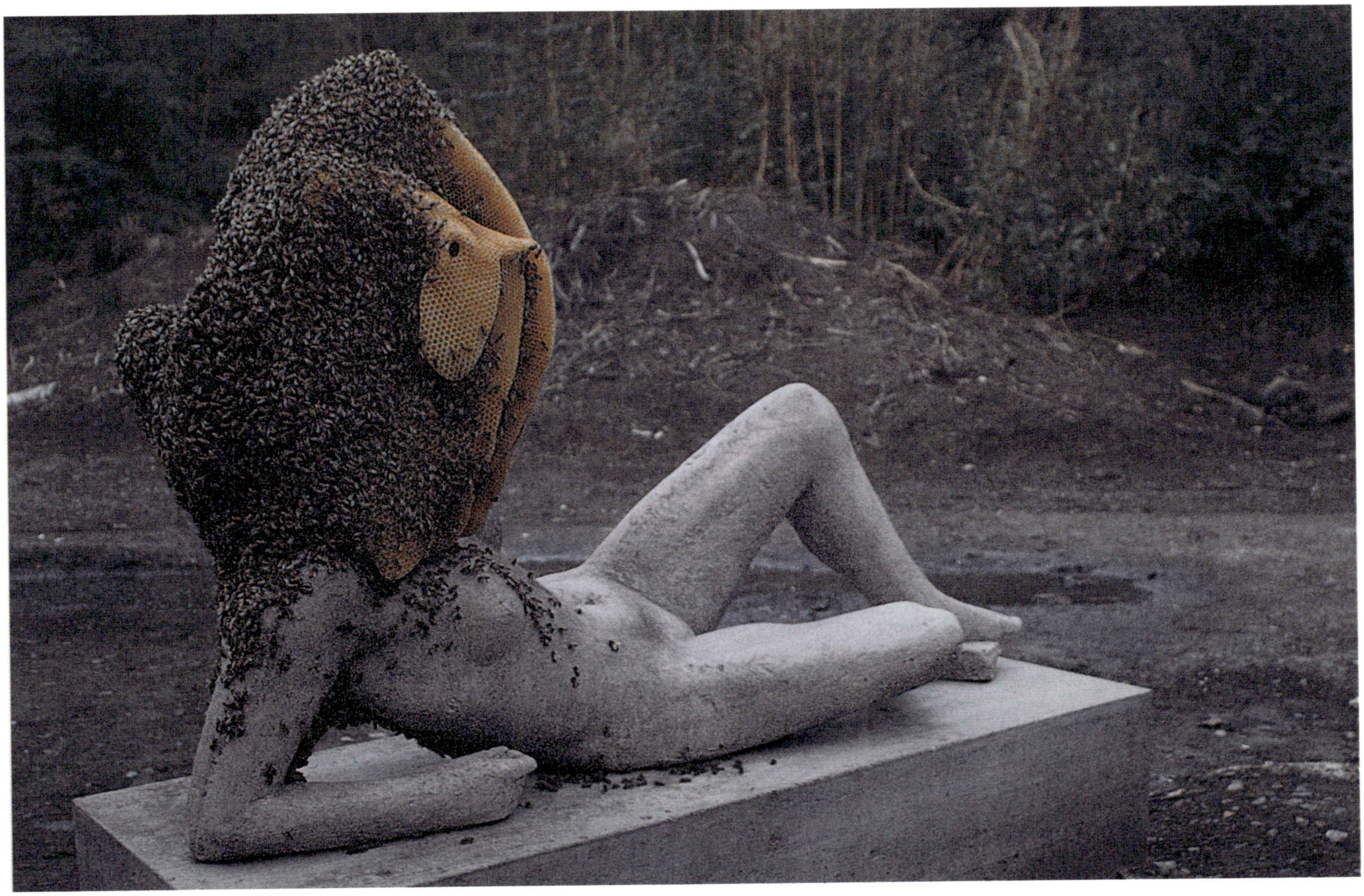

↑ ***Liegender Frauenakt (Untilled 2011–2012)*, 2012**

Jeff **Koons**

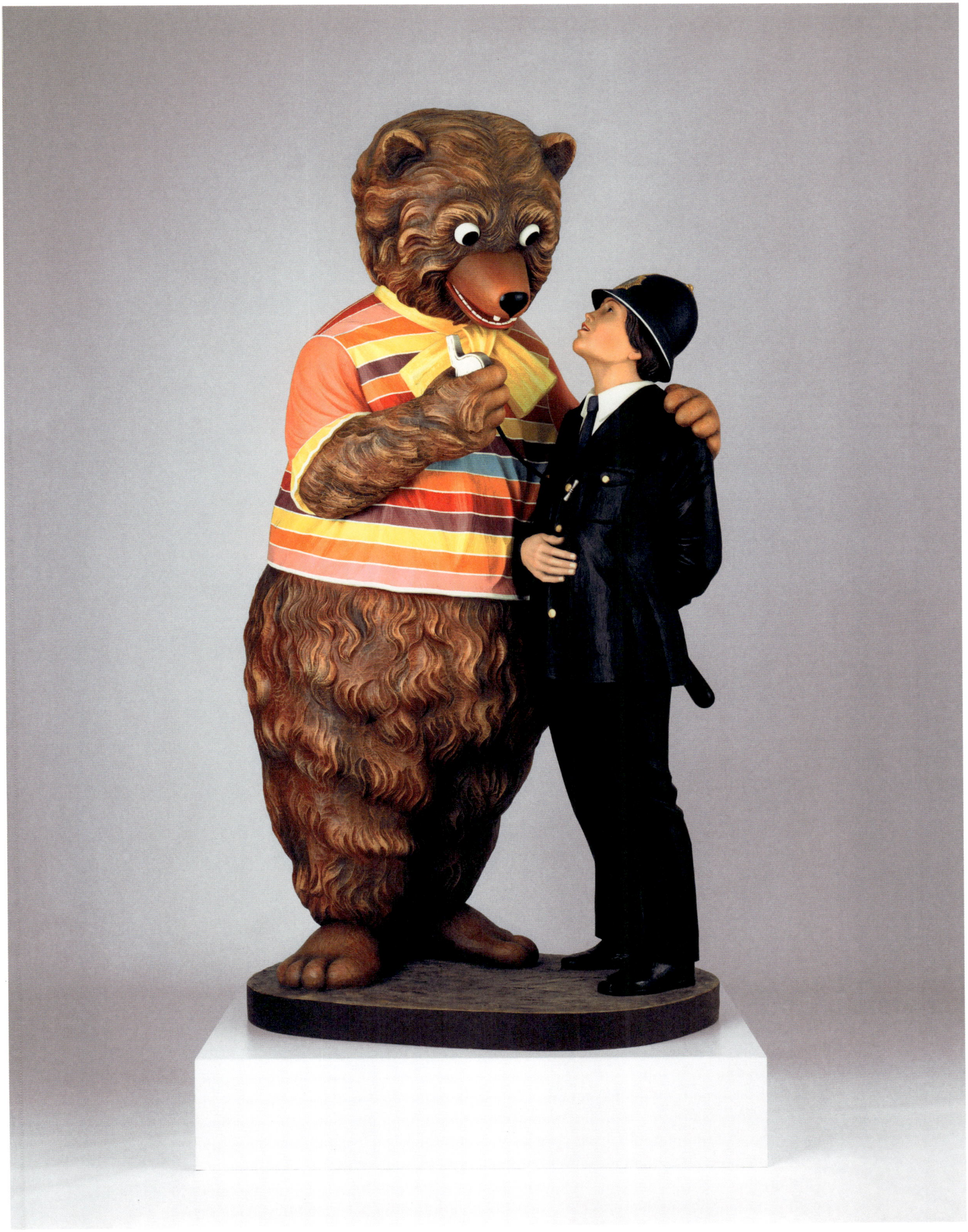

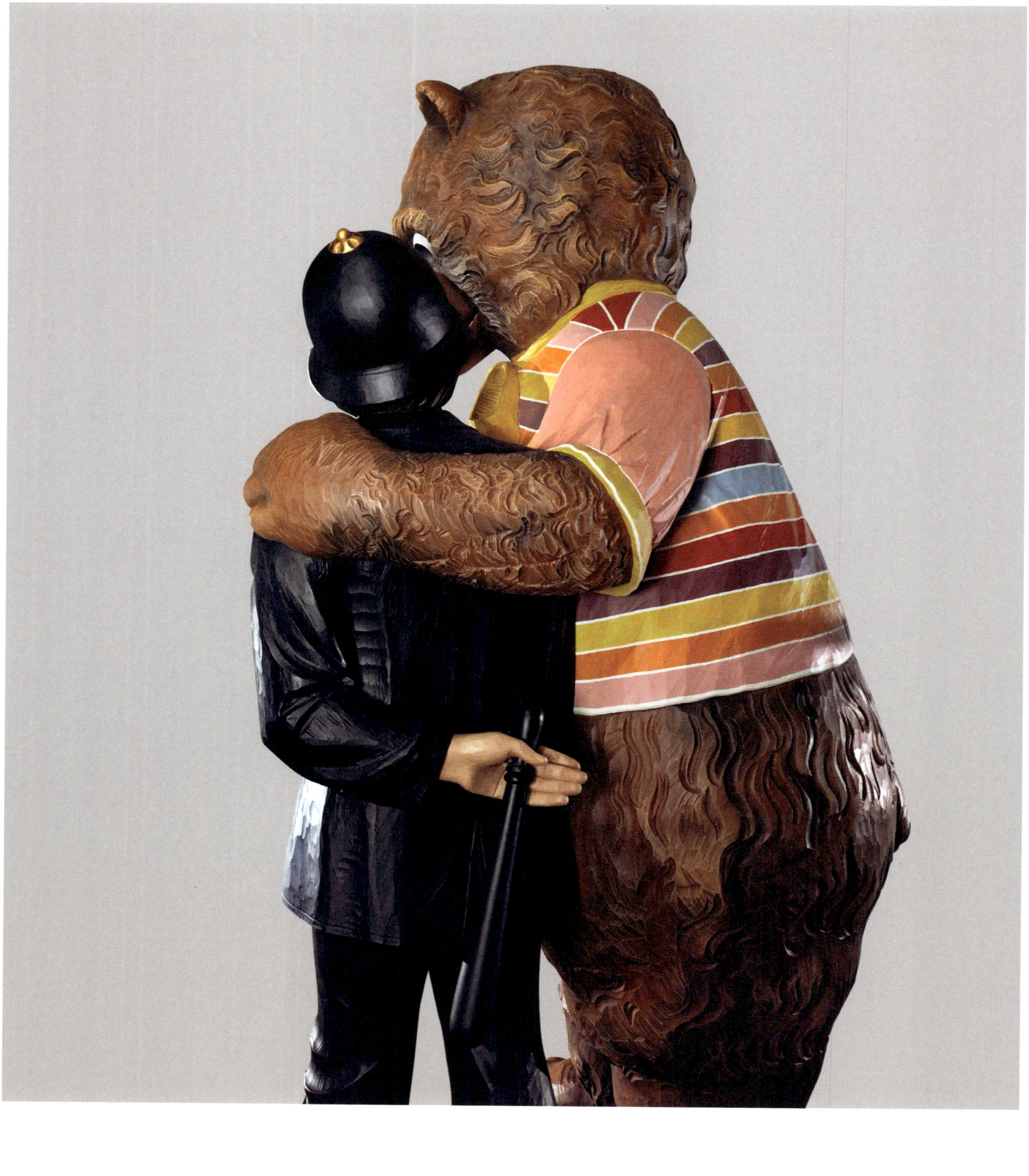

← *Bear and Policeman*, 1988

↑ *Bear and Policeman* (detail), 1988

When unveiled in 1988, Jeff Koons' 'Banality' series proved to be provocative on a number of levels. Exhibited simultaneously across three galleries in Europe and America, the 20 figurative sculptures included transformed images of gift shop knick-knacks, religious iconography and toy-inspired objects. Likening the works to 'what the Beatles would have made if they had made sculpture', Koons argued, without irony, for the kind of mass-appeal imagery shunned by self-conscious good taste. 'People respond to these types of things, but they still distance themselves from it', he observed. 'The "Banality" work is about the recognition of the response.'

The shock-factor of these sculptures came from their appearance as well as their content. In the post-conceptual art world of the late 1980s, Koons defied convention by using fabrication techniques and materials such as porcelain, wood and mirrored glass that were associated with collectible fine crafts and not the artistic traditions of modernist practice. *Bear and Policeman* (1988) is made from polychromed wood: a process through which wood is carved and painted naturalistically, developed originally by the sculptors of religious works in medieval Europe. The 'Banality' series was, Koons explained, based on the Garden of Eden. 'I've always tried to use materialism to seduce the viewer', he commented at the time, 'just like the church uses materialism. [...] The church uses the baroque and the rococo, you just go in there and you feel like you're participating in social mobility. [...] I've always tried to do the same thing with my work.'

The production of *Bear and Policeman*, as with the other 'Banality' sculptures, was outsourced to specialists in northern Italy (the chief craftsman has signed the sculpture's base; Koons' signature marks its underside). The sculpture depicts a huge bear wearing a striped t-shirt, standing beside a policeman, who is holding a nightstick, a symbol of authority. With one steadying paw on the bobby's shoulder, the bear has taken hold of his whistle, raising it up as if to blow it. Describing the sculpture's depicted situation as 'a man being sexually toyed with [...] to show "banality" out of control', Koons examines how banality and the power of an artist can have political value. The artist has said that the 'Banality' series is about embracing the power of communication to create a dialogue about the power of art, but also the moral responsibility of the artist that comes with that power.

Paul McCarthy

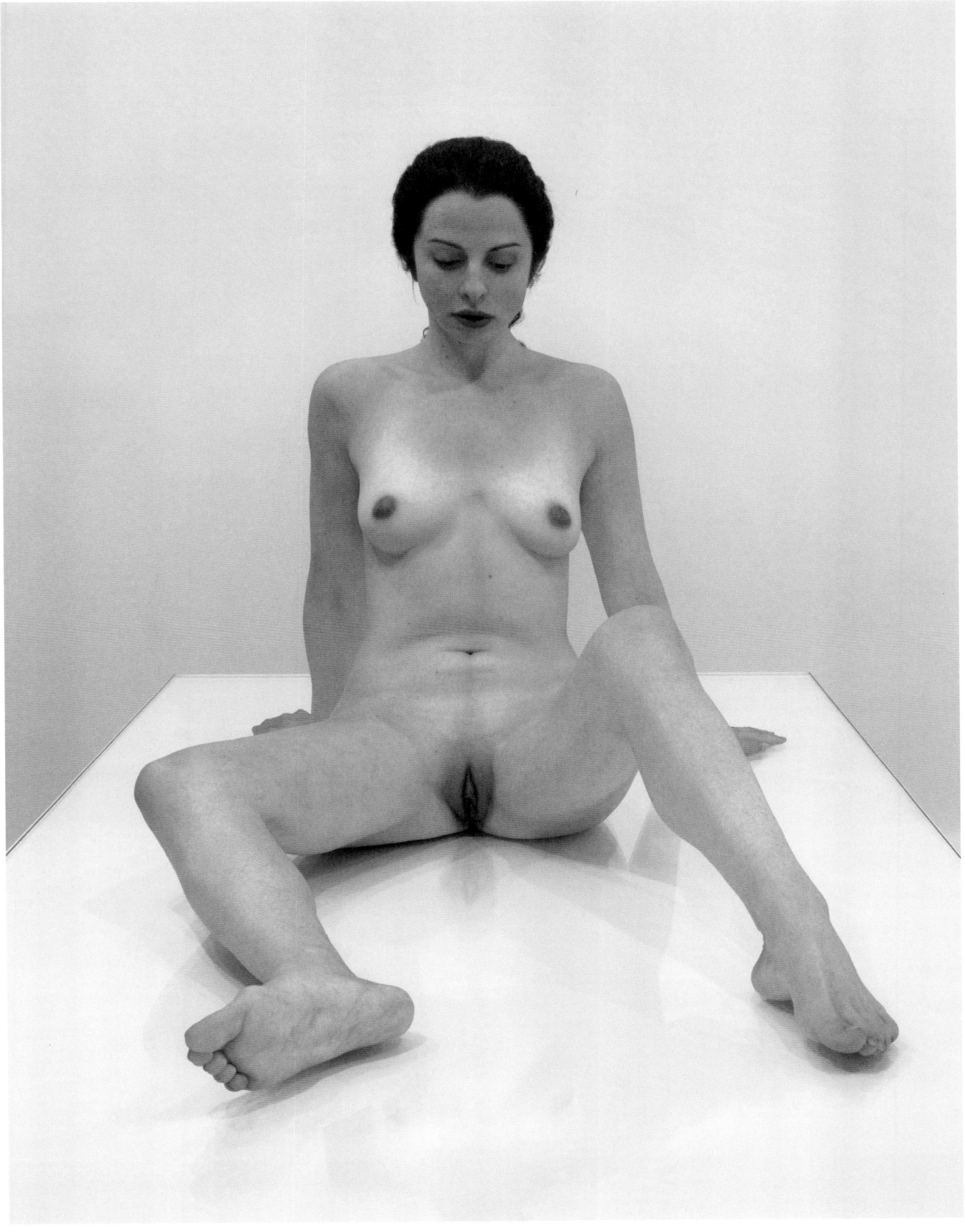

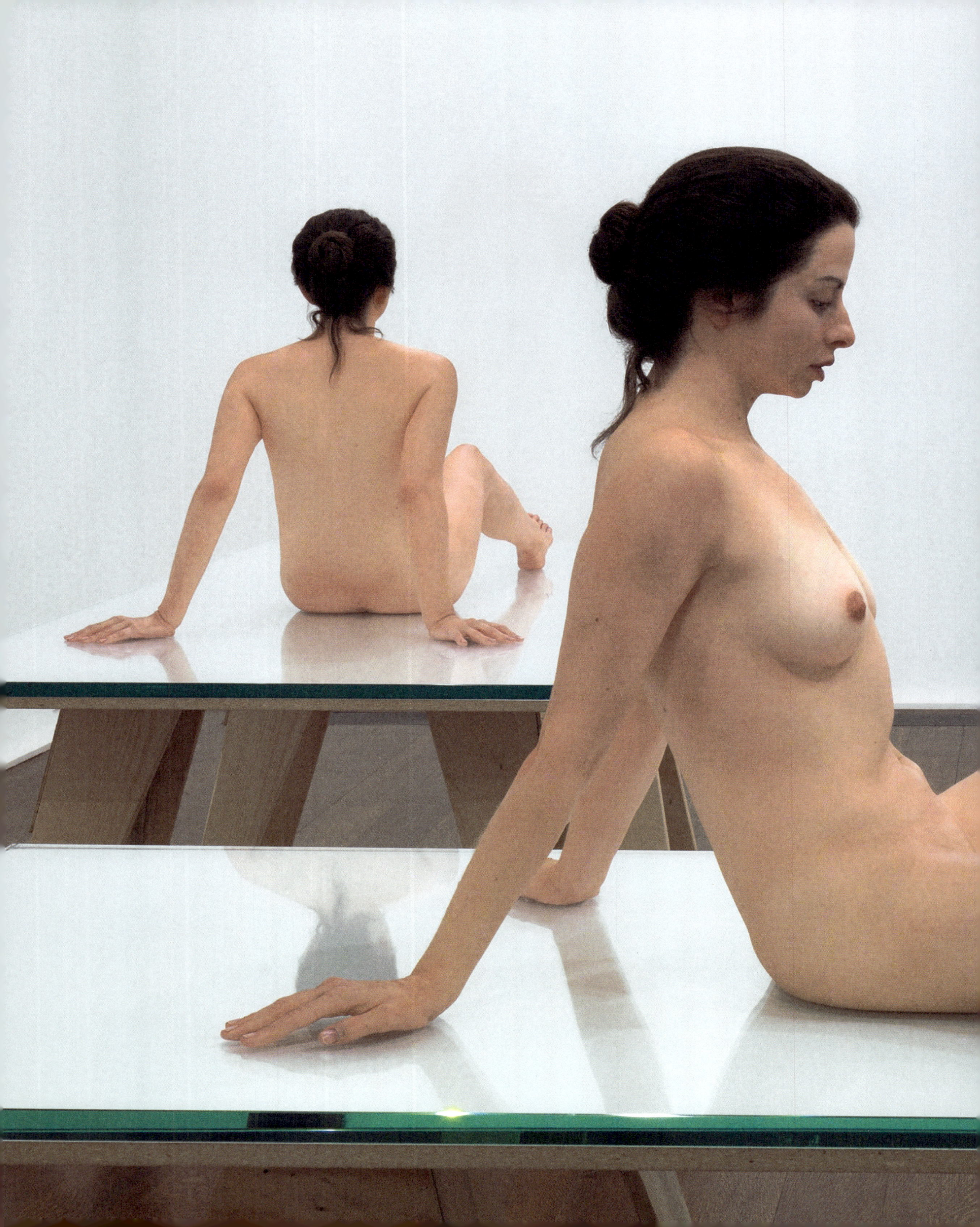

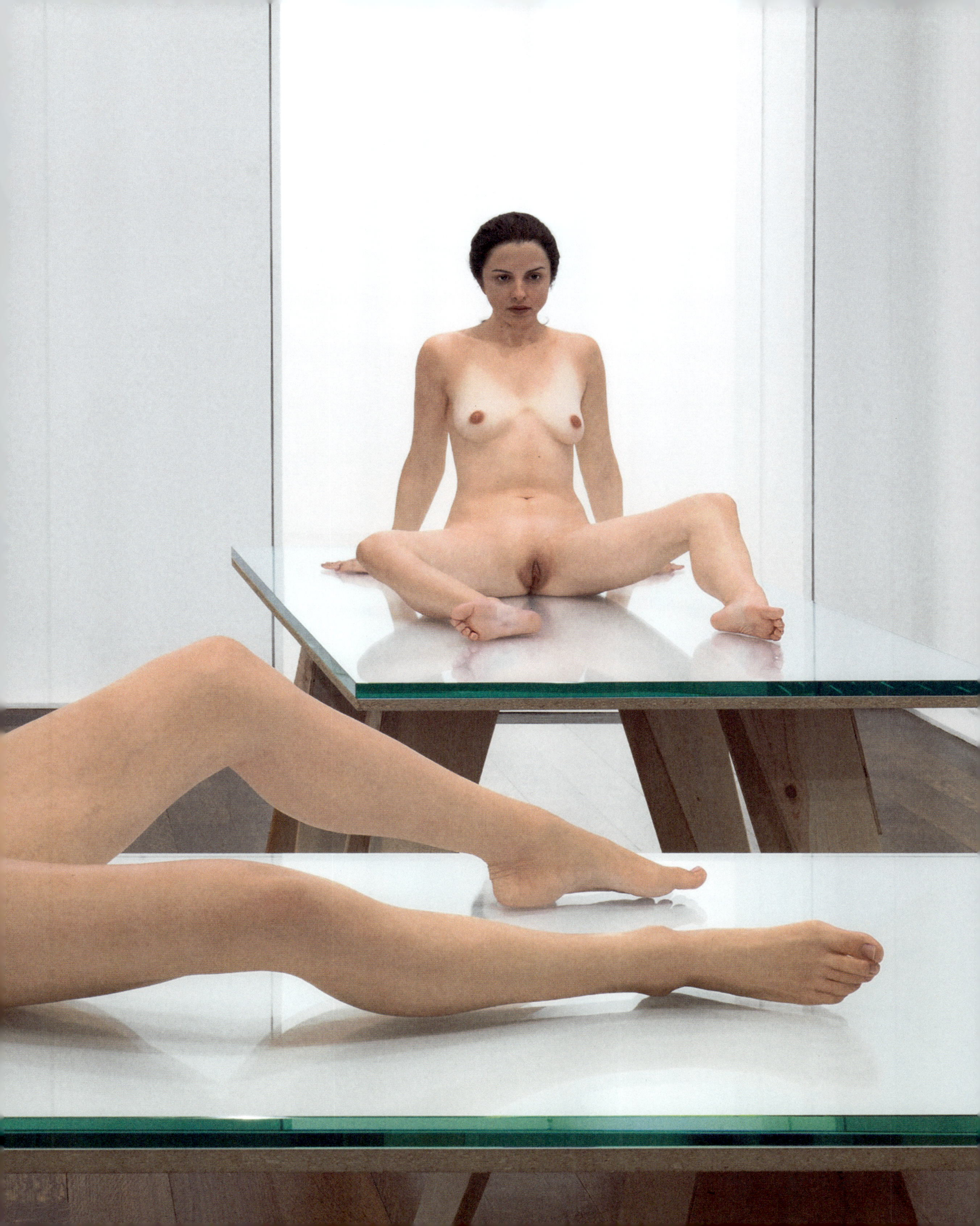

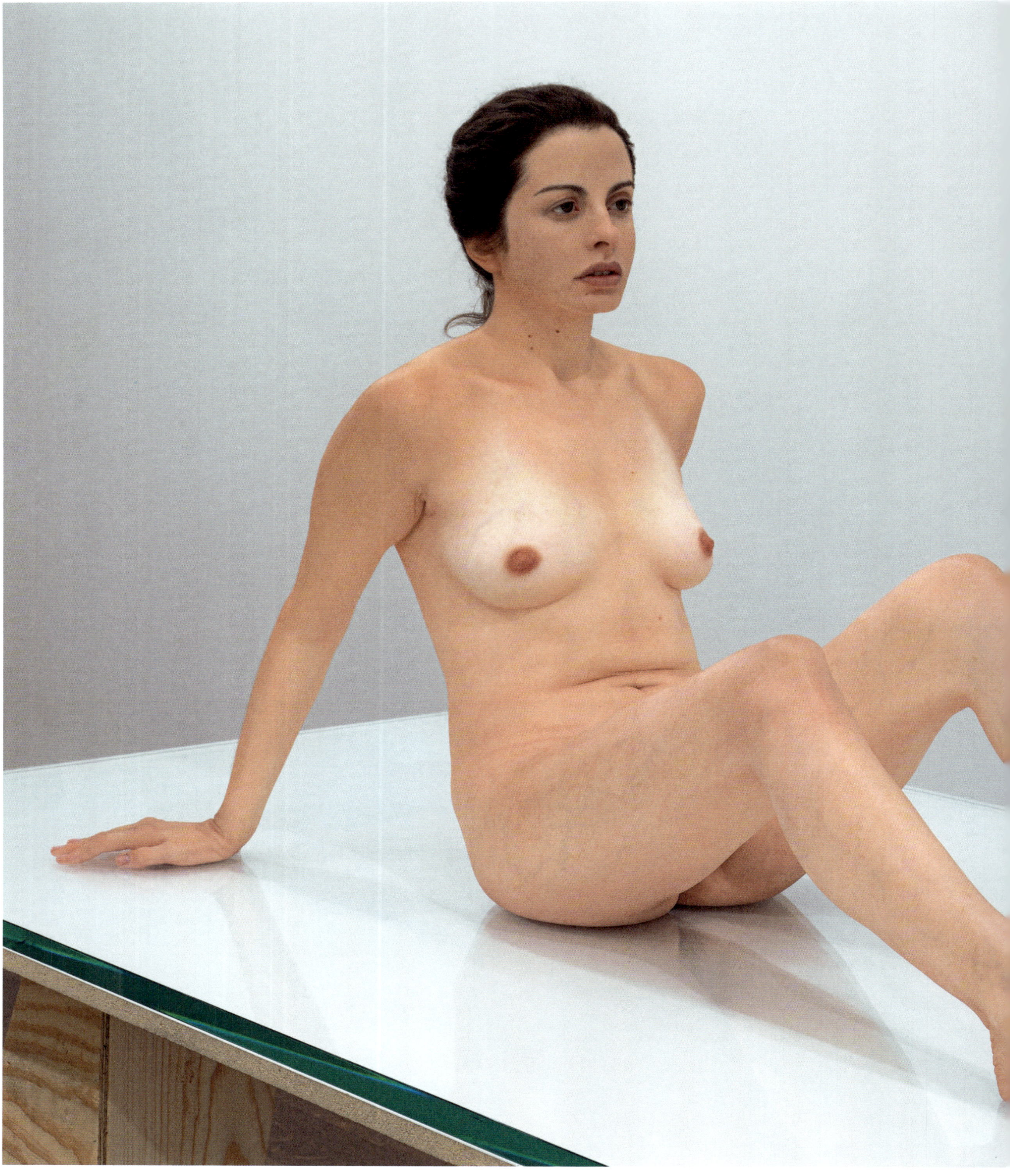

← *That Girl (T.G. Awake)* (detail), 2012–13
← *That Girl (T.G. Awake)* (detail), 2012–13

↑ *That Girl (T.G. Awake)* (detail), 2012–13

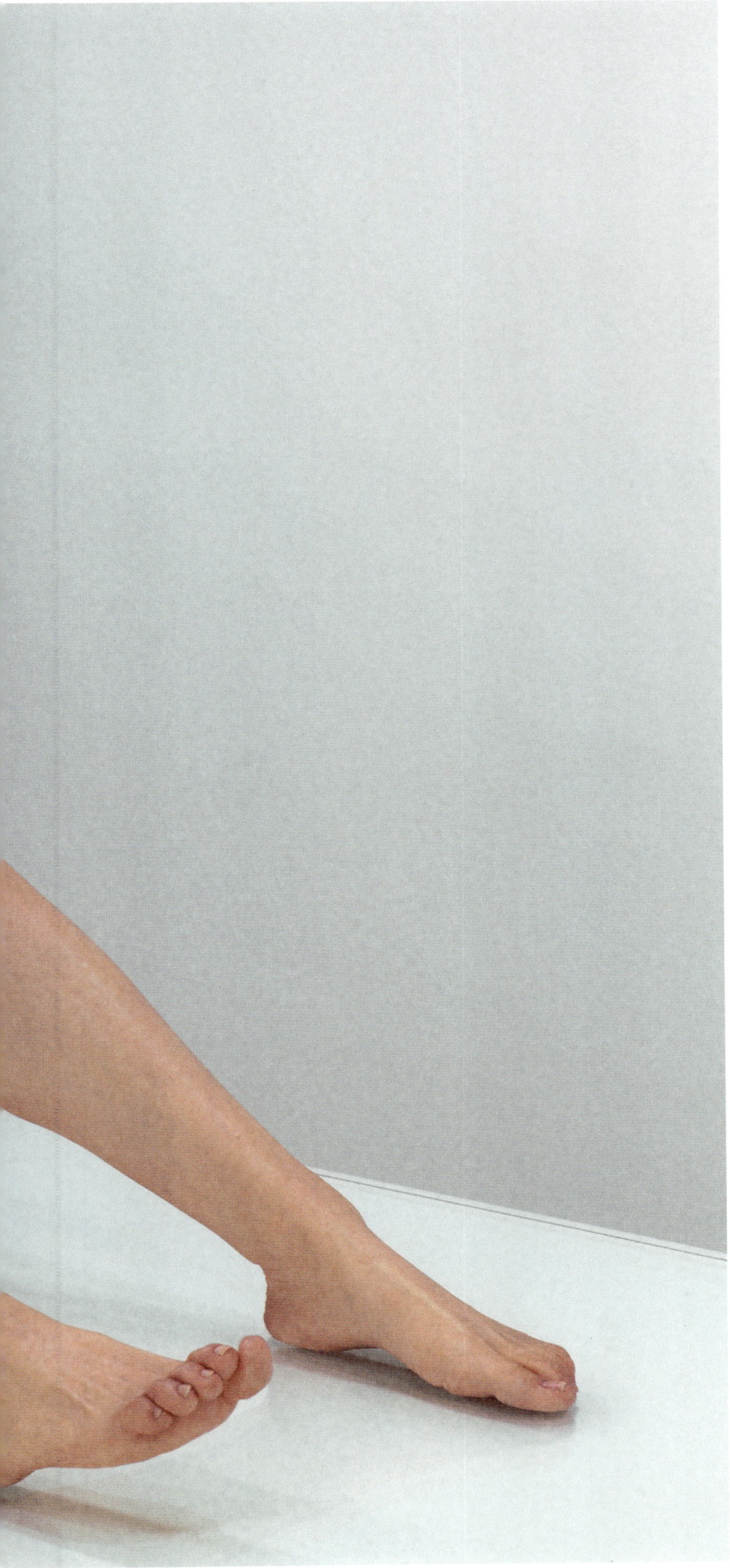

Over five decades, Paul McCarthy has used the body as a subject for exploring human desires and taboos in sculpture, performance, video and installation. McCarthy's own body frequently features in his work, but he also makes ample use of mannequins, dolls and life-casts to connect with 'a fear of the virtual, the fear of being unable to discern a real human from a mannequin. Wax figures, robotics or mechanised mannequins create this virtual reality, and you can't tell what is real'.

This blurring of physical and virtual experiences is nowhere more evident than in the three life-sized casts of *That Girl (T.G. Awake)* (2012–13). The platinum silicone life-cast nudes are exacting replicas of actress Elyse Poppers sitting upright, in slightly varied postures, atop three glass-topped trestle tables. Unnervingly lifelike, *That Girl* creates the urge both to stare and to look away in, raising questions about spectatorship and voyeurism. Despite the remarkable verisimilitude and technical virtuosity of the casts (realised by a team that included special effects artist Kazuhiro Tsuji), McCarthy is quick to point out that they are 'not exactly right', the-life-casting process having introduced its own almost imperceptible distortions.

The viewer's gaze takes centre stage in *T.G. Elyse* (2011). Here the onlooker is surrounded by a four-channel video documenting the intricate and messy process of moulding and casting the figures, as well as the moving and positioning of the model to generate the final pose. The model is laid out on a table, her body scrutinised by multiple cameras. The moulds are then created by covering her in blue silicone and plaster. Life-casting techniques are commonly used in the film industry (for special effects), the medical industry and the pornography industry, and these associations, which permeate McCarthy's overall practice, are aptly conjoined in this work. Life-casting verges on ritual and rite for McCarthy, who sees it as intersecting with painting, sculpture and performance. 'When we started the moulding process, which was always done in the middle of the room, a group of men and women gathered around her. It resembled surgery, with the body on an operating table. The pouring of the blue rubber over her became a painting [...] It was more than just the process of making a mould. You can read it like she's on an altar, an image of torture, whatever. I think the piece sits in an ambiguous position as a sculpture.'

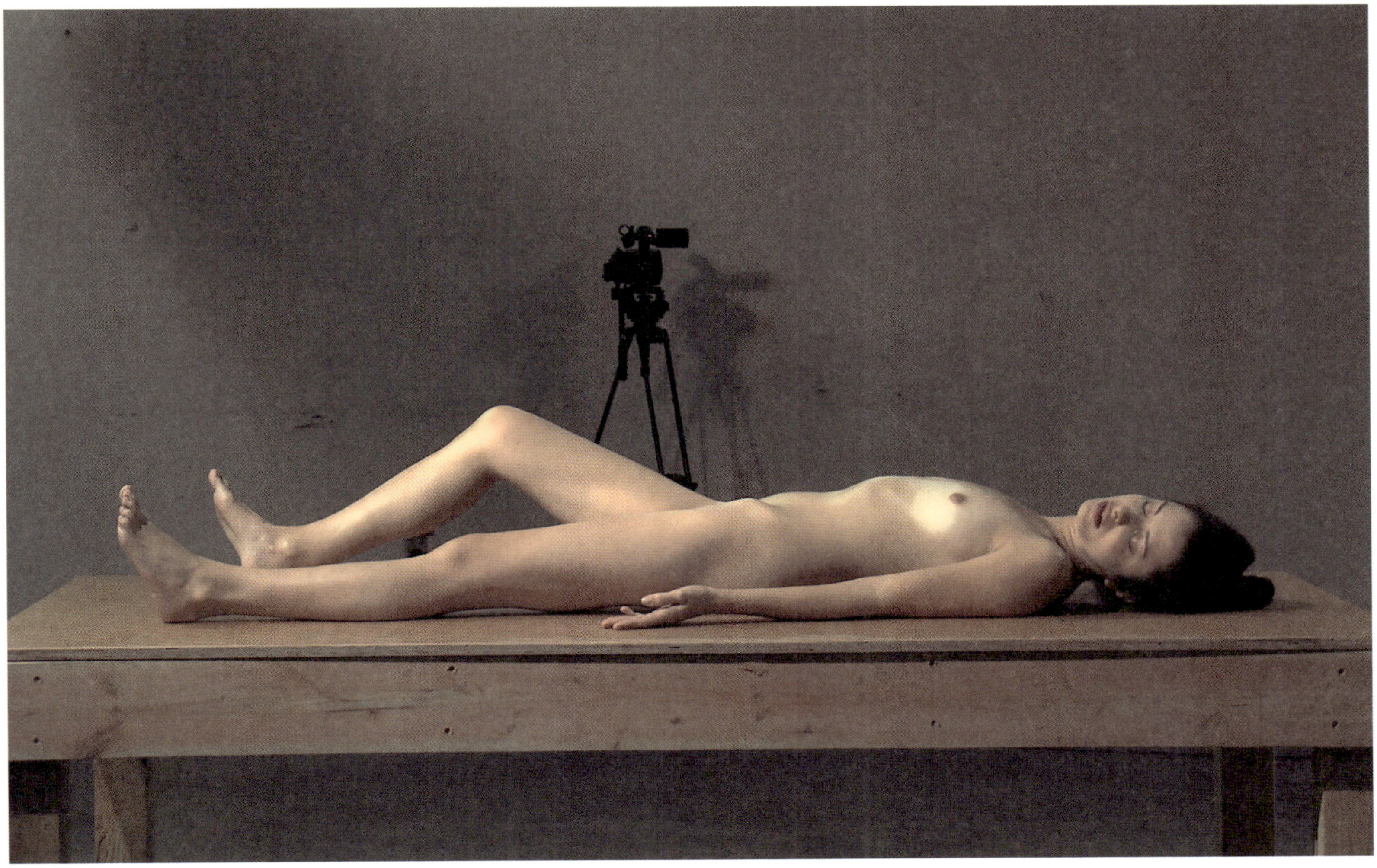

↑ ***T.G. Elyse*** **(film still), 2011**

John Miller

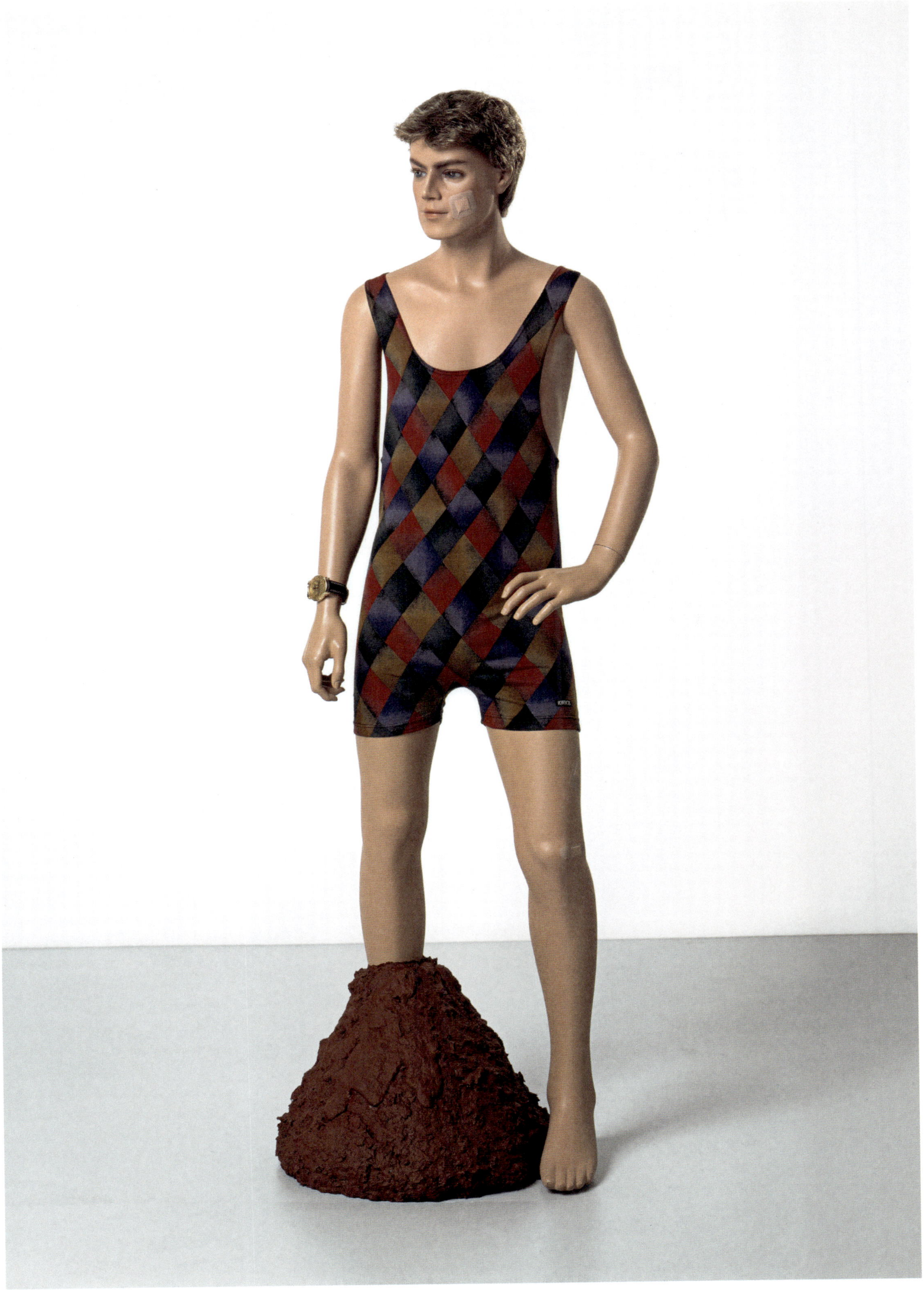

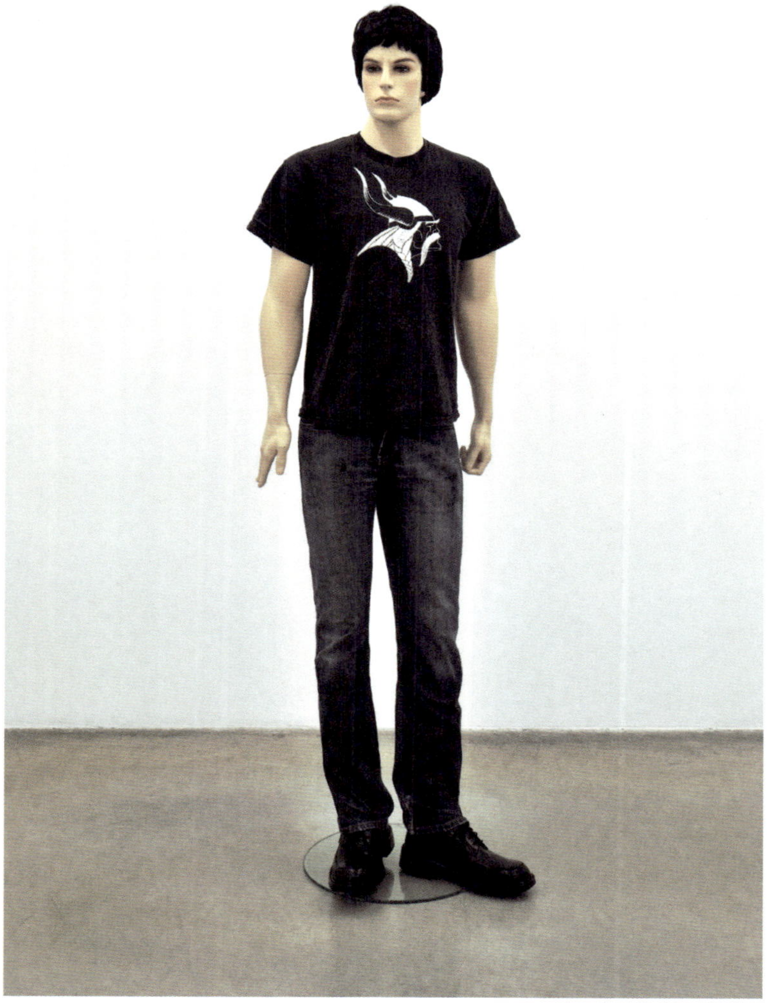

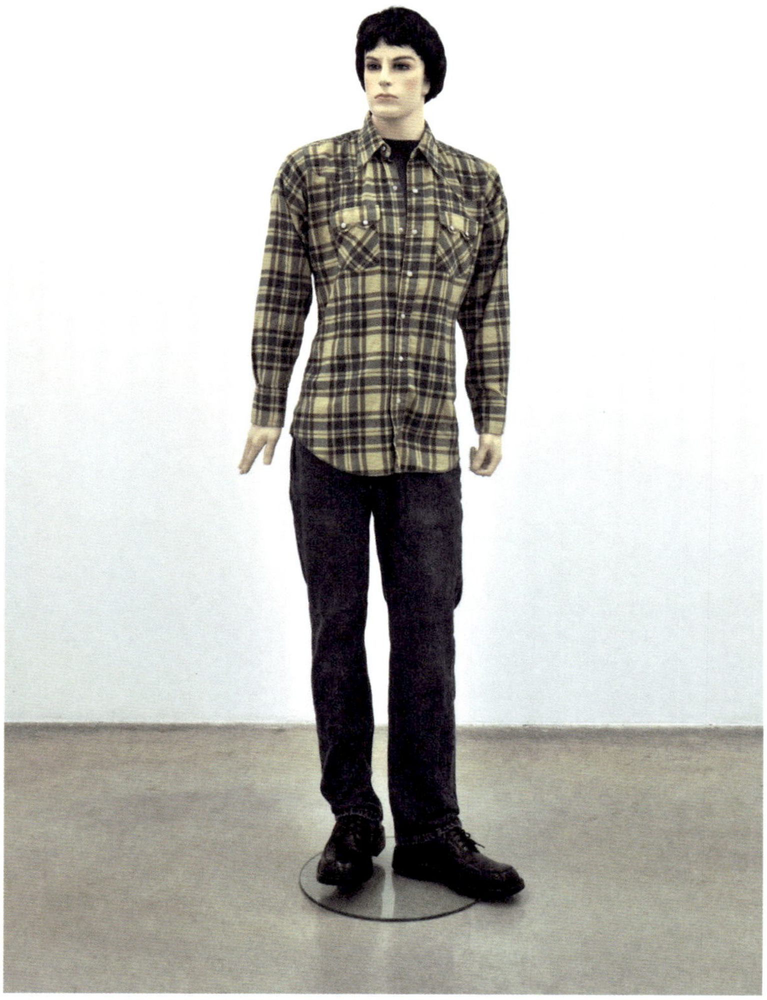

When John Miller made his first mannequin sculpture, using a second-hand display dummy, he did not expect to make another. This initial mannequin work, entitled *My Friend* (1989), was created as a 'gesture', a sort of human decoy to surprise or even supplant the viewer. Miller dressed a slightly outdated, generic male mannequin in his own clothes, which he then painted brown. He placed the work in the gallery so that the viewer, instead of walking into an empty room, came across a figure that was already there, effectively lying in wait. 'Installed like that', Miller felt, 'a mannequin might even direct the viewer's gaze, like an over-the-shoulder shot in cinema'. His realisation that this strategy had the ability to 'give voice to otherwise tacit conditions of display' led on to a whole series of works in which mannequins not only pre-empt the viewer and act as stand-ins for visitors, but sometimes become the focus of audience participation.

← ***Now We're Big Potatoes*, 1992**

↑ ***Mannequin Lover*, 2002**
↗ ***Mannequin Lover*, 2002**

Miller describes *Now We're Big Potatoes* (1992) as his 'first assault on youth culture'. It features a young male mannequin dressed in harlequin-patterned underwear, wearing an ostentatious gold watch and with a large sticking plaster hiding some hideous blemish on his otherwise perfect cheek. He seems oblivious to the fact that his right leg is anchored in a calf-high pile of brown muck, with a trail of smaller excremental deposits dumped in his wake. These dollops of dirt, it would appear, are an ironic nod towards — maybe even a farewell to — the thick brown impasto with which Miller had coated his earlier, highly textural monochrome reliefs, and which had inevitably reminded viewers of shit. Regarding the title, Miller explains that he made the work during the first year that he lived in Berlin, when he was especially alert to the differences between English and German: 'Small potatoes makes sense as an English idiom; big potatoes means nothing — except linguistic incompetence.'

The titles of many of Miller's mannequin works not only extend their implicit humour but also suggest a more caustic social critique. *Composition in Black and Tan* (2010) places a white, metrosexual type, wearing black bathing gear with his goggles pushed back on his head, in a child's paddling pool, reducing a serious swimmer to the status of life-size toy. With *Mannequin Lover* (2002), Miller gives other people the opportunity to dress a male mannequin in their own clothes and so, perhaps, in their own image, actual or imagined. As Miller says, 'More broadly, what's going on in these pieces is how various cultural texts cut across the body to define and re-define it. Of course, it's not a real body but a body displaced by an object of commercial display that may make this more apparent.'

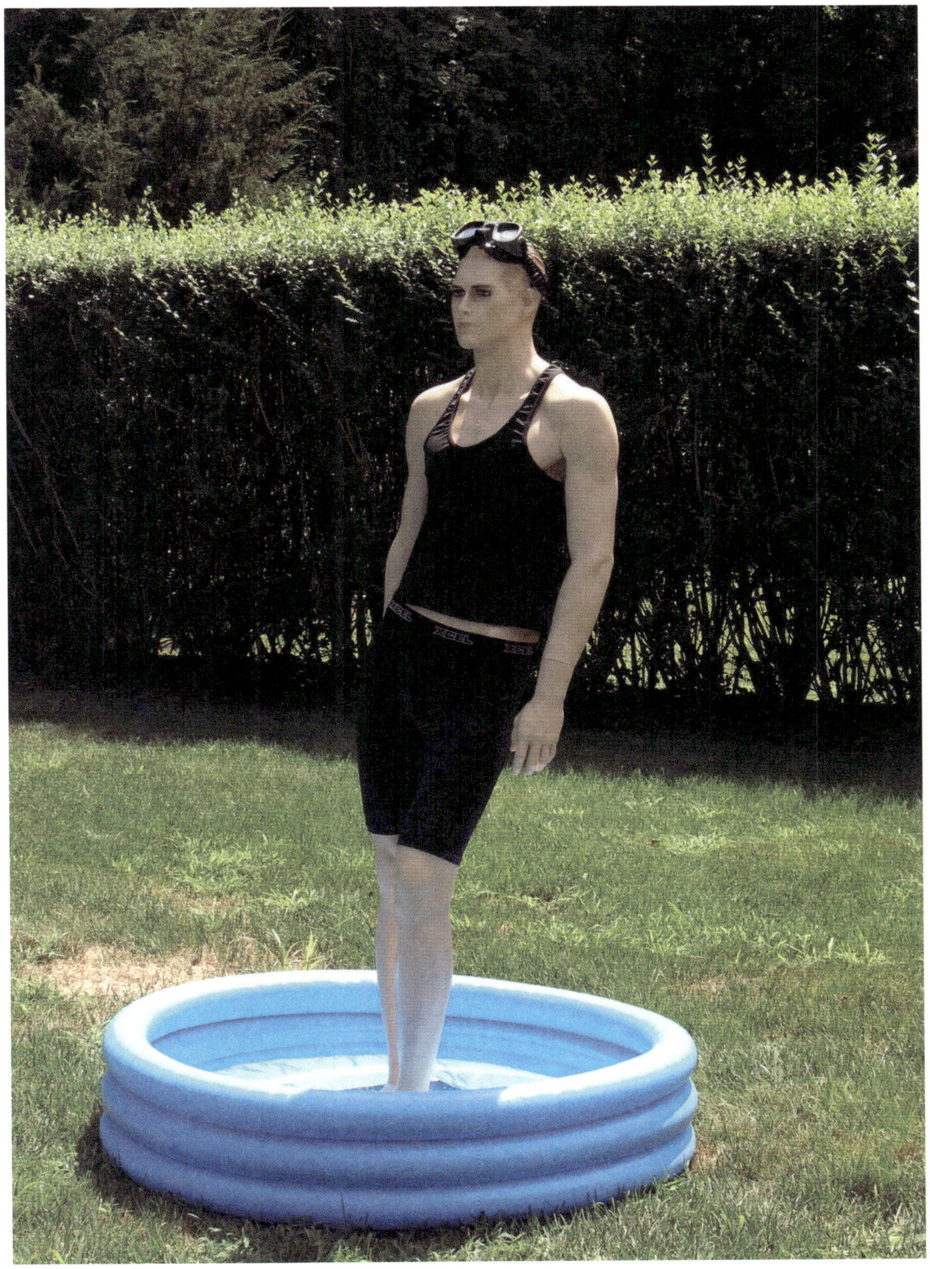

↑ ***Composition in Black and Tan*, 2010**

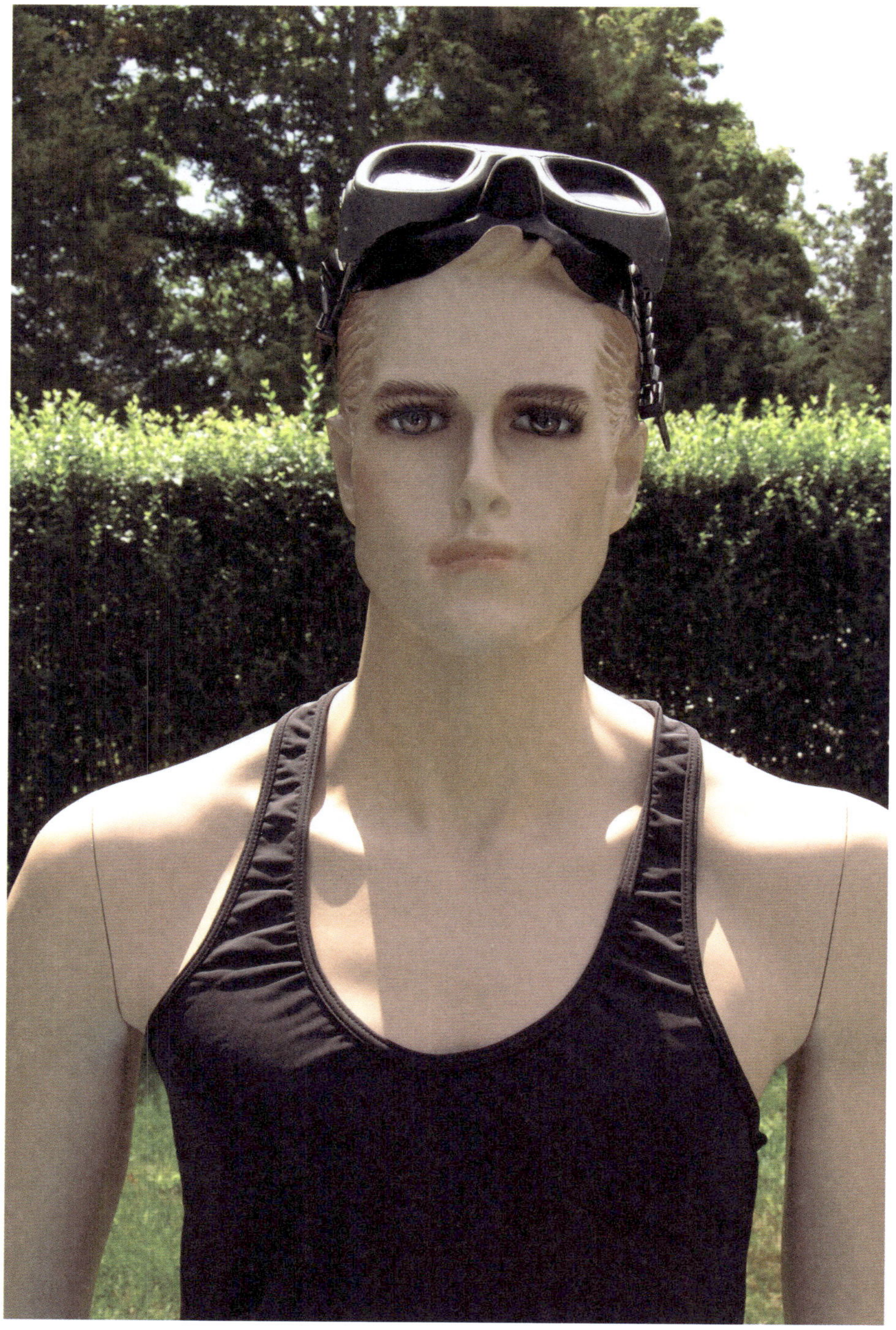

↗ *Composition in Black and Tan* (detail), 2010

Paul McCarthy

McCarthy created the group of three figures in *That Girl (T.G. Awake)* using life casts of the model Elyse Poppers. These were achieved through casting and careful moulding processes, using first the live model and then photography and film as a reference. The process was captured in this four-channel video, which is exhibited with the sculptures. By installing the film of its production as an artwork in its own right, McCarthy emphasises the labour, patience and skill involved, and provides the viewer with insight into the manner in which such uncannily lifelike work came about — a space in which, in the artist's words, 'reality and abstraction intersect'.

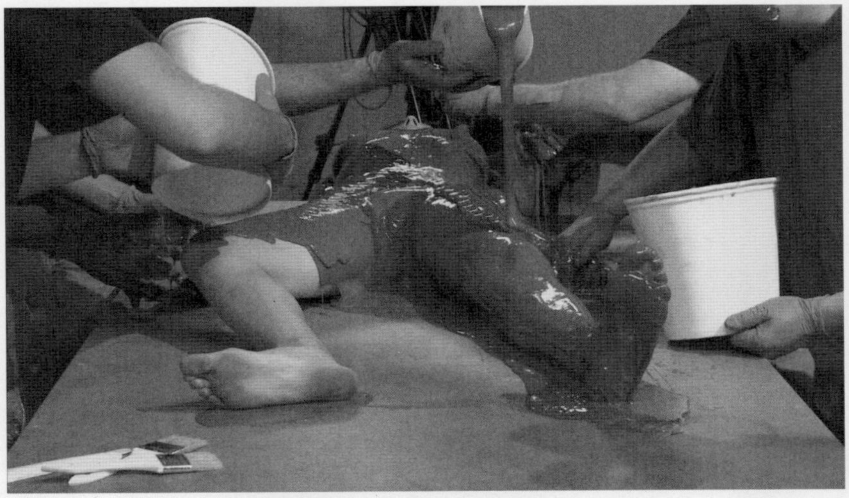

Paul McCarthy *T.G. Elyse* (film still), 2011

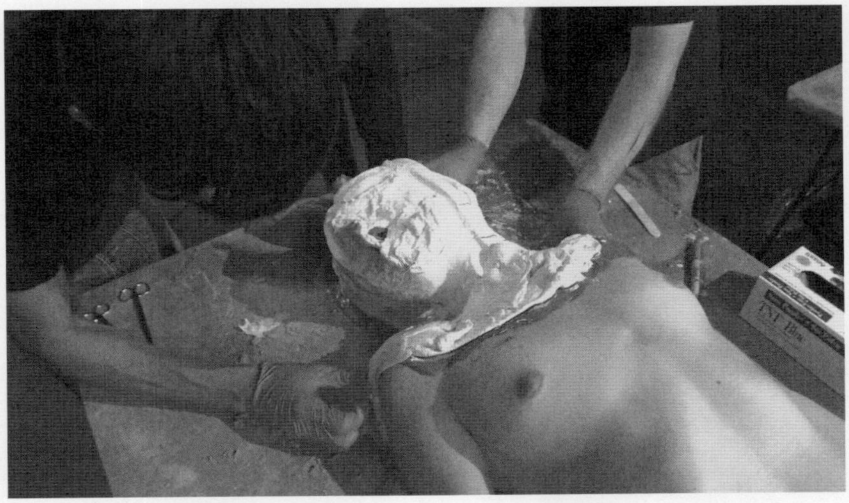

Paul McCarthy *T.G. Elyse* (film still), 2011

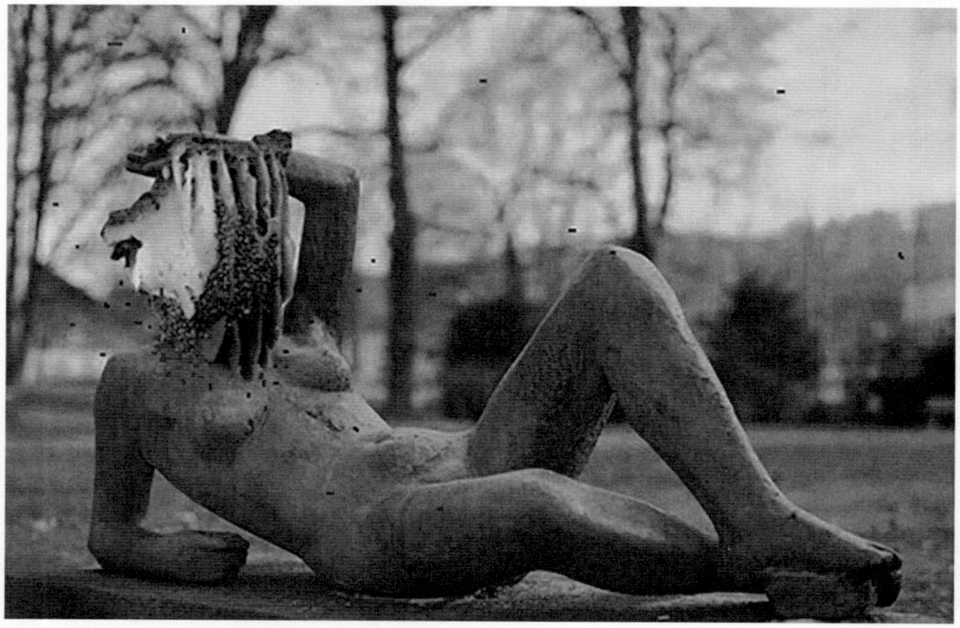

Pierre Huyghe Pierre Huyghe, *Liegender Frauenakt (Untilled 2011–2012)*, 2012 – preparatory collage

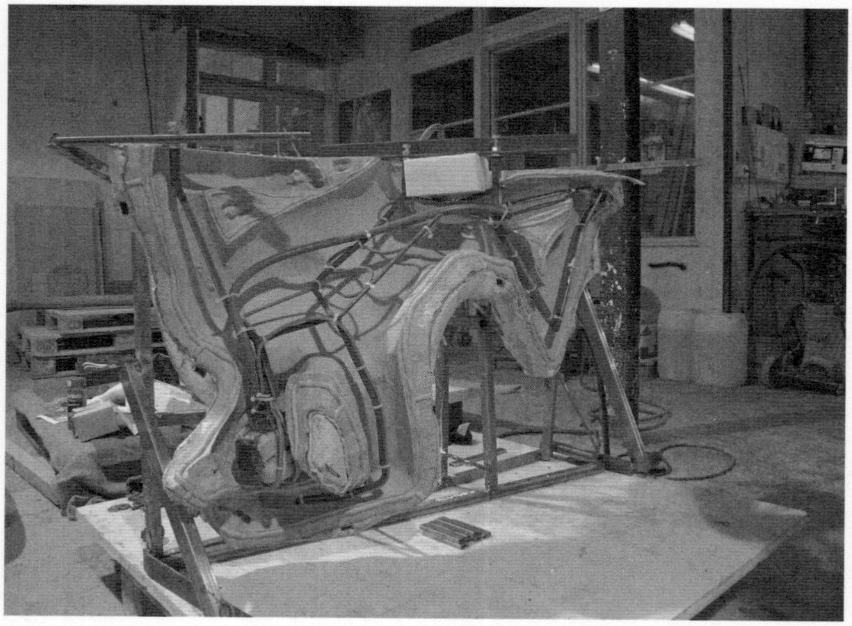

Pierre Huyghe *Liegender Frauenakt (Untilled 2011–2012)*, 2012 – interior of concrete cast showing heating system which brings the sculpture's temperature up to 37°C

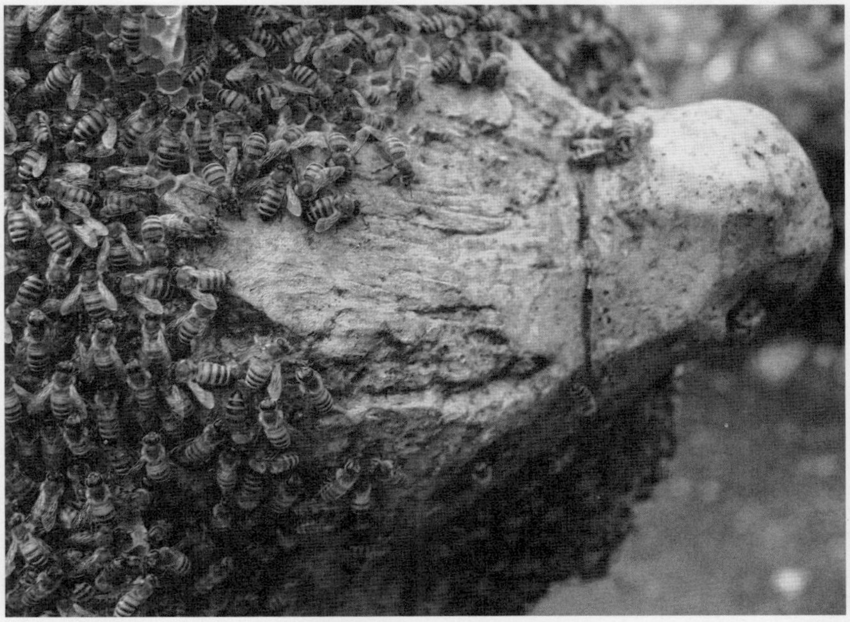

Pierre Huyghe *Liegender Frauenakt (Untilled 2011–2012)* (detail), 2012

Pierre Huyghe

These images depict four stages in the production process of Huyghe's sculpture. The original neo-classical bronze figure, created by Max Weber, an early twentieth-century Swiss sculptor, was cast in concrete on a steel armature. A heating unit has been placed inside the concrete cast and wired up so that the whole sculpture can be warmed to body temperature before the bees take up residence. Huyghe then installed a living beehive on the head, which grows throughout the duration of the exhibition. The sculpture was first presented at dOCUMENTA (13) as a part of a broader surrounding ecosystem in the composting area of Kassel's baroque park.

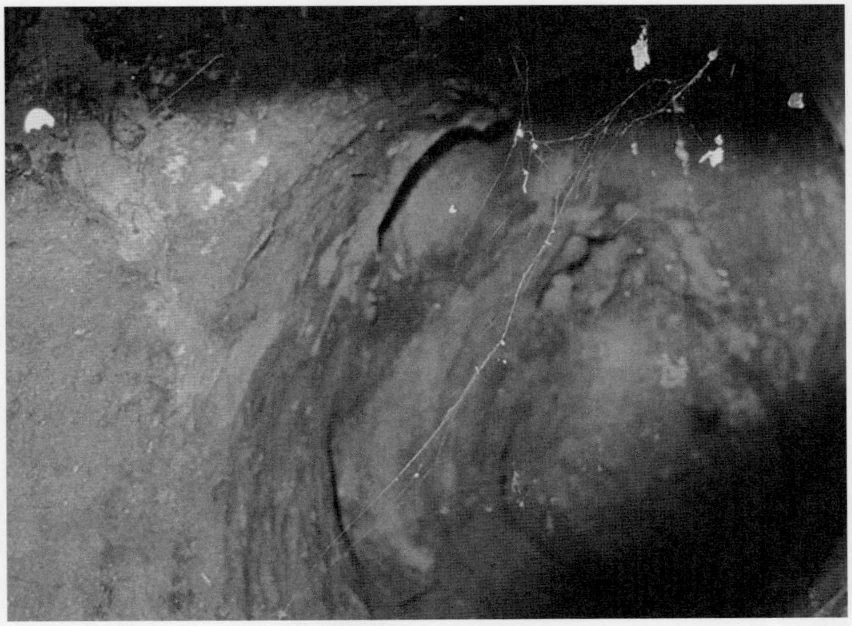

Pierre Huyghe Interior of the original bronze sculpture

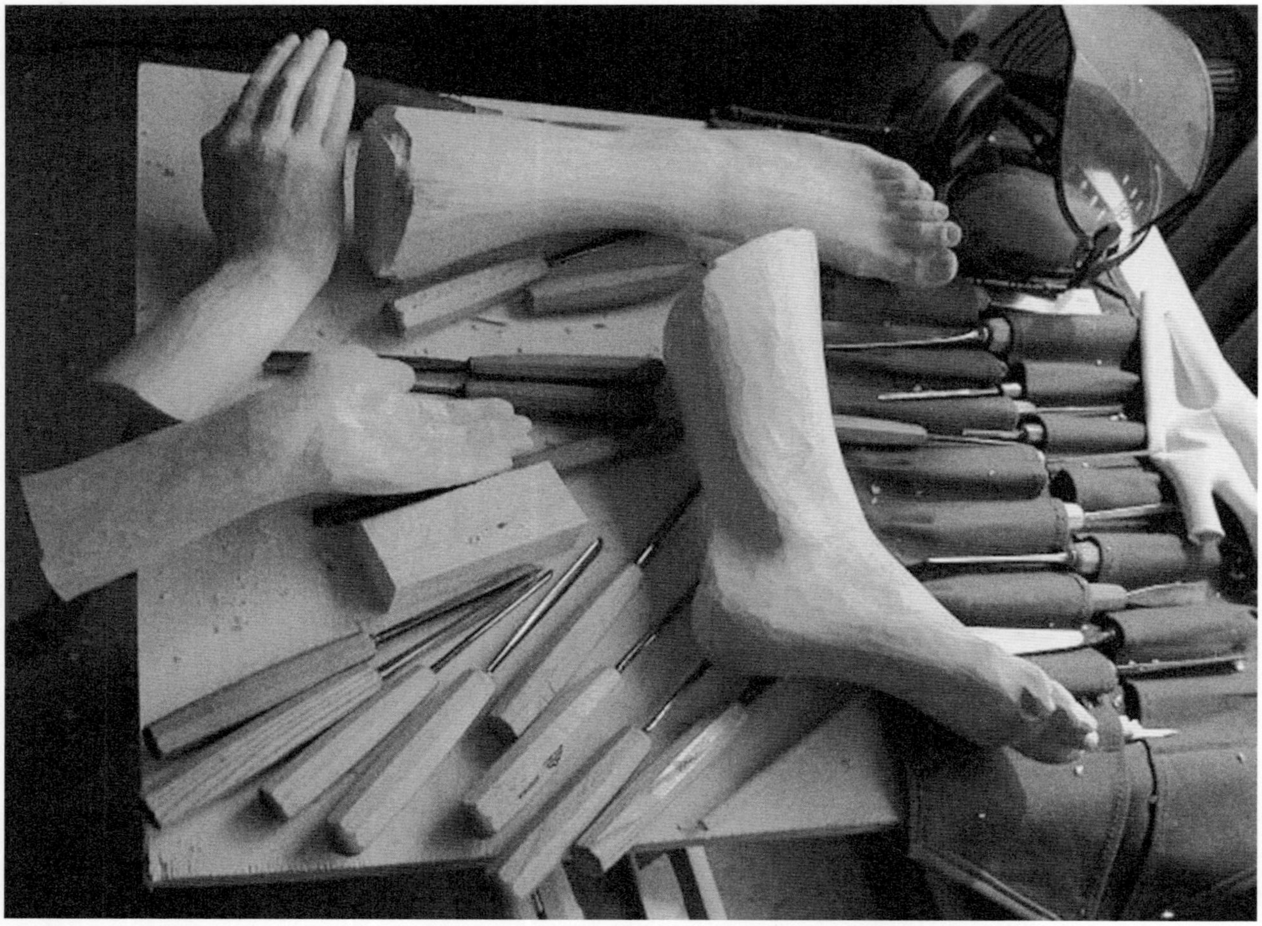

Paloma Varga Weisz Preparatory stages of
Fallende Frau, Doppelköpfig, 2004

Paloma Varga Weisz

The first step in the creation of *Fallende Frau, Doppelköpfig* was the casting from life of the artist's head, arms and legs in plaster. In Bavaria — where Varga Weisz trained as a woodcarver — the artist made use of traditional workshops that have mechanical 'shaper machines'. The plaster model is placed on one side of the machine and the wooden block on the other. By then tracing the plaster original, the machine shapes the limewood block with a drill-like tool that cuts away the wood. These wooden casts were then returned to the artist's studio for surface finishing, where the details could be newly interpreted.

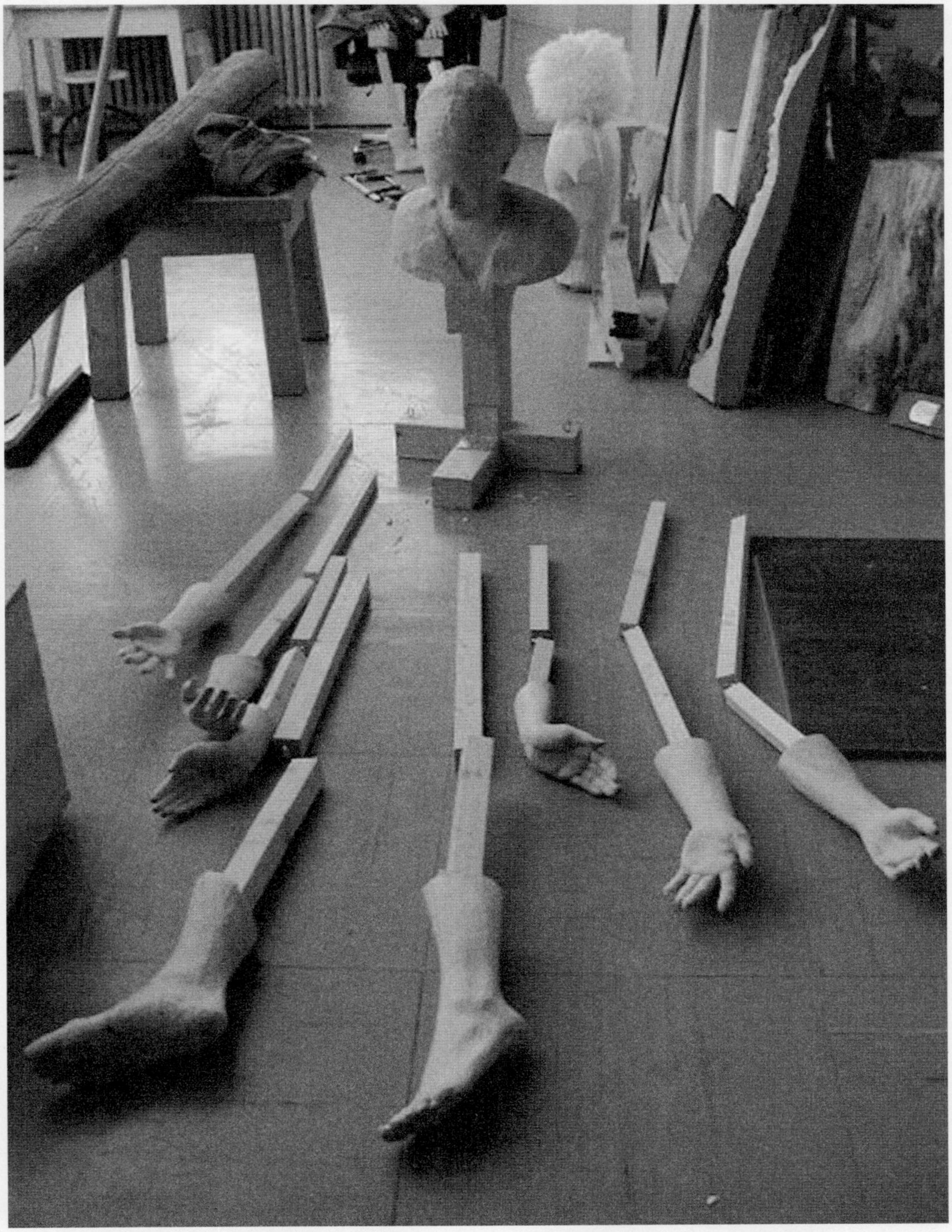

Paloma Varga Weisz Preparatory stages of
Fallende Frau, Doppelköpfig, 2004

John Miller

After developing the concept of the work in preparatory sketches, Miller sources second-hand shop window mannequins to use in his figurative sculpture and elaborates on them with his use of additional materials, clothing, make-up and accessories. In *Now We're Big Potatoes*, the ready-made figure is humorously de-idealised through the application of acrylic paint and a sticking plaster to its surfaces, and the embedding of the figure's right foot in a dung-coloured mound composed of Styrofoam, plaster, papier-mâché, modelling paste and acrylic.

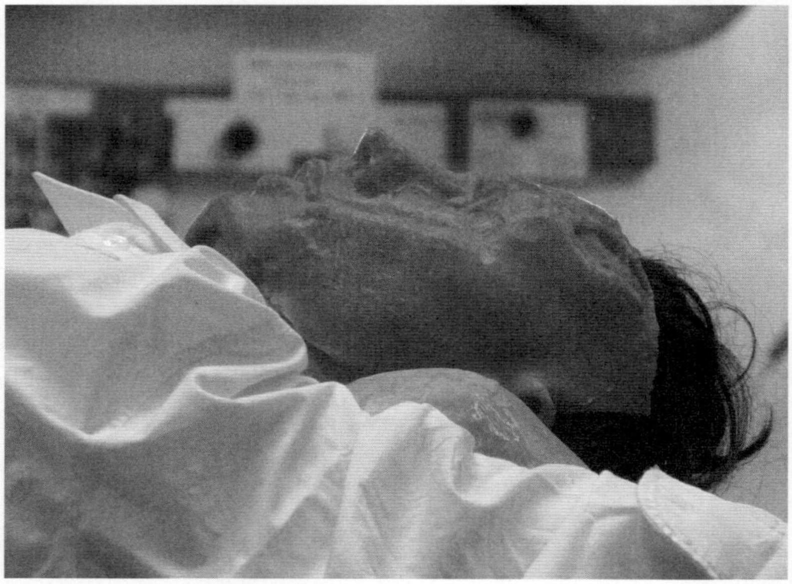

Andro Wekua Work in progress, *Sneakers 1*, 2008

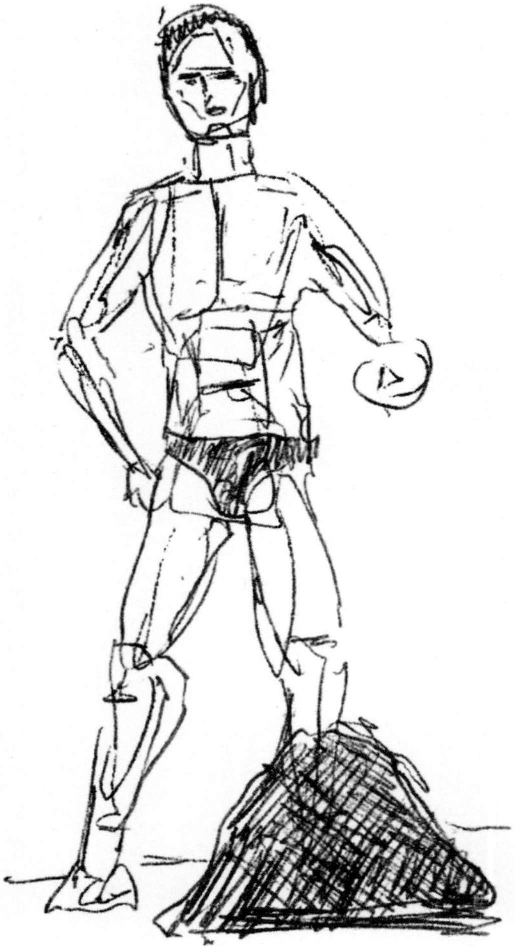

John Miller Preparatory sketch, *Now We're Big Potatoes*, 1992

Andro Wekua

Wekua casts live models in wax, producing sculptural work that disconcertingly appears simultaneously lifelike and unreal. In this work, a mass of artificial hair obscures the face and screens most of the front of the body, and the figure huddles on an Acrystal (a synthetic modelling material) board precariously balanced on a cast aluminium table base; on its back — where the fixing bolts are clearly visible — is a harlequin-like pattern, executed in coloured wax, while on its feet are the shoes referred to in the title, which are ceramic. The picture here shows the mask in being made, which in the final work is placed on the back of the bowed head.

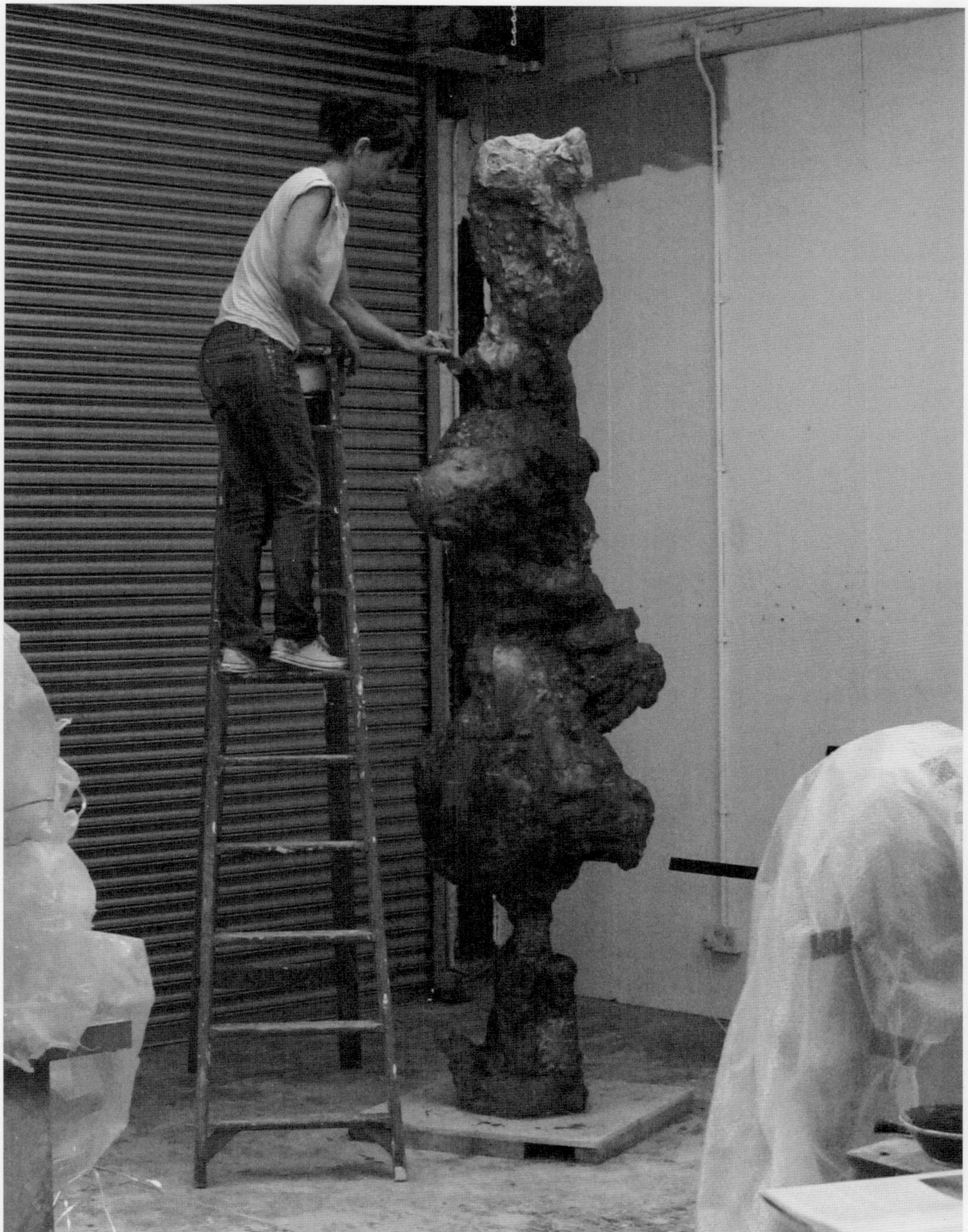

Rebecca Warren The artist at work on
The Main Feeling, 2009

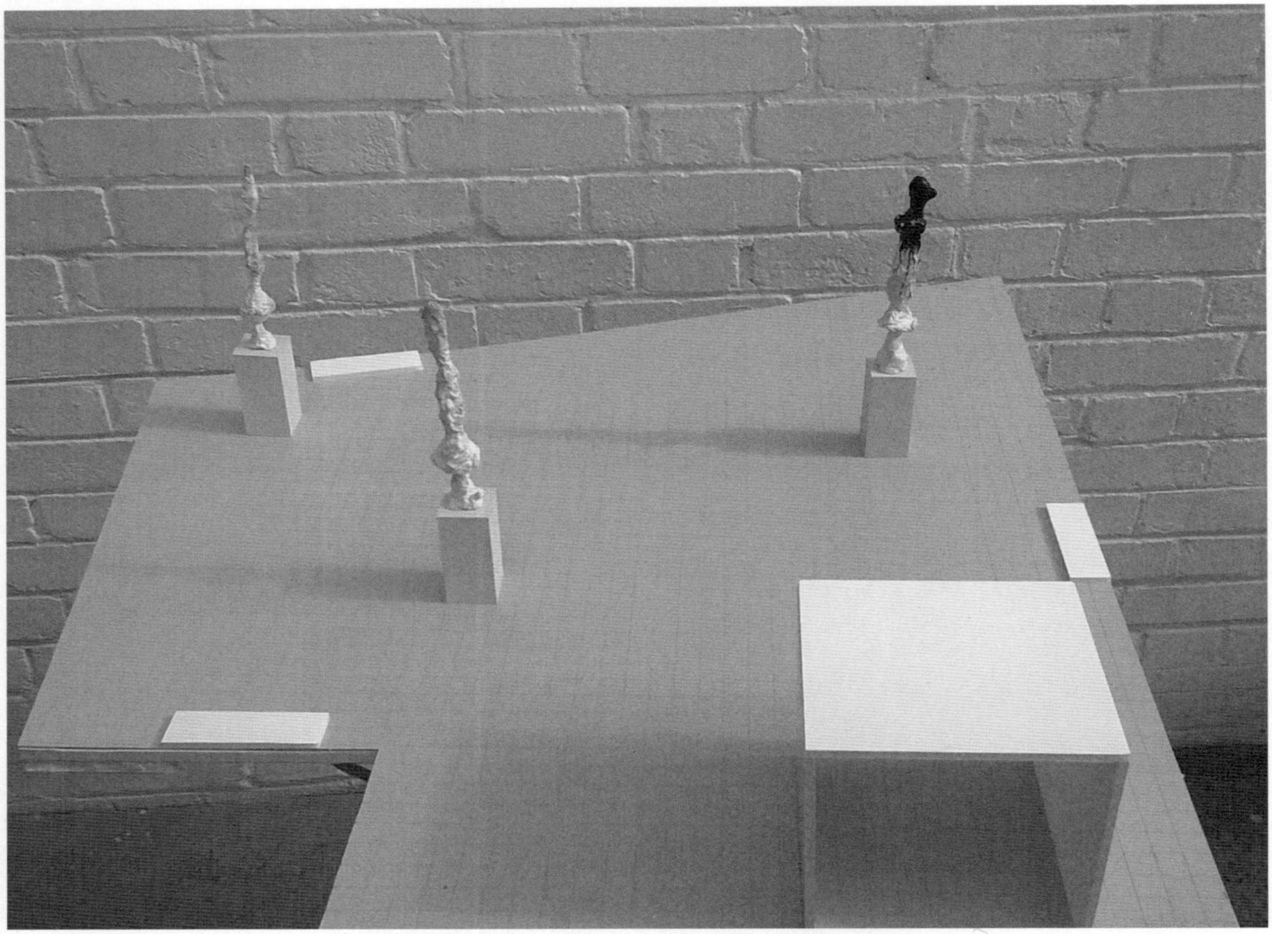

Rebecca Warren Scale model for the display of the sculptures *The Dane* (2011), *There is Another Way* (2011) and *Los Angeles* (2013), for their display on the Belvedere Terrace of the Hayward Gallery as part of *The Human Factor*, 2014

Rebecca Warren

Warren uses clay to make her life-size works, and roughly models the wet material in bulging and cinching forms, preserving, in the artist's words, the sense that they are 'alive and dynamic and fresh'. A contrasting practice, however, is to cast her clay works in bronze; as seen in *The Main Feeling* (2009), pictured on the previous page, the rigid surfaces of these structures deceptively mimic the soft pliant material that give them shape, and are further removed from traditional associations with the metal by the application of industrial paint in a range of pastel colours.

Cady Noland

Cady Noland's early work, produced during the late 1980s and early 1990s, probes the American psyche. Focusing on a national taste for violence, her sculptures, installations and silkscreened tableaux often feature firearms and incorporate found objects and materials such as flags, newspaper articles and advertisements. Their subjects are frequently people who have been pilloried in the press. Her sculpture *Bluewald* (1989) concerns the circumstances surrounding John F. Kennedy's death, a topic that continues to generate debate and speculation today.

On 24 November 1963, two days after the assassination of President Kennedy, America watched as Dallas nightclub owner Jack Ruby shot Lee Harvey Oswald — Kennedy's alleged killer — at point-blank range. The incident, witnessed by a hundred newsmen and the first murder ever broadcast live on television, immediately gave rise to suspicions of a conspiracy. A quarter of a century later, Cady Noland appropriated the image of Oswald from the Pulitzer Prize-winning photograph by Bob Jackson that had immortalised Ruby's act. Ignoring all the bystanders and focusing exclusively on the victim of the shooting and the instrument of his death, Noland cut out Oswald's half-length figure and blew it up to more than twice life-size. She then silkscreened it onto heavy-weight aluminium, punctured it with gigantic bullet holes, gagged it by stuffing an American flag where the mouth would have been, and set it up as if for target practice, or as a fairground attraction to be photographed with.

Shortly after *Bluewald* was made, Noland spoke about how her work had 'taken a pathological trend'. Mentioning her interest in 'how people treat other people like objects', she went on to say: 'I became interested in psychopaths, in particular, because they objectify people in order to manipulate them.' In this portrait of Oswald, she plays not only on our prurient, media-fuelled interest in violence, but also on the way the predatory tabloid press reduces its victims to 'photo-objects'. In other works, using the same cut-out 'standee' format, Noland turned her attention to the media's treatment of the terrorist Patty Hearst, a newspaper heiress who was kidnapped and then joined her kidnappers' cause.

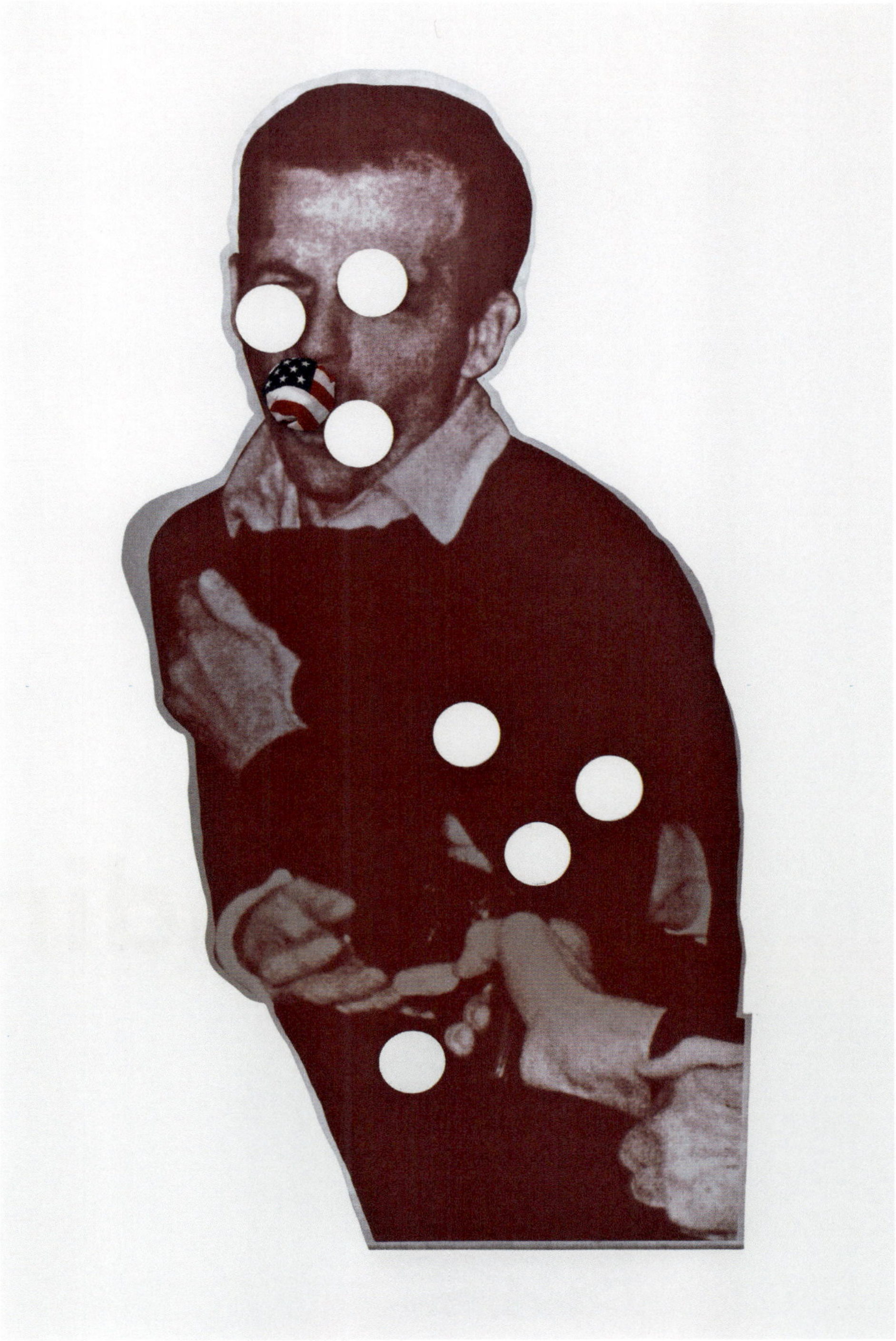

↑ ***Bluewald*, 1989**

Ugo Rondinone

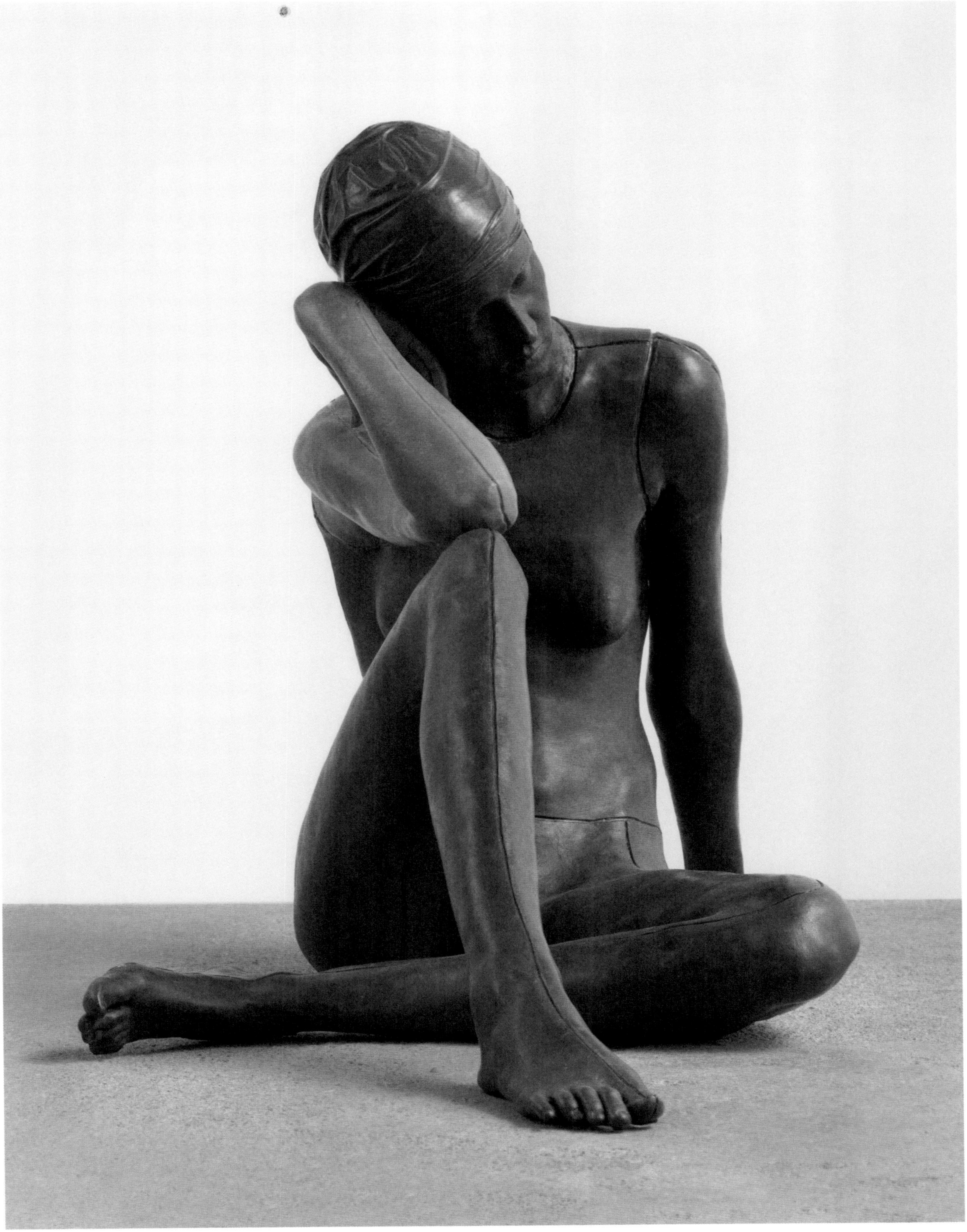

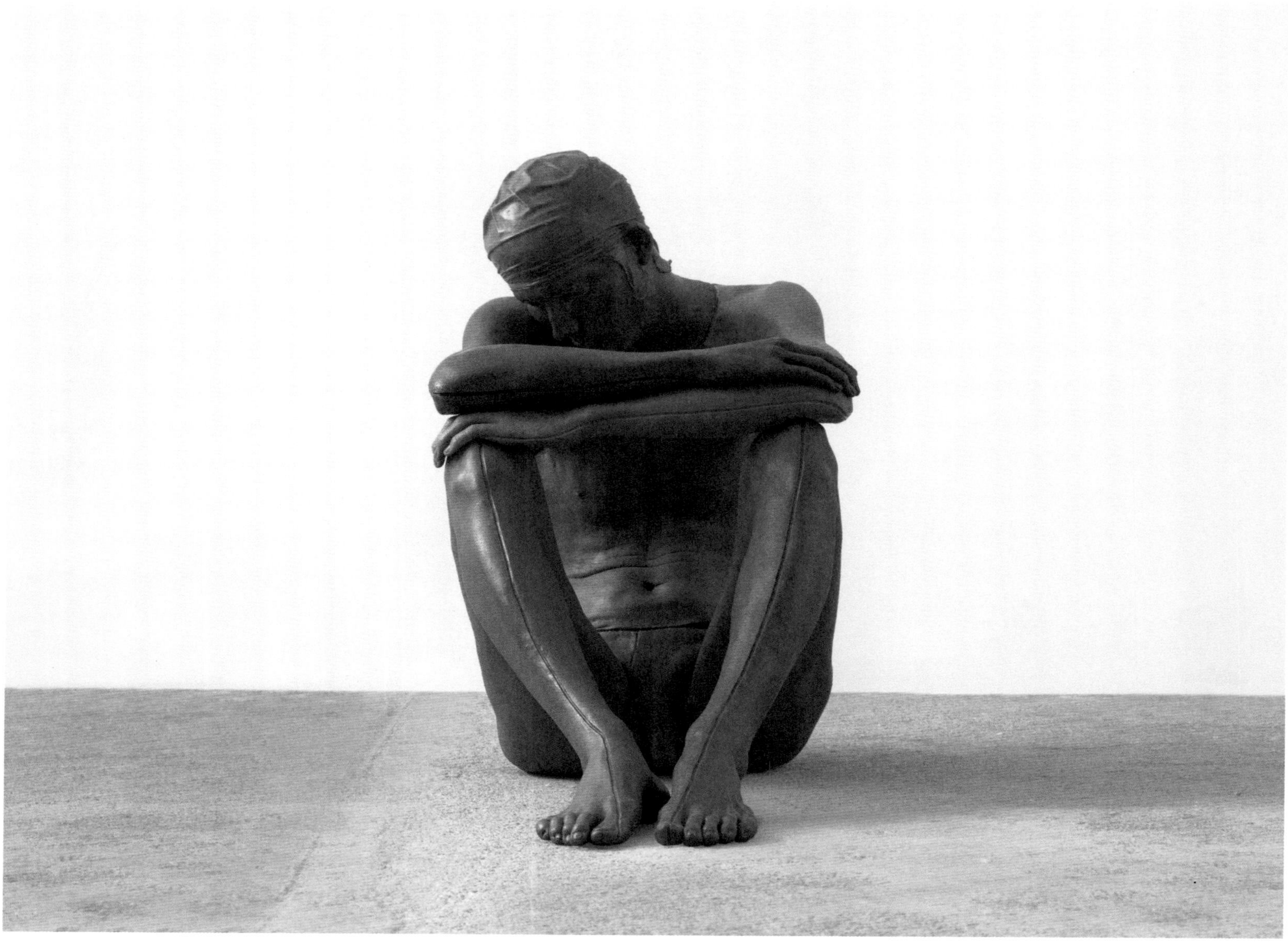

← *nude (xxxxxxxxxxxx)*, 2011

↑ *nude (xxxxxxxxxxxxxx)*, 2011

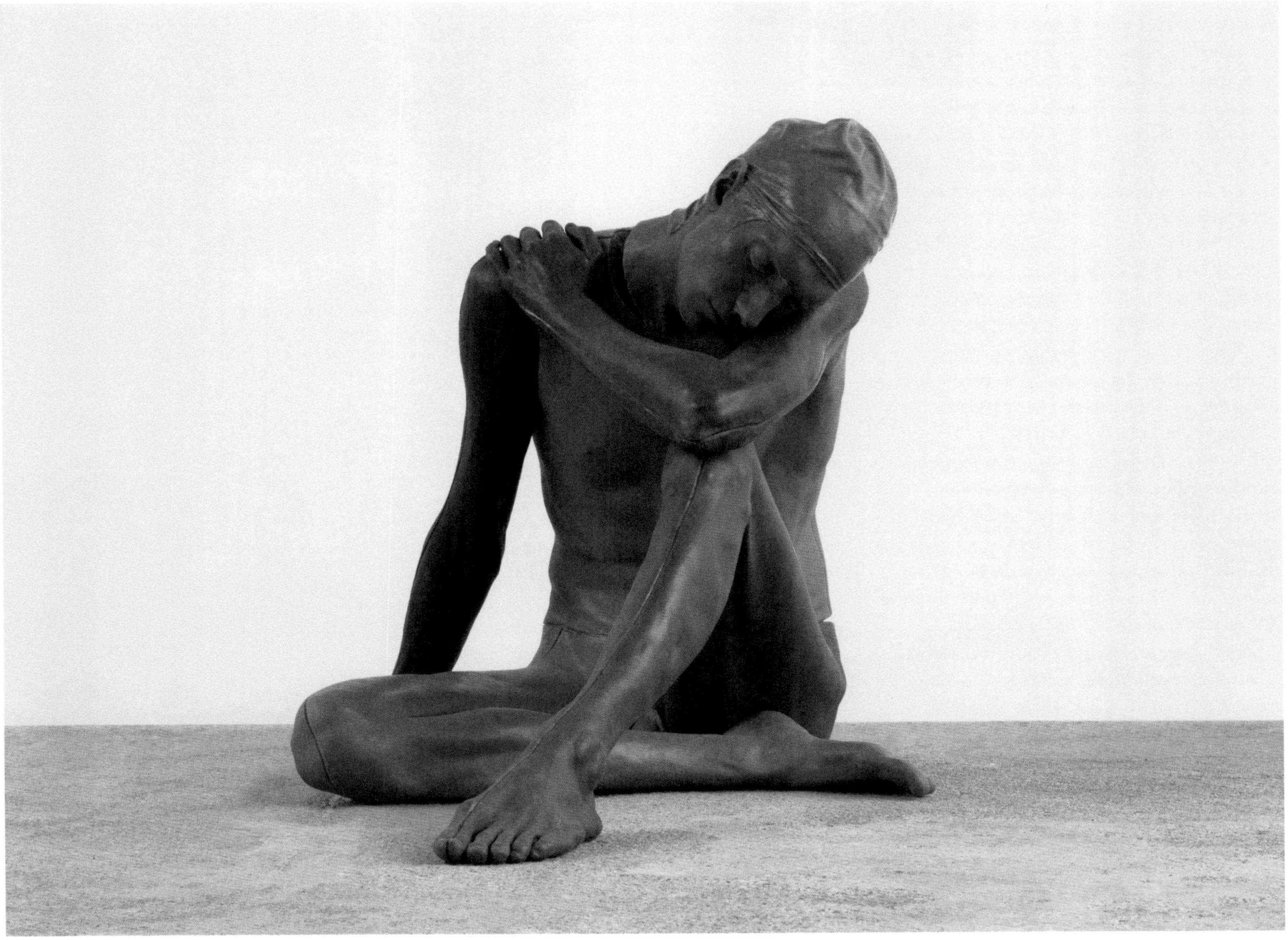

↑ ***nude (xxxxxxxxxxx)*, 2011**

With his 'nude' series (2010–11), Ugo Rondinone returned to an earlier preoccupation with the human figure. Previous investigations included castings of himself and a later series of moulded clowns (which stood in for effigies of the artist as entertainer and jester) in various slumped or reclining poses, evocative of sleep or dreaming. Here the life-size figures are cast in wax from the bodies of young dancers. Placed directly on the floor, the nudes are curled up, folded over or simply sitting, eyes closed, in a state of peaceful retreat and introversion; they might be at rest following a performance or rehearsal. The figures exude an atmosphere of silence and stillness, an essential element of Rondinone's practice. As he states, 'You will never see an expression in my work that indicates a movement or directness or an action. I understand art as essentially static; it creates its own artificial gravity system where the work states its own void or abyss.'

The exquisite detail of folds of skin and protruding veins, drooping hands and arched feet make Rondinone's figures appear strikingly lifelike and present. These sculptures hark back to an early modernist tradition of the nude; Rondinone has mentioned Aristide Maillol as an inspiration, citing his famous *La Méditerranée* (1905), whose restrained composition of interlocking triangles, smooth curves and meditative posture created a sensation in the 1905 *Salon d'Automne* in Paris, being praised for its 'silence'.

At the same time, these figures subtly disrupt a 'classical' reading. They are placed directly on the ground, having climbed down from the plinth. The use of wax for their final form (a material ordinarily used as a temporary stage in the casting of metal sculptures) only emphasises the sense of transience and vulnerability. The inner metal armature holding them together, visible in various joints, gives them the appearance of mannequins or puppets and introduces a distancing sense of the body as a dismembered entity.

The figures are made in a translucent wax mixed with 14 different earth pigments to create the muted grey, brown and russet hues, associating them with the organic and the telluric. For Rondinone, the 'nudes' are 'a crossing of nature and the human figure'. 'They are exposed and vulnerable because they are nude; but at the same time they are protected because the colour and the material act like a camouflage', or a second skin, adding to the overall effect of 'assemblage' and fragmentation.

The interplay and careful placement of the figures in space form a choreography that involves the viewer. Rondinone explains that he views the figures as a 'frozen performance and the floor as a stage' with the visitor an integral part; perhaps as a body in motion, the opposing binary to the slowness and stillness of the contemplative figures.

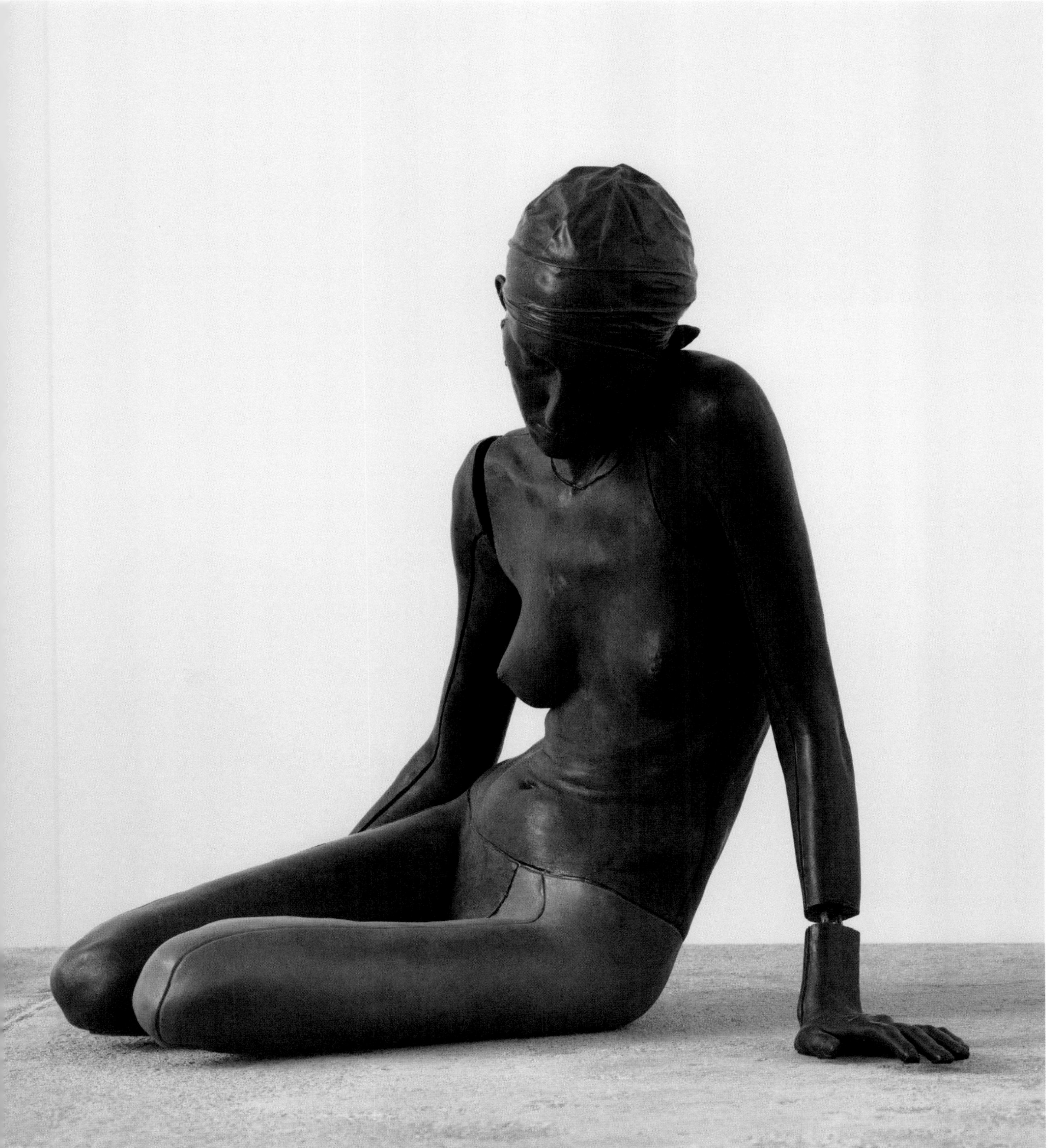

↑ *nude (xxxxxxxxxxxxx)*, 2011

→ **Exhibition view, M Museum, Leuven,**
***thank you silence*, 2013**

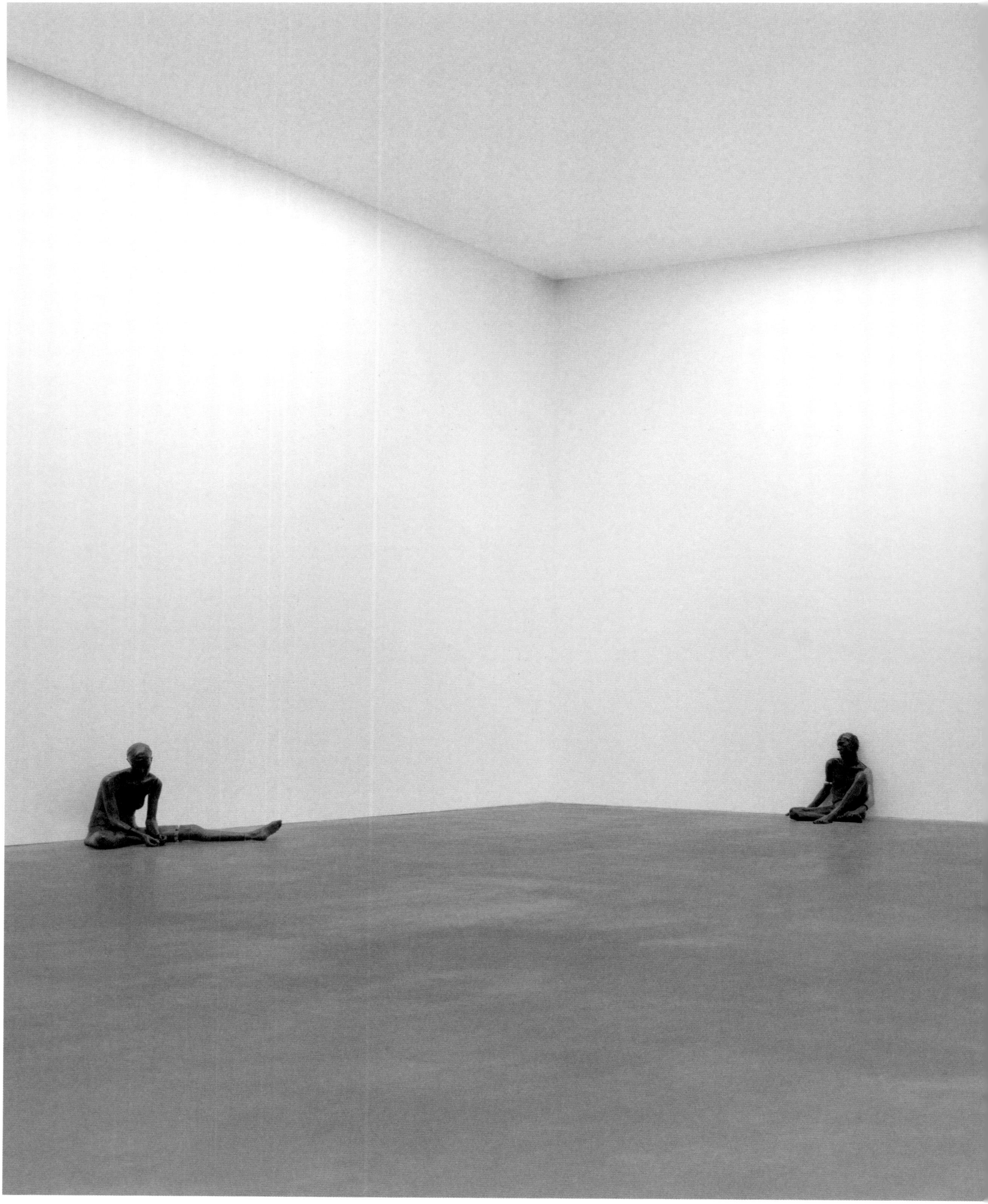

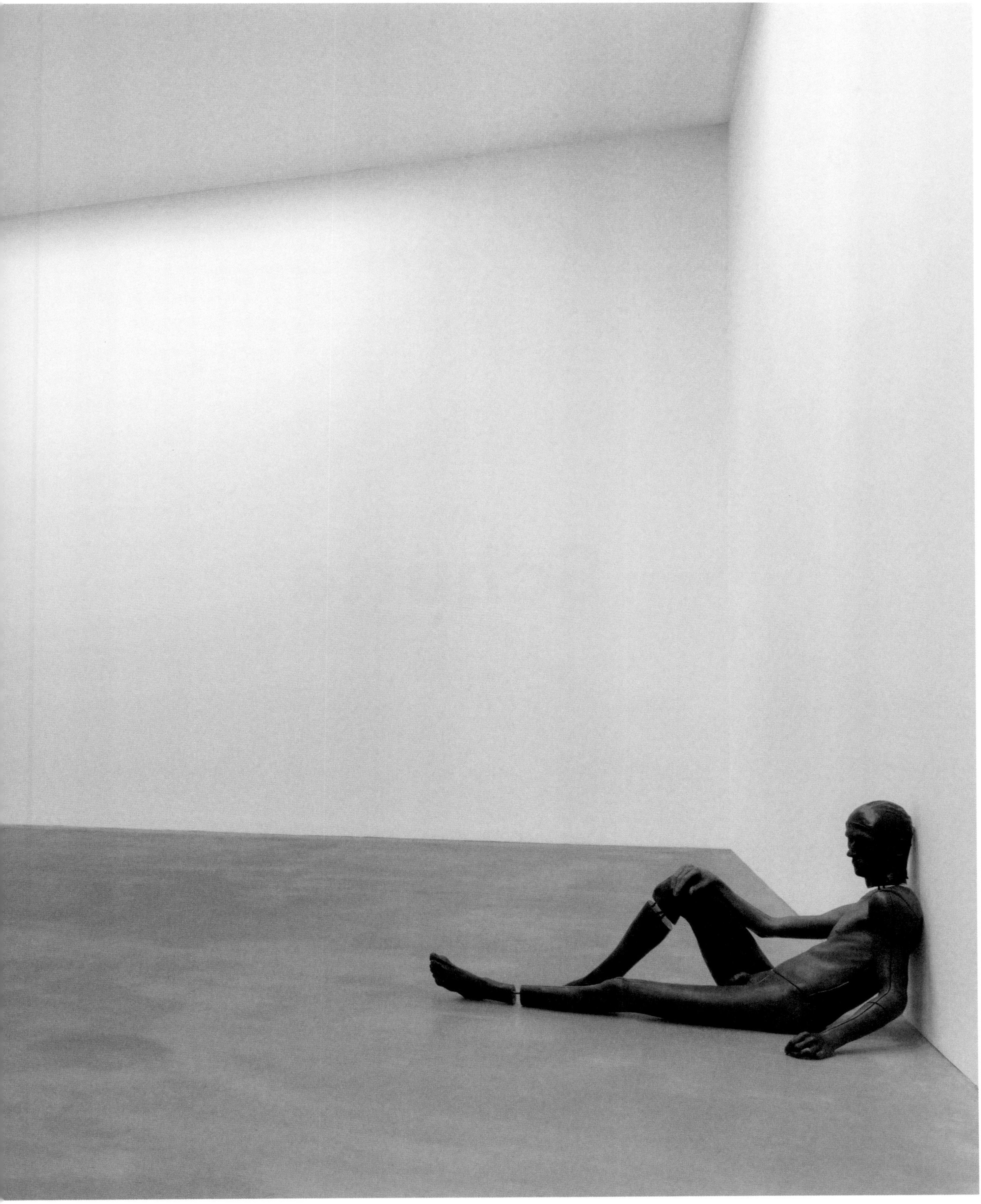

Thomas Schütte

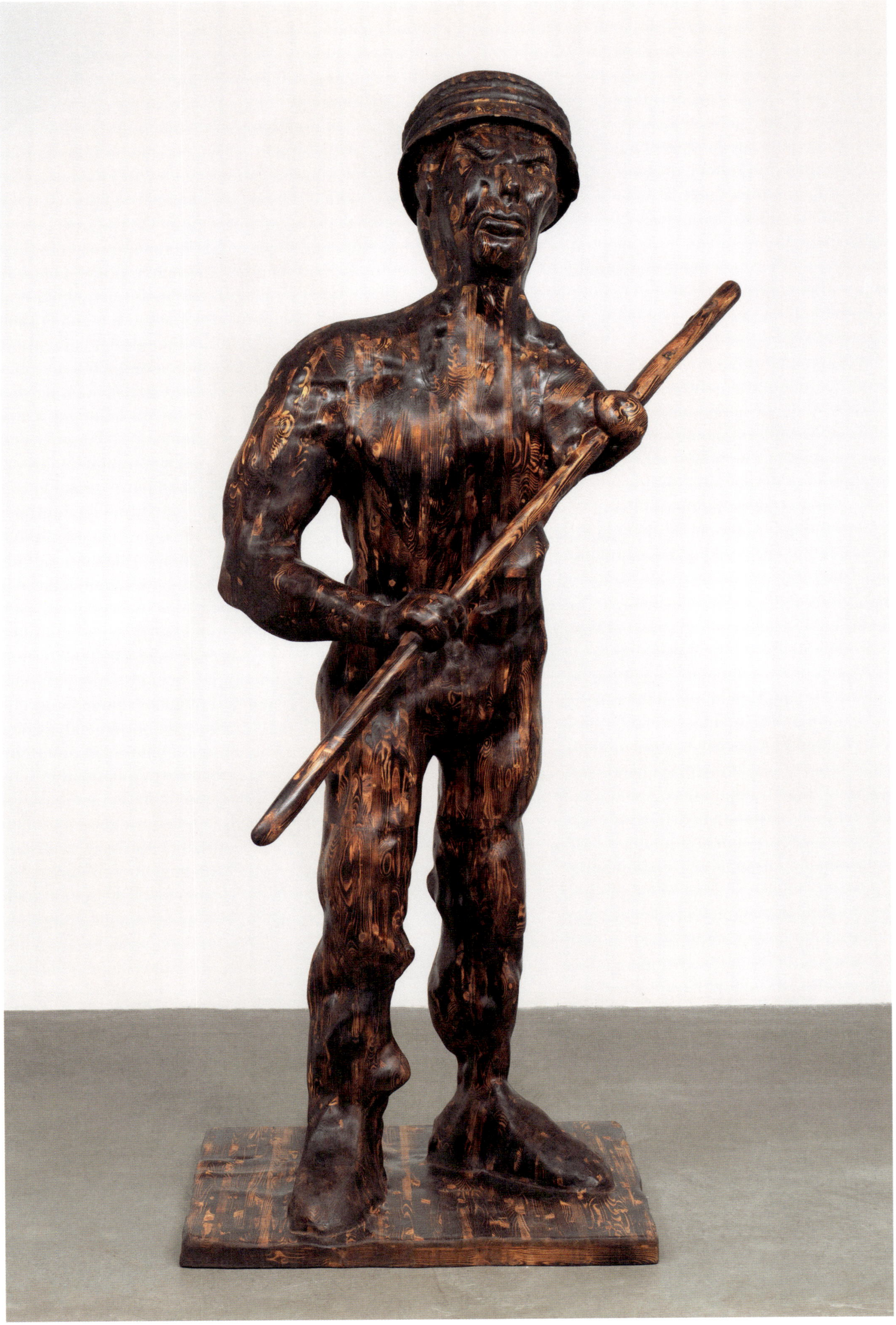

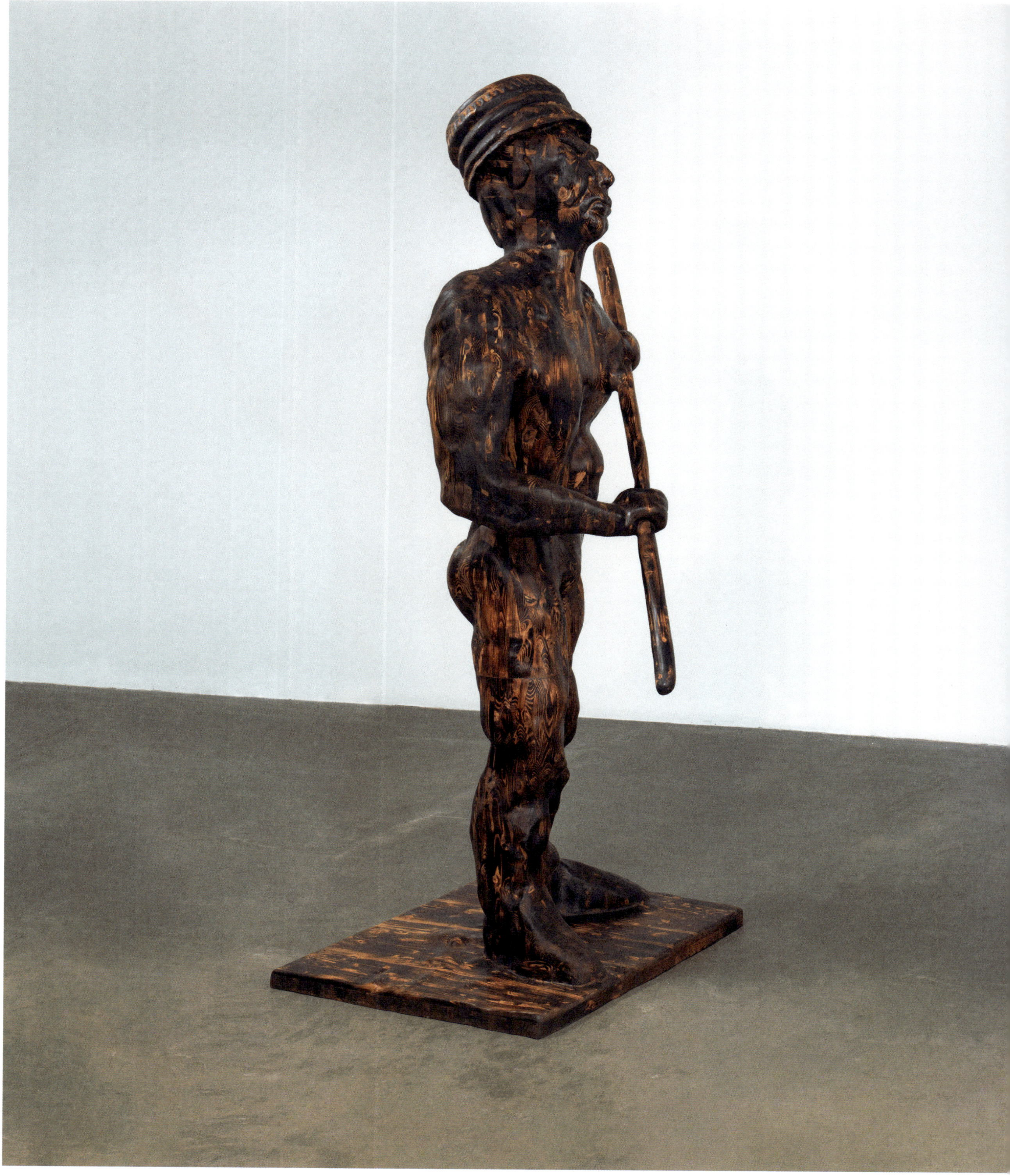

← *Krieger* (detail), 2012

↑ *Krieger*, 2012

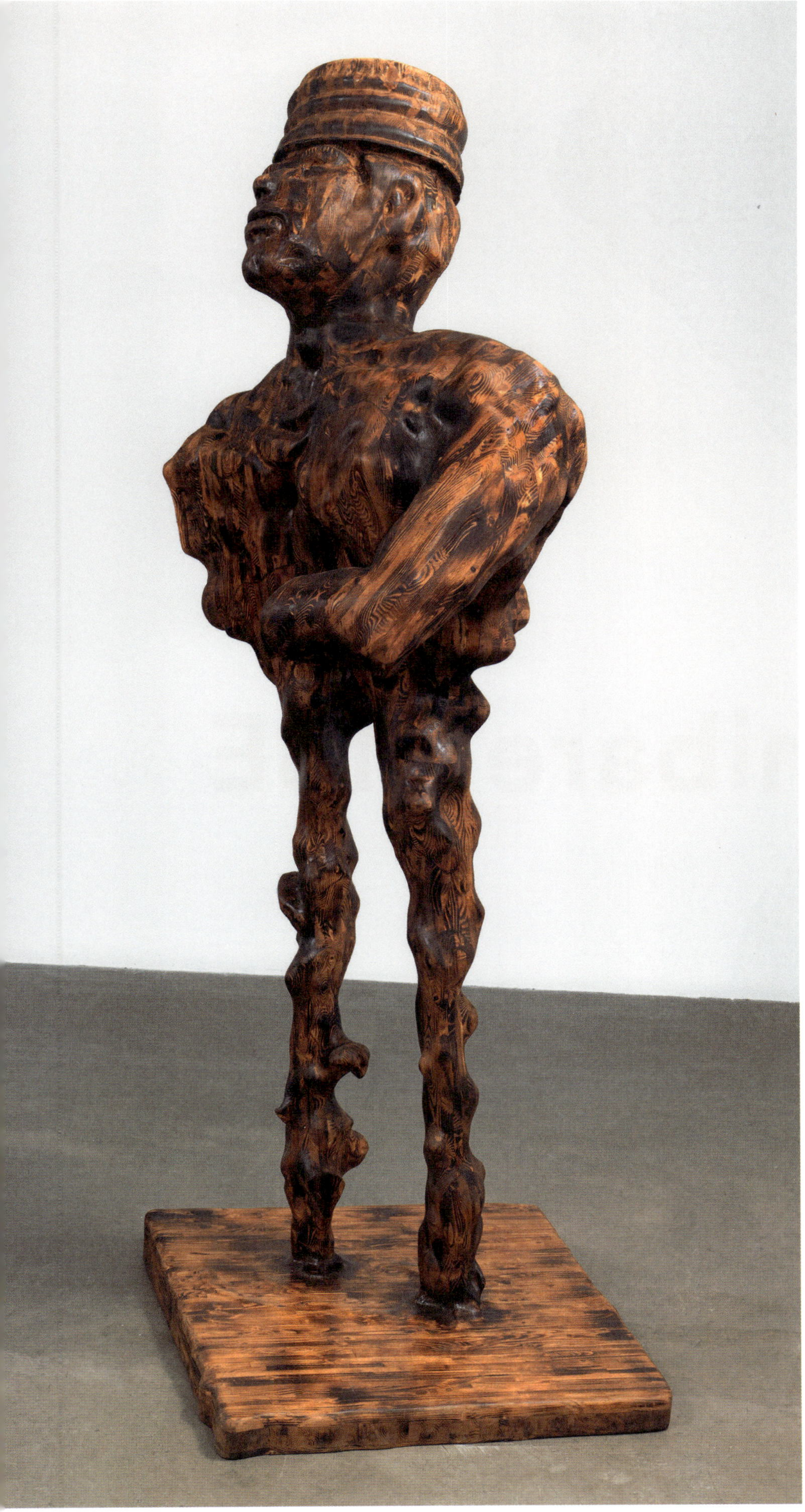

At around three metres high, Thomas Schütte's *Krieger* (2012) are very much larger than life. But though these gigantic warriors tower above humans, they themselves were originally created as tiny models — the clue to their original size lies in their helmets, which began life as screw-top bottle caps. Scanned, scaled-up and fabricated from laminated wood which has been stained and oiled, the figures become monstrous monuments; super-sized anti-heroes who are at once terrible and absurd.

The human figure has always been central to Schütte's sculptural work, and the problem of how to present humanity is a constant concern; as Schütte has said, 'I live in Germany and somehow have to face up to that fact'. The ancestry of *Krieger* dates back to the early 1990s, soon after the reunification of Germany and the end of the Cold War, when Communist-era monuments began to be toppled throughout Eastern Europe during a period in which Germany was experiencing a time of political uncertainty. At that time, Schütte started to make groups of small-scale figures as propositions for ironic war memorials. These personages were modelled mainly from clay and involved what Schütte calls 'thinking with one's thumbs'. (In their final, amplified form, the warriors are 80% cut by computers; Schütte only does the details.)

Enlarged to Brobdingnagian proportions, Schütte's *Krieger* lose any resemblance that they may have had to toy soldiers and become lumbering bogeymen instead. By choosing to recreate them in wood, rather than in metal, Schütte gives them an organic presence, redolent of fairytales and epic myths. They are monuments to aggrandisement, and to an idiotically staunch refusal to give up. Though these amputees are horribly disfigured and one of them is literally disarmed, they continue to stand their ground against all odds. Bringing to mind images of war by Otto Dix and George Grosz, these warriors are neither heroes nor victims, but evocations of intractable aggressiveness. However, as Schütte has said about other works: 'so far as meanings are concerned, I would rather let these creatures live and tell their own stories.'

Yinka Shonibare MBE

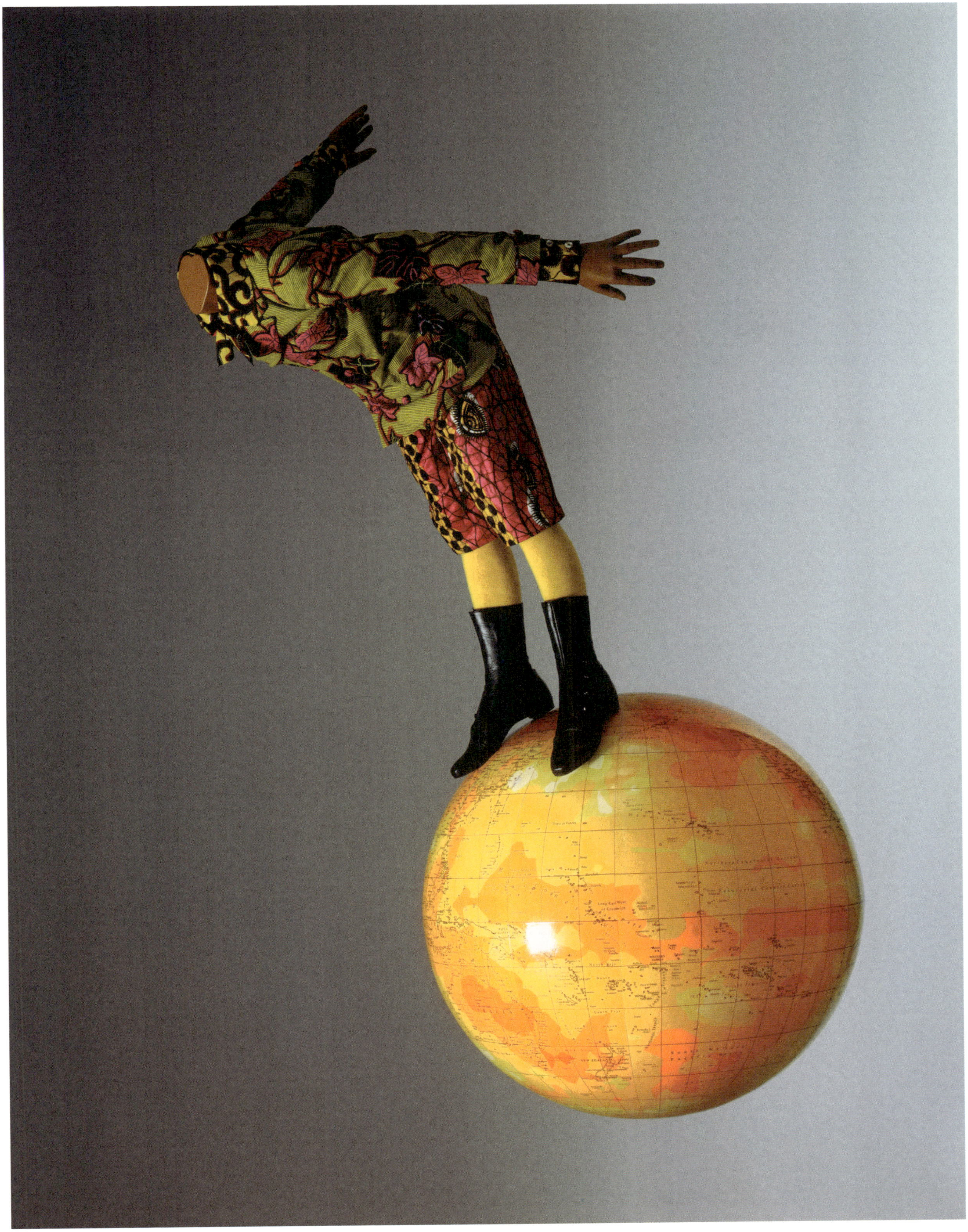

Masquerade, with all the ambiguity, subversion and paradox that it implies, lies at the heart of Yinka Shonibare MBE's art. His flamboyantly costumed mannequins challenge assumptions and stereotypes and raise questions about status, identity, power and governance. Shonibare describes himself as a 'postcolonial hybrid' and says that what he does is to 'create a kind of mongrel'. The coffee-coloured figures evade racial identity, and lack personal identities because they have lost their heads. (This motif began as a joke about the French Revolution and the guillotining of the aristocracy, and is an allusion to inherent mindlessness in the world today.) In a further act of 'mongrelisation', their Victorian-era frocks and suits are fashioned from 'African' textiles. As Shonibare explains, 'the fabric has a complicated history in its trade routes: it was originally designed as an Indonesian fabric, produced by the Dutch, and the British sold it into the African market. It's a perfect metaphor for multi-layered identities.'

As well as referring to history and, above all, being a critique of imperialism, Shonibare's sculptures often pay homage to other works of art. Even without a head, *Girl Ballerina* (2007) is instantly recognisable as Degas's *Little Dancer Aged Fourteen* (1880–81, cast c. 1922). Yet, under Shonibare's influence, she has become a different person; someone who might be thinking about taking up another profession, starting a revolution, or murdering the stage-door Johnnies who preyed on young dancers at the Paris Opera. Larger than Degas' sculpture, this life-size ballerina stands with a heavy handgun behind her back, and her finger is on the trigger.

With *Boy on Globe* (2008), Shonibare turns his attention to the impact and effects of climate change. Suspended in space, the boy struggles to keep his balance on a red-hot planet Earth. All the colours of the traditional political globe are gone, replaced by a red, orange and yellow heat map registering the effects of global warming. The world this child will inherit is already changed beyond recognition by the ecological legacy of global consumption and excess.

← ***Boy on Globe*, 2008**

→ ***Girl Ballerina*, 2007**

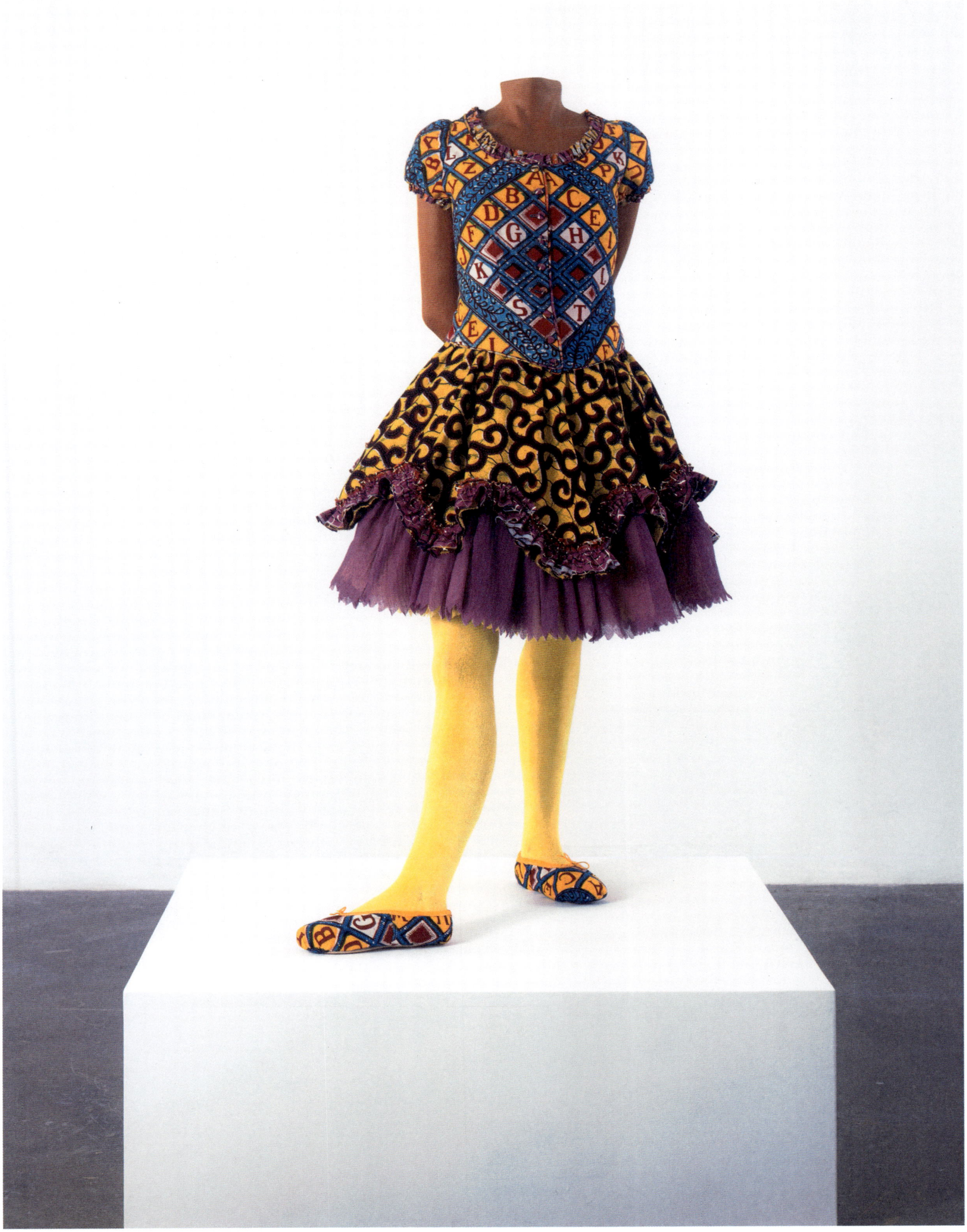

→ ***Girl Ballerina*** **(detail), 2007**

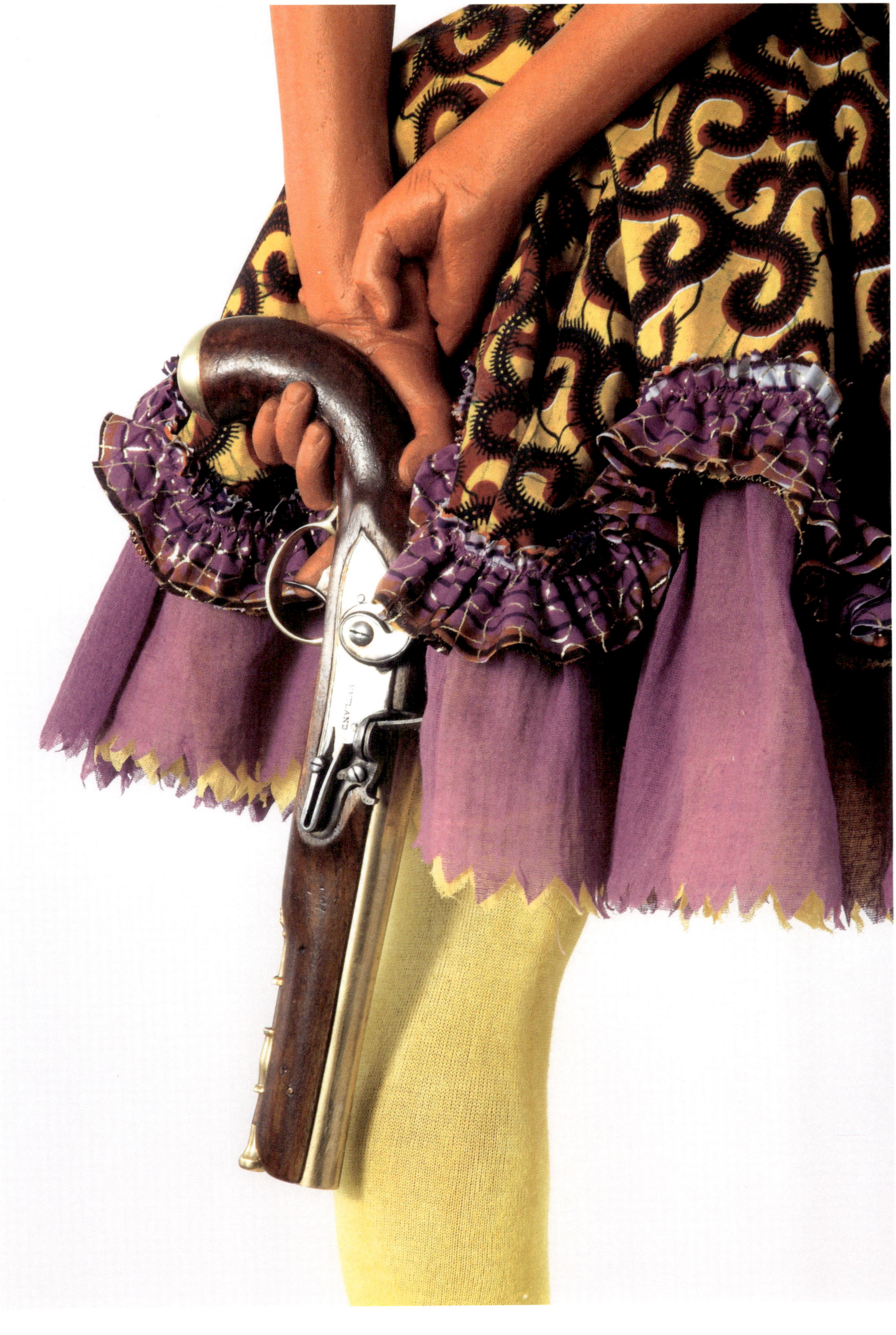

Paloma Varga Weisz

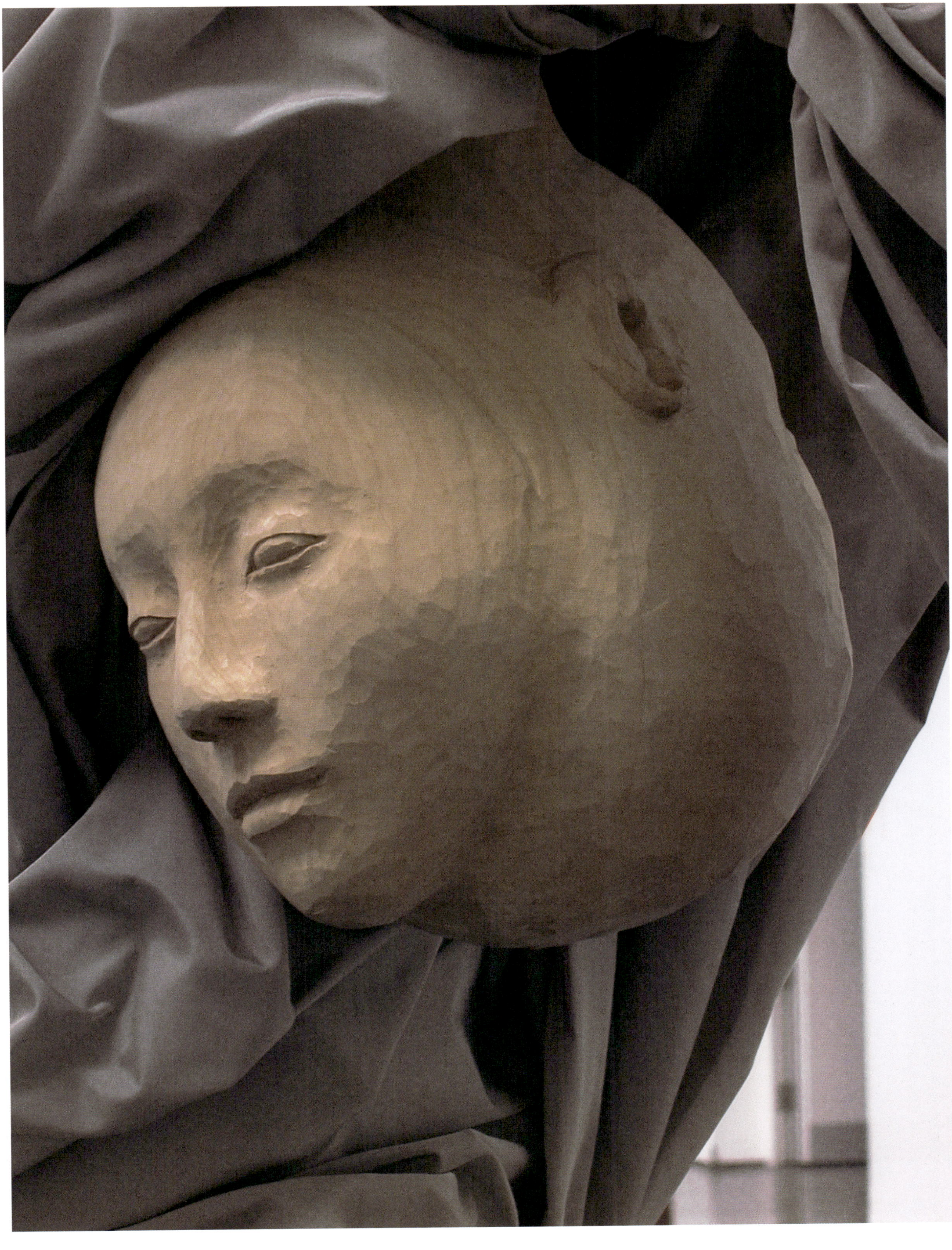

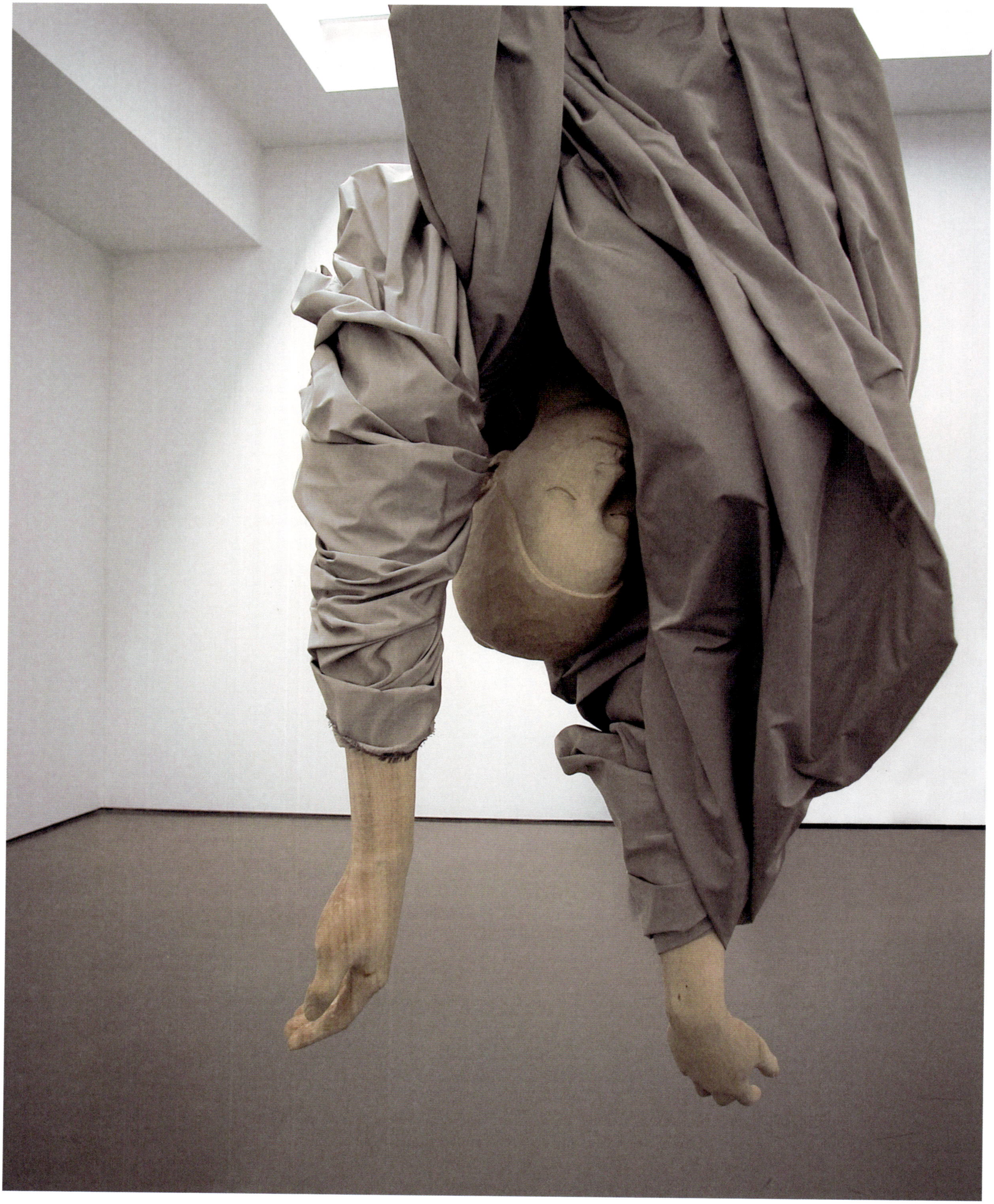

← *Fallende Frau, Doppelköpfig* (detail), 2004

↑ *Fallende Frau, Doppelköpfig* (detail), 2004

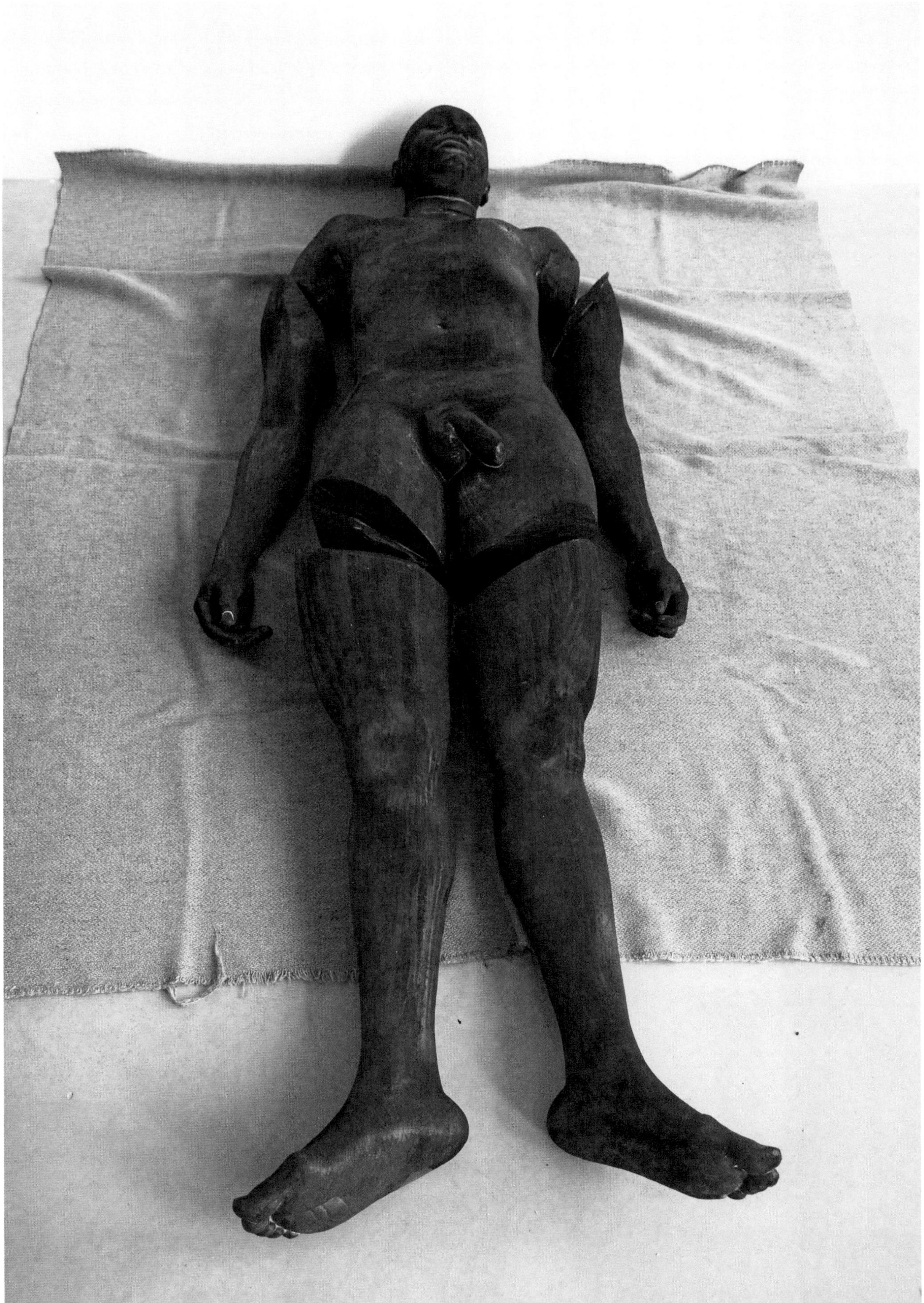

↑ *Lying Man*, 2014

Trained as a woodcarver as well as a fine artist, Paloma Varga Weisz creates handcrafted figures that draw on a rich repository of personal and collective motifs. In her hands the human form undergoes compelling and often enigmatic transformations, as she weaves together myriad elements from past art and craft iconographies and contemporary culture.

In *Fallende Frau, Doppelköpfig* (Falling Woman, Double-Headed) (2004), a life-size wooden female figure (made initially from plaster casts of the artist's body), swathed in a tangle of austere grey fabric, appears to be dramatically suspended head-first. Only her finely carved hands, face and feet are visible beneath the rich folds of fabric, which both conceal and define the body. The resulting image suggests simultaneously the movement of a falling or diving figure and the stillness of controlled suspension, but its meaning remains unresolved, evoking disparate motifs, from medieval executions to fallen angels. This ambivalence is reinforced by the figure's two-faced head — a flipped Janus with one face upright, eyes half open and peaceful, and the other upside down, eyes closed, perhaps in death. The figure does not yield unequivocal meaning; instead it suggests conflicting readings, refusing to settle for one over another. As Marcus Steinweg has put it: 'Perhaps Paloma Varga Weisz is inventing a new, unknown body [...] an acrobatic body of constant turning away from the self, a body that stages its presence as a kind of essential instability.'

In Varga Weisz's *Lying Man* (2014), a dismembered male nude, carved from burnt and blackened wood, is laid out on a blanket on the floor. As with *Fallende Frau, Doppelköpfig*, *Lying Man* was created using a full-body cast from a real person, which was then replicated in limewood, using a mechanical wood-copying lathe. But rather than uniting the individual body parts, which are separated in the process of releasing the subject from the cast, Varga Weisz has chosen to keep them slightly apart, as if hacked or butchered by a machete. She also submitted the severed head, body and limbs to a blowtorch in order to obtain the exact density and tone of the model's skin colour. Commenting on this recently completed work, Varga Weisz reflects: 'as I get more distance, I feel that it's more about a destructed soul than about a dissected body.'

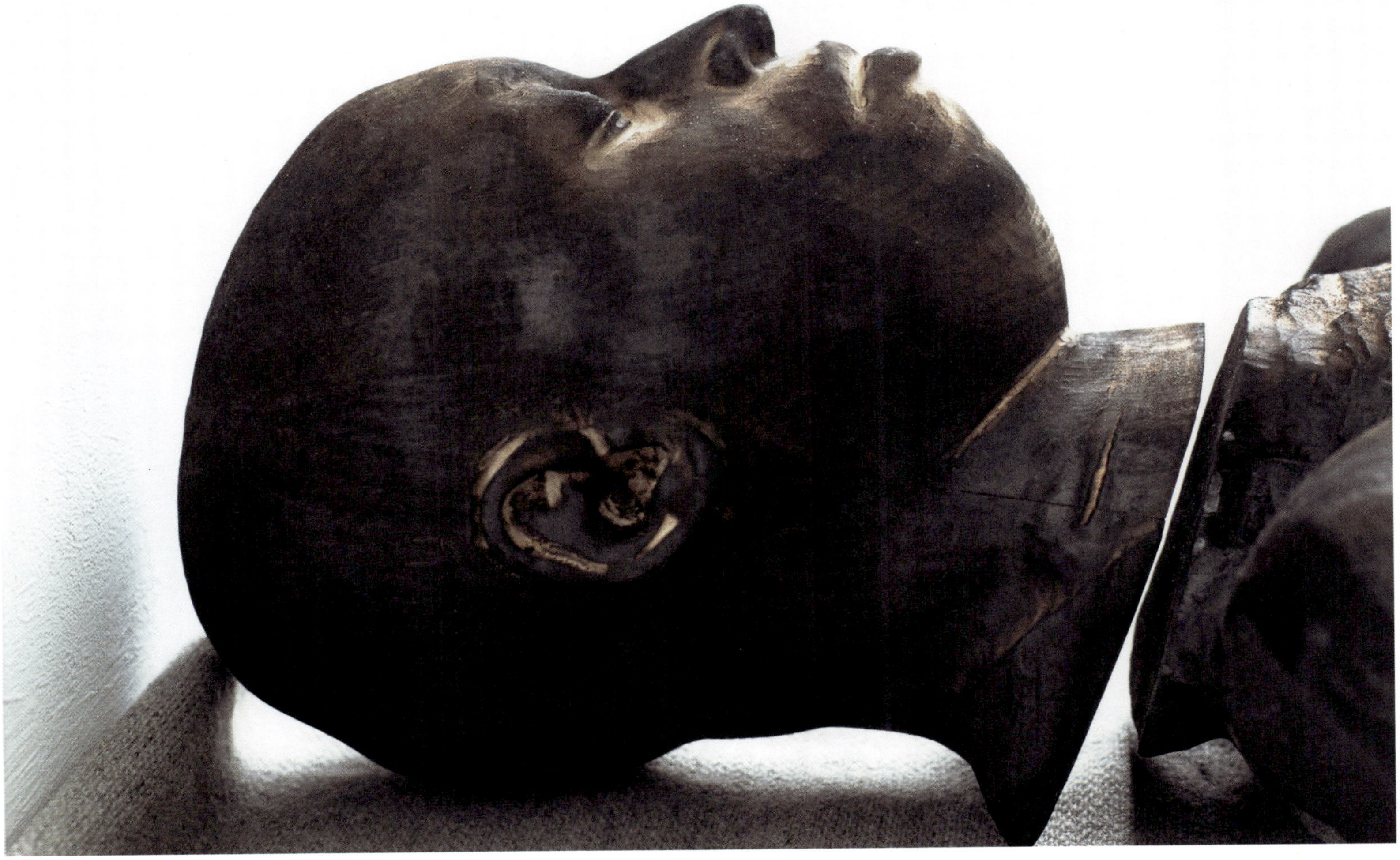

↑ *Lying Man* (detail), 2014

Mark Wallinger

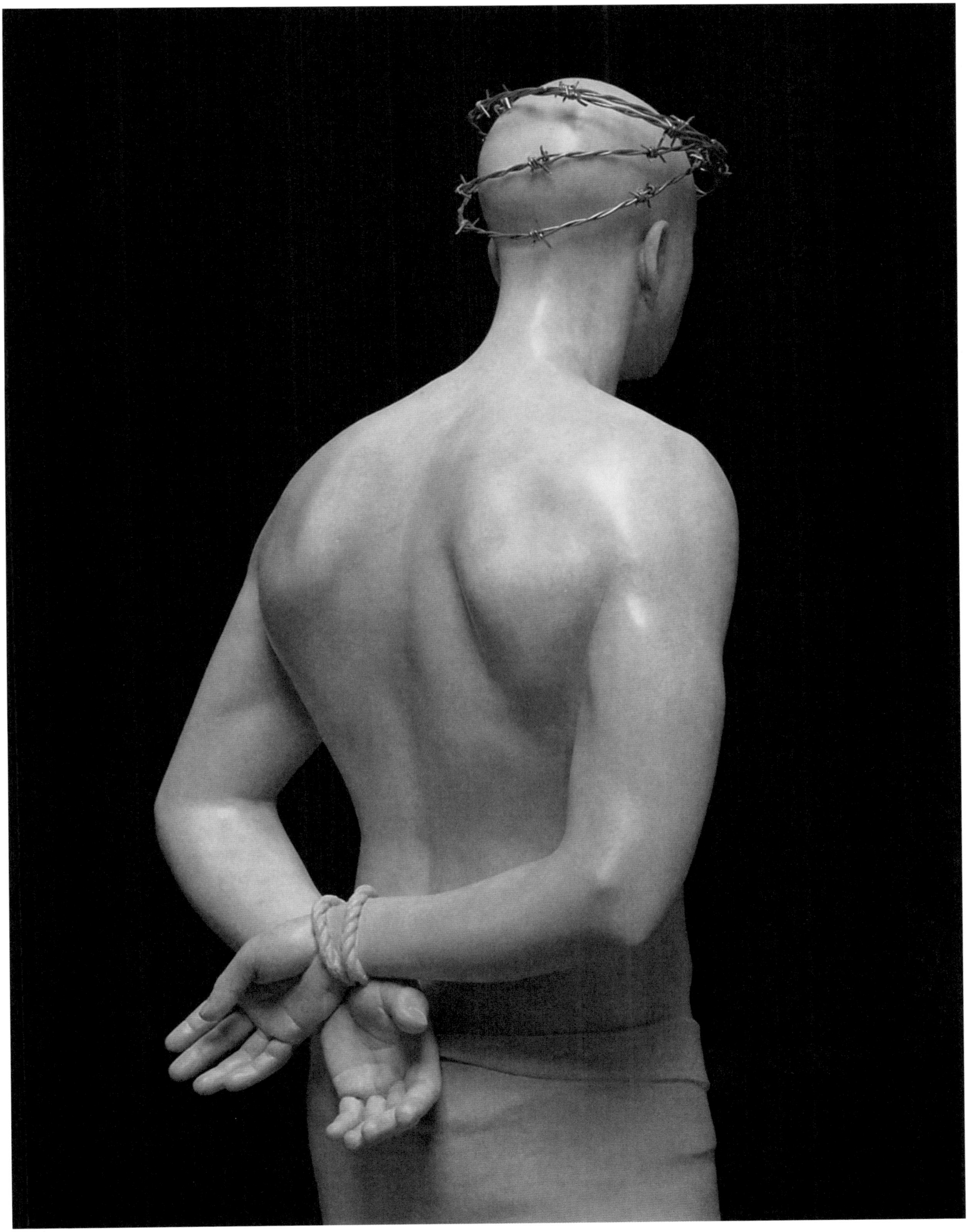

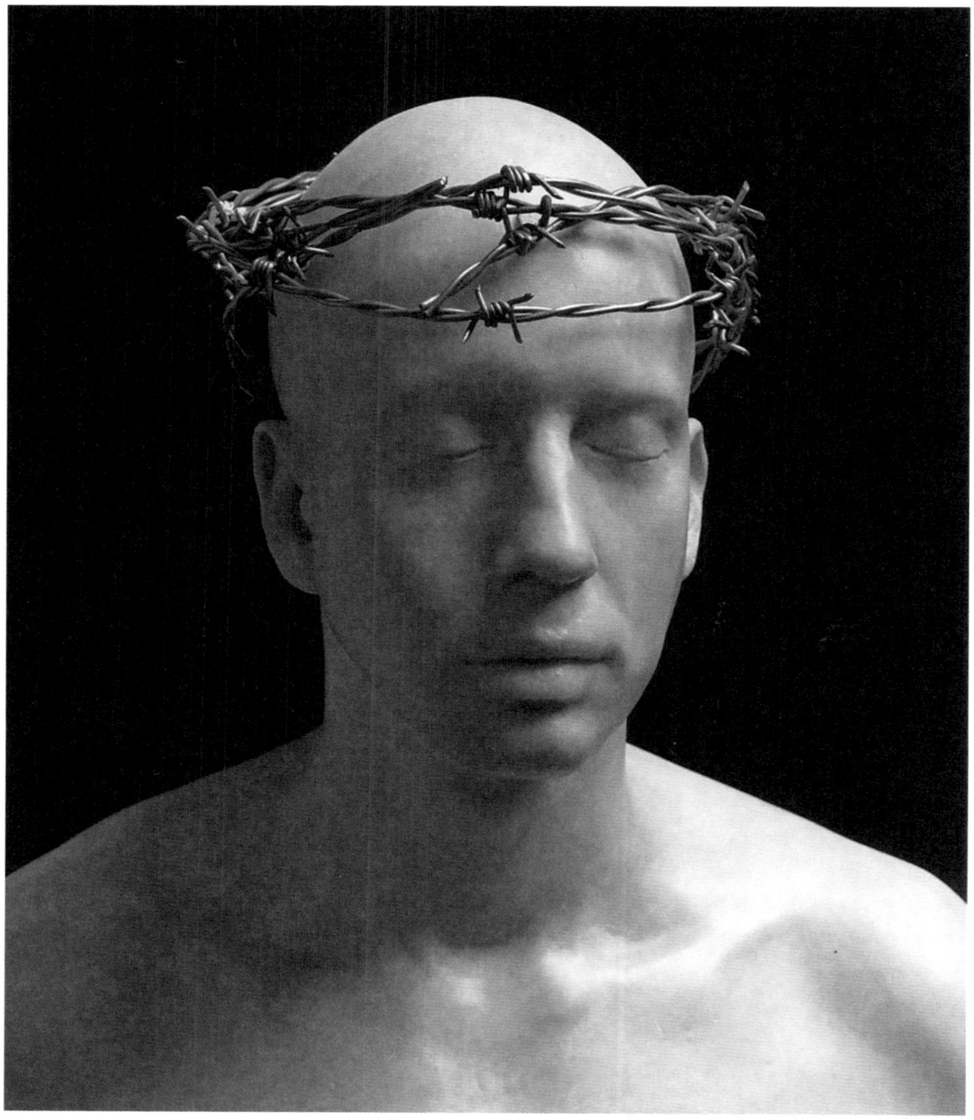

In choosing Jesus as his subject, Wallinger was addressing a topic fraught with contention and squeamishness. The government's plans for the Millennium ignored the fact that the date they were celebrating so extravagantly was the anniversary of two thousand years of Christianity. Wallinger, who is agnostic, therefore decided to present Christ to the people, in a place famous as a site of protest as well as revelry and which had, in the past, been the site of public hangings. Recent acts of genocide in Bosnia, where a person's religion and ethnicity was a matter of life and death, were also very much in his mind.

'Ecce homo' — 'Behold the man' — were the words with which Pontius Pilate brought Jesus, a political prisoner, before a lynch mob. In Wallinger's words, 'This figure aims to work as a spiritual reminder of our responsibilities as citizens. Democracy is about the rights of minorities to have free expression, not the majority to browbeat and marginalise.' Wallinger cast the figure from a real person, using an ex-art student as his model. The proxy Christ is posed with his hands tied behind his back, and has none of the usual iconographic attributes of the Christian Saviour or his Passion: no cross, no beard, no purple robe. In place of a crown of thorns he wears a circlet of gilded barbed-wire. His head is shorn because, according to Wallinger, 'that's the kind of humiliation they doled out during ethnic cleansing; it's what the Nazis did to the Jews'. He continues: 'I wanted a Christ that was both contemporary and kind of classical. I was trying to find a language that could be for that moment but also have a proper weight. He has his eyes shut because this is the moment where Christ is facing up to his destiny.'

Mark Wallinger's *Ecce Homo* (1999) was originally designed to be the first occupant of the Fourth Plinth in London's Trafalgar Square, where it stood from July 1999 to February 2000, memorialising the Millennium. Surrounded by monarchs, warmongers and heroes of British imperialism, the life-size figure of Christ was dwarfed, not only by the other statues' exaggerated scale, but also by the plinth itself, which was four times its height. The vulnerable appearance of the pale, near-naked body provided a striking contrast to the official civic monuments on plinths nearby: an equestrian statue of George IV, and the standing figures of General Sir Charles James Napier and Major-General Sir Henry Havelock.

← ***Ecce Homo*** **(detail), 1999**
↑ ***Ecce Homo*** **(detail), 1999**

→ ***Ecce Homo*, Trafalgar Square, 1999**

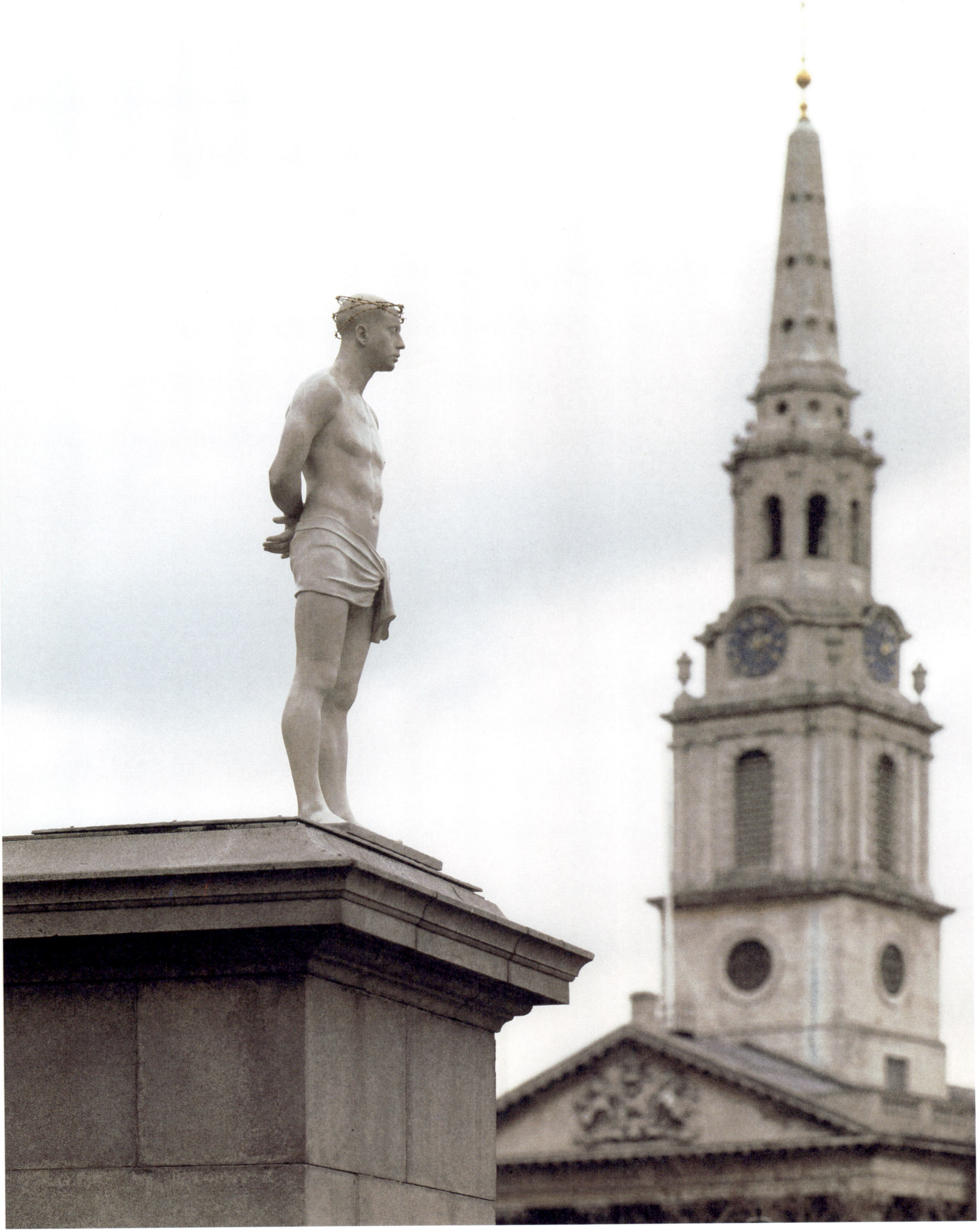

Rebecca **Warren**

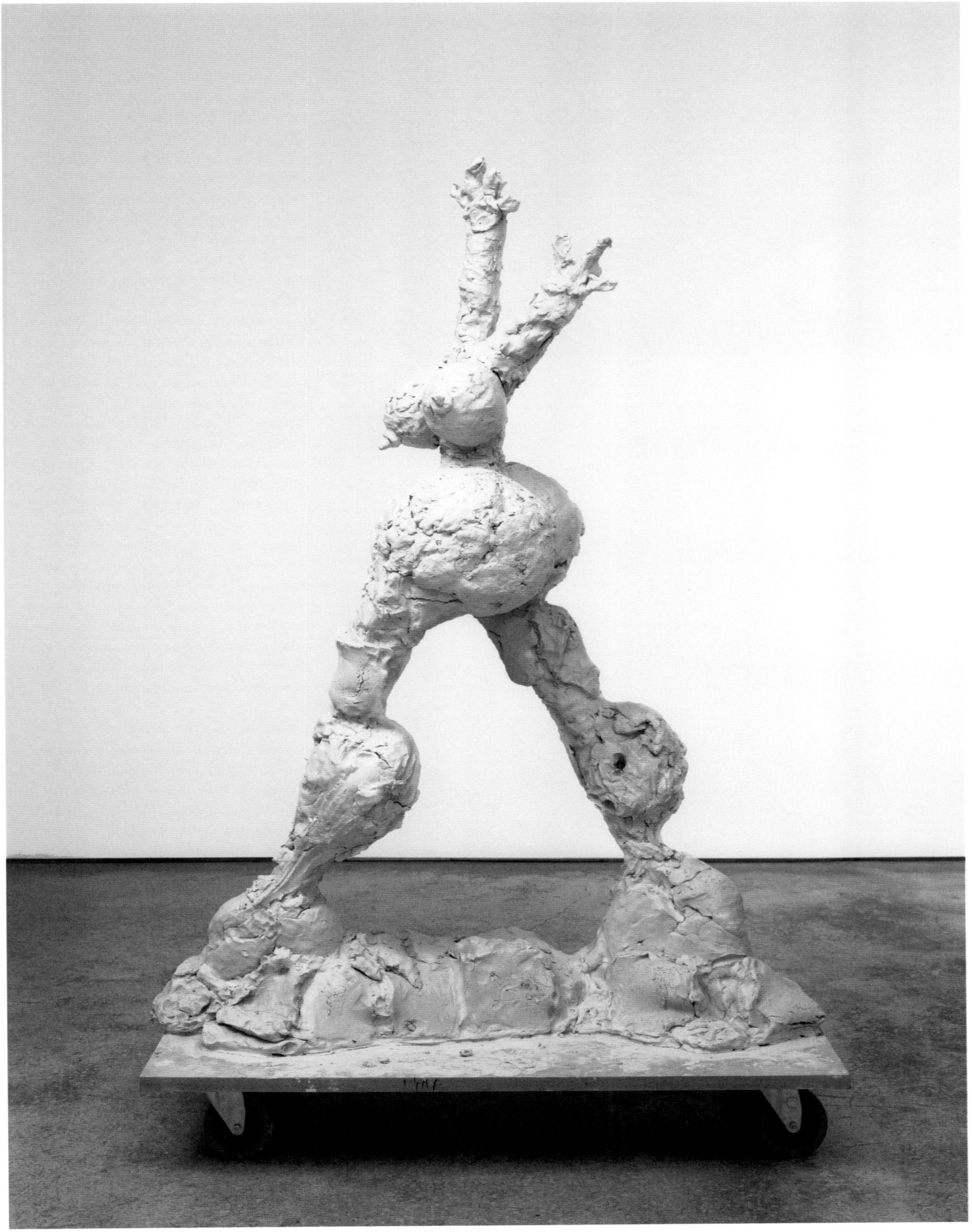

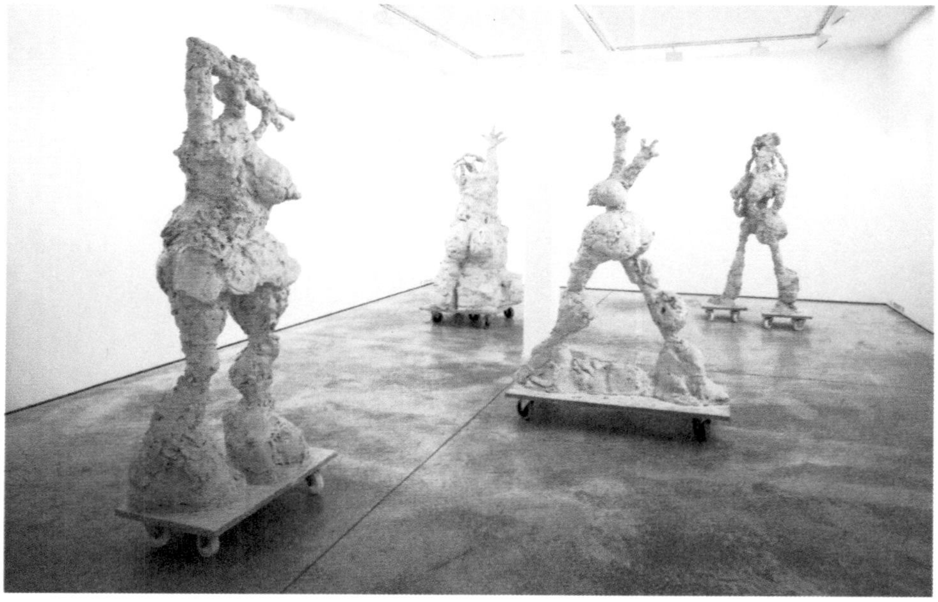

Roughly modelled in clay, Rebecca Warren's lumpen sculptures both represent and confound the human form. Her work draws on the long tradition of representing the female body through sculpture, a tradition almost exclusively mediated by male artists. Antagonising this inheritance, Warren mixes it with references to the ongoing distortion of female bodies in contemporary popular culture to produce what the artist has described as 'mad and ugly' sculpture that flouts conventional aesthetic ideals.

Warren's complex relationship with her subject is played out in works such as *SHE* (2003), an installation of six slightly bigger than life-sized clay figures, each mounted on MDF and set on castors. The title name-checks a Hammer film based on an H. Rider Haggard novel, whose female protagonist struck Warren as embodying a male 'idea of the archetypal woman'. Beginning with a concept of seeing 'what it's like to inhabit the space of the male artist', Warren presents through *SHE* a *reductio ad absurdum* of the female form as depicted by modern masters from Picasso (Warren has described her initial notion 'of reworking *Les Demoiselles d'Avignon* (1907) into three dimensions') and de Kooning through to Helmut Newton and R. Crumb. Sexualised to the point of ungainliness, Warren's figures sport grossly enlarged buttocks and unruly breasts that nearly defy recognition as such; heads are, for the most part, pointedly omitted.

Warren's atypical use of clay carries *SHE*'s experimentation with academic tradition further: visibly pushed and pulled, the churned-up surfaces are both fragile and technically unfinished. Warren has said of her sculptures: 'I like to keep the quality that they're breeding quite quickly, that there's a sense of them perhaps not being complete'. The figures' unorthodox, messy appearance is underlined by the wheels that support their bases: while practical (the heavy sculptures would be otherwise difficult to move), they also emphasise for Warren the 'plasticity' of the forms, 'that they're not fixed'.

← ***No. 6*, 2003**
↑ ***SHE*, exhibition view, Maureen Paley, London, 2003**

→ ***Homage to R. Crumb, My Father*, 2003**

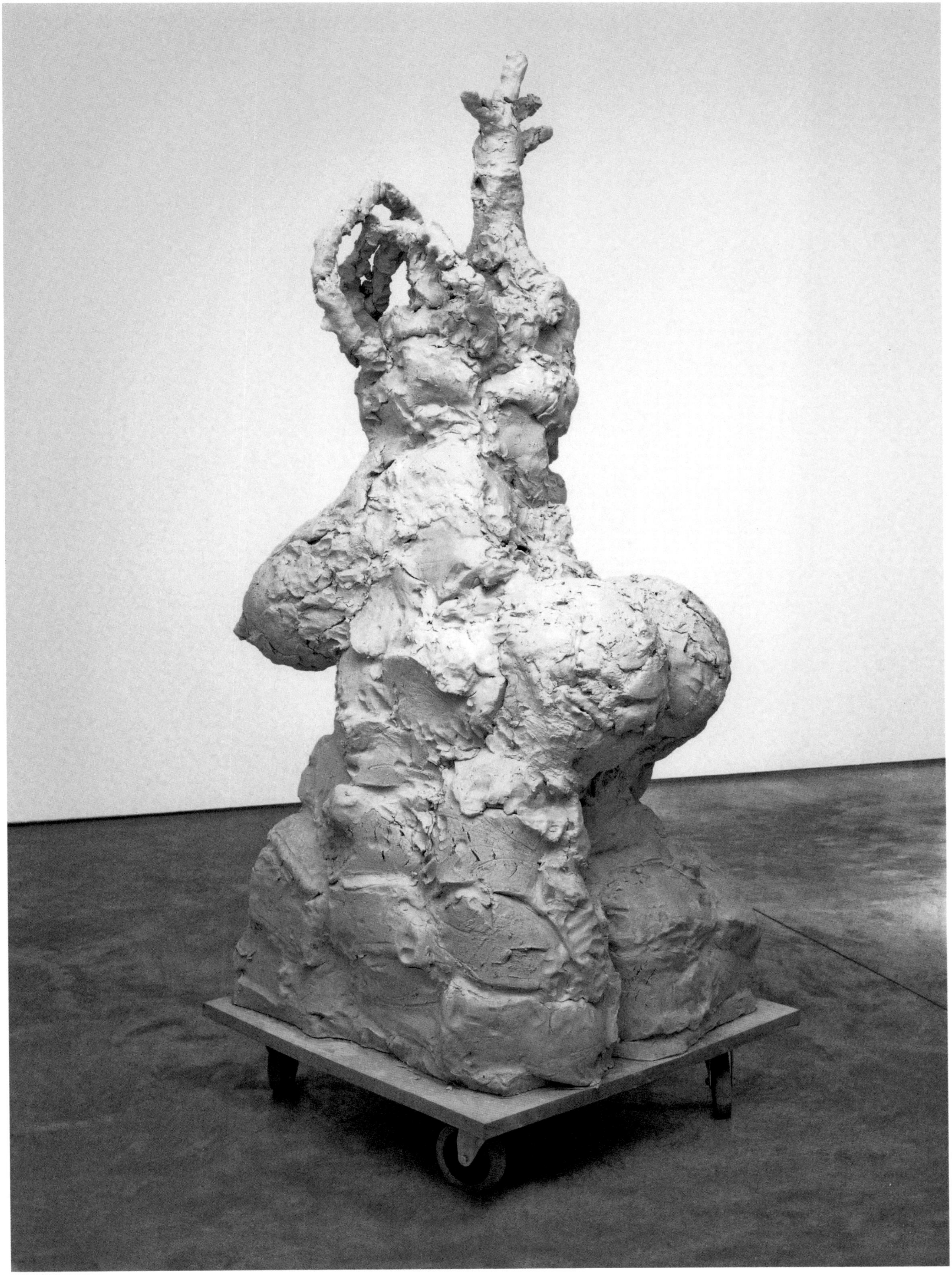

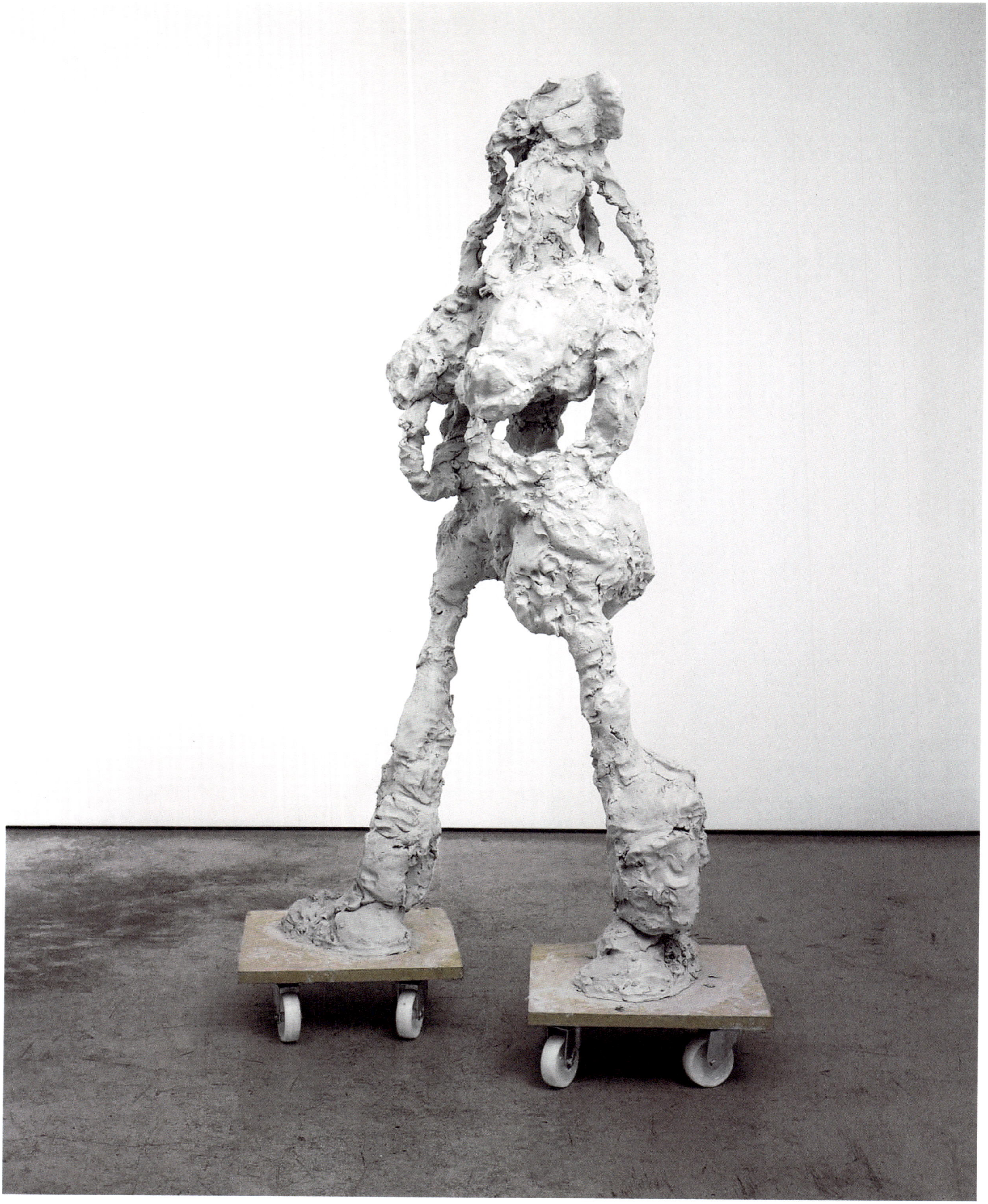

↑ ***South Kent*, 2003**

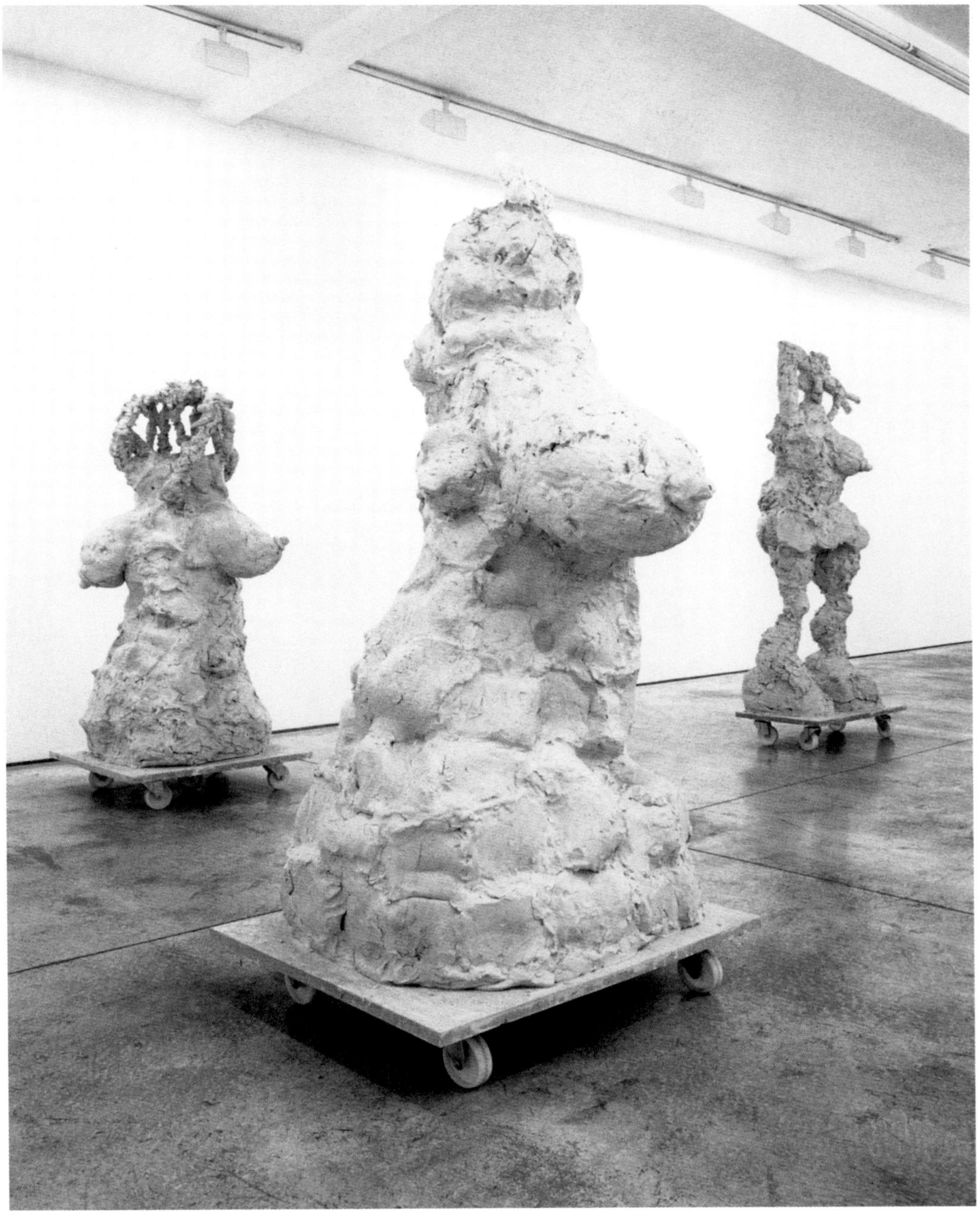

↑ **Works from left to right: *And Who Would Be My Mother*, 2003, *Valerie*, 2003, *Untitled*, 2003**

In Warren's recent bronzes, figuration proves more elusive. Though suggestive protuberances emerge from the surfaces of *The Dane* (2011), *There is Another Way* (2011) and *Los Angeles* (2013), they refuse to resolve into comprehensible human shapes. Teetering on the brink of abstraction, these pliant-looking forms are not all that they seem, the rigid bronze casts mimicking the quality of the clay surfaces that Warren is best known for. Working against the qualities traditionally associated with the metal, Warren daubs each upright form with a candy palette of industrial paint, belying its colour and heft.

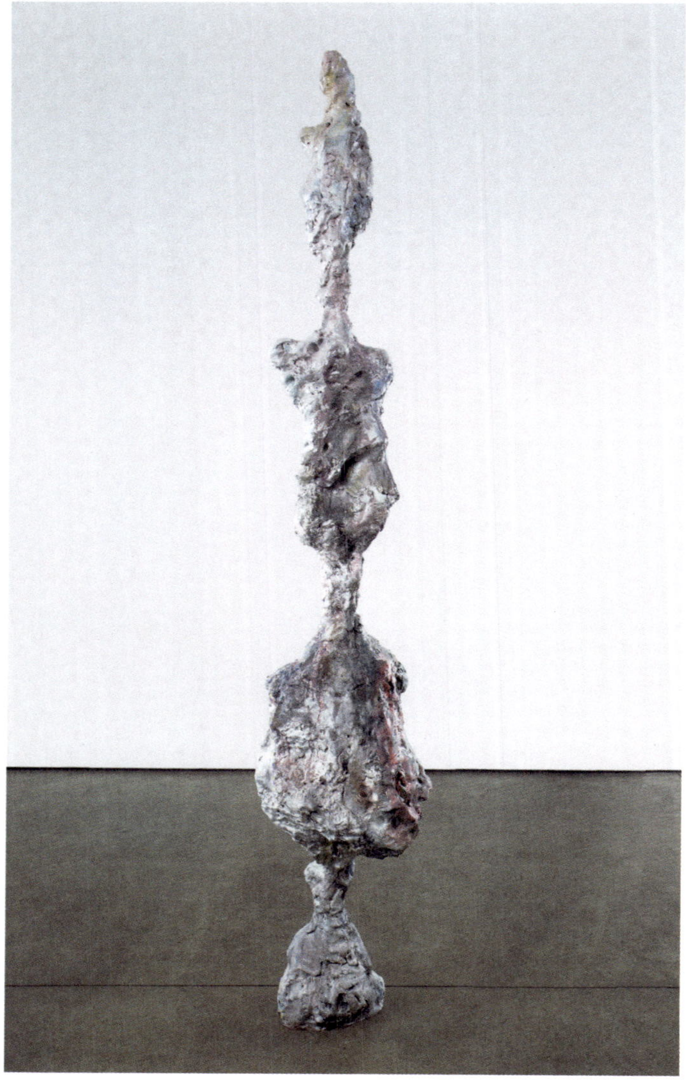

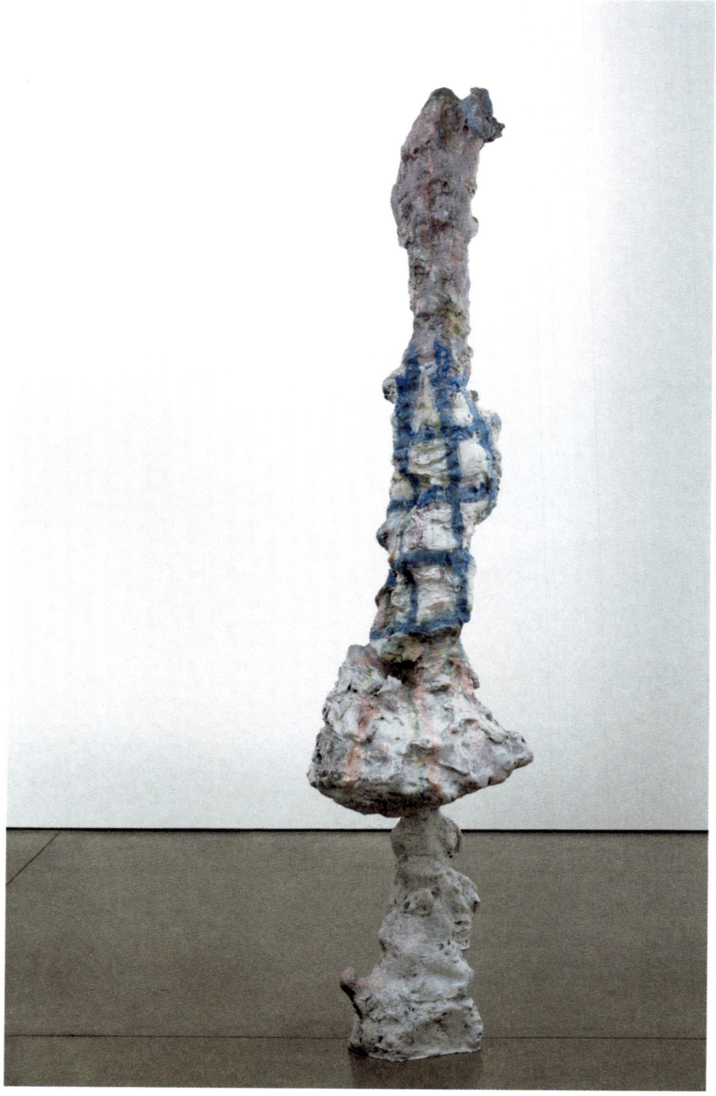

↑ ***The Dane*, 2011**
↗ ***There is Another Way*, 2011**

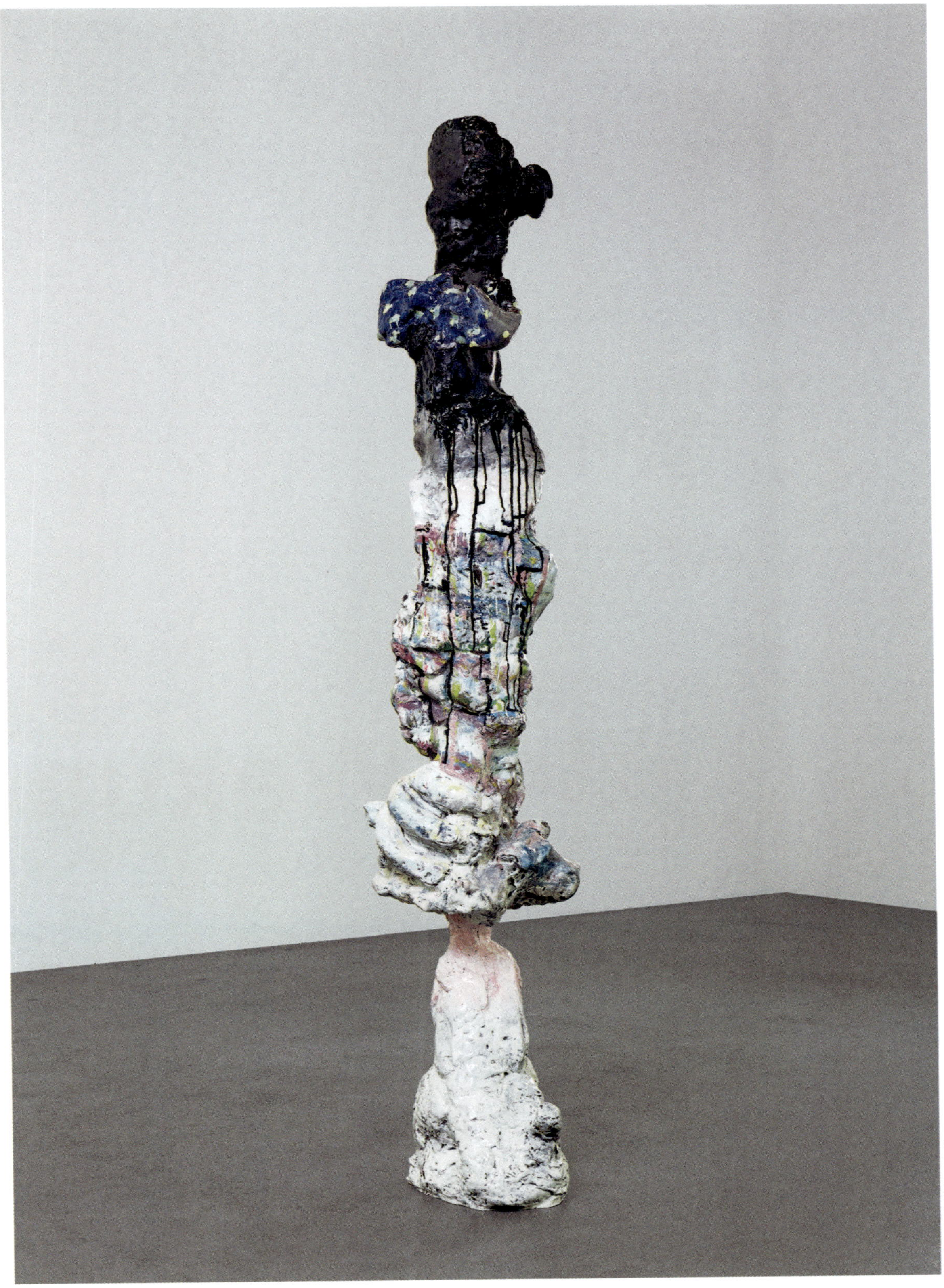

↑ ***Los Angeles*, 2013**

Andro Wekua

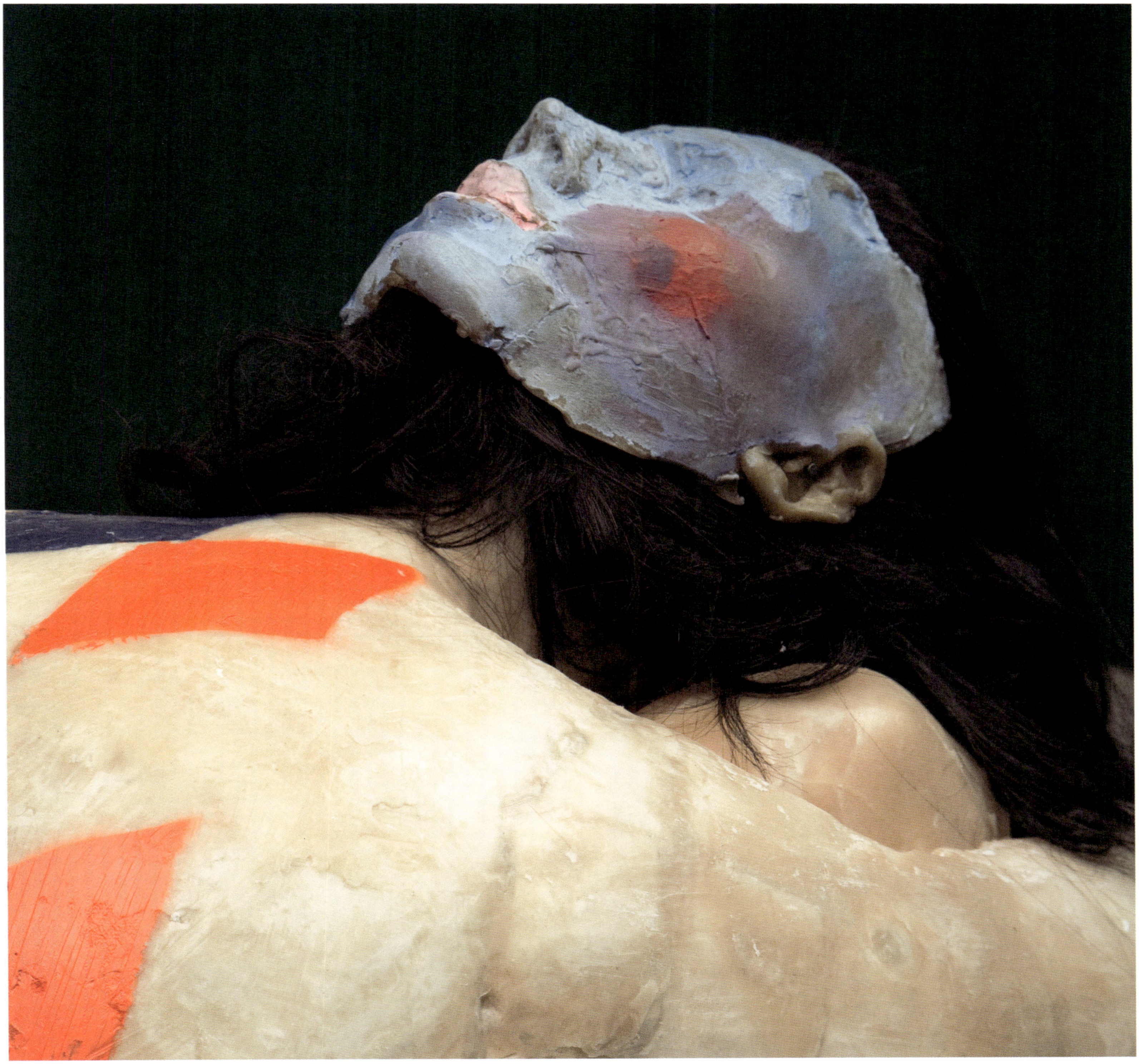

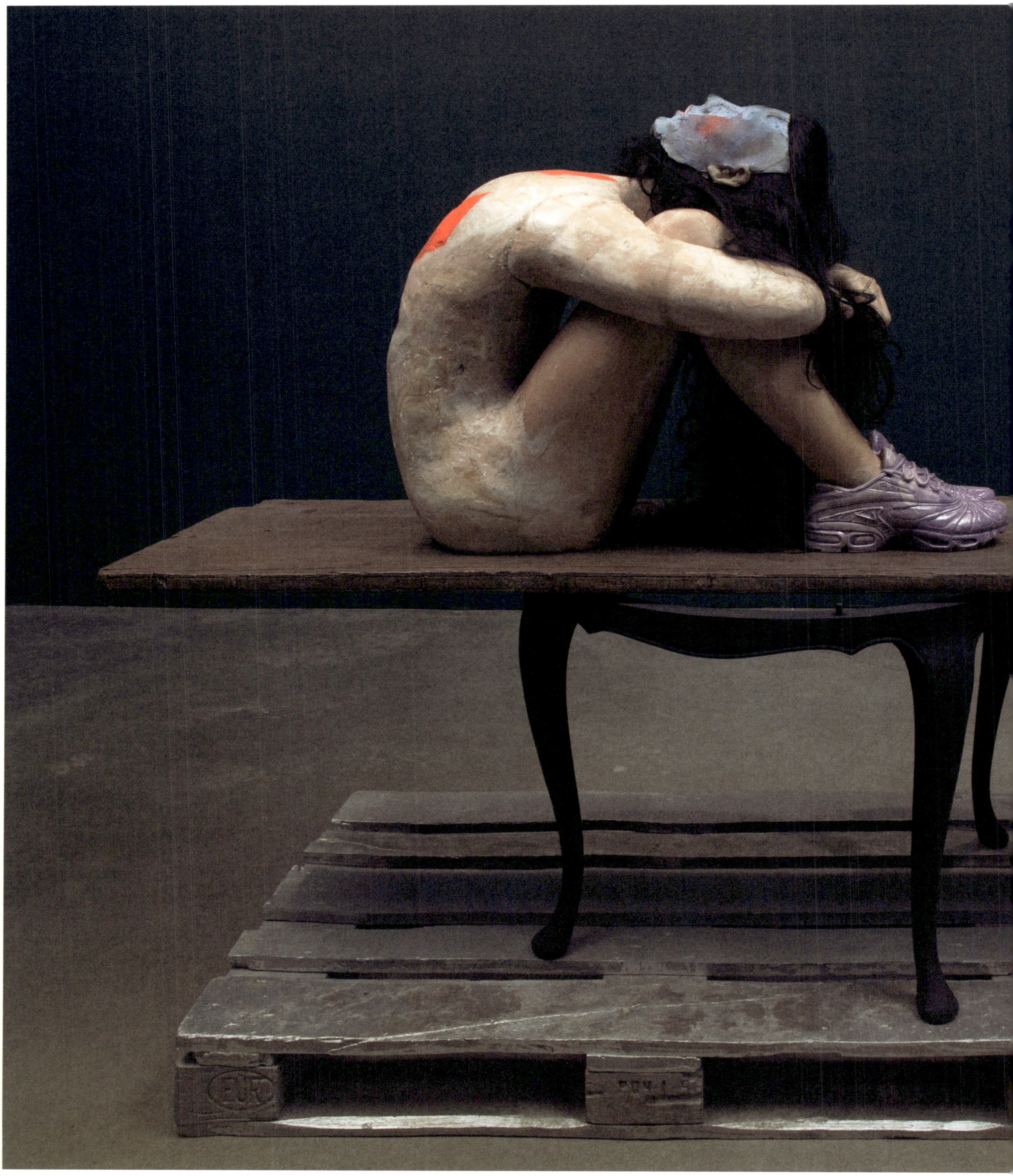

← ***Sneakers 1*** **(detail), 2008**

↑ ***Sneakers 1*, 2008**

The subjects of Andro Wekua's sculptures are conjured from the conflicted territory that lies between memory and dream. Explaining that he tries to create figures 'that function like actors', he goes on to say: 'they are intended to play all those roles I can't play myself; they act out what disturbs me.' While Wekua's sculptured scenes invite looking, they also frustrate it. His figures often hide in full view, refusing to return the viewer's gaze and keeping their identities secret.

Wekua creates his sculptures by casting live models in wax, a working method that makes his figures appear both disconcertingly lifelike and unreal. From a distance, the naked person huddled on a table top in *Sneakers 1* (2008) seems to be a hyper-realistic image of a young woman. Close up, the figure reveals itself as a sort of mirage: its back is punctured by two barely disguised bolts, its skin is not as perfect as it looks at first and even the gender of the figure is uncertain. Like many of Wekua's sculptures, the figure has a mask, but wears it back-to-front. The slapped-on colour on this Janus-like face, together with the harlequin pattern on the figure's back, suggests something from the *commedia dell'arte*. The ceramic sneakers — another recurring motif in Wekua's art — imply a different persona. As indicated by the title, these shoes are the most solid, factual and potentially enduring part of the figure.

Balanced on a board placed on top of a dilapidated table, which itself is supported by a cast aluminium pallet, the sculpture's precarious staging heightens its theatricality and the sense of something provisional that might suddenly be removed. Wekua characterises this as being like 'a little stage where a different, artificial reality comes into being, which isn't possible under normal conditions', and is concerned with creating a psychological distance between the work and the viewer. He applies this to himself as much as to his audience: 'I am happy when the work becomes autonomous and makes me into a distanced viewer. I am also happy when viewers interpret the different elements of the work for themselves.'

Cathy Wilkes

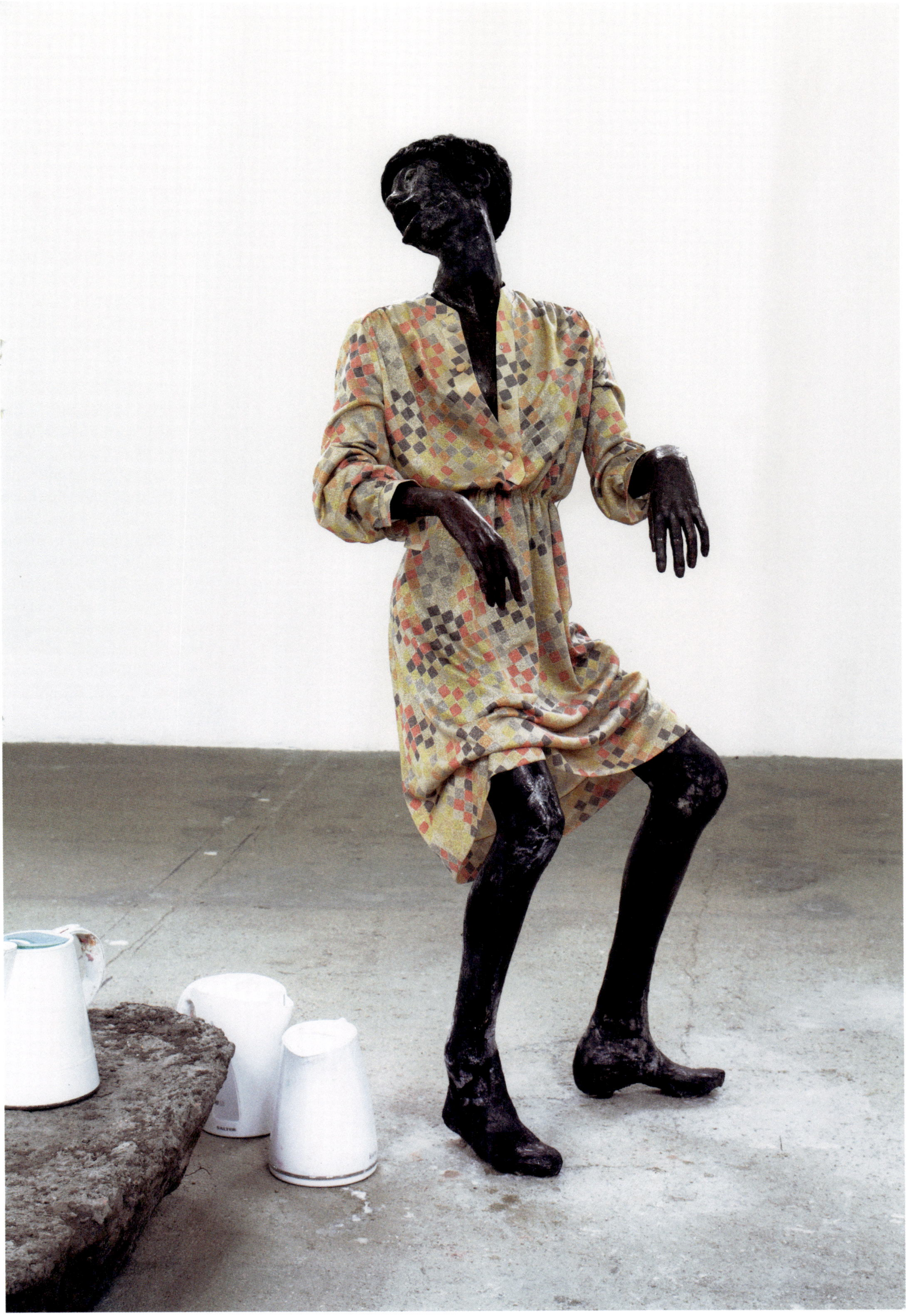

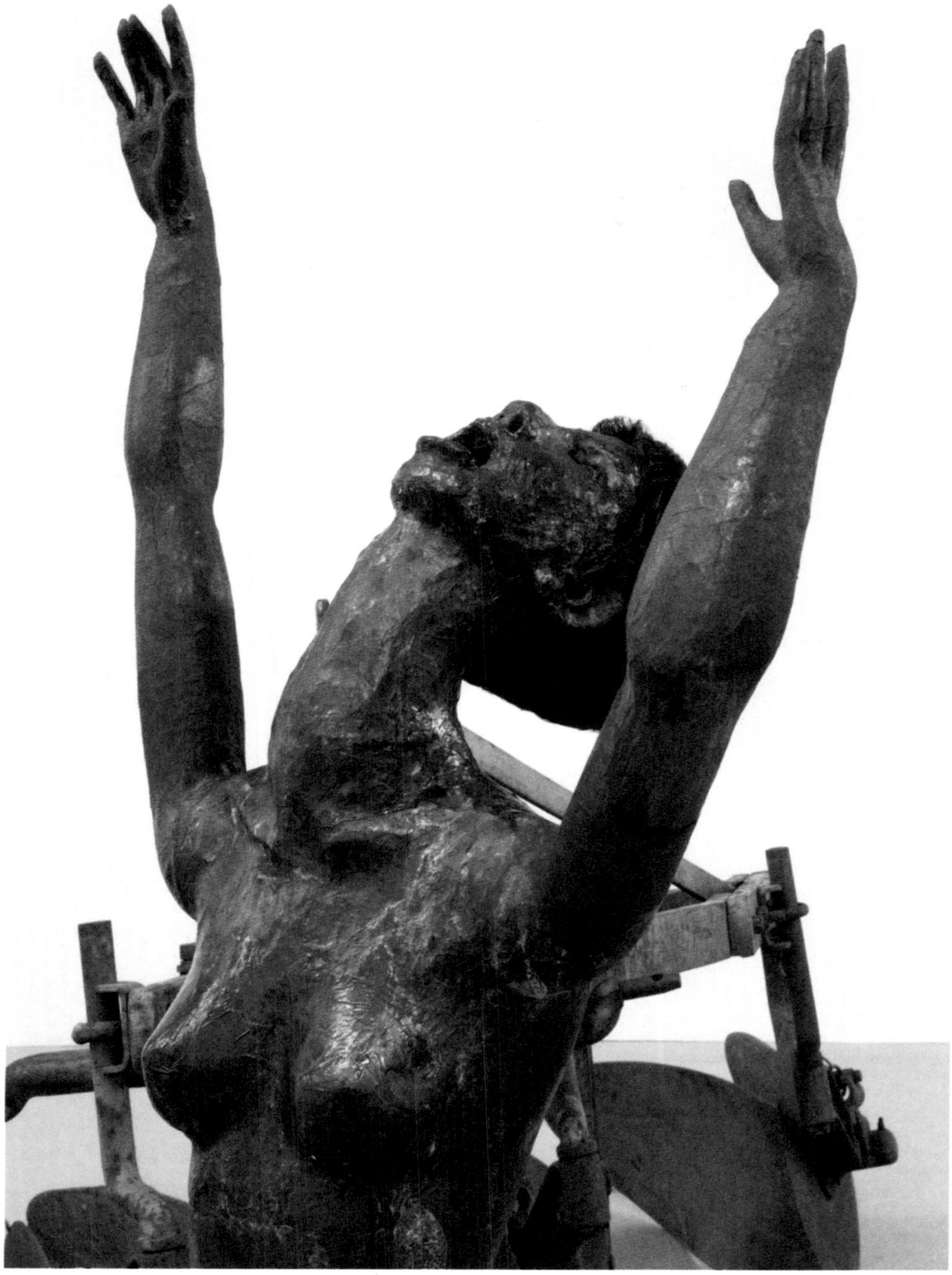

Cathy Wilkes' sculptural environments are deliberately enigmatic. The human body plays a central part in her meticulous arrangements of objects, but often in ways that leave us to reflect on moments of intense emotion. Though Wilkes resists attempts to explain her work directly, it is clear that her art speaks in abstracted and oblique ways of her own being and of those around her. 'I know that it's impossible to be objective', she has said, 'and being non-objective brings all the mysteries of my mind into my work. I think these parts are very important to any artwork: not knowing why something is exactly as it is or why it's there at all.'

Like many of her installations, *No Title* (2011) has an element of theatre-in-the-round; it needs to be seen from all angles. In this scene, three figures inhabit a landscape of desolation, where a plough lies idle and a standpipe has run dry. Various objects — toys, utensils and a wave-like sculpture — are scattered on the ground. It is only as you move around the work that the full extent of its lamentation is apparent. The grief-stricken female figures and the private anguish of the child become increasingly insistent, until the mourners' keening and ululation can almost be heard. The dislocation of the various elements, and the space surrounding them, amplifies absence and the sense of isolation surrounding the personages. And the treatment of the female figures — their papier-mâché skin, their blackness, their wild gestures and distorted anatomies, their palpable distress — gives them a universality that goes far beyond the personal, the local and the topical.

← ***No Title* (detail), 2011**
↑ ***No Title* (detail), 2011**

→ ***No Title*, 2011**

Speaking about the work, Wilkes emphasises the fact that, rather than being autobiographical or confessional, it broadly addresses mortality and loss: 'I don't want to share my story or something. I want to show suffering, frailty and compassion. The objects are part of each other's suffering; they are about openness and distance, the unknown distance between me and everything beyond me and inside me. Everything in the way the things are made and focused on measures this.'

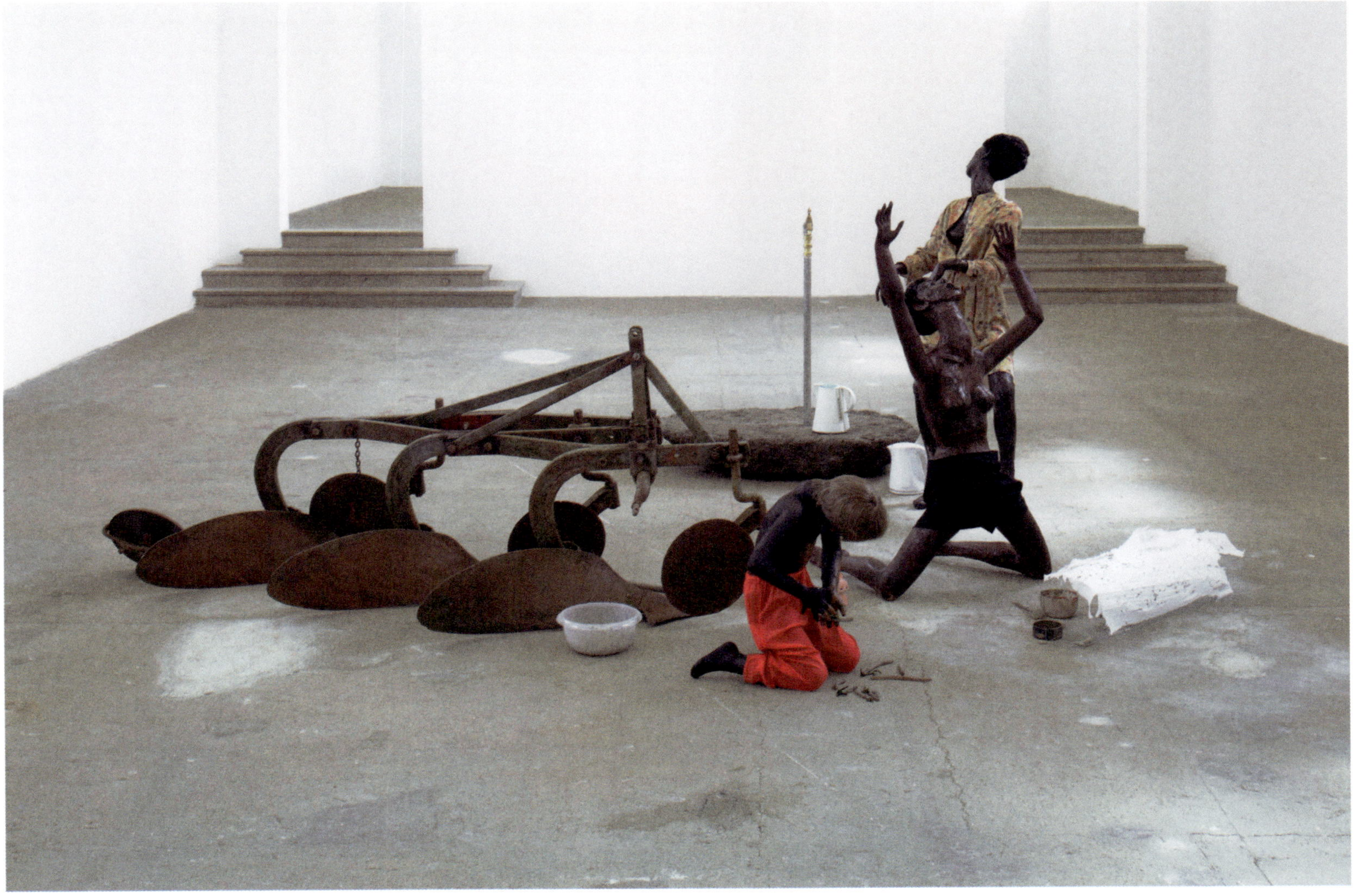

Appendix

List of Works

Measurements are given in centimetres,
height × width × depth

Paweł Althamer

Born 1967
Lives and works in Warsaw, Poland

pp. 51–52 ***Monika and Pawel***, 2002
Animal intestines, straw and hair over metal, plaster, porcelain, artificial wig, wooden floor, video camera, mobile phone, wrist watch, cotton thread and other materials. 176×73.5×111, Tate: Presented by Tate Patrons 2011

p. 53 ***Untitled***, 2006
Mixed media. Three figures, each 180 (height), Private Collection

Frank Benson

Born 1976
Lives and works in New York, USA

pp. 57, 59 ***Human Statue***, 2005
Forton MG, MDF, oil and acrylic paint. 173×50×30 Astrup Fearnley Collection, Oslo, Norway

p. 55 ***Human Statue (Jessie)***, 2011
Bronze and polyurethane acrylic. 201.5×96.5×76.2 Astrup Fearnley Collection, Oslo, Norway

Huma Bhabha

Born 1962
Lives and works in Poughkeepsie, USA

pp. 61–62 ***Bourne Darkly***, 2008
Clay, wood, wire, styrofoam, metal, acrylic paint. 173×36×36, Kopp Collection, Munich

p. 63 ***The Immortal Story***, 2007
Clay, wood, wire, foam, Styrofoam, cast iron, horn, acrylic paint. 122×244×107, Courtesy of Lehmann-Art Ltd. and Rashel-Art Ltd.

pp. 64–65 ***The Orientalist***, 2007
Bronze. 180×84.5×112, Courtesy of the artist, Stephen Friedman Gallery, London and Salon 94, New York

Maurizio Cattelan

Born 1960
Lives and works in New York, USA

pp. 67, 69 ***Him***, 2001
Polyester resin, wax, pigment, human hair and suit 101×41×53, Stefan T. Edlis Collection

pp. 70–72 ***Now***, 2004
Polyester resin, wax, pigment, human hair, clothing and coffin. 85×225×78, Private Collection

Urs Fischer

Born 1973
Lives and works in New York, USA

p. 85 ***Skinny Sunrise***, 2000
Polystyrene, wood, wood glue, dust, spray adhesive, flour, acrylic paint, silicone, screws, fabric 97×197×46, Ringier Collection, Switzerland

pp. 83–84 ***Untitled***, 2001
Wax, pigment, wick, brick, metal. 170×46×29 Edition 3 of 3 & 1 AP, Courtesy of Private Collection, London and Sadie Coles HQ, London

Katharina Fritsch

Born 1956
Lives and works in Düsseldorf, Germany

p. 90 ***Koch und 6. Foto (Schwarzwaldhaus)***
(Cook and 6th Photo [Black Forest House]), 2006/2008
Polyester, paint and oil-based ink and acrylic on plastic panel. Sculpture: 202×76×102; silkscreen: 280×375, Courtesy of the artist and Matthew Marks Gallery, New York

p. 88–89 ***Riese und 4. Postkarte (Franken)***
(Giant and 4th Postcard [Franconia]), 2008
Polyester, paint and oil-based ink and acrylic on plastic panel. Sculpture: 195×95×70; silkscreen: 280×400.1 Sculpture: Courtesy of the artist and Matthew Marks Gallery, New York, Silkscreen: Glenstone

p. 87 ***St. Katharina und 2. Foto (Efeu)***
(St. Katharina and 2nd Photo [Ivy]), 2007
Polyester, paint and oil-based ink and acrylic on plastic panel. Sculpture: 170×52×44; silkscreen: 280×400, Courtesy of the artist and Matthew Marks Gallery, New York

Ryan Gander

Born 1976
Lives and works in London, UK

p. 95–96 ***Come up on different streets, they both were streets of shame Or Absinth blurs my thoughts, I think we should be moving on***, 2009
Bronze and wood. Figure: 98×40×40; cube: 31×31×31; plinth: 100×40×40, THE EKARD COLLECTION

p. 93 ***I don't blame you, or, When we made love you used to cry and I love you like the stars above and I'll love you 'til I die***, 2008
Bronze and wood. Figure: 60×50×125; cube: 2×2×2; plinth: 80×50×50, Burger Collection, Hong Kong

p. 94 ***Tell my mother not to worry (ii)***, 2012
Marble. 80 × 175 × 60, Private collection, London

Isa Genzken

Born 1948
Lives and works in Berlin, Germany

p. 99 ***Untitled***, 2012
Mannequin and mixed media. 147×83×99, Courtesy of the artist, Hauser & Wirth, London Zürich and Galerie Daniel Buchholz, Cologne/Berlin

p. 101 ***Untitled***, 2012
Mannequin and mixed media. 287×115×153, Courtesy of the artist, Hauser & Wirth, London Zürich and Galerie Daniel Buchholz, Cologne/Berlin

Rachel Harrison

Born 1966
Lives and works in New York, USA

pp. 105–07 ***Jack Lemmon***, 2011
Wood, polystyrene, cement, acrylic, spray paint, mannequin, Dick Cheney mask, sweatshirt, sunglasses, glasses, butterfly net, and plastic lemon. 170.2×228.6×83.8, Collection of Barbara Lee, Cambridge MA

pp. 103–04 ***Schmatte with President***, 2006
Wood, chicken wire, polystyrene, cement, acrylic, scarf and Lincoln mask. 180.3×53.3×68.6 Marieluise Hessel Collection, Hessel Museum of Art, Center for Curatorial Studies, Bard College, Annandale-on-Hudson, New York

Georg Herold

Born 1947
Lives and works in Cologne, Germany

p. 111 ***Blühendes Leben***, 2009
Lath, canvas, lacquer, thread and screws. 373×132×102, Courtesy of the artist

p. 109 ***My Sweet Lord***, 2009
Lath, canvas, screws, core-board. 197×166×118, Courtesy of the artist

Thomas Hirschhorn

Born 1957
Lives and works in Paris, France

pp. 116–19 ***4 Women***, 2008
Perspex, wood, cardboard, polyurethane foam, paint, neons, printed matters, tape, transparents, felt pen, dummies, wigs. 223×306×81, Sammlung Migros Museum für Gegenwartskunst

pp. 113–15 ***Resistance-Subjecter***, 2011
8 mannequins with crystals, tape, wood, Perspex, aluminium foil, neon lights. 225×380 × 120, Courtesy of the artist and Gladstone Gallery, New York and Brussels

Martin Honert

Born 1953
Lives and works in Düsseldorf and Dresden, Germany

p. 123 ***Englischlehrer* (English Teacher)**, 2010
Polyurethane, sand, glass, and oil paint. 150×55×45, Olbricht Collection

p. 121 ***Foto* (Photo)**, 1993
Epoxy resin, wood, painted. Figure: 100 (height); table: 79×73×123, MMK Museum für Moderne Kunst Frankfurt am Main. Acquired with funding from the Donation Margarethe and Gustav Kober, Frankfurt am Main, prior to this on permanent loan at the MMK Inv. No: 2005/102

Pierre Huyghe

Born 1962
Lives and works in Paris, France

pp. 125, 127 ***Liegender Frauenakt (Untilled 2011–2012)***, 2012
Concrete cast on steel armature, beehive, wax, bees. Sculpture: 75×145×45; plinth: 30×145×55; beehive: dimensions variable, Sammlung Pulheim, Cologne, Esther Schipper, Berlin

Jeff Koons

Born 1955
Lives and works in New York, USA

pp. 129–30 ***Bear and Policeman***, 1988
Polychromed wood. 215.9×109.2×94
Kunstmuseum Wolfsburg

Paul McCarthy

Born 1945
Lives and works in Los Angeles, USA

pp. 139, 145 ***T.G. Elyse***, 2011
Position 1, Sleeping - posing, movement, form, Position 1, Sleeping - life molding, Position 2, Awake - posing, movement, form, Position 2, Awake - life molding, 2011, 4 channel video, colour, sound, Format: HD, BluRay, Posing, Position 1; Duration: 96:36 min, Posing, Position 2; Duration: 76:54 min, Molding, Position 1; Duration: 88:08 min, Molding, Position 2; Duration: 111:48 min, Friedrich Christian Flick Collection, Courtesy of the artist and Hauser & Wirth

p. 133–37 ***That Girl (T.G. Awake)***, 2012–2013
Group of three sculptures; silicone, paint, hair, wood, glass, melamine board. Figure 1: 78.1×74.9×141; Figure 2: 75×77.5×146.5; Figure 3: 77.5×72.4×138.4; each table: 76.2×101.6×228.6, D.Daskalopoulos Collection

John Miller

Born 1954
Lives and works in New York, USA and Berlin, Germany

p. 143–44 ***Composition in Black and Tan***, 2010
Mannequin, swimsuit, plastic pool. Dimensions variable, Courtesy of the artist

p. 142 ***Mannequin Lover***, 2002
Mannequin, assorted borrowed clothing. Dimensions variable. Rubell Family Collection, Courtesy of the artist, Metro Pictures and Praz-Delavallade

p. 141 ***Now We're Big Potatoes***, 1992
Mixed media. 168×90×40, Collection Gaby and Wilhelm Schürmann, Herzogenrath; Berlin

Cady Noland

Born 1956
Lives and works in New York, USA

p. 155 ***Bluewald***, 1989
Screen print (from original photograph by Bob Jackson) on aluminium, printed cotton flag. 182.8×85×90.1. Private Collection

Ugo Rondinone

Born 1964
Lives and works in New York, USA

p. 159 ***nude (xxxxxxxxxxx)***, 2011
Wax, earth pigments. 72×108×83, Courtesy of the artist and Esther Schipper, Berlin

p. 157 ***nude (xxxxxxxxxxxx)***, 2011
Wax, earth pigments. 77×128×60, Courtesy of the Dairy Art Centre, London

pp. 160–61 ***nude (xxxxxxxxxxxxx)***, 2011
Wax, earth pigments. 74×109×64, Courtesy of the artist and Galerie Eva Presenhuber, Zürich

p. 158 ***nude (xxxxxxxxxxxxxx)***, 2011
Wax, earth pigments. 76×99×45, Courtesy of the artist and Galerie Eva Presenhuber, Zürich

Thomas Schütte

Born 1954
Lives and works in Düsseldorf, Germany

pp. 165–67 ***Krieger***, 2012
Two statues, wood, coloured and oiled. Figure 1: 298.5×145×143; Figure 2: 303×126×115, Courtesy of the artist and Frith Street Gallery, London

Yinka Shonibare MBE

Born 1962
Lives and works in London, UK

p. 169 ***Boy on Globe***, 2008
Mannequin, Dutch wax printed cotton and globe. 180×125×100, Private Collection, London

pp. 171, 173 ***Girl Ballerina***, 2007
Mannequin, Dutch wax printed cotton, gun. 119×47×52, The Collection of John & Amy Phelan

Paloma Varga Weisz

Born 1966
Lives and works in Düsseldorf, Germany

pp. 175–76 ***Fallende Frau, Doppelköpfig (Falling Woman, Double-Headed)***, 2004
Carved limewood and fabric. 228.5×76×38, Installation dimensions vary. Courtesy of the artist and the Rachofsky Collection

pp. 177, 179 ***Lying Man***, 2014
Charred limewood, woolen blanket. Sculpture: 200 × 75 × 23; blanket: 170 × 140 × 0.5, Courtesy of the artist and Sadie Coles HQ, London

Mark Wallinger

Born 1959
Lives and works in London, UK

pp. 181–83 ***Ecce Homo***, 1999
White marbleised resin, gold-plated barbed wire. Life-size, Private Collection, Milan, Italy

Rebecca Warren

Born 1965
Lives and works in London, UK

p. 191 ***Los Angeles***, 2013
Hand-painted bronze on painted bronze plinth. Sculpture: 312.4×61×50.8; plinth: 147.5×68.5×68.5, Courtesy of the artist, Galerie Max Hetzler, Berlin and Maureen Paley, London

pp. 185–89 ***SHE***, 2003
Clay on MDF on wheels. Untitled: 198×77×46; Homage to R. Crumb, My Father: 213×81.5×81.5; No. 6: 186×61×122; South Kent: 206×127×66; And Who Would Be My Mother: 168×76×76; Valerie: 186×76×91, Private collection, Courtesy Galerie Max Hetzler, Berlin

p. 190 ***The Dane***, 2011
Hand-painted bronze on painted bronze plinth. Sculpture: 290×52×50; plinth: 147.5×68.5×68.5, Courtesy of the artist and Matthew Marks Gallery, New York

p. 190 ***There Is Another Way***, 2011
Hand-painted bronze on painted bronze plinth. Sculpture: 299.7×71.1×68.6; plinth: 155×67×67, Courtesy of the artist, Galerie Max Hetzler, Berlin and Maureen Paley, London

Andro Wekua

Born 1977
Lives and works in New York, USA and Berlin, Germany

pp. 193–95 ***Sneakers 1***, 2008
Wax figure, cast aluminium table and pallet, Acrystal board and ceramic shoes. 150×185×100, Private Collection

Cathy Wilkes

Born 1966
Lives and works in Glasgow, Scotland

pp. 197–99 ***No Title***, 2011
Mixed media, dimensions variable. Courtesy of the artist and The Modern Institute/Toby Webster Ltd., Glasgow

Illustrated Works

p. 10, Tilman Riemenschneider, *Saint Barbara*, c. 1510
p. 10, John Ide, *Bear and Policeman*, 1985
p. 10, Edward & Nancy Reddin Kienholz, *Sollie 17*, 1979–80. Courtesy LA Louver, Venice, CA. Collection of the Smithsonian Institute, Washington D.C.
p. 13, Edgar Degas, *Little Dancer Aged Fourteen*, 1880–81, cast c. 1922
p. 14, John de Andrea, *Untitled (Studio Scene)*, 1977. Courtesy Museum-Ludwig, Cologne
p. 14, Photographic basis for Martin Honert's *Foto (Photo)*, 1993. Courtesy Matthew Marks Gallery, New York and Johnen Galerie, Berlin
p. 19, Pierre Huyghe, *(Untilled 2011–2012)*, 2012. Courtesy the artist and Esther Schipper, Berlin
p. 21, Auguste Rodin, *The Age of Bronze*, c. 1876
p. 22, Mark Wallinger, *Ecce Homo*, 1999. Courtesy the artist and Hauser & Wirth
p. 22, Auguste Rodin, *The Burghers of Calais*, 1889
p. 25, Emmanuel Frémiet, *Gorilla Abducting Woman*, 1887
p. 25, John Gibson, *The Tinted Venus*, c. 1851–56. Walker Art Gallery, Liverpool, Bridgeman Art Library
p. 27, Rebecca Warren, *Head*, 2001. Courtesy the artist and Maureen Paley, London
p. 27, Rebecca Warren, *Cube*, 2003. Courtesy the artist and Maureen Paley, London
p. 28, Pablo Picasso, *Les Demoiselles d'Avignon*, 1907 MoMA New York/Giraudon/Bridgeman Art Library
p. 31, Ryan Gander, *The Artwork Nobody Knows*, 2011. Courtesy the artist and Staatliche Museen zu Berlin, Nationalgalerie
p. 32, Jeff Koons, *Gazing Ball (Centaur and Lapith Maiden)*, 2013. Courtesy the artist
p. 36, Charles Ray, *Male Mannequin*, 1990. Courtesy the artist and Matthew Marks Gallery, New York
p. 37, Thomas Schütte, *Three Capacity Men*, 2005 Courtesy the artist and the New Museum, New York
p. 39, Katharina Fritsch, *Madonnenfigur (Madonna Figure)*, 1987. Courtesy Matthew Marks Gallery, New York
p. 39, Juan Muñoz, *The Prompter*, 1988. Courtesy Tate Images and the Estate of Juan Muñoz
p. 39, Jeff Koons, *Kiepenkerl* at *Skulptur Projekte*, 1987. Courtesy the artist
p. 41, Martin Kippenberger, *Martin, ab in die Ecke und schäm dich* (Martin, into the Corner, You Should Be Ashamed of Yourself), 1989. Courtesy Estate of Martin Kippenberger, Galerie Gisela Capitain, Cologne
p. 47, John Heartfield and George Grosz, *Der wildgewordene SpieBer Heartfield (Elektro-mech. Tatlin-Plastik)* (The Petit-Bourgeois Philistine Heartfield Gone Wilde [Electro-Mechanical Tatlin Sculpture]), 1920. Courtesy Berlinische Galerie
pp. 74–75, Frank Benson, Digital preparatory images for *Human Statue (Jessie)*, 2011. Courtesy the artist and Sadie Coles HQ
p. 76, Katharina Fritsch, Photographs of the models for *Riese und 4. Postkarte (Franken)* and *Koch und 6. Foto (Efeu)*, 2006/2008. Courtesy the artist
p. 77, Ryan Gander, Preparatory images for *Come up on different streets, they both were streets of shame Or Absinth blurs my thoughts, I think we should be moving on*, 2009, and *Tell my mother not to worry (ii)*, 2012. Courtesy the artist
p. 78, Rachel Harrison, Installation images for *Jack Lemmon*, 2006. Courtesy the artist and Greene Naftali, New York
pp. 79–80, Thomas Hirschhorn, Preliminary sketches for 'Crystal of Resistance', 2011, Courtesy the artist
pp. 146–47, Pierre Huyghe, Preparatory stages for *Liegender Frauenakt (Untilled 2011–2012)*, 2012. Courtesy the artist
pp. 148–49, Paloma Varga Weisz, Preparatory stages for *Fallende Frau, Doppelköpfig (Falling Woman, Double-Headed)*, 2004. Courtesy the artist
p. 150, John Miller, Preparatory sketch for *Now We're Big Potatoes*, 1992. Courtesy the artist
p. 150, Andro Wekua, Preparatory stage, *Sneakers 1*, 2008, Courtesy the artist and Gladstone Gallery
p. 51, Rebecca Warren, *The Main Feeling*, 2009, Courtesy the artist and Maureen Paley, London
p. 52, Rebecca Warren, Scale model for the display of sculptures on the terrace of the Hayward Gallery, 2014. Courtesy the artist and Maureen Paley, London

Authors

Penelope Curtis
is Director of Tate Britain, London. Her books include *Sculpture 1900–45: After Rodin* (1999) and *Patio and Pavilion: The Place of Sculpture in Modern Architecture* (2007).

Martin Herbert
is a writer, critic and visiting lecturer in the sculpture department at the Royal College of Art, London. He is associate editor of *ArtReview* and European Editor of *Modern Painters*. He writes regularly for *Artforum*, *Art Monthly* and *Frieze* and is the author of a number of books including, most recently, *The Uncertainty Principle* (2014).

Lisa Lee
is an art historian and Collegiate Assistant Professor in the Department of Art History at the University of Chicago. She is a specialist in modern and contemporary art, with a focus on recent sculptural practice in Europe. She is co-editor, with Hal Foster, of *Critical Laboratory: The Writings of Thomas Hirschhorn* (2013).

James Lingwood
is Co-Director and curator of Artangel, London. His over 80 projects for the organisation include the celebrated *Rachel Whiteread: House* (1993–94), *Michael Landy: Break Down* (2001) and *Roger Hiorns: Seizure* (2008). Lingwood has also curated exhibitions for major museums including monographic shows on Juan Muñoz, Douglas Gordon and Thomas Schütte.

Ralph Rugoff
is Director of the Hayward Gallery, Southbank Centre.

Acknowledgments

Hayward Gallery is immensely grateful for all the help we have received in organising this exhibition, and would like to thank the following individuals, organisations, gallery staff and studios of the participating artists for their invaluable guidance and assistance.

Marcia Acita
Ulrike Baumgart
Florian Berktold
Kate Costello
Carole Courtillé
Eleanor Crabtree
Pauline Daly
Ulrike Duda
Holly Featherstone
James Green
Jessica Green
Carol Greene
Sarah Groothius
Jane Hamlyn
Louise Hayward
Matthias Heitbrink
David Hubbard
Danny Jöckel
Mario Kramer
Angela Kunicky
Jutta Küpper
Emily Lennox
Joanna Lisiak
Romain Lopez
Florian Lüdde
Phil Mayer
Rory Mitchell
Susanne Nolting
Alisa Ochoa
Anatol Orient
Francis Outred
Feodora Pallas
Natasha Polymeropoulos
Andrzej Przywara
Florian Rehn
Anthony Reynolds
Darren Rhymes
Lauran Rothstein
Benita Röver
Christina Ruf
Silke Schnellhardt
Sophie Scopes
Karin Seinsoth
Barnaby Shaw
Leonie Siroky
Sarah Sonderkamp
Anne Stenne
Cornelia Tischmacher
Aleksandra Urbanska
Ewout Vellekoop
Paola Vischetti
Ioanna Vryzaki
Linda Yun
Oleg Yushko

Southbank Centre is grateful to its Patrons for their generous support of the exhibition:

Edlis-Neeson Foundation
Gladstone Gallery
Dakis Joannou
Matthew Marks Gallery
Maureen Paley, London
Max Hetzler Gallery
Ringier Collection Zürich
Sadie Coles HQ
Stephen Friedman Gallery

The exhibition has also been generously supported by the Stanley Thomas Johnson Foundation and the Swiss Arts Council Pro Helvetia.

At Hayward Gallery and Southbank Centre for their contributions to the realisation of *The Human Factor: The Figure in Contemporary Sculpture*, thanks are given to:

Diana Adell, *Press and Marketing Officer, Hayward Publishing*
Grace Beaumont, *Hayward Administrator*
Alison Bowyer, *Head of Grants and Trusts*
Sarah Cashman, *Hayward Administrator*
Marcia Ceppo, *Operations Coordinator*
Bea Colley, *Participation Producer*
Peter Cooper, *Visitor Experience Manager*
Melford Deane, *Legal Advisor*
Helen Faulkner, *Marketing Manager*
Ben Fergusson, *Art Publisher, Hayward Publishing*
Matt Freeman, *Patrons Manager*
Catherine Gaffney, *Staff Editor, Hayward Publishing*
James Giffin, *Health and Safety Specialist*
Alex Glen, *Publication Sales Officer, Hayward Publishing*
Crystal Hinds, *Visitor Experience Manager*
Gareth Hughes, *Senior Technician, Hayward Production*
Nicola Jeffs, *Press Manager (Visual Arts)*
Debra Lennard, *Curatorial Assistant*
Lisa-Marie Lewis, *Website Manager*
Helen Luckett, *Interpretation Manager*
Thomas Malcherczyk, *Hayward Operations Manager*
Eimear Martin, *Assistant Curator*
Alison Maun, *Bookings and Transport Administrator*
Rachel Mellor, *Programming Assistant, Artistic Programming*
Filipa Mendes, *Press Officer*
Hannah Morrison, *Grants and Trusts Manager*
Joanna Newell, *Patrons Manager*
Ray O'Halloran, *Director, Estates & Facilities*
Sarah O'Reilly, *Hayward Gallery Manager*
Ruth Pelopida, *Production Manager*
James Runcie, *Head of Literature*
Julia Sawyer, *Health and Safety Manager*
Susannah Stevenson, *Marketing Assistant*
Luisa Summers, *Assistant to the Director, Hayward Gallery*
Adam Thow, *Head of Retail and Buying*
Sarah Toplis, *Digital Producer*
Katherine Walsh, *Buying and Merchandising Manager*
Henry Ward, *Head of Education*
Emily Webb, *Marketing Officer (Literature)*
Hilton Wells, *Head of Technical Services (Estates and Facilities)*
Louise Williams, *Marketing Officer*
Imogen Winter, *Registrar*
Matt Arthurs, Peter Avery, James Coney, Phil Gardner, Mark King, Kate Parrott, *Art Handling, Hayward Gallery*
Ali Brikci-Nigassa, Janet DeLuca, Pauline Dinis, *Security Team*

Lenders

The following individuals and institutions have kindly lent to the exhibition:

Astrup Fearnley Collection, Oslo, Norway
Burger Collection, Hong Kong
Collection of Barbara Lee, Cambridge MA
Collection of John & Amy Phelan
Collection Wilhelm and Gaby Schürmann, Herzogenrath; Berlin
Dairy Art Centre, London
D.Daskalopoulos Collection
Stefan T. Edlis Collection
Esther Schipper, Berlin
Frith Street Gallery, London
Friedrich Christian Flick Collection
Galerie Daniel Buchholz, Cologne/Berlin
Galerie Eva Presenhuber, Zürich
Galerie Max Hetzler, Berlin
Gladstone Gallery, New York and Brussels
Glenstone
Hauser & Wirth, London Zürich
Hessel Museum of Art, Center for Curatorial Studies, Bard College, Annandale-on-Hudson, New York
Kopp Collection, Munich
Kunstmuseum Wolfsburg
Lehmann-Art Ltd. and Rashel-Art Ltd.
Matthew Marks Gallery, New York
Maureen Paley, London
Metro Pictures, New York
Migros Museum für Gegenwartskunst
MMK Museum für Moderne Kunst, Frankfurt am Main
Olbricht Collection
Praz-Delavallade, Paris
Rachofsky Collection
Ringier Collection, Switzerland
Rubell Family Collection
Sadie Coles HQ, London
Salon 94, New York
Sammlung Pulheim, Cologne
Stephen Friedman Gallery, London
Tate
THE EKARD COLLECTION
The Modern Institute/Toby Webster Ltd, Glasgow

Together with those lenders who wish to remain anonymous

Text Credits

All texts are © the author.

pp. 56, 122, 131, 186–90
Original texts on the artists by Debra Lennard
pp. 53, 62, 68-70, 85, 94–97, 100, 104–05, 110, 126, 142–43, 155, 167, 170, 182, 195, 198–99
Original texts on the artists by Helen Luckett
pp. 91, 115–16, 138, 160, 178
Original texts on the artists by Eimear Martin
pp. 74–80, 145–152
Original texts by Catherine Gaffney

Copyright Credits

The publisher had made every effort to contact all copyright holders. If proper acknowledgment has not been made, we ask copyright holders to contact the publisher. All works are © the artist unless otherwise stated.

© ADAGP, Paris and DACS, London 2014, pp. 19, 44 (C), 79–80, 113–19, 125, 127, 146–47, front cover image
© DACS 2014, pp. 14, 37, 39 (C), 47, 76, 87–90, 109, 111, 121, 123, 148–49, 165–67, 169, 171, 173, 175–77, 179
© Estate of George Grosz, Princeton, N.J./DACS, 2014 / The Heartfield Community of Heirs/DACS, London 2014, p. 47
© Estate of Martin Kippenberger, Galerie Gisela Capitain, Cologne, p. 41
© Museum of Modern Art, New York/Giraudon/ Bridgeman Art Library, p. 28
© Succession Picasso/DACS, London 2014, p. 28
© Tate, London 2014 and the Estate of Juan Muñoz, p. 39
© The Rheinisches Bildarchiv, rba_c000213/Museum Ludwig Köln, p. 14
© Rex Features, p.10 (B)
© Walker Art Gallery, National Museums Liverpool / The Bridgeman Art Library

Photographic Credits

All images are courtesy the artist unless otherwise stated.

p. 10 (B): Courtesy Rex Features,
p. 10 (C): Courtesy LA Louver, Venice, CA
p. 14 (E): Courtesy the Rheinisches Bildarchiv/Museum Ludwig Köln
pp. 14 (F), 121, 123: Courtesy the artist, Matthew Marks Gallery and Johnen Galerie, Berlin
p. 19 (G): Courtesy the artist and Esther Schipper, Berlin
p. 22 (B): Courtesy the artist and Hauser & Wirth (Photo: Peter White); pp. 181–82: Courtesy the artist and Hauser & Wirth (Photo: John Riddy); p. 183: Courtesy the artist and Hauser & Wirth (Photo: Peter White)
pp. 27 (A, B), 151–52, 185–91: Courtesy the artist and Maureen Paley, London
p. 31: Courtesy the artist (Photo: Ken Adlard); p. 77t: Courtesy the artist (Photo: Nick Elphick); pp. 95–96: Courtesy the artist and Annet Gelink Gallery, Amsterdam (Photo: Peter Hauck); pp. 93–94: Courtesy the artist and Lisson Gallery, London
p. 36: Courtesy the artist and Matthew Marks Gallery
p. 37: Courtesy New Museum (Photo: Benoit Pailley);
p. 44 (B): Courtesy New Museum
p. 39 (C): Courtesy the artist and Matthew Marks Gallery
p. 39 (D): Courtesy Tate, London 2014
pp. 40 (F), 43 (A): Courtesy the artist and Metro Pictures
p. 41: Courtesy Estate of Martin Kippenberger, Galerie Gisela Capitain, Cologne (Photo: Lothar Schnepf, Cologne)
p. 44 (C), pp. 118–19: Courtesy the artist and Galerie Susanna Kulli, CH-Zürich; pp. 113–15: Courtesy the artist and Gladstone Gallery, New York, Brussels;
pp. 116–17: Courtesy the artist and Migros Museum für Gegenwartskunst
p. 47: Courtesy Berlinische Galerie
pp. 51–53: Courtesy the artist and Foksal Gallery Foundation
pp. 55, 57, 59, 74–75: Courtesy the artist, Sadie Coles HQ, London, and Andrew Krepps Gallery, New York
pp. 61–63: Courtesy the artist and Salon 94, New York;
pp. 64–65: Courtesy the artist, Stephen Friedman Gallery, London and Salon 94, New York
p. 67: Courtesy Maurizio Cattelan's Archive; p. 69: Courtesy Maurizio Cattelan's Archive (Photo: Attilio Matanzano); p. 70–71: Courtesy Maurizio Cattelan's Archive (Photo: Andrè Morin); p. 72: Courtesy DESTE
p. 78: Courtesy the artist and Greene Naftali, New York;
pp. 103–04: Courtesy the artist and Greene Naftali, New York (Photo: Jean Vong); pp. 105–07: Courtesy the artist and Greene Naftali, New York (Photo: John Berens)
pp. 83–85: Courtesy the artist, Sadie Coles HQ, London, and Galerie Eva Presenhuber, Zürich
pp. 88–89: Courtesy the artist (Photo: Ivo Faber)
pp. 99, 101: Courtesy the artist and Hauser & Wirth and Galerie Daniel Buchholz, Cologne/Berlin
p. 109: Courtesy the artist (Photo: Georg Herold/Jochen Littkemann); p. 111: Courtesy the artist and Petzel, New York
p. 125: Courtesy the artist and Esther Schipper, Berlin
pp. 133, 136–37, 139, 145: Courtesy the artist and Hauser & Wirth; pp. 134–35: Courtesy the artist and Hauser & Wirth (Photo: Genevieve Hanson)
p. 141: Courtesy the artist and CFA Berlin (Photo: Jochen Littkemann); p. 142: Courtesy the artist and Praz-Delavallade, Paris (Photo: Rebecca Fanuele);
pp. 143–44: Courtesy the artist and Metro Pictures, New York
pp. 148–49, Courtesy the artist and Sadie Coles HQ, London (Photos: Kristina Johlige Tolstoy)
p. 150t: Courtesy the artist and Gladstone Gallery
p. 155: Courtesy the artist and Wadsworth Atheneum Museum of Art/Art Resource, NY/Scala, Florence
pp. 157–61: Courtesy the artist and Galerie Eva Presenhuber, Zürich (Photos: Stefan Altenburger Photography Zürich); pp. 162–63: Courtesy the artist and M Museum, Leuven and Galerie Eva Presenhuber, Zürich and Gladstone Gallery, New York and Esther Schipper, Berlin
pp. 165–67: Courtesy Museum of Modern Art, New York/ Art Resource, NY/Scala, Florence
pp. 169, 171, 173: Courtesy the artist and Stephen Friedman Gallery
pp. 175–79: Courtesy the artist and Sadie Coles HQ, London (Photos: Stefan Hostettler)
pp. 193–95: Courtesy DESTE
pp. 197–99: Courtesy the artist and The Modern Institute/Toby Webster Ltd, Glasgow

Published on the occasion of the exhibition
The Human Factor: The Figure in Contemporary Sculpture

Hayward Gallery, London
17 June – 7 September 2014

Supported by:

swiss arts council
prohelvetia

STANLEY THOMAS
JOHNSON FOUNDATION

Exhibition curated by Ralph Rugoff
Organised by Eimear Martin, Assistant Curator, with Debra Lennard, Curatorial Assistant

This exhibition has been made possible by the provision of insurance through the Government Indemnity Scheme. Hayward Gallery would like to thank HM Government for providing Government Indemnity and the Department of Culture, Media and Sport and Arts Council England for arranging the indemnity.

Published by Hayward Publishing
Southbank Centre
Belvedere Road,
London, SE1 8XX, UK
www.southbankcentre.co.uk

Art Publisher: Ben Fergusson
Staff Editor: Catherine Gaffney
Sales Officer: Alex Glen
Press and Marketing Officer: Diana Adell

Catalogue designed by Atelier Dyakova
Printed in Spain by Grafos S.A.

A catalogue record for this book is available from the British Library

ISBN 978 1 85332 322 5

Distributed in North America, Central America and South America by D.A.P. / Distributed Art Publishers, Inc., 155 Sixth Avenue, 2nd Floor, New York, NY 10013
tel: +212 627 1999, fax: +212 627 9484
www.artbook.com

Distributed in the UK and Europe, by Cornerhouse Publications
70 Oxford Street, Manchester M1 5NH
tel: +44 (0)161 200 1503, fax: +44 (0)161 200 1504
www.cornerhouse.org/books

Front cover: Pierre Huyghe, *Liegender Frauenakt (Untilled 2011–2012)*, 2012
Back cover: Maurizio Cattelan, *Him*, 2001

SOUTHBANK CENTRE
HAYWARD PUBLISHING